Tulsa Baseball History 2024 Edition

A City's Love Affair with America's National Pastime

Elven Lindblad

Books About Tulsa

Tulsa Sounds: Contributions to American Music

Tulsa Baseball History: 2024 Edition

Coming Soon:

The 2025 A to Z Guide to Tulsa

Contents

This book is dedicated to the memory of Wayne McCombs, who left us far too soon but crafted a legacy of appreciation for the sport of baseball in general and for Tulsa sports teams in particular.

Introduction

Tulsa's longest relationship with any professional sport has been with baseball. And that love affair with its minor league teams has endured its share of peaks and valleys, of passionate embraces, periods of frustration and despair and joyous celebrations.

Baseball and Tulsa are currently living "happily ever after" with record-setting season attendance figures, more frequent appearances in postseason playoffs, having one of the finest stadiums on the Double-A level and its new partnership with one of baseball's most prestigious organizations, the Los Angeles Dodgers.

Ten major league teams, from powerhouses such as the Dodgers and St. Louis Cardinals to the woeful St. Louis Browns, have placed developmental teams in Tulsa with varying degrees of success.

Minor league baseball has connected with fans around the world and ranging in age three to 103 and Tulsa is certainly no exception. In addition to ticket and concession prices that are easier on the wallet and players who don't carry cocky attitudes often found in other professional sports, minor league baseball teams have always struck gold with plenty of clever and family-friendly promotions.

Back in the 1950s, there were the Oiler Frolics where the baseball players presented amateur talent shows and "talent" was sorely lacking. Youngsters flocked to grocery stores during the 1960s hoping to buy 16-ounce glass bottles of Pepsi-Cola that had autographed Oiler trading cards as part of a contest.

Nowadays, kids and grandkids eagerly await a chance between innings to run across the outfield grass in pursuit of the Drillers' big blue brahma bull mascot named Hornsby at a certain time during weekday home games or circle the bases just like their heroes following Sunday afternoon home games.

Most people, when stopped at Woodland Hills Mall, probably couldn't name three Tulsa Drillers players if asked. But ask those same three people if they've been to a game at ONEOK Field and their response, in so many words, is how enjoyable it was and that they can't wait to go there again.

For many years, a sign at the bottom of the entrance to the rickety and termite-infested Oiler Park had signs proclaiming it to be the proving ground for future stars of the St. Louis Cardinals.

This book tells the story of men who wore the uniforms of Tulsa's professional baseball teams and their contributions to the city's sports history. It also tells the story of opposing players and other men who came through town and left their mark on the sport, for better or for worse.

You can read about ...

How a crude invention by the manager of the 1966 Tulsa Oilers opened up baseball to be played and enjoyed by young boys and girls around the world.

How a fan got fed up with constant booing from others nearby and his response was a yell that became a battle cry for Tulsa baseball fans.

How a stadium usher at a 1923 home game helped a shorthanded umpiring crew and then become involved in some of major league baseball's memorable events during the 1930s and 1940s.

What happened when future Hall of Fame players and managers visited the Oil Capital of the World for exhibition games.

How the Oilers and their home stadium were involved in one of America's darkest hours, the 1921 Tulsa Race Massacre.

An exhibition game against the St. Louis Cardinals played in a college football stadium with softball-like ground rules.

Nine men with Tulsa connections are enshrined in the Baseball Hall of Fame in Cooperstown, New York.

Two teams comprised of young teenagers who became Babe Ruth League national champions along with the only Tulsa teams to reach the Little League World Series.

How a 12-year-old player captured the hearts of sports fans around the word with a heartfelt display of good sportsmanship shortly after being hit in the head by a pitch.

And how the 1966 Oilers lost nine games in a row and, incredibly, strengthened their hold on first place.

It's a glorious day so let's do what the home plate umpire just said...
Play ball.

Chapter One
The 1900s

This was the decade in which Henry Ford introduced the Model T automobile, the Wright Brothers made their first airplane flight, the first washing machine was built, plastic was invented and a new breakfast called Kellogg's Corn Flakes was sold for the first time.

Oklahoma became America's 46th state with the merger of the western Oklahoma Territory and eastern Indian Territory.

Tulsa became a boom town with the nearby discovery of large patches of oil. The local population skyrocketed, new business sprang up left and right, new money was flowing as freely as the newfound oil and local residents dreamed of bigger and better things. And the sooner those dreams turned into reality, the better.

In 1903, Major League Baseball created a best-of-seven series of games between the American and National League champions. Boston Americans defeated the Pittsburgh Pirates to win the first World Series.

Serious sports fans longed for a professional baseball presence in Tulsa. Many communities had what were called "town ball teams" where local residents played, mostly without pay, for the pride of representing their community and the love of the game.

Local residents desired to have a professional baseball team that was affiliated with an existing major league franchise, such as the Chicago Cubs or St. Louis Cardinals, for example. If Tulsa had a professional baseball team without a major-league affiliation, that was all well and good but many felt that it would neither be exciting nor successful.

Tulsa finally acquired a professional baseball team in 1905 and won its first professional baseball championship in 1908 in a Class D league, one of the lowest levels in minor league baseball history. The team's manager would be inducted into the Baseball Hall of Fame in 2013.

But off-the-field drama related to financial problems often drew more attention that what happened on the field in those days, not just in Tulsa but throughout minor league baseball. One prime example: Tulsa won a league championship in 1908 but could not field a team in 1909 due to money problems.

1905: Oklahoma City residents A.J. Bennett and Jimmy Bouldin had been stoking the fires of interest in baseball by the inclusion of a Tulsa team as part of a revival of the Southwestern League. Proposed teams would also be located in Oklahoma communities such as Enid, Guthrie, Muskogee, Shawnee along with Coffeyville, Kansas, located roughly 75 miles north of Tulsa.

Those Southwestern League dreams never came true. But two months later, C.E. "Charley" Shafft, a first baseman for a team in Pawnee, Oklahoma, put forth a plan for a Tulsa team to participate in the Missouri Valley League. Four days later, he was named as the player-manager for that Tulsa team.

The Missouri Valley Baseball League was a Class D league, the lowest in the minors at that time. It was comprised of teams from Missouri and Kansas along with four teams from Indian Territory, which covered the eastern one-third of what is now the state of Oklahoma. Indian Territory existed until 1907 when it merged with the Oklahoma Territory as part of Oklahoma became 46th state in the United States of America.

Those "state" teams were the Fort Scott (Kansas) Hay Diggers, Parsons (Kansas) Preachers, Pittsburg (Kansas) Miners, and Webb City (Missouri) Goldbugs. Teams from Indian Territory were the Muskogee Reds, South McAlester Giants (who moved to Fort Smith, Arkansas later that year), Tulsa Oilers and Vinita Cherokees.

A name-the-team contest was held and the winner was A.M. Fleshman, one of three Tulsans to suggest the Oiler nickname. That nickname was a tribute to the thriving oil production industry surrounding the city.

Home games were played at what was called Athletic Park at the intersection of East First Street and South Frankfort Avenue and on land that was part of the original Tulsa State Fairgrounds. Today, that plot of land is at the northeastern edge of the popular Blue Dome District and two long blocks south of ONEOK Field.

The most familiar names on Tulsa's roster were James Hugh McBirney and his younger brother, Sam. The McBirney brothers had been standout players on Tulsa's semi-professional town ball teams. In those days, town ball players held "day jobs" as well.

James was a pitcher while Sam played mostly at third base. James had moved from Coffeyville to Tulsa to work as the bookkeeper and assistant cashier with the Tulsa Banking Company. After that firm changed hands, the McBirney brothers founded the Bank of Commerce, which became the National Bank of Commerce in 1911.

James gave much of his time and money to the founding of Tulsa's First Methodist Church. The McBirney Mansion, located at the intersection of 14th and Galveston in downtown Tulsa, operates today as a bed and breakfast.

Sam later became the volunteer football coach of Henry Kendall College, which had moved the year before from Muskogee to Tulsa. That little college is today known as the University of Tulsa. Sam's TU football teams posted a 22-3-1 record from 1914 through 1916.

Some college football historians have opined that the short passing offense that Sam McBirney and others developed at TU would later be refined and enhanced by Texas Christian University quarterback and pro football legend "Slinging" Sammy Baugh.

What passed for spring training games didn't bode well for the Oilers. They lost three consecutive games to the Sapulpa Maroons before an error-plagued 8-1 home victory ended the losing streak. Tulsa made four fielding errors in that game but 12 errors were committed by Sapulpa.

Shafft had offered to quit six days before Opening Day but league officials did not take him up on that offer. A 7-5 Memorial Day victory over Muskogee lifted Tulsa into the upper half of the league standings. But after lost a three-game series at Parsons and also losing nine straight road games, the Oilers tumbled into last place.

This would be the first and final season for the Tulsa Oilers in the Missouri Valley Baseball League. It seemed that the Tulsa franchise and the league itself had two strikes against themselves before Opening Day and they kept fouling off pitches through the year in a valiant effort to stay alive. The Oilers survived after that season but the Missouri Valley League did not.

While individual records for Tulsa players from that team have not be found, Tulsa did lead the Missouri Valley Baseball League in attendance that year, drawing 25,000 fans.

The Pittsburg Miners, managed by H.O. Baldwin, were the league champions with a 75-26 record. Pittsburg had an outstanding pitching staff, led by Cy Stinson, a 22-game winner and William Burns

(21-3). Following Pittsburgh in the standing were the Parsons Preachers (61-40), Muskogee Reds (52-46), Fort Scott Hay Diggers (49-52), Webb City Goldbugs (47-54), Tulsa Oilers (44-58), Vinita Cherokees (41-63) and the South McAlester/Fort Smith Giants (33-63).

1906: The South Central League was a new Class D baseball league and the Oilers had plenty of good players and what appeared to be a bright future.

The six-team league spanned the Oklahoma Territory, Indian Territory and the western edge of the state of Arkansas. Indian Territory teams were the Tulsa Oilers, Muskogee Redskins and South McAlester Miners. The Oklahoma Territory teams were the Guthrie Senators and Shawnee Blues. Arkansas was represented by the Fort Smith Razorbacks.

Games were played in a newer version of Athletic Park, a three-acre site near the intersection of First Street and Frankfort Avenue. That site was roughly three blocks due south of Tulsa's current baseball stadium, ONEOK Field.

But Tulsa's home games were, essentially, played in a pasture much like minor league baseball was played elsewhere back then. The grounds where Athletic Park stood also served as the original site for the Tulsa State Fair.

Early newspaper photographs showed that spectator seating was located in a raised and covered wooden structure behind home plate that contained 10 rows of wooden bleachers. Additional seating was provided by 10 rows of ground-level, uncovered wooden bleachers adjacent to the main grandstand and running parallel to the first and third base lines.

Those photographs showed nothing resembling a modern press box, nor was there anything regarding a public address speaker system. The players wore billowing pants known today as knickers and the playing surface didn't have the infield outline common seen in today's baseball.

When financial problems arose prior to the start of the season, C.M. Casey stepped in to buy the Tulsa franchise and named F.H. "Cap" Smith as player-manager. Smith was a pitcher, also played in the outfield and helped Casey with the team's financial affairs.

The team's fan club printed 1,000 tickets for the home opener and sold the tickets at a dollar apiece to provide enough operating funds for the summer. The financial tumult did affect fan turnout with the season attendance of 19,750 being 5,000 fewer people than the previous season.

The South Central League's leadership was not immune from challenging times. League president J.B. McAllister resigned on May 29th to try to salvage the Shawnee team. Orville Frantz, the league's vice president and son of the Oklahoma Territory's governor, was promoted to president but resigned 17 days later. The *Tulsa Democrat* newspaper on June 22nd warned that the Oilers franchise was in danger of folding. The South Central League finally ceased operation during August.

The South McAlester Miners were the league champions with a 59-32 record, followed by the Muskogee Indians (50-38), Fort Smith Razorbacks (47-39) and Tulsa Oilers (45-42). The Shawnee Blues (29-42) and Guthrie Senators (18-55) disbanded on July 21st. Tulsa's season attendance was 19,750.

The South McAlester manager was Judson Grant "Jud" Smith, who was the first baseball player from Ohio State University to play major league baseball. He was a student there from 1888 through 1892 and later spent parts of four seasons with five National League teams.

1907: The Class D Oklahoma-Arkansas-Kansas League was Tulsa's third league in as many seasons. And just like in the previous two years, survival of the most financially fit was the priority. The eight-team league had shrunk to four teams when the season ended earlier than planned on September 15th.

The league's original teams were the Bartlesville (Oklahoma) Boosters, Coffeyville (Kansas) Glassblowers, Fort Smith (Arkansas) Soldiers, Independence (Kansas) Champs, Muskogee (Oklahoma) Redskins, McAlester (Oklahoma) Miners, Parsons (Kansas) Preachers and the Tulsa Oilers. Parsons and McAlester withdrew from the league on June 2nd while Fort Smith and Tulsa ceased operations on August 6th. Tulsa's season attendance increased to 24,000.

The Bartlesville Boosters, managed by Jack Love and Harry Truby, won the league championship with an 83-51 record. Pitcher Howard McClintock was by far the league's most valuable player with a 32-6 won-lost record. Teammate Ed Hutchison led the league in runs scored with 84. Hutchinson had played for the 1890 Chicago Colts, the predecessor to the Chicago Cubs.

The Coffeyville Glassblowers were next in the standings of the teams that finished the season at 71-57, followed by the Independence Champs (68-63) and Muskogee Redskins (63-70). When they ceased operation on August 6th, the Fort Smith Soldiers had a 40-46 record and the Tulsa Oilers were 37-59. When they withdrew from the league on June 2nd, the McAlester Miners were 11-17 and the Parsons Preachers were 10-19.

Harry C. "Ted" Waring had Tulsa's highest batting average (.266) and F.D. Mason led the Oilers with 112 base hits. Pitcher Marcus Hall later played in the majors with the St. Louis Browns (1910) and Detroit Tigers (1913-14).

Tulsa's manager that season was Jake "Eagle Eye" Beckley, who was a 1971 inductee into the Baseball Hall of Fame. More information about Beckley can be found on the Hall of Fame section of this book.

1908: This would be Tulsa's fourth professional baseball league in as many years but it would be a splendid season indeed as the Oilers won their first professional baseball championship. A future member of the Baseball Hall of Fame served as the Oilers' manager. And once again, Tulsa led the league in season attendance with 23,250 fans.

But just like in Tulsa's three previous seasons of professional baseball, the off-field drama almost kept those things from happening.

Prior to the start of the season, it appeared that Tulsa wouldn't have enough money to field a team and reverting to semi-pro town baseball appeared to be the only option. Twenty-five fans took a stand in behalf of baseball and made huge financial commitments for that point in time, forking over $25 apiece. The Oilers were saved and the march towards a title began.

The Class D Oklahoma-Kansas League began the season with six teams but only four remained when the season ended. Those teams were the Bartlesville (Oklahoma) Boosters, Independence (Kansas) Jewelers, Iola (Kansas) Champs, Muskogee (Oklahoma) Redskins and Tulsa Oilers. McAlester had a 17-47 record when the team ceased operations on July 5th and three days later, Iola (32-34) did likewise.

Of the teams completing the 1908 season, the Bartlesville Boosters had the best overall record (71-50), followed by the Tulsa Oilers (69-55), Independence Jewelers (66-58) and Muskogee Redskins (58-66). Tulsa then won three home games in a row against Bartlesville to claim the league championship.

Joe Kelly, a 21-year-old rookie outfielder, batted .302 in 65 games for Tulsa. Kelly spent 20 years playing minor league baseball but did have brief tenures with the major league Boston Braves, Pittsburgh Pirates and Chicago Cubs from 1914 through 1919.

The Oilers' manager that season was James Laurie "Deacon" White. More information about White can be found later in this book in Baseball Hall of Fame section.

1909: Tulsa did not field a professional baseball team due to not having enough money to field a team.

Chapter Two
The 1910s

World War I dominated the national and international news from 1914 through 1919. Tragedy struck again when on its maiden voyage, the *RMS Titanic* sank after hitting an iceberg in the northern Atlantic Ocean and over 1,500 people died. It was also the decade in which the first personal income tax was levied.

On the brighter side, this was the decade that saw the introduction of Oreo cookies, crossword puzzles, parachutes, self-serve grocery stores, Daylight Savings Time and the traffic light. The Panama Canal was opened and Charlie Chaplin made his movie debut.

The managerial genius of Connie Mack was on display during this decade as the Philadelphia Athletics claimed three World Series pennants. The city of Boston became a World Series power with the Red Sox and Braves combining to win five World Series.

Oklahoma experienced a second oil boom with the discovery of additional large oil fields. Tulsa's first skyscraper, the 16-story Cosden Building, was built. The state capital was relocated from Guthrie to its current home in Oklahoma City. The Green Corn Rebellion erupted in Pontotoc County in 1917 in opposition to a military draft related to World War I.

Tulsa's baseball melodrama of not having enough money to pay the bills continued but the quality of competition, both in Tulsa and in the Class D Western Association, kept improving. The 1912 Tulsa Oilers set what would be the record for the best winning percentage in a season in the city's professional baseball history. In 1913, Tulsa had to deal with a tragic collapse of its baseball stadium. That same misfortune would happen again nearly six decades later and came very close to ending professional baseball in the city.

The team changed its name from the Oilers to the Producers for the 1915-17 seasons then returned to being called the Oilers in 1918. Arch-rival Wichita had a player that set the professional baseball record of getting at least one base hit in 69 consecutive games and the Oilers were involving in that record being broken and its conclusion.

Major League Baseball teams began playing exhibition games in Tulsa and fans turned out in large numbers. Among the future Hall of Famers that played exhibition games in Tulsa were Rogers Hornsby, Tris Speaker, Honus Wagner, Walter "Big Train" Johnson, Christy Mathewson and managerial legend John McGraw. Even Oklahoma's greatest athlete, the former Olympian and future Pro Football Hall of Famer Jim Thorpe, participated in a couple of exhibition games.

The decade ended on a high note when well-heeled new ownership helped Tulsa move up to the Class A Western League, build a new baseball stadium and laid the foundation for a highly successful run during the 1920s.

1910: While the Oilers had a new home field and drew 31,200 fans that year, things didn't go well for them at all. They were one of four teams in the eight-team Class D Western Association, league that didn't finish the season.

Tulsa's home games from 1910 through 1913 were played at South Main Park, located at the intersection of East 18th Street and South Main Street on what is now the southern fringe of downtown Tulsa.

Things got off to a bad start when manager Gus "Cannonball" Weyhing was fired for unknown reasons after losing the opening game of the season. Conrad Harlow served as Tulsa's manager for the rest of the season.

Weyhing had been a major league pitcher in the late 1800s, winning 30 or more games in four consecutive years and won 32 games with the 1892 Philadelphia Phillies. He also hit more batters with a pitch (277) than anyone in major league baseball history.

Pitcher Ed Hawk, who started the season with Joplin before joining Tulsa, posted a 9-4 record. Hawk pitched briefly with the St. Louis Browns in 1911 and later managed three teams in the Class D Arkansas State League during the 1930s.

Another standout was shortstop John Desmond, who stole 38 bases despite a .208 batting average that year. Catcher Arthur "Jim" Jeffries led the team with a .311 batting average.

This season was dominated by the league champion Joplin (Missouri) Miners, who were ranked by the official website of Minor League Baseball (www.milb.com) as being among the 100 greatest teams in that sport's history.

Joplin won the pennant with an amazing 90-34 record and .726 winning percentage. Their march to the pennant was partially built on a 19-game winning streak during July, a streak which was snapped by a 5-4 loss to the last-place Oilers. Ironically the year before, the Miners had a 36-89 record and went through four managers.

Pitchers Ralph Bell and Mark Hall each won 21 games with Hall adding 241 strikeouts. Earl Hamilton went 19-8 that year and later spent 14 years with the St. Louis Browns.

Outfielders Bruce Ross and Harry Ellis were the offensive stars on a squad that posted a .287 team batting average and had four players that stole 40 or more bases. Ellis led the Western Association with 73 stolen bases and 104 runs scored while Ross batted .377 in just 70 games.

Following Joplin in the standings that year were the Enid (Oklahoma) Railroaders at 64-53, the Sapulpa (Oklahoma) Oilers at 65-61 and the Guthrie (Oklahoma) Senators at 47-73. The Muskogee (Oklahoma) Navigators had a 36-63 record when they and the Tulsa Oilers (28-68) ceased operations on July 22nd. Two other Oklahoma-based teams did likewise nine days later: the El Reno Packers (65-43) and Bartlesville Boosters (51-51).

1911: This Western Association season was a turbulent one, to say the least. The league started out with six teams but two went out of business after just five games. The Western Association had to cease operation on June 19th when it was down to two teams, which was a violation of the National Agreement of Baseball Rules.

Teams trying to play that year were the Coffeyville (Kansas) White Sox, Fort Smith (Arkansas) Scouts, Independence (Kansas) Packers, Joplin (Missouri) Miners, Muskogee (Oklahoma) Redskins, Springfield (Missouri) Jobbers and Tulsa (Oklahoma) Oilers.

The league's downfall began May 10th when Springfield (2-3) and Joplin (3-2) ceased operations. Then on June 14th, Independence (15-22) and Coffeyville (15-24) ceased operations. And five days later, Fort Smith (which had the league's best record at 29-14) and Tulsa (20-25) did likewise. That left Muskogee and Sapulpa tied with 23-21 records but because of National Agreement rules which do not recognize any league that has two teams, there was no league champion.

Despite the horrible results on the field, Tulsa led the league in attendance by drawing 6,800 fans for the abbreviated season. Statistics from that season for Oiler players could not be located after multiple attempts.

1912: The Oilers played in the short-lived Class D Oklahoma State League, a circuit whose season began in May and ended on June 29th. League members were the Anadarko Indians, Guthrie (whose nickname could not be found), Holdenville Hitters, McAlester Miners, Muskogee Indians, Oklahoma City Senators, Okmulgee Glassblowers and Tulsa Oilers.

The Okmulgee Glassblowers won the pennant with a 37-9 record. Under manager Howard Price, Tulsa finished second with a 34-14 record and their winning percentage of .708 still stands as the best season winning percentage in Tulsa's professional baseball history. The season attendance was 19,200. Statistics from that season for Oiler players could not be located after multiple attempts.

Following Tulsa in the OSL standings were the Anadarko Indians (24-23), Holdenville Hitters (21-23), McAlester Miners (21-25), Muskogee Indians (19-24), Oklahoma City Senators (15-33) and Guthrie (15-33).

During research for this book, it was discovered that several Internet resources for minor league baseball claimed that Tulsa's team was nicknamed the Terriers that year. Numerous clippings and microfilms from both the *Tulsa Democrat* and the *Tulsa World* newspapers confirmed that the team's nickname for the entire season was the Oilers.

1913: Tulsa did not field a professional baseball team that year but there were three memorable exhibition games.

The National League's Pittsburgh Pirates and the Western League's Sioux City Packers played on April 3rd and 4th at South Main Park, attracting estimated crowds of 1,000 for each game. The common bonds were that Pirates owner Barney Dreyfuss owned the Sioux City franchise and Pittsburgh's manager was Fred Clarke and his brother, Joe, was the Packers' skipper.

Sioux City won the first meeting, 4-3, and Pittsburgh took the second game, 6-1. Future Hall of Famers Honus Wagner and Max Carey played for the Pirates. In the first game, Wagner played first base and singled twice while Carey played left field and failed to get a hit in two at-bats. Wagner sat out the second game while Carey had a single and double but failed in an attempt to steal home plate.

That third exhibition game was a postseason event on Tuesday afternoon, October 28th, and drew an estimated 5,000 fans to South Main Park. The National League champion New York Giants, led by pitching legend Christy Mathewson and manager John McGraw, faced the Chicago White Sox.

Additional star power was provided when Washington Senators pitching ace Walter "Big Train" Johnson took a train from his Coffeyville, Kansas home and offered his services to the White Sox for free just for a chance to pitch against Mathewson. Johnson was considered baseball's premier power pitcher during his career with the Senators (1907-27).

But the game was nearly cancelled before the first pitch was thrown.

Part of the wooden grandstand collapsed without warning prior to the start of the game. A 20-year-old soldier from Arkansas was killed, over 50 people were injured and nearly 500 fans were buried in the debris. Local newspaper stories said the collapse was so quick and so quiet that no screams were heard when it happened. The bleachers had no roof and had been built just four years earlier.

After order was restored, Johnson's pitching prowess was a key in the 6-0 White Sox victory. Local newspaper stories told how Johnson's blazing fastball, sharply breaking curve ball and his famous drop pitch left many of the power-hitting Giants flailing at the air.

White Sox shortstop Buck Weaver went 5-for-5 with two doubles and three singles and played a key role in sending Mathewson to the bench after just four innings. Future Hall of Famer Tris Speaker belted a double and two singles.

The scenario of collapsing wooden stands and injured spectators during an exhibition baseball game in Tulsa would repeat itself in 1977, playing a nearly fatal role in the city's professional baseball history.

1914: Tulsa returned to the Class D Western Association with a new nickname (the Producers) and a new stadium (Association Park), both of which would last through the 1917 season. The Producers nickname was another acknowledgement of the importance of the oil industry and its related activities to the city of Tulsa.

Association Park was located close to the eastern edge of downtown Tulsa, just beyond the right field fence of Tulsa's current baseball stadium, ONEOK Field. The east-west borders were Cincinnati Avenue and Elgin Avenue and its north-south borders were East Archer Street and East First Street.

The Producers actually had the Western Association's best overall record but the league's schedule was split into half-seasons and they missed the playoffs by finishing in second place by two games in each half of the split season standings.

Despite missing out of the playoffs, the season attendance was 48,800. It was the highest total in the city's pro baseball history to that date and nearly doubled the combined attendance of the previous two Oiler seasons. The Producers were managed by Howard Price, who previous played for several minor league teams throughout Oklahoma.

The league had six franchises but played in eight cities that year. The more stable franchises were the Fort Smith (Arkansas) Twins, McAlester Miners, Muskogee Mets, Oklahoma City Boosters and Tulsa Producers. The Joplin-Webb City (Missouri) Miners had a 22-46 record before becoming the Guthrie Senators on July 10th and then turning into the Henryetta Boosters on July 22nd.

For the year, Tulsa had the best overall record at 74-49. They were followed by Oklahoma City (75-52), Fort Smith (73-52), Muskogee (74-54) and McAlester (47-79). The Joplin-Webb City/Guthrie/Henryetta franchise finished 35-92. Oklahoma City defeated Muskogee in the best-of-seven playoffs, 4-2.

Pitcher Nelson Jones led the league in victories with 29, a mark that still stands as the second-highest season total for pitching victories in Tulsa's professional baseball history. Roy Clements was another standout for the Producers with a 20-12 record in 34 games. Clements helped his own cause with 10 of his 22 base hits going for extra bases, four of those being home runs.

Shortstop Lee Morris led the league in runs scored (105) and stolen bases (62). Morris' stolen base total would stand for nearly 50 years in Tulsa's professional baseball history as a single-season record. The Producers had six players with 10 or more stolen bases. The team's batting average of .264 was the league's second highest mark and their fielding percentage of .940 ranked third in the league.

Outfielder Clyde Henry was runner-up for the league batting championship with a .301 average over the entire season and added nine home runs and 28 stolen bases. Catcher Charles Moneymaker batted .379 in 82 games (not enough games to qualify for the league title) and also stole 16 bases in what would be his final professional season.

The Pittsburgh Pirates and Sioux City Packers attempted to play two preseason exhibition games on April 3rd and 4th. The first game was rained out and the Pirates took a 3-0 victory over the Packers in the second game before an estimated 1,000 fans at South Main Park. Pittsburgh pitcher Babe Adams scattered two hits and struck out five batters. Max Carey had two base hits, scored two runs and stole two bases. Shortstop Honus Wagner went hitless in two at-bats.

1915: While the Producers weren't a winner on the field (finishing eight games below .500), they were big winners at the gate. The season attendance of 40,200 fans was the second-highest in Tulsa's professional baseball history to that time.

Western Association teams that year were based in Oklahoma, Texas and Arkansas. Texas was represented by the Denison Railroaders, Paris Snappers and Sherman Hitters. Arkansas was represented by the Fort Smith Twins. The Oklahoma teams were the McAlester Miners, Muskogee Mets, Oklahoma City Senators and Tulsa Producers.

Roy Clements posted his second straight 20-win season, going 21-16 with a 3.01 ERA and sharing the league lead in pitching victories with Fort Smith's Jerome Robertson.

Lee Morris split time between shortstop and third base while batting .263 with a team-leading 127 base hits and 38 stolen bases. Catcher Jim Burke led the Producers with 56 stolen bases and outfielder Ed Hopper belted 17 home runs. Catcher George Kelsey was the player-manager and batted .209.

Denison had a 76-53 record under player-manager Aldridge "Babe" Peebles, who led Denison teams to three league championships in five years during the 1910s. Following Denison in the standings were Oklahoma City (76-62), Sherman (70-65), Muskogee (68-66), Paris (68-66), Tulsa (63-71), Fort Smith (61-75) and McAlester (57-59).

Rogers Hornsby was a 19-year-old shortstop that played a key role in Denison's drive to the league championship. After the season ended, the St. Louis Cardinals paid Denison $600 to acquire his player contract. During his 23-year big-league career, Hornsby had a career batting average of .358, was a two-time Triple Crown winner (leading a league in batting average, home runs and runs batted in) and was a 1942 inductee into the Baseball Hall of Fame.

The Producers hoped to face the National League's New York Giants in preseason exhibition games on March 29th and 30th but both games were rained out. A postseason exhibition game between the Kansas City Packers of the Federal League and a team known as the Tulsa All-Stars, which included a few players from the Tulsa Producers, was won by Kansas City, 11-7.

1916: The Producers had a successful year, qualifying for the Western Association playoffs by a razor-thin margin and setting another single-season attendance record by drawing 62,100 fans.

The Denison Railroaders finished with an 86-49 season record with Tulsa in second place at 80-58. Denison continued its Western Association domination by defeating Tulsa in the best-of-seven playoffs, 4-2.

Following them in the league standings were the McAlester Miners (79-58), Oklahoma City Senators (64-73), Muskogee Mets (63-77), Fort Smith Twins (61-76), Sherman Lions (61-76) and Paris Survivors (56-83).

Tulsa first baseman James Stewart had the league's third-highest batting average at .347. Outfielder Lyman Lamb, one of the Tulsa Oilers mainstays in the 1920s, led the team with 146 base hits and batted .281.

Pitchers Clyde Geist and David Kraft were 20-game winners and had respective earned run averages of 2.19 and 2.75. Howard Price, who was Tulsa's manager in 1912 and 1914, played first base and batted .289.

Despite Sherman's subpar record, right fielder Ross Youngs was the league's best hitter with a .362 batting average and also led the league in base hits (193) and runs scored (105). Youngs played 10 years with the New York Giants, had a .322 major league career batting average and was an important player on the Giants' National League champions in 1921 through 1924. Tragically, he was stricken with Bright's disease (kidneys) and died in 1927 at the age of 30.

The Producers won the first exhibition game between a Tulsa-based professional team and a major league opponent, routing the St. Louis Browns, 11-1, on March 24th at Association Park before an estimated 1,000 fans. The Browns avoided a shutout when future Hall of Fame pitcher Eddie Plank hit a home run. Tulsa outfielders Ralph Heatley and Ed Hopper had three hits apiece, including a home run.

Baseball fans got a preseason treat in a March 29th exhibition game against the New York Giants and Hall of Fame manager John McGraw. The man widely regarded to be the best athlete to ever come from the state of Oklahoma, Jim Thorpe, played in that game for the Giants.

The former Olympic champion who later played professional baseball and football scored two runs as part of the Giants' 13-7 victory over the Producers before an estimated crowd of 600 fans.

Thorpe won gold medals during the 1912 Olympic Games in Sweden in the pentathlon (five different track and field events) and the decathlon (10 different track and field events). In addition to playing four baseball seasons with the New York Giants, he was a collegiate football All-American at Carlisle (Pennsylvania) Indian Industrial School and starred for one of earliest National Football League teams, the Canton Bulldogs. Thorpe was named to the NFL's 1920

All-Decade team and was inducted into the Pro Football Hall of Fame in 1963.

An April 7th exhibition game between the Producers and the Detroit Tigers and superstar Ty Cobb was rained out.

1917: America entered World War I and its related events drained interest in minor league baseball across the nation in general and in Tulsa, in particular. The Producers' season attendance fell to 45,600, a drop of nearly 25 percent. On the field, the Producers tumbled from the top of the Western Association into next-to-last place, 27 games champion McAlester Miners.

McAlester won the pennant with a 95-57 record. They were followed by the Muskogee Mets (89-69), Sherman Browns (80-72), Denison Railroaders (79-75), Fort Smith Twins (77-82), Oklahoma City Boosters (72-80), Tulsa Producers (68-84) and the Paris Athletics/Ardmore Foundlings (57-98).

No individual statistics for the 1917 Tulsa Producers were found after multiple search attempts. McAlester's Emmett Mulvey led the league with a .320 batting average. Sherman's Charlie Robertson went 26-6 and shared the league lead in pitching victories with Fort Smith's Doc Watson.

Muskogee's Ernie "Crazy Snake" Calbert was the league's best offensive player, leading the league in home runs (43), runs batted in (109), runs scored (101) and base hits (177). He also had a .297 batting average and stole 32 bases. Calbert won six minor league home run championships between 1911 and 1923.

The New York Giants defeated the Detroit Tigers, 8-4, in a preseason exhibition game on April 4th before an estimated 3,600 fans at Association Park. Jim Thorpe was one of four players to hit a home run that day for the Giants, who went on to win the 1917 World Series.

Ty Cobb did not play in Tulsa due to a suspension from manager Hughie Jennings for starting a bench-clearing brawl in an exhibition game against the Giants in Dallas, Texas, a few weeks earlier. Renowned for both his talent and temper, Cobb started the fight when he slid into second base and spiked Giants second baseman Buck Herzog.

1918: Local economic conditions connected with World War I prevented Tulsa from having a professional baseball team.

1919: This would be a pivotal season in Tulsa's professional baseball history, both on and off the diamond. The team moved into a new and very hitter-friendly baseball stadium. It was involved in two key moments during the longest hitting streak in professional baseball history. And several people who would be involved in the infamous Black Sox gambling scandal played in exhibition games in Tulsa.

Spencer Abbott was the manager-owner of the Hutchinson (Kansas) Salt Packers in the Western League, which had become a Class A minor league, three skill levels higher than Tulsa was accustomed to. But Abbott urgently needed additional financing to complete relocating his team from Kansas to Tulsa, which became the home for 50 millionaires thanks to the oil boom.

Lengthy negotiations with Irish-born businessman Jim Crawford resulted in a win-win situation for both gentlemen. Crawford, who would be the team's principal owner through 1929, acquired 50 percent ownership of the team and the franchise was rechristened as the Tulsa Oilers.

Abbott then met with Ed Stienger, who built Sportsman's Park in St. Louis where the Browns and Cardinals played, about building a new baseball stadium in Tulsa patterned after the dimensions of Sportsman's Park. Abbott returned with the blueprints and construction on McNulty Park was completed on March 3, 1919, just 22 days after the first spade of dirt had been turned.

McNulty Park would be the Oilers' home through the 1929 season, thanks to Crawford's friendship with St. Louis Browns owner Phil Ball. It was located at the intersection of East 10th Street and South Elgin Avenue, which today is at the southeastern corner of downtown Tulsa. Seating capacity was 5,000 for the 1919 season and 2,000 seats were added the following year.

Home plate was in the southwestern corner of the layout and the Midland Valley Railroad tracks abutted what would be right field. And just like Sportsman's Park, McNulty Park's dimensions were unique, to say the least. The left field fence at McNulty Park was only 310 feet away from home plate; it was only 320 feet to center field and a very inviting 274 feet to right field, thanks to the aforementioned railroad tracks.

That unique layout played a key role in the Oilers winning five pennants and six batting titles in the Roaring Twenties. But construction shortcuts resulted in a substandard facility and it would be demolished after the 1929 season.

The University of Tulsa played its home football games at McNulty Park, despite the gridiron being only 90 yards long. Newspaper articles said that on a long running play, game officials had to make a judgment call on whether or not a player would have scored. If not, the ball was placed back on the 10-yard line.

As for the 1919 Western League season, the St. Joseph Saints won the pennant with a 78-57 record and the Tulsa Oilers finished second at 77-63. Following them in the standings were the Wichita Witches (75-65), Des Moines Boosters (71-67), Oklahoma City Indians (69-69), Sioux City Indians (68-70), Joplin Miners (57-78) and the Omaha Rourkes (56-80).

Of hitters that spent more than half of the year in Tulsa, outfielder Stewart Diltz led Tulsa with a .308 batting average. Outfielder Yancy "Yank" Davis, batted .302 that year, the first of five seasons in which he hit .300 or better for Tulsa. Third baseman B.W. Cleveland led Tulsa in stolen bases with 23.

Bill Bayne, a 20-year-old rookie pitcher, led the Oilers pitching staff with an 18-8 record and joined the St. Louis Browns when the season ended. He spent six years with the Browns but managed only 24 total victories during that span.

Frank Sparks threw the first no-hitter in Tulsa's professional baseball history in a 6-0 victory over the Joplin Miners. He went on to post a 6-0 record that season. Pitchers H.A. Dennis and Roy Salisbury split time between Tulsa and Oklahoma City and posted identical 16-15 won-lost records.

Jesse "Pop" Haines had a disappointing 5-9 record that year but his baseball fortunes got a whole lot better after leaving Tulsa. More about his career can be found in the Baseball Hall of Fame section of this book.

Wichita Witches outfielder Joe Wilhoit led the Western League with a .422 batting average thanks to a 69-game hitting streak, the longest such streak in professional baseball history. During the historic streak, Wilhoit batted .512 (153 hits in 299 at-bats) and had two or more hits in 50 of those 69 games. He also had 38 extra-base hits and drew 34 walks.

By comparison, Joe DiMaggio hit safely in 61 consecutive games with the Triple-A San Francisco Seals of the 1933 Pacific Coast League and his 56-game hitting streak with the 1941 New York Yankees is still the longest in major league baseball history.

But the 1919 season didn't start so well for Wilhoit. He played in the majors during the three previous seasons and was batting under

.200 when he was traded from the PCL's Seattle Pilots to Wichita. The first step of his journey into baseball hitting history began with an infield single in his June 14th debut with Wichita.

The turning point came when the team's owner-manager Frank Isbell told Wilhoit to switch to a lighter bat that also had a smaller handle. Isbell knew more than a few things about hitting, being a standout on the 1906 Chicago White Sox's "Hitless Wonders" that had the American League's lowest batting average (.230) but beat the Chicago Cubs in the 1906 World Series. Isbell was so popular in Wichita that the team's nickname would become the Izzies during the 1920s.

When the Witches hosted the Oilers for a July 27th doubleheader at Island Park, Wilhoit had a chance to tie and break the existing professional baseball record for the longest hitting streak. That record was 45 consecutive games set by Jack Ness of the 1915 Oakland Athletics in the Pacific Coast League. Wilhoit legged out a bunt single in the first game to tie the record. Then in the nightcap, he ripped the first pitch he saw for a double and finished with four hits on the night.

Newspaper accounts said the overflow crowd of 4,600 fans, Wichita's largest of the season, tossed over $500 onto the field in appreciation of Wilhoit's achievement. Considering that most Class A baseball players that year earned less than $200 per month, Wilhoit had a very good night, indeed.

The streak continued during a rugged three-week road trip and Willhoit had a chance to extend it to 70 games when the Oilers and Witches faced off again on August 20th. He had walked but had no base hits in three attempts when pinch-hitter Yam Yaryan faced Oilers pitcher Bill Bayne in the bottom of the eighth inning with two outs.

Yaryan ripped an RBI double down the left field line that gave Wichita a 3-2 lead. Instead of being pulled for a pinch-hitter, Wichita pitcher Paul Musser batted and made the final out with Wilhoit waiting on deck. The Witches won the game but Wilhoit's hitting streak came to an end at 69 consecutive games.

Wilhoit moved up to the Boston Red Sox later that year but Boston had too many good outfielders (Babe Ruth among them) and he never got a chance to show what he could do. Boston released him the following year and he passed away in 1930 at the age of 38 following a short illness.

The Oilers faced three major league teams in exhibition games that season and lost all three contests.

On April 9th, Joe Gedeon was the star of the St. Louis Browns' 9-4 victory over the Oilers by swatting three base hits. Gedeon testified in the 1920 criminal trial about allegations that gamblers tried to pay members of the Chicago White Sox to lose the 1919 World Series against the Cincinnati Reds.

The White Sox lost that World Series and eight players faced criminal gambling charges. Those players were acquitted in court but later banned for life from baseball. The scandal was the basis for the 1988 movie *Eight Men Out*.

The Cincinnati Reds blanked the Oilers on April 10th, 8-0. Alfred "Greasy" Neale had two base hits for the Reds that day but he left a larger legacy in football. Neale later became the first coach to be inducted into both the College and Professional Football Halls of Fame. Neale took Washington and Jefferson College to the 1922 Rose Bowl and then guided the Philadelphia Eagles to the 1948 and 1949 NFL championships.

In an April 18th exhibition game, the Chicago Cubs roared past the Oilers, 10-3. Infielder Bill McCabe, who batted just .178 for the 1918 National League champions, homered that day to lead a 15-hit attack. Rookie first baseman William "Chief Bill" Wano homered for Tulsa.

Chapter Three

The 1920s

As dark as the mood was during World War I, The Roaring Twenties celebrated sustained economic prosperity, explosive industrial growth and major changes in culture and lifestyles, both in the United States and abroad. Breaking with tradition was the norm and everything seemed possible through new technology and thinking.

During this period, women earned the right to vote, Charles Lindberg made a historic flight across the Atlantic Ocean, penicillin and insulin were discovered, the first talking movie (*The Jazz Singer*, starring Al Jolson) was shown, the first commercial radio broadcast aired, the first Winter Olympics were held and liquor sales were prohibited.

Making their debuts were the Art Deco form of architecture, bubble gum, cartoons featuring Mickey Mouse and Felix the Cat, *Reader's Digest*, *Time* Magazine, the lie detector, car radios and sliced bread.

Babe Ruth made baseball history in 1927 by hitting an unheard-of 60 home runs for the New York Yankees. College football was surprised when coach "Gloomy" Gus Henderson left the prestigious University of Southern California to revive the football fortunes of the University of Tulsa.

The state of Oklahoma made national headlines during that decade when two governors, Jack Walton and Henry Johnston, were impeached and removed from office. The state got much better publicity in 1926 when Tulsa-born Norma Smallwood became the first Oklahoman to win the Miss American pageant.

This was also a decade where Tulsa's name was forever etched in American history with a deadly 1921 riot in the predominant African-American Greenwood District. Officially, 37 people were killed and over 10,000 others were left homeless in the two-day uprising but many historians have said those numbers were far too low.

And the Tulsa Oilers baseball team came closer than people realized to being involved in the early stages of that horrific event.

Baseball was on an upswing thanks to McNulty Park, a new baseball stadium on the southeastern edge of downtown. A new affiliation with the American League's St. Louis Browns provided top-notch playing talent. The Oilers won five league championships during this decade and won 100 or more games three times.

Pitcher George Boehler made minor league baseball history by winning 38 games in 1922. Slugger Lymon Lamb roared like a lion with his hitting prowess.

More major league exhibition games were played in Tulsa and near-record crowds came to see future legends such as Babe Ruth, Lou Gehrig, Rogers Hornsby, Hack Wilson and Ty Cobb. The new Commissioner of Baseball, Judge Kenesaw Mountain Landis, came to Tulsa for a speech but never said a word about his new sports-related job.

But when an agreement for a new stadium to replace McNulty Park couldn't be reached at the end of the decade, the Oilers left town and the city would not have minor league baseball for two years.

1920: The Oilers claimed the first of their five Western League championships during the Roaring Twenties with a dramatic 5-3 victory over the Sioux City Packers on the final day of the season. Sioux City rallied to put two runners on base with two outs but Oilers pitcher Joseph "Bugs" Bennett ended the game with a strikeout.

Tulsa finished with a 92-61 record, one-half game better than the Wichita Witches (92-62). Following Tulsa and Wichita in the final standings were the Oklahoma City Indians (82-68), Omaha Rourkes (76-77), St. Joseph Saints (74-80), Joplin Miners (73-81), Sioux City Packers (63-88) and Des Moines Boosters (58-93).

Bennett was 27-9 that year and was second only to Omaha pitching ace Emilio Palmero for most victories. Ironically, Bennett went 0-5 over parts of two major league seasons. Ray Richmond was another Tulsa pitching standout, posting a 20-12 record in 42 appearances.

Shortstop Cotton Tierney led the Oilers with a .335 batting average and shared the team lead in stolen bases (26) with outfielder James Burke. Yank Davis was the Oilers' home run king for the second year in a row, swatting 20 round-trippers compared to just nine in 1919. Tulsa's .275 team batting average was second in the league.

The Oilers were a very good defensive team, as well. They turned 125 double plays, a very high number for that era of minor league baseball, and led the league in fielding with a .958 percentage.

Field manager Spencer Abbott cited the declining price of oil and labor-related layoffs in selling his half-ownership of the Oilers franchise to co-owner Jim Crawford. But Abbott wasn't aware that Crawford had given 25 percent of the team's ownership to his good friend and St. Louis Browns owner Phil Ball.

Abbott's anger didn't last long because the following year, he led the Memphis Chicks to the 1921 Southern Association championship. Abbott finished with 2,180 career victories in 34 years as a manager, the fifth-highest total in minor league baseball history.

Two of the 1974 inductees into the Baseball Hall of Fame crossed paths with the Tulsa Oilers that year. Sioux City first baseman James "Sunny Jim" Bottomley had only one hit in 14 at-bats with the Packers, but he joined the St. Louis Cardinals two years later and played there for 11 of his 16 major league seasons and batted .300 or better in nine of those seasons.

Rookie center fielder John Bertrand "Jocko" Conlon batted .247 for the Wichita Jobbers. He was inducted into the Baseball Hall of Fame in 1974 but not for what he did at Wichita and not for being a member of the Chicago White Sox in 1934 and 1935.

Conlon became a New York state licensed boxing referee when he was not playing minor league baseball. His officiating background came in handy during a 1935 game between the White Sox and St. Louis Browns. Umpire Red Ormsby was overcome by heat and one of Conlon's teammates asked him to fill in for the ailing umpire.

Renowned for his fairness, professionalism, quick smile and polka-dot ties, Conlan was a National League umpire from 1941 through 1965 and was chosen to officiate in six World Series and six All-Star Games.

George Sisler of the St. Louis Browns put on an amazing hitting display in two preseason games against the Oilers. Sisler homered twice in an 8-7 loss to the Oilers on March 29th, then hit for the cycle and scored five runs in a 17-2 victory the following day.

That 1920 season was special for Sisler as he set a major league record with 257 base hits, a mark that stood until it was broken by Ichiro Suzuki with the 2004 Seattle Mariners. Sisler won American League batting championships in 1920 and 1922 and was a 1939 inductee into the Baseball Hall of Fame.

In the other two preseason games that year, the St. Louis Cardinals routed the Oilers, 13-3, on March 30th and the Chicago White Sox beat the Oilers on April 7th, 10-4. White Sox pitcher Dickie Kerr, who would win 21 games that year, pitched a complete game.

The newly-elected Commissioner of Baseball, Kenesaw Mountain Landis, delivered a speech on November 22, 1920 at the Tulsa Convention Hall, now known as the Brady Theater and five blocks due west of Tulsa's current baseball stadium, ONEOK Field.

The Chicago-based Landis was a stern federal judge as well as being a lifelong baseball fan. He had been hired as Commissioner of Baseball just 10 days earlier in a bid to restore baseball's credibility in the wake of the 1919 Black Sox scandal. But during his Tulsa speech, Landis never said a word about his new job which paid an astronomical (for the 1920s) annual salary of $50,000.

Landis told the Tulsa audience that gluttony, apathy and complacency since the end of World War I had put America on a rapid slide into cold and material selfishness. He also cites those things as being factors in a rising crime rate and businessmen getting away with shady deals.

Landis delivered equal and harsh criticism of both political parties but also had high praise for the sacrifices of American soldiers and declared his support for equal voting rights for women.

The only other Commissioner of Baseball to visit Tulsa while serving in office was Bowie Kuhn, who came to Oiler Park in August of 1971 for a ceremony honoring Oilers manager Warren Spahn.

1921: This would be one of the worst years in Tulsa's history, both for the Oilers on the field and the for the city's reputation. That Oilers team lost more games (103) than any team in Tulsa's professional baseball history.

But Tulsa's history was forever impacted by what would stand for nearly 70 years when America's worst race-related riot to that point in time erupted over 16 hours spanning May 31st and June 1st. And Oiler players almost found themselves in the midst of the violence.

None of the Oilers' nine pitchers that year had a winning record. Tom Lukanovic and George Boehler lost 21 and 20 games, respectively. The only bright spot for the pitching staff came on August 27th when Hub Pruett threw the second no-hitter in Tulsa baseball history in a 6-0 win against the St. Joseph Saints.

Tulsa had a decent hitting attack, ranking second in the league in home runs (106) and fifth in batting average (.290). Yank Davis was Tulsa's top hitter with a .364 batting average and 21 home runs. First baseman Phil Todt finished third in the league in home runs with 28.

The Wichita Witches (106-61) were the league champions, finishing with a flourish by winning their final 19 games. The Omaha Buffaloes (95-73) finished second and were followed by the Oklahoma City Indians (93-75), Sioux City Packers (81-83), St. Joseph Saints (79-88), Joplin Miners (76-88), Des Moines Boosters (71-92) and the Tulsa Oilers (65-103).

Three preseason games were played at McNulty Park. The Cincinnati Reds routed the Oilers, 14-3, on March 30th before about 1,500 fans. Sam Bohne and Ivey Wingo each hit home runs to lead Cincinnati's 13-hit attack. Reds pitcher Rube Marquard, a three-time 20-game winner and future Baseball Hall of Fame inductee, held Tulsa hitless over the last three innings.

Smooth-fielding shortstop Walter "Rabbit" Maranville scored two runs in a 13-7 victory by the Pittsburgh Pirates over the Oilers the following day. Maranville had been traded to the Pirates by the Boston Braves nine weeks earlier as part of a four-player transaction.

Ty Cobb, in his first season as player-manager of the Detroit Tigers, hit home runs in his first two at-bats as the Tigers shutout the Oilers, 8-0, on April 7th. Cobb's career batting average of .366 is the best in major league baseball history and The Georgia Peach was one of the first inductees into the Baseball Hall of Fame. Harry Hilmann, who became one of Cobb's hitting protégés, also homered twice for the Tigers, who had 14 base hits that day.

Entering the 1921 Memorial Day weekend, there was tension in the community in connection with 18 prisoners escaping from the Tulsa jail in two jailbreaks during the preceding week. Most people were likely looking forward to the holiday weekend and thought nothing would happen either at McNulty Park or downtown until the Oilers returned to open a homestand on June 4th.

The Tulsa Oilers and Oklahoma City Indians played an afternoon doubleheader on May 31st. The first game only took 95 minutes to play and resulted in a 2-1 victory for Oklahoma City. After a short rest period between games, the Oilers rallied for a 6-5, 10-inning victory in a contest that lasted two hours.

The Oilers then hit the road for a three-game series against the Wichita Witches. But the spark that would set the city ablaze was struck with a seemingly innocuous event a few hours earlier. And just a few hours after that doubleheader ended, McNulty Park became one of the city's detention facilities for large numbers of black men, women and children displaced by what would be known as the 1921 Tulsa Race Massacre.

The Drexel Building was located roughly seven blocks north and four blocks northwest of McNulty Park. The major tenants were business offices and retail stores. Most of the downtown businesses were closed for Memorial Day but the Drexel Building was open.

Dick Rowland was a 19-year-old black male who worked at a shoe shine stand. He had been given permission by the Drexel Building's owner to use a racially-segregated restroom on the top floor and went to take an elevator to get to that restroom. Sarah Page was a 17-year-old white female who operated the elevator and knew Rowland.

Suddenly, what sounded like a woman's scream was heard and a department store clerk quickly contacted Tulsa police after seeing an unidentified young black man running from the Drexel Building.

But multiple investigations, including a 2001 report commissioned by the Oklahoma Legislature about the 1921 Tulsa Race Riot, said that Rowland never assaulted Page, either physically or sexually. The report speculated that the scream came after Rowland grabbed Page's arm after stumbling while getting on the elevator.

Page later told officers that she would not press charges and left Tulsa shortly thereafter. Rowland fled to his mother's home and would be arrested the following morning. One of the two arresting officers was a black patrolman. Rowland would later be exonerated and moved from Tulsa to Kansas City.

During the evening and the following morning, rumors and heated gossip were spreading throughout the community about what allegedly happened at the Drexel Building. Then a mob described by historians as white supremacists marched from the downtown courthouse into the predominantly black Greenwood district with guns blazing.

The ensuing looting, gunfire and arson resulted in the destruction of nearly 1,300 structures; among those being homes, schools, family businesses, churches and a hospital. American Red Cross officials estimated that between 100 and 300 people were killed during the violence.

1922: As awful as 1921 turned out to be, the 1922 season was one of the greatest in Tulsa's professional baseball history as the Oilers went from worst to first.

Their 103 victories and .617 winning percentage were the best by any Tulsa professional baseball team and their amazing team batting average of .323 was tops in the Western League. Attendance grew for the second straight year with 135,000 fans. The Oilers later defeated Southern Association champion Mobile Bears, 4-1-1, in a playoff series.

Following Tulsa in the league standings were the St. Joseph Saints (98-70), Wichita Izzies (94-73), Omaha Buffaloes (91-77), Sioux City Packers (86-79), Oklahoma City Indians (73-94), Denver Bears (63-105) and Des Moines Boosters (61-107).

Pitcher George Boehler had one of the greatest seasons in professional baseball history, minor league or major league, with an amazing 38-13 record. Two pitchers won 39 games in the Pacific Coast League during the 1900s but back then, the PCL then played 200-game seasons.

Boehler set franchise season records for victories (38), innings pitched (441) and strikeouts (333). He would win 20 or more games in seven of his 17 minor league seasons but won only six games with four teams over nine major league seasons.

Player-manager Jack Lelivelt was in the first of his three seasons with the Oilers and was also one of seven Oilers who batted .300 or higher. Lelivelt played first base and batted .369 with 16 home runs that year.

Outfielder Herschel Bennett led Tulsa with a .370 batting average and swatted 24 homers. Bennett also set the Tulsa professional baseball single season record of 717 at-bats. Yank Davis hit a team-leading 35 home runs, the first of three straight seasons that he would hit 30-plus homers in Tulsa and also scored 161 runs. Outfielder Lyman

Lamb, a cornerstone of the Oilers' dynasty of the 1920s, hit a career-high 32 home runs.

The Cincinnati Reds routed the Tulsa Oilers, in exhibition games on March 27th and 28th at McNulty Park. Cincinnati won the first meeting, 12-2, and took the second contest, 6-2. Jake Daubert, whose 22 triples led the National League that year, had four hits for Cincinnati in the first meeting. Reds pitchers Pete Donohoe and John Gillespie held Tulsa hitless over the first six innings of the second game. Donohoe won 20 or more games three times for Cincinnati during the 1920s.

Outfielder Henry "Heinei" Manush, a future Hall of Famer who batted .330 over 17 major league seasons, played for Omaha in 1922. Another outfield standout on that Omaha squad was Floyd "Babe" Herman, whose .416 batting average that year was his career high. Herman spent 13 years in major league baseball and while playing for Brooklyn in 1929 and 1930, was the runner-up for the National League batting title in each of those years.

1923: How can a team win 101 games, lead the Western League in hitting (.327) and fielding percentage (.968) and miss the playoffs? Just ask the 1923 Tulsa Oilers. Those 101 victories are tied for the second-highest season total in Tulsa's professional baseball history and the .601 winning percentage is second-highest as well.

Karl Black and Hollis McLaughlin were the aces of Tulsa's pitching staff and two of eight Western League pitchers with 20 or more victories that year. Black led the Western League with a career-high 29 victories while McLaughlin went 23-16. That duo picked up the slack for George Boehler's free fall from a 38-13 record in 1922 to a lackluster 7-9 in 1923.

Yank Davis and Lyman Lamb packed the big bats for the Oilers, who had 11 players with batting averages of .300 or higher. Davis batted .352 with 240 hits and 32 home runs, the latter figure ranking second in the league that season. Lamb led the league with 241 hits and batted .341.

Attendance at McNulty Park increased for the third straight year with 142,228 fans, the best single-season attendance in Tulsa's pro baseball history to that point.

The Oklahoma City Indians, Oilers and Wichita Izzies each won 100 or more games. Oklahoma City won the pennant with a 102-64 record, followed by Tulsa (101-67) and Wichita (100-68). That trio was followed by the Omaha Buffaloes (92-74), Des Moines Boosters (87-79), St. Joseph Saints (65-101), Sioux City Packers (59-105) and Denver Bears (59-107).

Oklahoma City's success was remarkable considering that their home field, located along the banks of the North Canadian River, was destroyed during that season by a major flood. The team finished the season at the Oklahoma State Fairgrounds, playing on an improvised baseball diamond that frequently had issues with water and mud.

Des Moines' Shags Horan led the Western League with a phenomenal .411 batting average and played briefly with the New York Giants the following year. Wichita's Jim Blakesley batted .359 and put on an unprecedented display of power with 105 of his 246 hits going for extra bases, including a league-leading 36 home runs. Blakesley never reached the major leagues but hit .333 over 15 minor league seasons.

McNulty Park was the site of two memorable exhibitions games that year. On April 5th, the Pittsburgh Pirates trounced the Oilers, 10-1. Future Hall of Famer Pie Traynor homered twice and former Oilers Max Carey, Cotton Tierney and Bob Russell also homered.

Nine future Hall of Famers played in an April 10th exhibition game in which the New York Yankees edged the Brooklyn Dodgers, 5-4. The Yankees scored three runs in the eighth inning to pull out the victory.

An overflow crowd of 8,319 fans saw the game, a figure that would be the largest exhibition attendance in Tulsa's baseball history until 1965.

Yankee third baseman Joseph "Jumping Joe" Dugan had a home run and a double among his game-leading four base hits and first baseman Wally Pipp added two base hits. Diehard baseball fans remember that Pipp was replaced in the Yankees' starting lineup on June 2, 1925 by Lou Gehrig, who went on to play in 2,130 consecutive games. Brooklyn left fielder and future Hall of Famer Zac Wheat homered in that game.

Even though he struck out in all four at-bats, Babe Ruth caused the biggest commotion among McNulty Park spectators. Fans cheered loud and long for the Yankee right fielder at the start of each inning and "The Bambino" would grin and wave back every time. When the game ended, a group of 400 youngsters swarmed Ruth in right field in hopes of shaking his hand or getting an autograph. Ruth held his arms above his head and waded through the crowd to get into a waiting taxi.

1924: The Oilers had a league-leading team batting average of .326 but inconsistent pitching was their downfall, resulting in a third-place finish. Nevertheless, it was a Lamb named Lyman that roared mightily throughout the Western League.

Lamb had a .373 batting average with 261 base hits but his claim to fame was setting a single-season professional baseball record by hitting 100 doubles; a feat which has never been matched on the major league or minor league levels. He batted .304 in 16 minor league seasons but hit .272 with just one home run and 21 RBIs over parts of two seasons with the 1920 and 1921 St. Louis Browns.

Second baseman Royce "Mule" Washburn led the league with 48 home runs and set Tulsa's professional baseball record for the most games played in a season, 169. Yank Davis swatted 42 home runs that year, the third-highest total in Tulsa professional baseball history.

Karl Black was Tulsa's top pitcher with a 20-15 record and Russ Pence provided fireworks of his own with a 22-0 no-hit victory over the Omaha Buffaloes on the Fourth of July. That game also set a Western League record for the largest victory margin as Tulsa scored in every inning except the second and third and capitalized on 15 base hits, 10 walks by Omaha pitchers and three fielding errors.

This would be Jack Lelivelt's final season as Tulsa's player-manager. His record with the Oilers was 293-200. As a minor league manager from 1920 through 1940, Lelivelt's 1,861 career victories ranks 19th in minor league baseball managerial history.

The Omaha Buffaloes won the pennant with a 103-61 record led by three hurlers who won 20 or more games. Herb Hall was the ace of the Buffaloes' staff with a 26-13 record. Trailing Omaha in the standings were the Denver Bears (100-67), Tulsa (89-69), St. Joseph Saints (86-79), Oklahoma City Indians (82-86), Wichita Izzies (79-88), Des Moines Boosters (59-106) and Lincoln Links (57-108).

Infielder Tony Lazzeri, who played on five of the New York Yankees' World Series championship teams during the 1920s and 1930s, batted .329 and hit 28 home runs that year for last-place Lincoln. Lazzeri drove in 100 or more runs seven times in his major league career and was a 1991 inductee into the Baseball Hall of Fame.

The Oilers played preseason exhibition games on three consecutive days. The Chicago Cubs banged out 25 base hits in a 25-8 rout of the Oilers on April 8th, the most lopsided exhibition score in Tulsa's professional baseball history. Future Hall of Fame catcher Charles "Gabby" Harnett went 4-for-4 and third baseman Barney Friberg homered twice for the Cubs.

Jack Lelivelt delivered a two-out, two-run double in the bottom of the ninth inning for a 5-4 victory over the St. Louis Browns on April 9th. Marty McManus, who would be the Oilers' manager in 1936, gave the Browns an early lead with a three-run home run.

The Browns avenged the loss the next day, aided by 13 hits in a 9-3 victory. Ken Williams went 3-for-4 and George Sisler went 2-for-3 while Urban Shocker held Tulsa scoreless over the first four innings.

Late in the 1924 season, rumors circulated that Tulsa and Oklahoma City wanted to move to the Texas League. It did not happen that season but those whispers wouldn't stop for another five years.

1925: Lyman Lamb assumed the Oilers' managerial duties but one of the greatest hitters in Tulsa's baseball history didn't have a winning touch in the dugout and he was fired in July. The Oilers' 91 losses that year is the third-highest total for losses in a season in Tulsa's professional baseball history.

Marty "Pepper" Berghammer replaced Lamb and from that point through the 1929 season, he would earn 373 victories and two Western League championships with the Oilers.

Infielders Sam Simon was Tulsa's top hitter with a .360 batting average and 22 home runs. First baseman Guy Sturdy had a .353 batting average, the sixth straight minor league season in which he hit .300 or higher.

Outfielder Joe Riggert batted .348, led the Western League with 57 doubles and also hit 21 home runs. Baseball historian Bill James once wrote that during the 1910s, Riggert was the best minor league baseball player of that decade. Riggert finished with 2,717 hits in 2,403 minor league games.

Stew Bolen led the Western League in strikeouts (184) and had a 17-13 record. Karl Black had the dubious distinction of leading the Oilers' pitching staff in wins (18) and losses (20).

The Des Moines Demons (98-70) edged the Denver Bears (97-71) to win the pennant. They were followed by the Oklahoma City Indians (88-76), Wichita Izzies (80-84), St. Joseph Saints (77-87), Omaha Buffaloes (74-89), Tulsa Oilers (75-91) and Lincoln Links (70-91).

Oklahoma City manager Fred Luderus took a young left-handed pitcher under his wing and taught him how to throw a screwball. That pitch would turn Carl Hubbell into the National League's top left-handed pitcher during the 1930s with the New York Giants.

Hubbell attended high school in Meeker, Oklahoma (approximately 75 miles southwest of Tulsa) and he won 17 games that season for Oklahoma City. He went on to be a nine-time National League All-Star during his time with the Giants (1928-43) and led that league three times in victories and lowest earned run average. His best seasons came in 1933 through 1937 when he won 20 or more games in each year.

But the pinnacle of Hubbell's success came during the 1934 All-Star Game played at the Polo Grounds in New York City. The pitcher nicknamed "King Carl" consecutively struck out five future Hall of Famers: Babe Ruth, Lou Gehrig, Jimmie Foxx, Al Simmons and Joe Cronin. Hubbell spent 60 years in the Giants' organization, overseeing their minor league teams and scouting for potential players. He was inducted into the Baseball Hall of Fame in 1947.

1926: A full season with Marty Berghammer as the manager did wonders for the Oilers. They finished fourth in the Western League (86-78), won 11 more games than in the previous year and gathered many of the players who would play key roles in the successful three seasons that followed.

First baseman Guy Sturdy and outfielder Pete Casey each set single-season records for Tulsa professional baseball. Sturdy hit a career-high 49 home runs while scoring 163 runs. Sturdy played parts of the following two seasons with the St. Louis Browns but a shoulder injury in 1929 reduced his power hitting stroke to almost nothing. Casey's batting average of .393 still stands as the season record for Tulsa players having a minimum of 330 at-bats.

George Blaeholder, who was instrumental in creating the baseball pitch now known as the slider, won 27 games for the Oilers. Blaeholder spent 10 of his 11 major league seasons with the St. Louis Browns and led the American League with four shutouts in 1929.

Despite walking 170 batters and hitting 21 others, Walter Beck posted an 18-17 record and earned the nickname "Boom Boom" because he hit four home runs, had a .315 batting average and 14 of his 39 hits that year went for extra bases. Beck went on to win 20 or more games twice during an 18-year major league career.

For the second straight season, the Des Moines Demons won the pennant by a razor-thin margin, posting a 99-64 record with the Oklahoma City Indians second at 100-66. Following them in the standings were the St. Joseph Saints (89-75), Denver Bears (88-80), Tulsa Oilers (86-78), Omaha Buffaloes (77-89), Lincoln Links (64-101) and Wichita Izzies (58-108).

Two-run home runs by future Hall of Famers Chick Hafey and Bob O'Farrell gave the St. Louis Cardinals a 4-0 exhibition victory over Tulsa before 2,183 fans at McNulty Park on April 6th. Cardinal pitcher Bill Hallahan pitched a complete game and struck out seven Oilers. St. Louis would defeat the New York Yankees in seven games to win the 1926 World Series.

1927: Babe Ruth got the national headlines by hitting 60 home runs for the New York Yankees that season but the Tulsa Oilers were making history of their own by winning the first of three consecutive Western League championships.

Except for an Opening Day rainout, Tulsa led the league wire-to-wire and finished with a 101-53 record. The Oilers' .333 team batting average was the best in the city's professional baseball history. The season attendance of 140,000 was the second-highest in Tulsa's baseball history to that point.

The Oilers' 101 victories that year are tied for the second-highest season total in Tulsa's professional baseball history and their .656 winning percentage ranks third in Tulsa professional baseball history.

Following Tulsa in the standings were the Wichita Larks (91-63), Des Moines Demons (82-72), Denver Bears (77-75), Oklahoma City Indians (68-86), Amarillo Texans (66-87), Omaha Buffaloes (66-88) and Lincoln Links (63-90).

The Oilers faced the Texas League champion Waco Cubs in the Dixie Series, but lost that series, 3-2 with one tie. Waco's star player was 39-year-old Del Pratt, who was the Texas League's first Triple Crown batting champion as the league's leader in batting average, home runs and runs batted in.

Outfielders Fred Bennett and Joe Munson sparked the Oilers offense. Munson led the Western League with 32 home runs and batted .383. Munson's last name was actually Carlson and he had played the previous two seasons for the National League's Chicago Cubs. Amazingly, that .383 batting average wasn't good enough to lead the Oilers that year because Bennett hit. 385. Bennett had a sensational .343 batting average over his 14-year minor league career.

Guy Sturdy batted .347 and also hit 23 home runs, then replaced George Sisler as the St. Louis Browns' first baseman near the end of the 1927 season. Eleven years later, Sturdy gained unwanted fame when as manager of the Marshall (Texas) Tigers, his physical assault of an umpire drew a 90-day suspension.

George Blaeholder posted his second straight 20-win season by going 26-9 as the Oilers' pitching ace. Stewart Bolen won a career-high 19 games in 35 pitching appearances.

The Oilers lost preseason exhibitions on consecutive days to the Chicago Cubs and St. Louis Browns.

Future Hall of Famer Hack Wilson went 5-for-5, including a home run, and scored three runs in the Cubs' 16-4 victory over the Oilers on April 5th. Joe Munson led the Oilers with three doubles. The next day, the Browns scored five runs in the top of the ninth inning to pull out an 8-5 victory over the Oilers. Left fielder Harry Rice went 4-for-4 and George Sisler added two hits for St. Louis.

After the 1927 season ended, Tulsa and Oklahoma City tried again to jump to the Texas League. That move was stopped by the combination of a ruling from the National Arbitration Board and Texas League officials believing that Tulsa did not have an adequate baseball stadium.

1928: Tulsa won its second consecutive Western League pennant as the Oilers participated in their first split season competition in 12 years. This was one of the better hitting teams in Tulsa's baseball history as those Oilers had a team batting average of .323 and led the Western League in runs scored, total base hits, doubles and home runs.

And two players off that Tulsa championship squad would achieve athletic notoriety in following years.

The Oklahoma City Indians won the first half pennant with a 51-29 record while Tulsa went 43-39. The Oilers won the second half pennant with a 53-30 record, holding off a late surge by the Wichita Larks (52-32). Tulsa won the playoff series against Oklahoma City, 4-1-1. A season attendance record of 145,000 was set and would be matched the following year.

Oklahoma City had the best overall season record at 95-67 with Tulsa second at 96-69. Then came the Wichita Larks (94-70), Pueblo Steeler Workers (85-78), Denver Bears (81-84), Omaha Crickets (71-86), Amarillo Texans (60-93) and Des Moines Demons (63-98).

Outfielders Fred Bennett and Joe Munson put the pop in Tulsa's hitting attack while Chad Kimsey and Rollie Naylor were the pitching aces. Munson led the league with a .385 batting average, hit 39 home runs and also led the league in runs scored and base hits. Bennett batted .371 and hit 35 home runs, the third and final time in his career that he would have 30-plus homers.

Kimsey, a 21-year-old right-handed power pitcher, had a career best 23-7 record. He pitched for the St. Louis Browns, Chicago White Sox and Detroit Tigers over the next six seasons, but won only 24 games over that span. Naylor, the greybeard of Tulsa's staff at age 36, went 19-12.

Bennett did not play baseball in 1929 but made baseball history in 1930 as the sport's first free agent, laying a philosophical foundation for what would lead to high player salaries about a half-century later.

Baseball commissioner Kenesaw Mountain Landis ruled that St. Louis Browns owner Fred Ball unfairly stymied Bennett's career and that Bennett could seek a contract to play for whatever team he wanted. A federal court upheld the commissioner's ruling and 200 other players followed Bennett's footsteps into free agency during that decade.

Bennett played only one major league season after that legal hubbub, batting .281 with one home run and seven RBIs in 32 games with the 1931 Pittsburgh Pirates.

A future Hall of Famer in another sport was the Oilers' right fielder that year. Morris "Red" Badgro had been a baseball and football standout at the University of Southern California. He played one year with the National Football League's New York Yankees and then retired but came to Tulsa hoping to revive his baseball career.

Badgro did well with the Oilers, batting .334 with eight home runs and 10 stolen bases. The St. Louis Browns promoted him to the major leagues and he played for them for two years.

But after seeing how inept the Browns were, Badgro gave the NFL another try and played for the New York Football Giants as a wide receiver and defensive end in the 1930-35 seasons. He caught 16 touchdown passes in 1934, a significant statistic given the NFL's emphasis of the running game back then. In 1981, Badgro would be the oldest inductee into the Pro Football Hall of Fame at the age of 78.

Tulsa was on the losing end of two preseason games against the St. Louis Browns that year. Ralph Kress had three hits and Heinie Manush added two hits in the Browns' 9-8 victory before 1,500 fans on April 2nd. The Oilers scored four runs in a ninth-inning rally but it wasn't enough. The next day, the Browns blitzed the Oilers with a 28-hit attack in a 23-8 rout. Former Oilers Fred Bennett and Guy Sturdy combined for nine hits and two home runs.

1929: Tulsa baseball dreams came true and also died that year. The good news was that the Oilers won their third consecutive Western League championship. The bad news was the financial collapse of the team which, combined with political bickering about a new baseball stadium, would leave the city without professional baseball until 1932.

Everything looked rosy when the Oilers posted a preseason victory over the defending World Series champion New York Yankees on April 8th. Over 8,000 spectators jammed into McNulty Park to see the Oilers defeat the Yankees, 12-8. Irv Burns of the Oilers went 4-for-4 and scored three runs.

Lou Gehrig and Babe Ruth were the hitting stars for the Yankees. Gehrig ripped a three-run home run in the first inning, a towering shot which cleared the railroad tracks beyond the short right field fence. Ruth singled twice and nearly created a riot in the seventh inning while playing left field.

After a ground-rule double down the foul line rolled into a group of standing-room only fans, a spectator tossed the ball back to Ruth. But Ruth tossed the ball back into the crowd and chaos erupted when a scuffle to get the ball spilled onto the playing field close to where Ruth stood. Tulsa police officers intervened to restore order.

The parent St. Louis Browns defeated the Oilers in preseason games on April 10th and 11th. Future Hall of Famers Heinie Manusch and Rick Ferrell led the Browns' 7-5 victory on April 10th. George Blaeholder pitched a six-hit shutout and hit a home run against his former team in the Browns' 14-0 victory on April 11th.

Shortstop Ralph "Red" Kress, a member of the 1927 Oilers, also homered for St. Louis. As a big-league rookie with the 1928 Browns, Kress led the American League in defensive magic (assisting on 400 putouts) and defensive misery (committing 55 errors).

Artemus Ward "Nick" Allen was the Oilers' new manager and he promptly guided Tulsa to another pennant. He previously was the minor league manager for baseball legends Leo Durocher and Chuck Dressen and also had genealogical linkage to Daniel Boone and former American President Harry Truman.

The Oilers posted a 95-66 regular season record, leading the Western League in batting average, runs scored, total base hits, doubles and home runs. Following Tulsa in the standings were the Oklahoma City Indians (88-68), Omaha Crickets (81-75), Wichita Aviators (77-79), Denver Bears (73-81), Topeka Jayhawks (75-85), Des Moines Demons (72-86) and Pueblo Steel Workers (69-90).

First baseman Irving Burns led Tulsa in home runs (36) while batting .337. Outfielders Joe Munson and Ted Gullic each hit 32 homers.

Munson led the league in runs scored (167) and also hit three home runs in a single game.

Second baseman Lin Storti led the league with 230 base hits, including a career-high 61 doubles. Len Stiles was the pitching ace with a 22-11 record in 45 appearances and threw a no-hitter against the Des Moines Demons.

Things got very ugly off the field after winning the pennant. Five days after the season ended, Stiles was sold to the major league St. Louis Browns. Munson's contract was sold to the Waco Cubs of the Texas League.

It turned out that the Oilers had lost $26,000 in each of the past two pennant-winning seasons, which was very big money back in those days. And coupled with the Wall Street financial collapse in October of 1929, baseball wasn't the only business facing extremely grave circumstances.

During minor league baseball's winter meetings in December, Allen was fired as the Oilers' manager, all of Tulsa's infielders were sold to other teams and the franchise was relocated to Topeka, Kansas during the following month.

The Oilers had hoped the year before to win approval to build a new stadium near the intersection of East 21st Street and South Lewis Avenue, which is now part of midtown Tulsa. Those plans fell through in 1929 when the city of Tulsa annexed that land and costs for taxes and rentals made building a baseball stadium financially prohibitive.

In an ironic twist, on the same day that the 1929 demolition of McNulty Park began, the man who brought professional baseball back to Tulsa in 1919, Jim Crawford, passed away. The land where McNulty Park once stood is today occupied by one of three Tulsa locations for a national chain of home improvement stores.

Chapter Four
The 1930s

This would be one of the darker periods in American history with the widespread economic impact of the Great Depression and the beginning of World War II in 1939. National unemployment reached 25 per cent of the work force and personal financial wealth plummeted. President Franklin Delano Roosevelt created the New Deal to put Americans back to work through numerous construction projects.

Western Oklahoma became known as the Dust Bowl because of a widespread drought. Countless families lost their farms and moved westward to California to seek a new start. Those people would be known as Okies and the subject of John Steinbeck's best-selling novel as well as a popular movie, *The Grapes of Wrath*.

The 1930s did have some bright spots with the adoption of *The Star-Spangled Banner* as the National Anthem, the debut of *The Wizard of Oz* and *Snow White and the Seven Dwarfs* movies and *The Adventures of Superman* cartoon books. There was also the introduction of air conditioning, cheeseburgers, parking meters (Oklahoma City had the first one in 1935), Zippo lighters, *Gone with the Wind* (both the novel and the movie), the Volkswagen Beetle automobile and the debut of Little League baseball.

Bob Wills and his Texas Playboys took their highly danceable music called Western Swing to Tulsa in 1934 with Cain's Ballroom in downtown Tulsa becoming their headquarters.

The hearts of Oklahomans were heavy in 1935 after the death of their Favorite Son, Will Rogers, in an Alaska plane crash that also took the life of aviation legend Wiley Post. Born in the nearby town of Oologah, Rogers was also a movie actor, newspaper columnist, cowboy, vaudeville star, humorist and social commentator.

After not having minor league baseball for the 1930 and 1931 seasons, the sport returned to Tulsa with a bang in 1932 and a new home in the Texas League. The Oilers would win three league championships and make five playoff appearances. Local sports fans benefitted from one of the New Deal construction projects with the building of a new baseball stadium on the Tulsa State Fairgrounds.

Joe DiMaggio, Lou Gehrig and Lefty Gomez were among the major league baseball stars appearing in exhibition games played in Tulsa. Other big-league standouts coming to Tulsa back then included Joe "Ducky" Medwick, Paul and Lloyd Waner, Dizzy and Paul Dean, Pie Traynor and Luke Appling.

1930: A dispute between the Oilers' management and the city of Tulsa over land rights for a new baseball stadium resulted in no professional baseball that season.

On February 11th, the Western League relocated Tulsa's franchise to Topeka, Kansas and it would be known as the Topeka Senators during the 1930 and 1931 seasons, placing seventh in the eight-team league in each of those seasons.

The team's manager was a veteran of minor league baseball known as Christian Frederick Albert John Henry David Betzel. Fortunately, he went by the nickname of Bruno.

The Wichita Aviators won the league championship with an 89-56 record. Forrest Jensen provided Wichita's offensive punch by leading the league in batting average (.354) and runs scored (207). Pitcher Charles Wood led the league in wins (22) and strikeouts (197). Art Griggs, who figured prominently in Tulsa baseball history just two years later, was Wichita's manager.

Following Wichita in the standings were the Omaha Packers (76-66), Oklahoma City Indians (79-71), Des Moines Demons (79-71), Pueblo Braves (75-75), Denver Bears (74-74), Topeka Senators (66-84) and St. Joseph Saints (53-92).

Had there been a Tulsa Oilers team in 1930, they would likely have been among the first professional baseball teams to play a game at night under permanent lights.

Des Moines defeated Wichita, 13-6, in a night game on May 2nd before a crowd of about 12,000 fans, which included baseball commissioner Kenesaw Mountain Landis. The NBC Radio Network broadcast the game but couldn't carry it live due to its prior commitments for other radio shows. The broadcast didn't begin until 10:30 that night and it ended around 1:00 a.m.

Future Hall of Famer pitcher Jay Hanna "Dizzy" Dean was a hotshot 20-year-old rookie pitcher for the lowly Saints that year. Blending a lightning-like fastball with a sharply bending curve ball, Dean posted a 17-8 record in 32 appearances with a 3.69 earned run average and made the Western League All-Star team.

That resulted in a quick promotion to the St. Louis Cardinals' Houston affiliate in the Texas League where he won the 1931 Texas League Player of the Year award with a 26-10 record and 1.57 ERA.

Dean became a four-time National League All-Star (1934-37), won 30 games in 1934 and was one of the stars of the Cardinals' teams of that era known as "The Gashouse Gang." Baseball fans coming out of the Great Depression era took to the Cardinals because their blue-collar work ethic was the opposite of the rich and powerful teams such as the New York Giants.

Fans and sports media alike were drawn to Dean's colorful persona of a not-too-bright country bumpkin with an equal flair for making bold statements then backing up those words with actions. Dean became a radio and television baseball announcer after retiring as a player. His broadcast career was renowned for his enthusiasm as well as his frequent mangling of proper and correct English grammar.

Dean would play for the 1940 Tulsa Oilers in the twilight of his professional baseball career before being inducted in the Baseball Hall of Fame in 1953.

1931: Lucille Thomas acquired a Western League franchise for Tulsa and Howie Gregory, who played briefly for the St. Louis Browns in 1911, was tabbed to serve as Tulsa's business manager. Thomas wanted to build a new stadium near the intersection of Admiral Boulevard and South Utica Avenue, roughly two miles due east of the current home of the Tulsa Drillers, ONEOK Field. The Tulsa team held a spring training camp in Ponca City, Oklahoma and even practiced against the St. Louis Browns.

Finding a financial investor willing to build a stadium during the second year of the Great Depression was just too much for Thomas to overcome and professional baseball in Tulsa had to wait one more year. Just 10 days before Opening Day of the season, Western League management moved the Tulsa franchise back to Topeka.

The booming bat of Sean Keys lifted the Des Moines Demons to a 94-51 record and a 4-2 victory in the best-of-7 championship playoff against the runner-up Wichita Aviators (92-58). Keys led the league with 38 home runs and a .369 batting average. Following Des Moines and Wichita in the standings were the St. Joseph Saints (79-64), Pueblo Braves (76-69), Oklahoma City Indians (79-80), Denver Bears (64-77), Topeka Senators (58-86) and Omaha Packers (49-79).

Future Hall of Famer Joseph Floyd "Arky" Vaughn was a 19-year-old shortstop with Wichita that year. He led the league with 167 base hits with 58 of those going for extra bases. Vaughn joined the Pittsburgh Pirates the following year and played 14 years in the majors, won the 1935 National League batting title with a .385 average and was a nine-time All-Star selection.

1932: Tulsa returned to professional baseball in grand style with the opening of a new stadium along with one of the best teams in the city's baseball history winning a championship in their final season in the Western League.

An article on the official website of Minor League baseball (www.milb.com) ranked the 1932 Tulsa Oilers 83rd among the Top 100 teams in the history of minor league baseball for its amazing collection of talented players.

The Oilers had five players that scored 100 or more runs apiece with two of them batting over .350 and lashing over 60 extra base hits apiece. Pitching was another strong point with the Oilers having five of the Western League's top nine pitchers in total victories, all of them being age 25 years or younger.

The Oilers' regular-season record of 98-48 represents the fourth-highest total for wins in a season in Tulsa and their winning percentage of .671 is the second-best mark in Tulsa professional baseball history. Tulsa defeated the Oklahoma City Indians for the league championship after a heated battle to end the regular season and through the playoffs but both teams jumped to the Texas League after the season ended.

Tulsa won the first half title with a 46-32 record, eight games better than Denver while Oklahoma City went a lackluster 31-41. But the Indians came alive in the second half and tied the Oilers for the second half title with a sizzling 52-26 record. Oklahoma City won a best-of-three mini-series to determine the second half regular season champion.

But the championship series didn't have the drama of the previous meetings with Tulsa sweeping that best-of-seven series, 4-0. Oklahoma City protested one of those victories and the protest was upheld by Western League officials but the torrid Tulsans won again when the game was replayed.

The final Western League standings saw Tulsa at 98-48, followed by the Oklahoma City Indians (83-67), Denver Bears (83-64), Des Moines Demons (71-72), St. Joseph Saints (72-75), Pueblo Braves (62-75), Wichita Aviators (63-86) and Omaha Packers (58-88).

Outfielder Stan Schino led the Oilers in batting average (.354), runs batted in (143), doubles (32) and shared the team lead in home runs (18) with outfield teammate John Stoneman. The 23-year-old Stoneman batted .352 and added a team-leading 28 triples. Second baseman Cecil Stewart and first baseman Bobby Hipps led the Oilers in runs scored with 148 and 147, respectively and shortstop Floyd Young scored 102 runs.

Another Tulsa standout was Leo Najo who was one of the first Mexican players in Organized Baseball and the first player inducted into the Mexican Baseball Hall of Fame back in 1939.

Najo was a 5-foot-9, 155-pound outfielder who batted leadoff and his knack for drawing walks proved invaluable for Tulsa that year. He batted .323 with 33 extra-base hits and was third on the Oilers in runs batted in (94). Najo was a defensive standout as well, making numerous acrobatic catches and displaying a strong and accurate throwing arm.

He was drafted by the Chicago White Sox in 1925 but baseball historians have written that the combination of a leg injury, racial prejudice and a desire to help his impoverished family during the Great Depression kept Najo from achieving the level of fame for Hispanic baseball players in the way that Jackie Robinson did for African-American baseball players.

Andy Bednar was Tulsa's pitching ace with a career-best 22-4 record in 33 appearances. Pinpoint control was Bednar's strongest suit as he walked just 64 batters over 234 innings pitched.

Due to family and economic pressures related to the Great Depression, Bednar left Organized Baseball shortly thereafter and was working for his uncle in oil fields south of Graham, Texas when he died in an auto accident on November 26, 1937 at the age of 29.

Jim Bivin went 15-7 that year but has long held a place in baseball trivia for what he did three years later. He was the Philadelphia Phillies' starting pitcher in a game against the Boston Braves on May 30, 1935. Babe Ruth went hitless in his only at-bat against Bivin and the Sultan of Swat never played after that, meaning that Bivin was the last pitcher that Babe Ruth faced in his baseball career.

Bill Posedel went 16-10 with Tulsa in 37 appearances but walked more batters (121) than he struck out (70). But his impact on baseball was profound nearly 40 years later. Posedel worked with the pitching staff of the World Series champion Oakland Athletics in the early 1970s and played key roles in the development of All-Star pitchers Jim "Catfish" Hunter, John "Blue Moon" Odom and relief ace Rollie Fingers.

Games that year were played at the newly-built Fairgrounds Park, located on a former horse racing track on the Tulsa State Fairgrounds to the south-southwest of the intersection of East 15th Street and South Yale Avenue. (Little did anyone know that Tulsa's baseball stadium-horse racing connection would resurface nearly 50 years later.) Fairgrounds Park had seating for 4,000 fans and served as the Oilers' home field for two years.

While season attendance topped six figures at 101,450, that figure was nearly 44,000 lower than 1929; the last season in which Tulsa had a professional baseball team. The Great Depression was no small factor, illustrated by the stock market's Dow Jones average bottoming out at 41.22 on July 8th.

1933: An April 6th exhibition game at Fairgrounds Park was part of the festivities connected with the Tulsa Oilers moving up to the Texas League. Tulsa's parent team, the Pittsburgh Pirates, erased an 8-0 fourth inning deficit and pulled out a 9-8 victory over the Chicago White Sox before 4,016 fans. It would be the first of three consecutive annual exhibitions between those two teams in Tulsa.

Pittsburgh tied the game with six runs in the seventh inning and scored the winning run in the eighth. Pie Traynor and Paul Waner had two hits apiece and Waner scored twice. Waite Hoyt pitched the last three innings in relief to pick up the win. Jimmy Dykes went 2-for-3 for the White Sox while Luke Appling went 0-for-4. The game was called after eight innings because the Pirates had to make a train connection.

Pittsburgh delivered when it had to in that exhibition game but failed to do the same for the Oilers when it counted most midway through the season. The Pirates' financial problems, coupled with Oilers owner-manager Art Griggs spending more money than planned on stadium repairs and player salaries, led to Pittsburgh unplugging the Oilers' financial lifeline. Griggs sold three players to Pittsburgh and made a small financial profit but the Oilers finished 29 games out of first place in their Texas League debut.

Outfielder John Stoneham became the first Tulsa player named to the Texas League's postseason All-Star Team. He played every inning of every game that year, led the Oilers in batting average (.304) and shared the team's RBI leadership with third baseman Sam Hale (81). Stoneham's outfield teammate, Chuck Hostetler, led the Texas League in triples with 20.

A.F. Johns and Frank Barnes were the only Tulsa pitchers with winning records, going 17-14 and 12-11 respectively.

Charles Wood was only 2-11 that year but one of his victories was a no-hitter which came in a 9-2, seven-inning triumph over the Houston Buffaloes in the second game of a July 23rd doubleheader. The Oilers were on the losing end of the first recorded nine-inning no-hitter by an opposing pitcher when Galveston's Henry Thormahlen wove a 2-0 gem on June 9th.

The San Antonio Missions were the Texas League champions, defeating the Galveston Buccaneers in the championship series, 4-2. San Antonio swept Houston in a three-game semifinal series. Galveston advanced with a 3-2 series victory over the Dallas Steers, who reached the playoffs despite going through three managers and starting the year with a 23-30 record.

Houston had the best season record at 94-57, followed by Galveston (88-64), Dallas (82-70), San Antonio (79-72), the Beaumont Exporters (73-79), Tulsa Oilers (65-86), Fort Worth Cats (63-88) and Oklahoma City Indians (62-90).

Dallas first baseman Henry John "Zeke" Bonura was the Texas League Player of the Year, leading the league with 24 home runs, finishing second in batting average (.357) and tied for third in doubles

(43). Bonura spent his first four major league seasons with the Chicago White Sox but his defensive shortcomings led to his playing sparingly over the final three seasons.

Galveston's George Darrow was the Texas League Pitcher of the Year, posting a 22-7 record and a 2.61 ERA. The left-handed hurler tied Houston's Ed Greer for the league lead in victories and ranked fourth in innings pitched (272). Darrow's major league career was short-lived, however, posting a 2-6 record the following year with the Philadelphia Phillies before returning to the minors until retiring in 1943.

1934: Despite finishing just two games over .500 at 77-75, this was a significant season for the Oilers. They moved into a new stadium and three players were named to the Texas League's postseason All-Star team, as chosen by *The Sporting News* magazine.

The honorees were first baseman Alex Hooks, shortstop Skeeter Newsome and outfielder Chuck Hostetler. Hooks led the Texas League with 24 triples and his .340 batting average was third-highest in the league. Hostetler led the league with 124 runs scored. Newsome batted .286 and had 33 doubles.

Texas League Park was opened on July 11, 1934 at the southeast corner of East 15th Street and South Sandusky Avenue in the northeastern section of the Tulsa State Fairgrounds. The wooden structure seated 4,000 fans and measured 355 feet down each foul line and 380 feet to center field.

The stadium was one of many construction projects under the auspices of the Works Progress Administration, the ambitious program which was part of the New Deal vision of President Franklin Delano Roosevelt to re-employ unskilled workers following the Great Depression. Between 1934 and 1977, Texas League Park would be expanded and later renamed as Oiler Park and Driller Park.

Jake Atz had a 77-75 record in his only season as a Tulsa Oilers manager. That would be one of the few blemishes on the record of the winningest manager in Texas League history. He served as manager of the Fort Worth Panthers (1914-29, 1933), Dallas Steers (1930), Shreveport Sports (1931) and Galveston Buccaneers (1936).

Among the 14 Texas League managerial career records set by Atz are the most managerial seasons (21), most games (3,838), most victories (1,566), most winning seasons (12), most consecutive winning seasons (10), most league championships (6, all consecutive in 1920-25) and most Dixie Series championships (5).

He claimed to have a birth name of John Jacob Zimmerman but changed it to Jacob Henry Atz because earlier in his minor league career, players were paid alphabetically by last names but owners would run out of money for those whose last names came later in the alphabet. His major league career consisted of three games with the 1902 Washington Senators and three years (1907-09) with the Chicago White Sox.

Outfielder John Stoneham played every inning of every game for the second straight season and finished with a .313 batting average and 39 doubles. He also led the Texas League in bases on balls (91) and ranked third in RBIs (109).

Pitcher Mace Brown was the Texas League leader in strikeouts (168) while posting a 19-12 record and a 3.53 ERA. That earned a quick promotion to the Pittsburgh Pirates, with whom he spent seven of his 10 major-league seasons. He pitched the final three innings of the National League's 4-1 victory in the 1938 All-Star Game.

But on September 28, 1938, Brown became part of baseball infamy, giving up the legendary two-out, two-strike "Homer in the Gloamin'" in a nearly-dark Wrigley Field to Chicago Cubs catcher Gabby Harnett. That walk-off home run played a key role in the Cubs reaching the 1938 World Series.

Brown later worked as Boston Red Sox scout and convinced them to sign Jim Rice, a promising but raw outfielder from South Carolina. Rice became an eight-time American League All-Star and was a 2009 inductee into the Baseball Hall of Fame.

Future Texas League Baseball Hall of Fame outfielder Paul Easterling had a league-leading 29 home runs as an Oiler that year. That was even more remarkable considering that the right-handed hitting Easterling used a cross-handed batting grip.

Nicknamed "Pound 'Em Paul" for his hitting prowess, Easterling is the Texas League's career leader in games played (1,777), at-bats (6,502), runs scored (1,134), total base hits (1,922), extra-base hits (667), total bases (3,101), strikeouts (852), doubles (378), home runs (223), and runs batted in (1,136).

He spent 13 years in the Texas League and played for three pennant-winning teams: the 1932 Beaumont Exporters, the 1935 Oklahoma City Indians (who also won the Dixie Series that year) and the 1941 Dallas Rebels. Surprisingly, Easterling only played 76 major league games over three years (the 1928 and 1930 Detroit Tigers and 1938 Philadelphia Athletics) and hit just four big-league home runs.

Pitcher Jim Bivin, who played that year for Tulsa and Galveston, led the Texas League with eight shutouts. Bivin went 20-14 that year with a 2.79 ERA.

Beaumont Exporters pitcher Steve Larkin threw a 7-inning no-hitter against the Oilers in the second game of a doubleheader on September 1st.

Pittsburgh pounded out 17 hits in a 10-4 rout of the Chicago White Sox in an April 12th exhibition game at Fairgrounds Park before 2,169 fans. Arky Vaughn swatted a two-run home run while Oklahoma natives Paul "Big Poison" Waner and Lloyd "Little Poison" Waner added three hits apiece for the Pirates. Luke Appling had two hits for the White Sox.

The Galveston Buccaneers won the 1934 Texas League regular season by one thousandths of a point over the San Antonio Missions and then defeated San Antonio in the postseason series, 4-2. The Buccaneers had earlier eliminated the Dallas Steers, 3-1, while San Antonio knocked out the Beaumont Exporters, 3-2.

Galveston went 88-64 in the regular season while San Antonio finished 89-65. Then came Beaumont (81-69) and Dallas (80-73), followed by the Tulsa Oilers (77-75), Houston Buffaloes (76-78), Fort Worth Cats (59-92) and Oklahoma City Indians (59-93).

Buccaneers second baseman Charlie English was the Texas League Player of the Year, batting .326 and lashing 42 doubles. English played 2,156 minor league games from 1931 through 1949, finishing with 2,499 hits and a career minor league batting average of .305.

San Antonio pitcher Harold Ashley "Ash" Hillin was the Texas League Pitcher of the Year, leading the league with a 24-12 record and posted a 3.66 ERA. Hillin would play for the Oklahoma City Indians in 1937 and 1938, posting respective records of 31-10 and 23-10. That would be the last Texas League Pitcher of the Year award until it was brought back in 1946.

1935: The Oilers made their first appearance in the Texas League playoffs and drew 74,069 fans, an increase of nearly 9,000 over the previous year. Art Griggs, Tulsa's manager in 1932 and 1933, returned after a one-year absence to lead the team to an 82-79 record. Tulsa's season record could have been much better (or much worse, depending on one's viewpoint) had they not split 22 doubleheaders, a feat which still stands as a Texas League season record.

The Oilers lost in the playoff semifinals to the Oklahoma City Indians, 3-1. Oklahoma City went on to win its first postseason championship since joining the Texas League two years earlier. The Indians defeated the Beaumont Exporters in the championship series, 4-1. Beaumont reached the finals by eliminating the Galveston Buccaneers, 3-2.

Oklahoma City had the best regular season record at 95-66, followed by Beaumont (90-69), Galveston (86-75), Tulsa (82-79), the Houston Buffaloes (77-84), San Antonio Missions (75-84), Dallas Steers (71-88) and Fort Worth Cats (64-95).

Oilers third baseman Ernie Holman played every inning of every game and was the only Tulsa player named to the Texas League's postseason All-Star team which was chosen by *The Sporting News* magazine. Holman batted .294 and led Tulsa in games played (162), at-bats (598), runs scored (96), base hits (176), doubles (37).

Al Shealy threw the first perfect game by a Tulsa pitcher in a 7-0, seven-inning victory over San Antonio in the second game of a June 23rd doubleheader. Then for the second time in three years, the Oilers were on the losing end of a no-hitter authored by the Galveston Buccaneers. Eddie Cole threw a nine-inning perfect games in a 2-0 victory over the Oilers on July 10th.

There have been just two other nine-inning perfect games in Texas League history. They were by Shreveport's Dave Wilhelmi (1983 against Arkansas) and the Frisco trio of A.J. Murray, Steve Karsay and Scott Feldman (2005 against Corpus Christi).

Oilers outfielder Elias "Liz" Funk led the Texas League in the most times being hit by a pitch (14). Funk attended the University of Oklahoma during the 1920s and was the Detroit Tigers' center fielder in 1930, ranking third in the American League in putouts by an outfielder that year.

Beaumont catcher Rudy York was the Texas League Player of the Year, leading the league with 32 home runs while batting .301. He played for the Detroit Tigers in 1937-45 and his switch to first base allowed future Hall of Famer Hank Greenberg (the 1932 Texas League Player of the Year with Beaumont) to move to the outfield. York hit 20 or more home runs eight times in his big-league career and had six seasons with 100 or more runs batted in.

Luke Appling led the way in the Chicago White Sox's 3-2 victory over the Pittsburgh Pirates in the first exhibition game played at Texas League Park before about 1,000 fans on April 8th.

The defending American League batting champion had a base hit, stole a base and scored the decisive run. The Pirates didn't have much punch at the plate with Arky Vaughn and Babe Herman going without a hit. Paul Waner chose to go to Oklahoma City to visit his parents but Lloyd Waner did play and went 1-for-3.

1936: Tulsa earned its first Texas League pennant by defeating the regular season champion Dallas Steers, 4-3, in the championship series. The Oilers then went on to sweep the Southern Association champion Birmingham Barons in four games to win the Dixie Series.

Marty McManus, an infielder with the 1920 Oilers who played for the American League's St. Louis Browns later in that decade, returned as the team's manager. The Oilers finished third during the regular season but upset the Houston Buffaloes in the semifinals, 3-1, while Dallas advanced by eliminating Oklahoma City, 3-1.

Dallas had the best regular season at 93-61, followed by Houston (83-69), Tulsa (80-74), Oklahoma City (79-75), the Fort Worth Cats (76-78), San Antonio Missions (73-77), Beaumont Exporters (69-80) and Galveston Buccaneers (57-96).

Two Oilers outfielders were Texas League leaders that year. Red Howell had 127 runs batted in while batting .319 with 23 home runs. Hal Patchett drew 90 bases on balls while batting .305.

Newt Kimball, a 21-year-old right-hander, was Tulsa's pitching ace that year, posting a 16-7 record and a 3.87 ERA and struck out 109 batters. George "Cowboy" Milstead, who spent 25 years in minor league baseball, had a 13-12 record but led Tulsa in complete games (14).

The first recorded triple play in Tulsa's professional baseball history happened on August 7th in Oklahoma City in an 8-7 victory over the Oklahoma City Indians.

Attendance increased for the third year in a row, drawing 80,778 fans during for regular season games and nearly 31,000 for the playoff contests.

This was also the first year for Tulsa Oilers games to be broadcast by a local radio station, KTUL-AM (1430). It would be the first of six consecutive seasons that Oilers baseball was broadcast by that station. Ironically, Tulsa Drillers baseball games are carried today on that same radio frequency but the call letters are KTBZ-AM, also known as "AM 1430: The Buzz."

Dallas second baseman Les Mallon was the Texas League Player of the Year, leading the league with a .344 batting average and added 36 doubles. He later played two years apiece with the National League's Philadelphia Phillies and Boston Braves.

The Oilers played three exhibition games in a four-day span during April. The first one was against the St. Louis Cardinals and the other two were against the Tokyo Giants, one of the powerhouse teams in Japanese baseball.

The Oilers let the air of the St. Louis Cardinals' "Gas House Gang" with a 10-4 victory before 4,648 fans on April 9th. It was the largest crowd for an exhibition baseball game in Tulsa in 13 years. Oilers left fielder Babe Howell and first baseman Bernie Cobb had three hits apiece with Howell belting a home run and driving in three runs. Future Hall of Famer Joe "Ducky" Medwick doubled home two runs for St. Louis.

Then on April 11th, the Tokyo Giants defeated the Oilers, 9-8, in a controversial contest. The Oilers led after seven innings, 4-3. Tokyo capitalized on its speed and clutch hitting to score six runs in the top of the eighth inning. Winning pitcher Tosho Hatafuka capped the Giants' scoring geyser with a three-run double.

Tulsa fought back in the bottom of the ninth inning to score four runs with Stan Schino driving in three of those runs with a double.

When the inning ended, the manually-operated scoreboard showed that the game was tied, 8-8, so the Oilers got their gloves and went back onto the field for what they thought was the top of the 10th inning. The confusion arose because the person out in the manually-operated outfield scoreboard had credited Tokyo with five runs scored in the eighth inning instead of six runs.

Amazingly, Tokyo manager Sotaro Suzuki failed to notice the mistake until the Oilers took the field. Suzuki wrote a note to home plate umpire Zeke Johnson that showed the inning-by-inning score and Johnson declared that the game was over, an action that caused Oilers manager Marty McManus to charge out of the dugout to protest the decision.

Since there was no telephonic communication between the field and the official scorer in the press box back then, McManus yelled and used hand gestures to ask what the score was. When the response came back that Tokyo had won, he shrugged his shoulders and shook hands with Suzuki.

The April 12th contest was a pitcher's duel with Tulsa defeating Tokyo, 3-1. Oilers pitchers Max Thomas and Ed Selway combined to scatter eight hits and Bill Jackson's RBI single proved to be the game-winning hit.

1937: The Oilers had the Texas League's second-highest victory total but fell to the eventual league champion Fort Worth Cats in the playoffs. Fort Worth won its best-of-five semifinal series with Tulsa, 3-2, while Oklahoma City eliminated San Antonio, 3-2.

Fort Worth defeated Oklahoma City in the championship series, 4-2, for its first Texas League championship since the Cats claimed league pennants from 1919 through 1925.

Oklahoma City had the best season record at 101-58 and those 101 victories would be the most by that franchise during its membership in the Texas League.

The Oilers were next at 89-69, followed by Fort Worth (85-74), the San Antonio Missions (85-76), Beaumont Explorers (82-77), Galveston Buccaneers (73-86), Houston Buffaloes (67-91) and Dallas Steers (55-106). Dallas took quite a tumble from going 93-61 the previous year and also had four different managers in 1937.

Pitching was Tulsa's strongest weapon with a pitching staff that tossed 13 shutouts and six pitchers winning 10 or more games apiece. Clyde Lahti and Max Thomas each won 16 games, Irving Stein and Eddie "Lefty" Carnett each won 15 games while George Milstead and Leo Twardy respectively added 14 and 12 wins. Twardy tied a Texas League record by helping turn three double plays in a game on April 17th.

Carnett later played a role in enhancing the career of Cleveland Indians pitcher and future Hall of Famer Bob Feller. In June of 1945, Carnett and Feller were stationed at the Great Lakes Naval Base just north of Chicago. Feller's fast ball and curve ball were legendary back then but Feller wanted to learn more about how to throw a slider.

When Feller heard that the former Oiler threw a very good slider, he sent a jeep to pick up Carnett for a meeting. Carnett not only taught Feller the proper hand grip and arm motion for throwing the pitch, he even put on catcher's gear to work with Feller.

During his 18-year major league career with the Cleveland Indians, "Rapid Robert" Feller led American League pitchers in strikeouts seven times, won 20 or more games in a year six times, pitched three no-hit games and 12 one-hitters and won 266 games. Feller would later be a frequent visitor to Tulsa for exhibition games and autograph sessions.

Outfielder Stan Schino was Tulsa's power-hitter, leading the team with 17 home runs (tied for third-highest in the Texas League) and driving in 114 runs.

Bruce Connatser was in the first of his three seasons as the Oilers' player-manager. Connatser, who spent parts of the 1931 and 1932 seasons with the Cleveland Indians, played first base for Tulsa and was third on the team in runs batted in (71) while batting .286.

Oilers shortstop Tony York made big news in the Texas League, both in a good way and in a bad way. The good news was York's reaching base 14 consecutive times (12 base hits and two walks) between June 24th and June 27th was a Texas League record. The bad news was that York's 119 strikeouts that year were the most by any Texas League player to that point in time.

York finished the season with a .292 batting average, 81 RBIs and ranked second in the league in doubles (46). He spent 23 years in the minor leagues and played 28 games for the 1944 Chicago Cubs.

Tulsa's regular-season attendance cracked six figures for the first time in six years with 104,898 fans coming to Texas League Park.

Oilers baseball games were broadcast for the second year in a row on KTUL-AM radio (1430) with Don Hill and Eddie Gallagher calling the action.

Oklahoma City pitcher Ash Hillon was the Texas League Player of the Year. He had a career-high 31 victories and he would become the fifth and final Texas League pitcher to win 30 games in a season. Hillin also led the league in lowest earned run average (2.35) and winning percentage (.756).

Two exhibition games were played at Texas League Park that year. The Oilers fell to the defending World Series champion New York Yankees, 8-3, before 4,477 fans on April 9th. The Yankees' offense capitalized on Oilers mistakes and scored all eight of their runs with two outs while their pitchers held Tulsa to just six hits.

Lou Gehrig went 2-for-5, scoring three runs and drawing three walks. Tony Lazzeri had two hits and stole a base but Joe DiMaggio went 0-for-1 as a pinch hitter. Those Yankees would win 102 games and then defeated the New York Giants to win their second consecutive World Series championship.

On April 13th, Chicago White Sox pitcher Monty Stratton pitched seven strong innings in a 12-5 victory over the Pittsburgh Pirates before 1,135 fans. Luke Appling and Jack Hayes homered for the White Sox. Paul "Big Poison" Waner and Arky Vaughn had three hits apiece for Pie Traynor's Pirates.

Tragedy struck Stratton the following year when his right leg had to be amputated after a hunting accident. After receiving an artificial leg, Stratton played in the lower levels of the minor leagues from 1946 through 1953. His comeback attempt was the inspiration for the 1949 movie, *The Stratton Story*, in which legendary actor Jimmy Stewart portrayed Stratton and June Allyson portrayed his wife.

1938: The Oilers kept moving upward, both on the field and at the turnstile. The Oilers reached the Texas League playoffs for the third year in a row and it was also the fifth consecutive season of increased attendance.

Tulsa had claimed the fourth and final playoff berth with an 86-75 record. Unfortunately, they would face a Beaumont Exporters team that went 99-53 during the year and the Oilers were swept in their three-game semifinal playoff series.

The Beaumont Exporters defeated the San Antonio Missions in championship finals, 4-3-1. Beaumont and San Antonio reached the finals with respective three games sweeps of the Tulsa Oilers and Oklahoma City Indians.

Beaumont's regular season record was 99-53, followed by San Antonio (93-67), Oklahoma City (89-70), Tulsa (86-75) the Houston Buffaloes (74-84), Shreveport Sports (69-90), Dallas Steers (65-94) and Fort Worth Cats (61-99).

Tulsa outfielders Morris "Red" Jones and Stan Schino led the Texas League in two hitting categories. Jones had 189 base hits and played for the St. Louis Cardinals two years later. Schino led the league with 25 home runs and 118 RBIs.

Tulsa's Max Thomas and Oklahoma City's Ash Hillin shared the league lead in pitching victories with 23. Thomas also led the league with a 1.94 ERA and 29 complete games. Vern Olsen had a fine year for Tulsa, posting a 19-9 record and a 3.05 ERA. He later spent five years with the Chicago Cubs.

Oilers baseball games were broadcast for the third consecutive season on KTUL-AM radio (1430) with Don Hill and Eddie Gallagher calling the action.

It's not unheard of for Tulsa to have snow in the early part of the baseball season and that is what kept the New York Yankees and Tulsa

Oilers from playing an exhibition game on April 8th. It was the only exhibition game scheduled in Tulsa that year.

Beaumont pitcher Paul Howard "Dizzy" Trout was the Texas League Player of the Year. He was 22-6 that year with a 2.12 ERA, ranking third in victories and lowest earned run average. Trout played 14 of his 15 major league seasons with the Detroit Tigers and was a two-time American League All-Star. His son, Steve, played for the Chicago White Sox and Chicago Cubs during the 1970s and 1980s.

1939: The death of Oilers owner Art Griggs prior to Opening Day cast a pall over the season. The team had a 78-82 record and the season attendance of 81,290 fans was a drop of nearly 30,000 from the previous year.

General Manager Don Stewart, a business partner who accompanied Griggs from Wichita to Tulsa in 1932, became the team's owner. Stewart, whose in-laws lived in the southwestern Tulsa suburb of Sapulpa, ran the Oilers franchise successfully until 1942 when the Texas League suspended operations in connection with World War II; a move that Stewart did not support.

Stewart had a reserved demeanor but more importantly, a widely-respected reputation for personal and professional integrity. Bill Veeck, the flamboyant baseball owner/promoter, once said that Don Stewart "is one of the three men in baseball I'd turn my money over to without counting it."

Oilers left fielder Lou Novikoff led the Texas League with a .368 batting average and was honored as Minor League Baseball's Player of the Year. Nicknamed "The Mad Russian" and known for an eccentric personality, Novikoff led the Oilers that year with 154 base hits and added 14 home runs and 77 RBIs. When the season ended, his contract was purchased by the Los Angeles Angels of the Pacific Coast League.

Novikoff was one of the best hitters in minor league baseball history, batting .337 over 11 minor league seasons. He played for the Chicago Cubs in 1941-44 when the major league baseball talent level was diluted by several top players left to serve in America's armed forces during World War II.

Vern Olsen was the ace of a sub-par Tulsa pitching staff that year. His 18-11 record was one of just two winning records on the 10-man Oilers pitching staff. Olsen also led the team in strikeouts (110) and had a 3.10 ERA.

Oilers baseball games were broadcast once again on KTUL-AM radio (1430) but Vic Rugh handled the play-by-play duties by himself. Rugh was one of the announcers for local radio broadcasts of professional wrestling matches at the downtown Tulsa Coliseum and announced football games and boxing matches.

Joe DiMaggio singled twice in the New York Yankees' 5-2 victory over the Tulsa Oilers before 4,652 fans at Texas League Park on April 7th. Tulsa was held to six hits by Yankee hurlers Wes Ferrell and Oral Hilderbrand.

But the game's low light was the appearance and performance of Yankees star Lou Gehrig. He had no base hits in five at-bats, dropped an easy infield popup that resulted in Tulsa's two runs and was just not "The Iron Horse" that baseball fans everywhere knew and loved.

Three weeks after that Tulsa game, Gehrig retired from baseball in a memorable and moving ceremony at Yankee Stadium. He died on June 2, 1941 from amyotrophic lateral sclerosis (ALS), a fatal disease that attacks the muscles as well as the ability to swallow or speak. In the United States, ALS is also known as "Lou Gehrig's Disease."

The Fort Worth Cats won their second Texas League championship in three years by defeated the Dallas Rebels in the playoffs, 4-1.

Fort Worth and Dallas advanced with 3-2 semifinal victories over the Houston Buffaloes and San Antonio Missions, respectively.

Houston had the best regular season record (97-63), followed by Dallas and San Antonio (each at 89-72) and Fort Worth (87-74). Trailing those teams were the Shreveport Sports (86-75), Tulsa Oilers (78-82) and Oklahoma City Indians (59-102). The defending champion Beaumont Exporters went from first in 1938 to worst in 1939, finishing 58-103.

Houston left fielder Nick Cullop was the Texas League Player of the Year, leading the league with 25 home runs and 290 total bases. Nicknamed "Tomato Face", 1939 would be the 18th of Cullop's 23 seasons in minor league baseball.

Chapter Five

The 1940s

The oppressive clouds of World War II hovered over America and the entire world through 1945. When they parted, Tulsa and the rest of America celebrated with a new era of financial prosperity and industrial growth.

This was the decade that gave us t-shirts, nylon stockings, bikini swimsuits, ball point pens, the first computer, the Slinky toy, the Polaroid camera and the Mount Rushmore monument. Legendary books were published by George Orwell (*1984*) and Dr. Benjamin Spock (*The Common Book of Baby and Child Care*).

A monumental mistake in journalism happened when the *Chicago Tribune* proclaimed Thomas Dewey's victory over Harry Truman in the 1948 Presidential election. Biblical prophecy was fulfilled when the nation of Israel was formed during the decade and the Dead Sea Scrolls were also discovered.

Despite the Texas League not operating from 1943 through 1945 due to World War II, this was one of the better decades in Tulsa's professional baseball history. The Oilers were affiliated with the National League's Chicago Cubs and Cincinnati Reds, made five playoff appearances and won the 1949 Texas League championship.

The player who inspired the novel and movie *The Natural*, Eddie Waitkus, was a rising star for the Oilers while the sun began to set on the career of pitching legend Dizzy Dean. Russell "The Muscle" Burns and his booming bat left indelible marks on Tulsa's baseball history books.

Jackie Robinson and Roy Campanella were among the major league baseball stars appearing in exhibition games played in Tulsa. Other big-league standouts coming to Tulsa back then included Casey Stengel, Earl Averill, Johnny Mize and the Negro League powerhouse Kansas City Monarchs and their ageless wonder of a pitcher, Leroy "Satchel" Paige.

1940: The Oilers began their first long-term affiliation with a major league baseball team, signing an eight-year contract with the Chicago Cubs. But because the Texas League ceased operation from 1943 through 1945 due to World War II, that relationship actually lasted for five years. Nevertheless, the Cubs' player development system had enough good players that Tulsa reached the Texas League playoffs in three out of those five years.

Roy Johnson served as the Oilers' manager from 1940 through 1942. He was no stranger to the city, having pitched for the Oilers in 1924 and 1925 when they played in the Western League. Johnson had a 243-218 managerial record during that period but the Oilers' only playoff appearance under his leadership came in 1941.

Outfielder Gordon Donaldson became the second Oiler in as many years to win the Texas League batting championship, posting a .319 batting average. Surprisingly, Donaldson's final professional baseball season would be in 1941, splitting time between the Oklahoma City Indians and the Pacific Coast League's Los Angeles Angels.

Julian Tubb had the best record among Tulsa pitchers, posting a 15-11 record and a 3.03 ERA. Jack Bertram played for Tulsa and Shreveport that year and led Texas League pitchers in losses (21).

First baseman Eddie Waitkus led the Texas League in triples (18) and being hit by a pitch (12), was the league's co-leader in doubles (39) and played in every inning of the Oilers' 162-game schedule. He also batted .303 and stole 18 bases.

Waitkus later spent three years as the Cubs' first baseman and was traded to the Philadelphia Phillies after the 1948 season; a transaction that led to a life-changing experience.

Ruth Ann Steinhagen was a 19-year-old typist who lived in Chicago and had an obsession about Waitkus when he played for the Cubs. On June 14, 1949, Waitkus was staying with the Phillies at the Edgewater Beach Hotel in Chicago. She checked into that hotel under the name of one of Waitkus' former high school friends and left an urgent note for Waitkus to come to her room. After entering her room, Waitkus was shot in the chest with the bullet lodging in one lung and barely missing his heart. Doctors said Waitkus nearly died four times during life-saving surgery.

Following the release of his stalker, Waitkus declined to press charges in an attempt to move on with his life and played major league baseball through the 1955 season. But he was never the same person, suffering from what is considered today as post-traumatic stress syndrome and later developing a drinking problem. Steinhagen was declared legally insane and sent to a mental hospital in Kankakee, Illinois until 1952. She eventually moved to Chicago and lived with family members before passing away in 2012.

That incident was a key part of a 1952 novel written by Bernard Malamud called *The Natural*. And that novel was the inspiration for the 1984 movie of the same name which starred Robert Redford

as a baseball player named Roy Hobbs and was nominated for four
Academy Awards.

Legendary pitcher Dizzy Dean spent part of the 1940 season with
the Oilers in a comeback attempt. He suffered a toe injury during the
1937 All-Star Game and overcompensating for the ailing toe led to
arm injury that altered how he threw the ball. So the Cubs sent Dean
to Tulsa, hoping that he could learn a sidearm delivery that would
revive his career.

Over 7,500 fans saw Dean pitched a complete game victory in his
Oiler debut. But he finished 8-8 that year, averaged just two strikeouts
a game and it was obvious that the powerful pitching style that would
make him a Hall of Famer was a thing of the past.

Oilers games were still on KTUL-AM Radio (1430) but Don
O'Brien was the new play-by-play announcer.

The Oilers were scheduled to host the St. Louis Cardinals in an
exhibition game on April 11th but the game was rained out.

The New York Yankees played what would be their final exhibition
game in Tulsa, losing to the Oilers, 10-6, before an overflow crowd of
6,500 fans on April 4th. Joe DiMaggio went 1-for-4 and Charlie Keller
hit a two-run home run for the Yankees. Tulsa broke the game open
by scoring seven runs in the fourth inning. Eddie Waitkus, Stan Schino
and Ed Zydowski had three hits apiece for the Oilers.

The Houston Buffaloes made Texas League history that year by
winning 105 games, setting a virtually unbreakable league record for
the most victories in one year. Then they stampeded to their first
Texas League championship by trouncing the Beaumont Exporters in
the championship series, 4-1. Houston reached the finals by defeating
the Oklahoma City Indians, 3-1, while Beaumont blanked the San
Antonio Missions, 3-0.

Following Houston were San Antonio (89-72), Beaumont (88-72), Oklahoma City (82-78), the Tulsa Oilers (76-82), Dallas Eagles (75-83), Shreveport Sports (72-88) and Fort Worth Cats (52-108).

Hall of Famer Rogers Hornsby provided a spark for Oklahoma City when he replaced manager Jim Keesey after a 26-35 start. Hornsby went 56-43 the rest of that season but he was fired the following year after his own sluggish (31-37) start. "The Rajah" regained the winning touch in the dugout in 1942 when he took the Fort Worth Cats to the Texas League playoffs.

1941: The Houston Buffaloes topped 100 victories for the second year in a row. But it would be the Tulsa Oilers and Dallas Rebels fighting for the Texas League pennant.

Dallas earned its first Texas League championship since 1929 by defeating Tulsa in the best-of-seven championship series, 4-2. Dallas had upset Houston in the best-of-five semifinals, 3-1, while Tulsa swept the Shreveport Sports, 3-0.

Pitcher Hank Wyse and third baseman Glenn "Rip" Russell were Tulsa's brightest stars. Nicknamed "Hooks" for a sharply breaking curveball, Wyse went 20-4 with a 2.40 ERA and followed that effort with a 20-11 record and 2.56 ERA in 1942. He also suffered from spinal problems that at times forced him to wear a corset while pitching.

Wyse's best major league season was with the 1945 Chicago Cubs when he went 22-10 with a 2.68 ERA. As a the final pitcher in Chicago's Game 7 World Series loss to the Detroit Tigers, he became the last Cubs pitcher to appear in a World Series game. Wyse lived in Pryor, Oklahoma, roughly 50 miles north-northeast of Tulsa, when he died in 2000.

Russell was the Texas League's Most Valuable Player, finishing third in the league in home runs (20) and sixth in batting average (.313).

He played for the Chicago White Sox and Boston Red Sox during the 1940s but spent most of his minor league career with the Pacific Coast League powerhouse Los Angeles Angels.

The Oilers played three exhibition games in a five-day span at Texas League Park during early April.

The Boston Braves fought off a ninth-inning rally by the Tulsa Oilers for an 11-10 victory on April 6th. The game was a slugfest with the two teams belting out a combined 31 base hits. Bill Capps, Don Johnson and Goober Crawford had three hits apiece for Tulsa but catcher Chico Hernandez struck out with the bases loaded to end the game.

The Braves were managed by future Hall of Famer Casey Stengel, later renowned for his New York Yankees championship teams and the fun-loving futility of the early days of the "Amazin'" New York Mets.

Center fielder Earl Averill hit one of Boston's three home runs in what turned out to be one of his last baseball games. A six-time All-Star with the Cleveland Indians during the 1930s and who still holds four of that team's career offensive records, Averill retired after going 2-for-17 in the Braves' first eight games that year. He was inducted into the Baseball Hall of Fame in 1975.

St. Louis Cardinals pitcher Johnny Mize tossed a five-hit shutout in a 5-0 victory over the Oilers before an estimated 1,100 fans on April 10th. Cardinal center fielder Terry Moore scored two runs.

They played again the following day and St. Louis had its hands full but escaped with an 8-5 victory before 2,500 fans. Tulsa scored three runs in the bottom of the ninth inning but it was too little, too late. All nine of Tulsa's hits went for extra bases, highlighted by home runs from first baseman Ed Zykowski and catcher Goober Crawford. Terry Moore swatted a pair of two-run home runs for the Cardinals.

Houston's 103-50 record and was nearly 17 games better than the Oilers (86-66) during the regular season. Trailing those two teams were Shreveport (80-71), Dallas (80-74), the Fort Worth Cats (78-76), Oklahoma City Indians (69-85), Beaumont Exporters (58-94) and San Antonio Missions (58-96).

Before being decimated by call-ups to the major leagues, Houston had three 20-game winners who pitched for the St. Louis Cardinals. The 1941 Houston Buffaloes were ranked by the official website of minor league baseball (www.milb.com) as the 65th-best team in minor league history.

Fred Martin, a master of the split-finger fastball and a mentor for Chicago Cubs/St. Louis Cardinals bullpen legend Bruce Sutter, was the Buffaloes' pitching ace with a 23-6 record and a 1.54 ERA, leading the Texas League in victories and having the league's second-lowest ERA.

Equally impressive was Howie Pollet's 1.16 ERA being the second-lowest ERA in Texas League history, along with having a 20-3 record and throwing a no-hitter in a 7-0 home victory over Shreveport on April 25th. Ted Wilks rounded out the talented trio with a 20-10 record.

Houston second baseman Danny Murtaugh, who became one of the most beloved managers in Pittsburgh Pirates history, batted .316 in 69 games. Murtaugh was the manager of Pittsburgh's World Series champions in 1960 and 1971 and also guided the Pirates to three National League Eastern Division titles.

Don O'Brien was in his second and final year as the play-by-play announcer for Oiler games KTUL-AM Radio (1430). But this would be the year that another man's voice became part of Tulsa's baseball heritage for nearly 30 years.

Andy Andrews lived in Barnsdall, Oklahoma and worked for a small oil company in that city during the day. He and several friends would then make a 90-mile roundtrip journey, whether hitchhiking or by car, to see the Oilers play and seldom missed a game. Andrews had actually attended baseball games since 1936 but also frequently came to town to see University of Tulsa football and the city's minor league hockey team, also known as the Oilers.

During one game in the 1941 season, Tulsa pitcher Clare Bertram (who went 13-11 with a 2.91 ERA that year) was not pitching very well and several fans sitting around Andrews were giving Bertram a hard time. Andrews frequently said that fans should support the home team and in that game, he finally had enough of the bellyaching by the spectators surrounding him.

Andrews cut loose with an ear-splitting yell of "Let's Go, Bertram!" and was able to hold the "o" for more than 10 seconds. Those fans giving grief to Bertram were quickly silenced. Then the others fans in Texas League Park, as well as players from both teams started looking around to see who was guy doing that cheer.

Before the 1941 season ended, Andrews replaced "Let's Go, Bertram" with "Let's Go, Tulsa" in his cheer, doing it over the ballpark's public address system prior to the Oilers coming to bat in the bottom of the first inning. He eventually added the word "Hey" to the start of the cheer and held the vowel portion for what seemed like an eternity. Then he did then did the same routine with the "o" in "Go" before finishing with a flourish after yelling, "Tulsa!!"

In real life, Andrews spoke softly but once said that his increased volume came from his days in the Boy Scouts when he learned to yell as long and loud as his scoutmaster.

Andrews later worked in the team's front office and handled season ticket sales, sold advertising and did various other jobs with an ever-present smile. He was also an active participant in fund-raising campaigns for Tulsa-area civic organizations and sometimes performed a spot-on vocal impersonation of actor-comedian W.C. Fields.

An event near and dear to Andrews' heart was an annual talent show called Oiler Frolics. To say that there was talent and that it was a show was being far too kind.

The Oiler Frolics featured players performing comedy sketches in unusual costumes or trying to sing like Elvis Presley or The Beatles. Among the former "stars" were infielder Ed Knoblauch (1949-51 Oilers) and current St. Louis Cardinals radio announcer Mike Shannon, an outfielder on the 1961 Oilers.

Andrews passed away in 1972 but the echo of his "Hey, Let's Go, Tulsa!!" cheers will always be part of Tulsa's baseball history.

1942: The call of military service in connection with World War II depleted the talent levels for all minor league teams and Tulsa was hit especially hard. In addition, the Oilers' season attendance of 59,176 was the lowest in Tulsa's professional baseball history since 1933. The Oilers had a winning record but finished in sixth place in their eight-team league.

Outfielder-first baseman Marvin "Twitch" Rickert was Tulsa's best hitter, batting .310 with 79 runs batted in and his 35 doubles ranked fourth in the league. Rickert later played for five major league teams. Outfielder Hershel Martin tied for second in the league in doubles (39) and batted .292.

Hank Wyse won 20-plus games for the second year in a row, posting a 20-11 record along with a 2.56 ERA. He was also the ironman of Tulsa's pitching staff with 23 complete games in 40 appearances. Joe Berry's 1.88 ERA was the lowest of any Oiler pitcher that year. He also had an 18-11 record and threw a nine-inning no-hitter in Tulsa's 1-0 victory over Oklahoma City on August 11th.

The Oilers were on the losing end of one of the fastest games in Texas League history. In a nine-inning game on July 12th that took just 69 minutes to play and with people lined up to buy tickets when it ended, the Fort Worth Cats defeated the Oilers, 7-0, with Ed Greer being the winning pitcher.

Shreveport snared its second Texas League title and first since 1919 by defeating the Beaumont Explorers, 4-3. The Sports had eliminated the Fort Worth Cats, 4-3, while Beaumont beat the San Antonio Missions, 4-2.

The Chicago Cubs and Chicago White Sox were scheduled to play an exhibition game at Texas League Park on April 9th but it was rained out.

Beaumont had the league's best regular season record at 89-58. Shreveport was second (83-61), followed by Fort Worth (84-68), San Antonio (80-68), the Houston Buffaloes (81-70), Tulsa Oilers (76-75), Oklahoma City Indians (58-95) and Dallas Rebels (48-104).

That 1942 Beaumont team had a light-hitting utility player (.219 batting average) who not only played a key role in Tulsa's baseball history 24 years later, but his invention still helps children learn how to play baseball.

That device was the batting tee, the foundation of baseball leagues for children ages four years old and up.

Charles Moreskonich went by the name Charlie Metro with his adopted last name actually being the first name of his father. Metro would become a successful minor league manager with four championship teams and also led the 1966 Tulsa Oilers to the Pacific Coast League Eastern Division title.

In a 2011 interview, Metro's said the concept of a batting tee came to him as a high school student in Nanty Glo, Pennsylvania. He cut down a pair of tall and hollow bushes, stuck them back into the ground, put a baseball between them and then hit the ball into a nearby mattress.

After his awful 1942 season in Beaumont, Metro worked in the Pennsylvania coal mines and pretty much followed the same principles as his original contraption. A rubber base was the foundation with spare pieces of rubber tubing stacked atop each other and then a baseball was put on top.

Metro claimed he filed a patent for the batting tee but never paid the processing fee because he was between jobs back then. He strongly disputed claims from other people that they invented the batting tee, stating that they were not even alive when he created the concept and filed the patent's paperwork.

Today, there are millions of children around the world playing in tee ball leagues. So when you see a youngster wearing a huge smile after hitting the ball off that tee or if you're watching an older baseball player working on his hitting stroke, a tip of the proverbial baseball cap is in order for the creativity of Charlie Metro.

As for managing major league baseball teams, his tenures with the 1962 Chicago Cubs (as part of the infamous "College of Coaches") and the 1970 Kansas City Royals were far from successful, posting a 62-102 record over parts of two seasons.

During the Royals' 1968 expansion draft, Metro said he had opportunities to draft New York Yankees superstar Mickey Mantle, who was far past his prime due to numerous injuries. When Royals owner Ewing Kauffman threatened to fire Metro if he actually drafted Mantle, the idea was dropped.

1943: The Texas League did not operate due to World War II.

1944: The Texas League did not operate due to World War II.

1945: The Texas League did not operate due to World War II.

1946: Baseball returned to Tulsa after World War II in grand style. The Oilers reached the Texas League playoffs and were rejuvenated by an infusion of new money and new front-office leadership.

Six Tulsa businessmen purchased the team franchise and Texas League Park received $100,000 ($1.2 million in today's money) worth of repairs for the termite-infested wooden structure as well as the pockmarked playing field. The Texas League was upgraded from Class A-1 to Class AA, reflecting a higher level of competition.

Five of the six owners were Tulsa-based oil and petroleum executives. They were William G. "Bill" Skelly, William K. Warren, Sr., John Mabee, P.C. Lauinger, and W.L. Kistler. The sixth man was Grayle Howlett, who would serve as the Oilers' general manager in 1946-47 and team president in 1948-61.

Skelly built one of America's strongest independent oil businesses during the 1920s and was a visionary of what Tulsa could become in aviation, business, culture and education. Skelly Oil Company later merged with Getty Oil and, eventually, with Texaco.

Warren was the founder of the Warren Petroleum Corporation, which became an industry leader in producing and selling LPG, which was a byproduct of the refining of petroleum and the purification of natural gas. In the largest energy industry merger prior to 1953, Gulf Oil acquired Warren Petroleum for $420 million (in today's money, roughly $3.5 billion.)

Mabee developed a successful oil drilling company and then branched out into banking, real estate, ranching and insurance. He and his wife, Lottie Jane, were renowned philanthropists whose gifts benefitted numerous hospitals, community groups, churches and universities.

Lauinger led the PennWell Corporation, which published the Oil and Gas Journal and was reverenced by oil industry experts. PennWell also handled the publication of numerous trade magazines and various business periodicals.

Kistler was vice president of one of Oklahoma's largest oil drilling firms, Producers and Refiners Corporation and vice president of the Economy Oil Company of Tulsa.

Skelly served as the Oilers' president for the 1946 season and Warren did likewise for the 1947 season.

Howlett came to Tulsa from Chicago, where he had worked with the parent Chicago Cubs after previously working as a *Chicago Tribune* sportswriter and on WGN Radio's Cubs broadcasts with Baseball Hall of Fame announcer Jack "Hey-Hey" Brickhouse.

During Howlett's tenure, the Oilers topped 200,000 in season attendance for the first time (1948) and averaged over 200,000 fans per year in 1947-50. And when the St. Louis Cardinals took Howlett up on his offer for Tulsa to be their Double-A affiliate starting in 1958, the Oilers would lead the Texas League in attendance for the following seven years.

Promotion could easily have been Howlett's middle name because his work in drumming up interest in baseball among fans and local media was highly effective. A key tool in his work was a monthly newsletter promoting the team and upcoming events.

Another of Howlett's innovations, The Diamond Dinner, began in 1947 and honored major league baseball players as well as former Tulsa Oilers who were doing well in the major leagues. The Diamond Dinner was held for 30 years, mostly at the Mayo Hotel in downtown Tulsa.

Among the baseball legends appearing at the Tulsa Diamond Dinner during its heyday were Mickey Mantle, Johnny Bench, Casey Stengel, Warren Spahn, Allie Reynolds, Dizzy Dean, Jim Brewer, Joe Garagiola and Joe "Ducky" Medwick. A variation of that event continues today as a fundraiser for the Oral Roberts University baseball program.

Another priority for Howlett was eliminating racially segregated seating arrangements at Texas League Park. Colored people were restricted to an entrance/exit behind third base with bleacher seating and their main concession stand and restrooms were also behind third base. Smaller restrooms behind first base were also designated for colored people.

Howlett was fascinated by statistics illustration how good or poorly a player performed well against opposing pitchers. In essence, he pursed the fundamental purpose of "Moneyball" long before it was made popular by the Oakland Athletics or into a movie. Howlett was one of the first minor league executive to arrange for players to journey to road games on a sleeper bus.

One of Howlett's first hires was a groundskeeper named John Tabor and he worked at the baseball park for nearly 20 years. He also wore many other hats during that time, working as a scout, assistant coach, clubhouse manager, team trainer, traveling secretary and accountant.

Tabor spent nine years as a minor league pitcher and later managed a semi-professional team in Oklahoma City. Two players from that Oklahoma City team would become sports stars in their own right: Pepper Martin as a St. Louis Cardinals shortstop and Henry "Hank" Iba as the basketball coach at Oklahoma State University.

After being hired, Tabor found out that not only was the playing surface was full of weeds and rocks, it was actually built over an abandoned coal mine. But through hard work and unusual practices, he turned the lump of coal that was the baseball field into a thing of beauty and even drew high praise from baseball legend Leo Durocher.

When the nearby Tulsa State Fair ended, Tabor collected leftover straw and animal bedding to cover the entire playing surface. The dugouts were converted into chicken coops with glass-covered fronts. The chicken poop from the dugout became fertilizer for the baseball field.

Tabor also ran hoses from a hot water tank in the clubhouse to soak the field with warm water and all of this was covered by a tarpaulin whenever bad weather threatened. The result was a rich, green grass which stood up to Oklahoma's blistering summer heat.

As for the chickens in those dugouts, Tabor provided them as springtime gifts for players, front office staff and local sportswriters. Both dugouts were cleaned so thoroughly before the baseball season began that many visiting players never knew what they were sitting in, literally.

Regular season games were not carried by a local radio station but playoff games were carried on KVOO AM (1170), the station which would be the Oilers' home during most of the 1960s. John Henry, who would be part of the radio crew for University of Oklahoma football broadcasts in 1953, was the play-by-play announcer.

On the diamond, Tulsa was an offensive power and led the Texas League with a .280 team batting average as well as leading the league in doubles, hits, stolen bases and runs batted in.

Third baseman Hank Schenz was the Texas League's Most Valuable Player, leading the league in batting average (.333), doubles (44) and runs scored (102).

Outfielder Clarence Maddern had a league-leading 184 base hits and later played parts of four seasons with the Chicago Cubs and Cleveland Indians. Maddern and teammate Wilmer Skeen also led the Texas League in singles (133). Shortstop Sal Madrid was a Texas League leader but in a category hitters don't want to be known for: most strikeouts (95).

Tommy Warren was one of the league's best pitchers, leading Tulsa's mound staff with a 20-6 record with a 2.86 ERA.

Tulsa earned the fourth and final playoff spot but was swept in four games by the Fort Worth Cats in the semifinals. Dallas won its semifinal series with the San Antonio Missions, 4-1, then defeated Fort Worth by the same margin in the finals.

Fort Worth had the league's best regular season record at 101-53. Dallas was second (91-63), followed by San Antonio (87-65), Tulsa (84-69), the Beaumont Exporters (70-83), the Houston Buffaloes (64-89), Shreveport Sports (61-92) and Oklahoma City Indians (54-98).

The Oilers had a baseball oddity in their 10-6 victory over Houston on July 29thh with two inside-the-park home runs in a single game. Outfielder Wilmer Skeen hit one in the first inning and Jack Richards hit one in the seventh inning.

Texas League Park hosted seven exhibition games during April and May, giving Tulsa baseball fans plenty to cheer about.

The defending National League champion Chicago Cubs lost to the St. Louis Browns, 1-0, before 2,713 fans on April 8th. Cubs pitcher Hank Wyse was one of five former Oilers to play for the Cubs and scattered six hits over six innings. Junior Stephens of the Browns drove in the game's only run with a sixth-inning single.

An April 9th exhibition between the Pittsburgh Pirates and Chicago White Sox was called off due to rain after two innings with Pittsburgh leading, 1-0. The two teams faced each other the following day with the Pirates pulling out a 3-2 victory. Future Hall of Famer Ralph Kiner drove in the game-winning run with a sacrifice fly. The White Sox had a future Hall of Famer of their own in shortstop Luke Appling. That day, the 37-year-old Appling played like a man half that age, turning two double plays and stealing a base.

The St. Louis Cardinals administered a football-style pounding to the Tulsa Oilers in a 14-0 rout. St. Louis struck for seven runs in the first inning and pounded Oilers pitchers for 20 base hits. Meanwhile, the Cardinal pitchers held the Oilers to just two base hits. Del Wilber led the Cardinal offense with four base hits while future Hall of Famers Stan Musial and Red Schoendist added two hits apiece.

The first Negro League exhibition game in Tulsa saw the Kansas City Monarchs defeating the Chicago Giants, 19-6, before 2,114 fans on May 7th. The Monarchs were the Negro League's equivalent of the New York Yankees' dynasty teams with legendary players such as pitcher Leroy "Satchel" Paige (who worked in a front-office capacity with the Oilers in later years) and first baseman Buck O'Neill.

Kansas City, which had 21 hits in the contest, scored four runs in the first inning and added eight runs in the second inning and was never challenged. Outfielder Willard "Home Run" Brown had two singles and scored three runs. Baseball historian Bill James once likened Willard Brown's baseball talents to those of modern-day stars Andre Dawson and Juan Gonzalez, among others. Brown would be inducted into the Baseball Hall of Fame in 2006. O'Neill went 3-for-4 and scored three runs.

The All-American Girls Professional Baseball League played their only game in Tulsa on May 9th, with the Kenosha Comets defeating the Rockford Peaches, 4-2, before nearly 2,000 fans.

The field dimensions for women's baseball were different than those for the men's game. It was 70 feet between the bases (90 feet for men) and 43 feet from the pitching rubber to home plate (60 feet and 6 inches for men). The baseball for women's play measured 11 inches around, slightly bigger than the men's baseball but smaller than a softball. Pitches in the women's game were thrown underhanded compared to overhand or sidearm for men's game. Otherwise, the rules were the same as in the men's game.

Rockford, the 1945 AAGPBL champions, was in a tight game when rookie relief pitcher Verna Wilson entered the game in the seventh inning. Kenosha greeted her by scoring eight runs in the inning with a three-run triple by Alice Hohlmeyer being the key blow.

A May 10th rematch in Tulsa was rained out so both teams journeyed to Ponca City, Oklahoma for another exhibition game.

The 1992 movie *A League of Their Own* was a fictionalized version of life in the AAGPBL. The movie starred Tom Hanks as Jimmy Duggan, the manager of the Rockford Peaches and a former Chicago Cubs player trying to redeem himself. The movie also starred Geena Davis, Rosie O'Donnell, Lori Petty and Madonna.

During one scene in the movie, Duggan (Hanks) expresses his frustration with a player with one of the more memorable quotes in the annals of sports-related movies: "There's no crying in baseball!"

The Kansas City Monarchs returned to Texas League Park on May 23rd and defeated an outclassed House of David team, 19-6 before 1,684 fans. The House of David hurt their own cause by making eight fielding errors. Willard Brown went 4-for-5 with a home run and Monarchs catcher Earl Taborn stole home.

Josh Gibson, a legendary player with the Negro League's Homestead Grays, joined the Monarchs for that Tulsa contest. Gibson died of a stroke the following year.

Elsewhere in the Texas League, Oklahoma City's lone bright spot was rookie leftfielder Dale Mitchell, one of the greatest baseball players to suit up for the University of Oklahoma Sooners. Mitchell hit .337 in 108 games with Oklahoma City before moving up to the majors. He batted .300 or higher in six of his seven years with the Cleveland

Indians and was a key member of their 1948 World Series championship team.

Ralph Houk was a catcher that year with Beaumont, the Double-A affiliate of the New York Yankees. After replacing Casey Stengel as manager, Houk led the 1961 and 1962 Yankees to World Series championships.

1947: Tulsa qualified for the Texas League playoffs for the second year in a row but the story of this season was the miraculous turnaround of the Houston Buffaloes.

After finishing nearly 37 games out of first place in 1946, the Buffaloes stormed back to win their first Texas League pennant since 1940 by defeating the Dallas Eagles in the finals, 4-2. Houston swept the Tulsa Oilers in the semifinals, 4-0, while Dallas squeaked past the Fort Worth Cats in their semifinal series, 4-3.

Houston had the league's best regular season record at 96-58 with Fort Worth hot on their heels at 95-58. They were followed by Dallas (79-74), Tulsa (79-75), the Shreveport Sports (75-79), Oklahoma City Indians (71-83) with the Beaumont Exporters and San Antonio Missions tied at 60-94.

Oilers third baseman Jack Cassini led the Texas League in runs scored (116), stolen bases (52) and finishing second in batting average (.319). Outfielder Elwood Grantham provided Tulsa with clutch hitting, leading the team in doubles (27), triples (13) and home runs (12).

Bill Stewart was Tulsa's best pitcher with a team-leading 2.77 ERA and also won 15 games. Tom Warren and Lee Anthony had good years as well, each of them winning 14 games.

Tulsa's John Vernon "Rocky" Stone led Texas League pitchers by appearing in 51 games. Despite a 9-11 record, Stone pitched seven complete games and had a 3.42 ERA.

Gus Mancuso was in his second and final year as Tulsa's player-manager. Mancuso was a two-time National League All-Star catcher with the New York Giants (1935 and 1937) and was also the catcher for five pitchers who later became Hall of Famers: Carl Hubbell, Grover Cleveland Alexander, Dizzy Dean, Burleigh Grimes and Jesse Haines.

The second stop in Bob Murphy's historical baseball journey came during this season when he was part of a three-man broadcast crew for Oiler baseball games on KAKC AM (970). The other announcers were Mack Creager and Bill Hyden.

Murphy attended the University of Tulsa and began his radio sports career in 1946 as the play-by-play announcer for the Muskogee (Oklahoma) Reds of the Class C Western Association. He moved to Oklahoma City in 1948 and joined another broadcasting legend, Curt Gowdy, as the radio announcers for University of Oklahoma football games.

Murphy spent 50 years covering major league baseball games on television and radio. He was renowned for his skillful use of words in painting a picture for radio listeners and always had a sunny disposition about life and the game of baseball. Murphy was the voice of the New York Mets from their first game in 1962 through the end of the 2003 season and was inducted into the Baseball Hall of Fame in 1994.

Except for the 1952 season, Creager would be part of Oiler radio broadcasts from 1947 through 1971 and announced over 3,000 games. He was the sports director at KOTV (Channel 6), the CBS television affiliate in Tulsa. Creager, who also did play-by-play on high school football and minor league hockey, was a football star at Oklahoma A&M University (now Oklahoma State University) during the 1940s prior to entering sports broadcasting.

Hyden was a long-time newscaster at KOTV and mentored several Tulsa newscasters who went on to have success in larger media markets. Hyden also founded KTBA-FM (92.1), a radio station in the Tulsa suburb of Broken Arrow that originally played instrumental music then became one of Tulsa's first progressive rock music stations.

Oklahoma City third baseman Al Rosen was the Texas League's Most Valuable Player, winning the batting title with a .349 average. Rosen went on to win the 1953 American League Most Valuable Player award with the Cleveland Indians and later served as an executive with the New York Yankees, Houston Astros and San Francisco Giants. Rosen was inducted into the Texas League Baseball Hall of Fame in 2005.

The Kansas City Monarchs, winners of six Negro League championships over the previous 10 years, defeated the Indianapolis Clowns, 5-3, before 2,500 fans on April 30th. Kansas City jumped to an early 3-0 lead and then held off a late Indianapolis rally.

Monarch shortstop Henry Thompson had a single, double and triple and turned two double plays. Pitcher Lefty LaMarque, a veteran of the Cuban League, pitched six shutout innings. First baseman Reece "Goose" Tatum, who later played for basketball's Harlem Globetrotters, entertained the crowd with several acrobatic defensive plays.

1948: The Oilers began a seven-year affiliation with the Cincinnati Reds, a period that would be one of the more successful periods in Tulsa's professional baseball history. The Reds owned 75 percent of the team with Grayle Howlett, one of the six businessmen who purchased the Oilers in 1946, owning the remaining 25 percent.

Tulsa played for the Texas League championship four times during those seven years as a Reds affiliate. Season attendance topped 200,000 for the first time in the city's history with 223,569 fans coming to

Texas League Park. That latter total stood as the best single-season attendance in Tulsa's professional baseball history until 1990.

Al Vincent, manager of Texas League championship teams in Beaumont and Dallas, was hired as Tulsa's manager. His 354 managerial victories from 1948 through 1951 ranks fourth in Tulsa's professional baseball history. Vincent also holds Texas League career managerial records for most playoff victories (50), most consecutive playoff seasons (five) and most total playoff seasons (eight).

Pitcher Harry Perkowski was the Texas League's Most Valuable Player, leading the league with 22 victories and 21 complete games while posting a 2.98 ERA. Perkowski also set a Texas League record that year with 15 pinch-hits in 30 at-bats. He later spent eight seasons with Cincinnati, winning 12 games in 1952 and 1953.

Second baseman Johnny Lane was the Texas League leader in runs scored (115). His on-base percentage of .452 also led the league and is also the best by any player in Tulsa's professional baseball history.

Seven Oilers were named to the Texas League's postseason All-Star Team, which was chosen by *The Sporting News* magazine. It also represented the most Tulsa professional baseball players ever named to a league's postseason All-Star Team. The honorees were pitchers Buddy Lively and Perkowski, catcher Al Unser (no relation to the famous auto racing family), first baseman Chuck Kress, third baseman Bill Capps, outfielder Russ Burns and Tatum.

Lively led the Texas League that year with a .789 winning percentage, thanks to a 15-4 record. During the previous year with the parent Cincinnati Reds, he came within two batters of pitching a perfect game against the Brooklyn Dodgers in Ebbets Field on July 14, 1947. Lively was a World War II veteran who marched with General George Patton's Third Army through France, Belgium and Holland. A shoulder injury forced Lively into an early retirement from baseball.

Tatum led the Texas League in batting average (.333) and in stolen bases (37). He would be the Oklahoma City Indians' player-manager in 1951-55.

Burns hit 26 home runs that year, the fourth out of nine minor league seasons in which he would hit 20 or more homers. A Tulsa professional baseball player would not lead the Texas League in home runs until Dean Palmer hit 25 for the 1989 Tulsa Drillers.

Unser batted .274 and was among the Texas League's best catchers in throwing out runners trying to steal a base. He played in the minor leagues for 25 years and parts of four seasons in the major leagues during the World War II era. Unser served for eight years as a manager in the St. Louis Cardinals' minor league system, taking four teams to their league's playoffs and winning two championships. His oldest son, Del, played for the Philadelphia Phillies' 1980 World Series champions.

Capps, who was born in Lawton, Oklahoma, batted .295 and had 24 doubles. He played 20 years in the minor leagues and spent most of the 1950s as a player-manager in the lower levels of minor league baseball and led the Tyler East Texans to the 1952 Big State League (Class B) championship. Capps also worked for 20 years as a scout for the Chicago Cubs.

A left-handed hitter, Kress led the Texas League in triples with 12 and extra base hits (66) while batting .312 with 13 home runs, 85 RBIs and 27 stolen bases. Kress finished his career with the 1954 Brooklyn Dodgers and also spent five years as a minor league manager.

Pitcher Eldred "Bud" Byerly, who split time that year between the Oilers and the Houston Buffaloes, had the league's lowest ERA (2.20). A teammate of Hall of Famer Stan Musial on the St. Louis Cardinals' 1944 World Series champions, Bylerly was released by the

Cardinals on May 5, 1948 then the Cincinnati Reds quickly signed him and sent him to Tulsa. Byerly played 11 years in the major leagues.

Oilers radio broadcasts moved to KAKC-FM (95.5) and switched to a two-man announcing crew of Bob Murphy and Mack Creager.

An April 7th exhibition game between the Brooklyn Dodgers and Tulsa Oilers drew the largest attendance for a professional baseball game in Tulsa to that point in time. Brooklyn banged out 13 hits and blasted the Oilers, 12-1, before 8,892 fans.

Future Hall of Famer Duke Snider led Brooklyn's hit parade by driving in three runs. A rookie catcher named Roy Campanella had two hits and drove in two runs. Jackie Robinson, who became the first modern-era African-American major league baseball player 51 weeks earlier, played that day for the Dodgers.

The Fort Worth Cats won their first Texas League pennant since 1939 and spoiled Tulsa's championship dreams by defeating the Oilers, 4-2-1. The Cats had eliminated the Shreveport Sports in the semifinals, 4-2, while Tulsa eliminated the Houston Buffaloes by the same margin in their semifinal series.

Fort Worth had the league's best regular season record at 92-61 with Tulsa close behind at 91-63. They were followed by Houston (82-72), Shreveport (76-77), the San Antonio Missions (75-76), Oklahoma City Indians (70-84), Dallas Rebels (64-89) and Beaumont Exporters (61-90).

Fort Worth pitcher Carl Erskine went 15-7 with a 2.59 ERA and earned a quick promotion to the Brooklyn Dodgers. Erskine spent 12 years with the Brooklyn and Los Angeles Dodgers, pitching no-hitters in 1952 and 1956 and struck out 14 New York Yankee hitters in Game 3 of the 1953 World Series, a single-game World Series record that stood for 10 years.

1949: Tulsa won its second Texas League title by beating the Fort Worth Cats in the best-of-seven championship series, 4-1. Tulsa reached the finals by defeating Oklahoma City in the semifinals, 4-2, but did it the hard way by losing the first two games to the Indians and then winning four in a row. Fort Worth had eliminated Shreveport, 4-1.

Fort Worth won the first two games of the series then Tulsa won three in a row. Fort Worth won Game 6 to set up a dramatic Game 7. After power-hitting outfielder Russell "The Muscle" Burns was walked intentionally in the 11th inning, first baseman Joe Adcock belted a two-run home run and the Oilers won, 4-1.

Adcock went on to play for the Milwaukee Braves in the 1957 and 1958 World Series. On May 26, 1959, he broke up a 12-inning perfect game by Pittsburgh Pirates pitcher Harvey Haddix, which would be the longest no-hitter in baseball history. Adcock returned to Tulsa in 1968 as the manager of the Seattle Angels in the Triple-A Pacific Coast League.

The Oilers went on to face the Southern Association champion Nashville Vols in the best-of-seven Dixie World Series. Nashville won that best-of-seven series, 4-3, when the game-winning run scored in the 10th inning on a bases-loaded infield ground ball that rolled between the legs of Oilers second baseman Johnny Lane. Carl Sawatski, who served as president of the Texas League from 1976 until his death in 1991, hit a home run against Tulsa in that series.

A key part in Tulsa's success that year was winning 15 consecutive road games, a Texas League record which still stands.

The Dallas Eagles jumped to a 16-1 start that year and seemed to be a shoo-in to win the Texas League, led by Jerry Witte who went on to hit 50 home runs. But the Fort Worth Cats finished with the best regular season record at 100-54 with Tulsa second at 90-64. They were followed by the Oklahoma City Indians (81-72), Shreveport Sports (80-74), Dallas (76-77), San Antonio Missions (70-83), Houston Buffaloes (60-91) and Beaumont Exporters (55-97).

Burns left his mark on Tulsa baseball history with the most runs batted in during a single season with 153 that year. It still stands as the third-highest RBI season in Texas League history. Burns also hit 27 home runs and batted .340 that year and would be among the first players inducted into the Texas League Baseball Hall of Fame when it was created in 2004.

Second baseman Johnny Lane was the Texas League's co-leader in triples with 13. Lane also led the Oilers in runs scored with 134 while batting .303 in what would be his final professional baseball season. He never played in the majors.

Frank Smith led Texas League pitchers in appearances with 57. A 6-foot-3 right-handed pitcher with a sidearm delivery, Smith made 23 starts and had 15 complete games before becoming a relief pitcher, a move that made him one of baseball's first closers during the 1950s. Smith was 17-11 with Tulsa that year and then spent six of his seven major league seasons with the Cincinnati Reds, highlighted by a career-high 20 saves in 1954.

Catcher Walt Wrona hit .344 in 76 games that year and would leave a strong baseball legacy in Tulsa through his sons. Ron Wrona was a baseball standout at Tulsa's Bishop Kelley High School and starred at the University of Tulsa. Rick Wrona was a college standout at Wichita State University and spent parts of six seasons with four major league teams.

Oilers radio broadcasts remained on KAKC-FM (95.5) with Mack Creager becoming the lead announcer after Bob Murphy's departure and Bill Hyden returned after a one-year absence.

Season attendance topped 200,000 for the second year in a row, but the final total of 221,176 was a slight drop from the previous year.

The Brooklyn Dodgers and Duke Snider continued their love affair with Tulsa and exhibition games, posting a 10-0 shutout victory on April 6th before 7,153 fans with the Oilers being held to just three base hits. Snider went 3-for-4, including a home run, while Jackie Robinson went 2-for-5.

Elsewhere in the Texas League, center fielder Dick Williams enjoyed his finest season out of the four he spent with the Fort Worth Cats. The fleet-footed Williams batted .310, drove in 114 runs and scored 109 runs. Williams went on to be one of just two major-league managers to lead three different teams to the World Series: the 1967 "Impossible Dream" Boston Red Sox, the two-time World Series champion Oakland Athletics (1972-73) and the 1984 San Diego Padres.

As a manager, Williams had a knack for turning teams around upon his arrival with a no-nonsense approach in game strategy and in the clubhouse. Five out of the six teams that he managed had improved won-lost records in his first season there. Williams was inducted into the Baseball Hall of Fame in 2008.

Chapter Six
The 1950s

Many historians refer to this period as "The Golden Age" because of America's ongoing prosperity after the end of World War II. Military hero Dwight Eisenhower served two terms as President of the United States and technology promised a bright tomorrow. It would also be a decade of profound changes.

The United States Supreme Court ruled that racial segregation was unconstitutional and the civil rights movement began with an equal emphasis on non-violent tactics and the proposition that all people are created equal. Exploration of outer space began with the launch of the Soviet Union's Sputnik satellite and then the United States quickly followed suit.

This would be the decade that gave us *Playboy* magazine, the *Peanuts* comic strip, color televisions and remote controls, a vaccine for polio, the first medical reports linking cigarette smoking with cancer, seat belts in cars, credit cards, hula hoops, the opening of Disneyland, Lego toys, McDonald's restaurants and the tragic death of actor James Dean.

But the most profound change was a new form of music called "Rock and Roll." It drew passionate fans, mostly teenagers and young adults and equally passionate critics, mostly adults and religious organizations. Elvis Presley's dancing while singing on *The Ed Sullivan Show* sent the nation into a tizzy with some saying it wouldn't last and other decrying it a tool of the devil himself. Nearly two-thirds of a century later, somebody has been proven wrong.

The University of Oklahoma football team made history under the leadership of coach, Bud Wilkinson. The Sooners won national championships in 1950, 1955 and 1956. And their achievement of winning 47 consecutive games from 1953 through 1957 is a collegiate football record which has never been broken.

Thanks to the development of a master plan for city-wide parks, civic improvements and overall prosperity during the decade, *Reader's Digest* bestowed the title of "America's Most Beautiful City" upon Tulsa.

While the Tulsa Oilers made five playoff appearances in this decade, the era was far from golden for local baseball fans. The team went through affiliations with the Cincinnati Reds, Cleveland Indians, Chicago Cubs (again), Philadelphia Phillies and St. Louis Cardinals. They reached the playoffs five times but failed to win a pennant. Season attendance was on the decline and tensions between the ballpark's landlords and team ownership were close to boiling over.

Willie Mays, Hank Aaron and Ted Williams were among the major league baseball stars appearing in exhibition games played in Tulsa. Other big-league standouts coming to Tulsa during that time were Leo Durocher, Pee Wee Reese, Enos Slaughter and Eddie Stanky.

1950: Tulsa reached the Texas League championship series for the third straight year under manager Al Vincent, but the San Antonio Missions prevailed in the best-of-seven finals, 4-2. Tulsa eliminated the Fort Worth Cats, 4-0-1, in their semifinal series while San Antonio swept the Beaumont Exporters in four games.

Under manager Rogers Hornsby, Beaumont had the league's best regular season record at 91-62. Fort Worth was next (88-64) followed by Tulsa (83-69) and San Antonio (79-75). Then came the Dallas Eagles (74-78), Oklahoma City Indians (72-79), Shreveport Sports (63-91) and Houston Buffaloes (61-93).

Despite success on the field, it was a different story for the Oilers' front office. Season attendance fell by nearly 15 percent to 184,677.

Jim "Bones" Blackburn led Texas League pitchers in winning percentage (.750, 21-7 record) and shared the league lead for most victories in what would be his best professional baseball season. He also tied the Texas League record of four consecutive shutouts originally set by Harry "The Cat" Breechen of the 1930 Houston Buffaloes and duplicated by Don Ferrarese of the 1955 San Antonio Missions.

A slender, 6-foot-4 right handed pitcher, he played briefly with the parent Cincinnati Reds but baseball was easy compared to his challenges from a few years earlier.

Blackburn became a prisoner of war on December 23, 1944 after being wounded by German soldiers during World War II's Battle of the Bulge. While in captivity and weakened by a lack of food, a brutal German POW guard would pull out Blackburn's toenails with a pair of pliers. Blackburn was freed in April of 1945 by members of the 69th Infantry Division and resumed his baseball career following an extended hospitalization.

Outfielder Wally Post, who later played for the Cincinnati Reds, set a Tulsa professional baseball record by driving in nine runs in a game on September 1st. By comparison, the Texas League record for most RBIs in a game is 16 by Jay Clarke of the Corsicana (Texas) Indians on June 15, 1902.

Second baseman Jack Baumer provided Tulsa's long-ball threat by hitting 22 home runs that year, tops on the Oilers and fifth-best in the Texas League.

Outfielder Eddie Knoblauch, an uncle of future Minnesota Twins-New York Yankees infielder Chuck Knoblauch, led the Texas League in triples with 15.

The radio broadcasts switched back to KAKC-AM (970) with Mack Creager handling all of the announcing duties by himself.

The largest crowd to see a Texas League baseball game watched the Oilers' season opener against the Dallas Eagles on April 11, 1950 in the historic Cotton Bowl football stadium. Eagles owner Dick Burnett, considered to be a cross between baseball executives Bill Veeck and Tom Yawkey, was dead set on making history for himself and his team.

No baseball-related changes were made in the Cotton Bowl's seating configuration. That meant home plate was likely in the corner of one of the end zones with the left field and right field foul poles about 200 feet away from home plate. That also led to a ground rule where any ball hit into those sections was automatically ruled to be a double.

A crowd of 53,378 (out of 54,151 tickets sold) saw a star-studded Dallas lineup take batting practice. The Eagles that night featured four members of the Baseball Hall of Fame and three future Cooperstown inductees.

The batting order had John "Home Run" Baker (age 64) at third base, Duffy Lewis (age 61) in left field, Charlie Grimm (age 51) at third base, Tris Speaker (age 62) in center field, Charlie Gehringer (age 46) at second base, Travis Jackson (age 46) at shortstop and Ty Cobb (age 63) in right field. Mickey Cochrane (age 47) was the catcher and Dizzy Dean (age 40) was the pitcher.

Tulsa's Harry Donabedian was walked by Dean to start the game and then the baseball legends were replaced by the regular Dallas line-up. The Oilers won the game, 10-3.

The only major league exhibition game in Tulsa that year saw Eddie Stanky and Wes Westrum ignite a 27-hit attack as the New York Giants routed the Cleveland Indians, 18-8, on April 10th before 7,369 fans. Stanky had three hits and scored two runs while Westrum homered and drove in three runs. Future Hall of Famers Lou Boudreau and pitcher Bob Lemon each had a hit for the Indians.

Because the game ran longer than expected with all of the base hits, umpires ended the game during the bottom of the ninth inning to allow both teams to make train connections.

The Negro League's Kansas City Monarchs played three exhibition games in Tulsa that year: May 21st against the Philadelphia Stars, June 9th against the Memphis Red Sox and June 14th against the Memphis Red Sox. Unfortunately, newspaper articles containing the results of those games could not be found.

Monarchs catcher Elston Howard was featured in advertisements promoting each game. Howard went on to play for the New York Yankees and after splitting time with incumbent catcher Yogi Berra, became one of many standouts on the Yankees' World Series championship teams during the early 1960s.

Beaumont infielder Gil McDougald was the Texas League Player of the Year, leading the league with 187 base hits, tying for the league lead in games played (152) and finishing second in batting average (.336). McDougald played for the New York Yankees from 1951 through 1960, winning the 1951 American League Rookie of the Year award and was a five-time American League All-Star.

McDougald earned an unfortunate spot in baseball lore on May 7, 1957 in a game against the Cleveland Indians when he hit a line drive that accidentally struck Cleveland pitcher Herb Score in the right eye. Score eventually regained 20/20 vision in the eye but he was never the same pitcher afterwards.

Dallas pitcher Wayne McLeland was the Texas League Pitcher of the Year, sharing the league lead in victories (21) and having the third-lowest ERA among starting pitchers (2.49). A relatively successful pitcher over 11 minor league seasons, McLeland made big-league baseball infamy during his 10 appearances with the 1951 and 1952 Detroit Tigers by never striking out an opposing batter, setting the major league record for most pitching appearances without a strikeout.

1951: A major stadium renovation was completed prior to Opening Day with much needed repairs done to the playing surface and the wooden seating structure. Huge amounts of dirt were spread over the infield and outfield to stabilize a sinking playing surface.

That sinking feeling carried over to the Oilers' performance. Their 94 losses was the second highest season total in Tulsa's professional baseball history to that point in time. And the season attendance of 147,907 was Tulsa's lowest since the Texas League resumed operations in 1946.

Second baseman Johnny Temple was the only bright spot for local fans that year. He led the Texas League in base hits (180), singles (151) and stolen bases (30). An above-average defensive player as well, Temple was a three-time National League All-Star with the Cincinnati Reds during the 1950s.

Outfielder Fletcher Robbe led the Texas League in on-base percentage (.424) and his 101 walks were second only to teammate Harry Donabedian (102).

Pitcher Joe Nuxhall led the Oilers in victories with 13, but his 22 losses that year led the Texas League. He also became the last Texas League pitcher to lose 20 or more games in one season.

Nuxhall was the youngest player to make a major league debut during the 20th Century, playing as a 15-year-old for the 1944 Cincinnati Reds. He fared much better once he rejoined the Reds and spent 15 years with them and being a National League All-Star team in 1955 and 1956.

Left fielder Bob Nieman, who started the 1951 season with the Oilers before joining Oklahoma City, won the Texas League batting championship with a .324 average. Nieman made baseball history on September 14th of that year in his major league debut with the St. Louis Browns by hitting home runs in his first two big-league at-bats.

San Antonio Missions pitcher Tommy Fine threw a seven-inning no-hitter against the Oilers in a 2-0 victory in the first game of a doubleheader on June 24th. It would be the last time the Oilers were on the losing end of a no-hitter for 13 years. Fine also tossed a no-hitter for the 1952 Caribbean Series champion Havana Lions (Leones de la Habana) and was chosen as the series' Most Valuable Player.

Oilers radio broadcasts remained on KAKC-AM (970) with Mack Creager handling all of the announcing duties by himself.

An April 8th exhibition game between the Oilers and the National League Boston Braves was a high-scoring and lengthy affair. Boston needed 10 runs in the seventh inning to pull out a 16-11 victory in a contest that had 11 walks in addition to 30 base hits plus five fielding errors.

Future major league manager Gene Mauch hit a home run on the game's second pitch. Sid Gordon drove in four runs for Boston and Sam Jethero, a former Negro League star, added four hits and scored four runs. Tulsa's Harry Donabedian had four hits in the contest.

Johnny Temple added two hits, pitcher Joe Nuxhall drove in two runs and Eddie Knoblauch scored four times.

The Negro League's Kansas City Monarchs and Indianapolis Clowns played at Texas League Park on April 28th with Indianapolis taking an 11-9 victory before 1,336 fans. Kansas City scored four runs in the first inning but they also made six errors which led to their downfall. Indianapolis took the lead for good by scoring three runs in the fifth inning.

The Indianapolis Clowns lived up to their nickname by providing non-stop laughter during the contest. Infielder Richard "King Tut" King alternated between wearing his game uniform, dressing up as the Egyptian pharaoh of that same name or sporting a tuxedo and top hat, as though headed to a high-society event. A midget named Spec Bebop was King Tut's sidekick during those skits.

Houston went from worst to first by winning the Texas League pennant as well as having the league's best regular season record. Houston swept the San Antonio Missions, 4-0, in the finals. The Buffaloes won their semifinal series against the Beaumont Exporters, 4-2. Beaumont made the postseason by defeating the Fort Worth Cats in a one-game playoff for that final spot. San Antonio advanced by eliminating the Dallas Eagles, 3-2.

Houston posted a 99-61 record followed by San Antonio (86-75), Dallas (85-75) and Beaumont and Fort Worth each at 84-77. Then came the Oklahoma City Indians (75-86), Tulsa Oilers (67-94) and Shreveport Sports (63-98).

San Antonio dominated the postseason awards with Bob Turley winning the Texas League Pitcher of the Year award and Jim Dyck earning Player of the Year honors.

Turley's nickname of "Bullet Bob" was well-deserved. His 20-8 won-lost record put him second in the league in victories and he also ranked among the league's top 10 pitchers in lowest earned run average and most strikeouts.

Despite giving up more bases on balls than any American League pitcher three times during his career, Turley was a three-time American League All-Star selection and played eight of his 12 major league seasons with the New York Yankees. He won the 1958 American League Cy Young Award (the league's best pitcher), aided by league-leading totals of 21 victories and 19 complete games.

Dyck was a versatile player who batted .284 that year and finished second in the Texas League in home runs (27) and had 60 of his 167 base hits going for extra bases. During 16 years in the minor leagues and five major league seasons, Dyck played every position except pitcher and catcher.

Beaumont infielder Dorrel Norman Evert "Whitey" Herzog was not one of that team's memorable players in 1951, batting an anemic .198 over 35 games. That was in sharp contrast to when he was an 18-year-old infielder with the 1950 Sooner State League's McAlester (Oklahoma) Rockets, a class D farm club of the New York Yankees and had that league's fourth-highest batting average that year. 351.

Herzog would achieve fame not on the playing field but in the dugout, becoming one of major league's baseball premier managers during the 1980s. His baseball teams were rooted in strong pitching, good defense, hitters with a high on-base percentage and overall team speed instead of relying on dramatic home runs.

Herzog won 822 games managing the St. Louis Cardinals from 1980 through 1990, leading them to three National League championships and a 1982 World Series title. He had won 410 games over five seasons with the American League's Kansas City Royals, guiding them to consecutive AL divisional championships from 1976 through 1978. Herzog was a 2010 inductee into the Baseball Hall of Fame.

1952: The Oilers fared better in the first year of Joe Schultz's three-year run as the team's manager. Despite a losing record of 78-83, it was 11 more victories than the year before. Attendance improved as well with a season total of 155,064.

In 1969, Schultz was the manager of the Seattle Pilots in their only year of existence. That team had a 64-98 record and became the Milwaukee Brewers the following year.

Tulsa's baseball fortunes almost went up in smoke on July 8th when a fire broke out in the team offices behind the third base grandstand. Had there been the typical summertime wind from the southwest, the fire would have quickly spread into the aging wooden structure. Fortunately that day, the wind was blowing out of the north and damage was kept to a minimum.

The ballpark's age created another problem when a spectator suffered minor injuries after falling through a broken area of the wooden bleachers. That same type of event would happen again in 1977, but with many more spectators being injured and Tulsa's professional baseball livelihood would once again hang in the balance.

Johnny Vander Meer, a baseball legend for throwing two no-hitters as a young superstar with the Cincinnati Reds, threw another no-hitter in Tulsa's 12-0 victory over the Beaumont Roughnecks on July 15th. It was the first no-hitter by a Tulsa pitcher in nearly 10 years.

Earl York was Tulsa's hitting standout that year, leading the team with 15 home runs and driving in 101 runs while batting .307.

Minor league veteran Tom Reis was the ace of the Oiler pitching staff, posting a 15-6 record and a 3.08 ERA, despite walking more batters (77) than he struck out (43).

The Oilers turned two triple plays that year, both of which were in road games and the only time Tulsa ever turned two triple plays in a single season. Shortstop Alex Grammas, who later starred with the Cincinnati Reds, was the key player in those triple plays.

The first came in an 8-4 win over the Shreveport Sports in Shreveport, Louisiana on April 28th. Six consecutive Sports batters had singled in an eighth-inning rally with no outs. Then Grammas snagged a line drive, stepped on second base and threw to first baseman Earl York to end the play. Then on August 27th in an 8-1 road win over the Dallas Eagles, Grammas caught an infield grounder which resulted in putouts at second base, first base and home plate.

Oilers catcher Hobie Landrith batted .300 that year and later made baseball history as the first player chosen in a draft to stock the expansion New York Mets. Landrith batted .289 in 23 games in 1962 and also hit the game-winning home run in the Mets' first-ever regular season victory. But Landrith was later part of a trade to the Baltimore Orioles for what many Mets fans considered to be one of the infamous Mets, "Marvelous" Marv Thornberry.

Two memorable exhibition games were played at Texas League Park and those would be the last exhibitions in Tulsa for four years. On April 7th in one of his last appearances before serving in the military during the Korean War, future Hall of Famer Ted Williams hit a game-winning three-run home run in the ninth inning as the Boston Red Sox edged the Tulsa Oilers, 5-3, before 6,562 fans.

Three days later, Wes Westrum and Hank Thompson had two hits apiece in the New York Giants' 4-0 win over the Cleveland Indians. Giants pitchers Larry Jansen and Max Lanier combined on a six-hit shutout. Future Hall of Fame outfielder Willie Mays wasn't with the team that day due to military duty.

With Mack Creager taking a one-year hiatus, Tulsa baseball games moved to KOME-AM (1300) with Hugh Finnerty and Blaine Triplett calling the action. This move helped lay the foundation for Finnerty's key role in the success of Tulsa Oilers baseball during the 1960s.

Finnerty had moved to Tulsa earlier in the year to handle sales and public relations work at Tulsa's CBS affiliate, KOTV. That led to the Oilers being one of the first minor league teams to have its baseball games televised on a regular schedule.

Finnerty later served as the team's general manager for three years in the early 1960s and earned the 1963 Minor League Executive of the Year award from *The Sporting News* magazine. He also served as president of the Texas League from 1965 through 1969 and president of the National Association of Baseball, which oversaw all of minor league baseball.

After leaving the Oilers, Finnerty promoted auto racing at the Tulsa Fairgrounds Speedway adjacent to Oiler Park. While Finnerty's promotional magic drew record crowds, the engine noise from those Friday and Saturday night dirt track races could be a nuisance for nearby baseball fans and local residents.

Shreveport won its third Texas League championship and first since 1942, defeating the Oklahoma City Indians in the playoffs, 4-2. The Sports swept the Fort Worth Cats, 4-0, in their semifinal series while Oklahoma City ousted the Dallas Eagles, 4-2.

Dallas had the best regular season record at 92-69, followed Fort Worth (86-75), Shreveport (84-77) and Oklahoma City (82-79). Following those teams were the San Antonio Missions (79-82), Tulsa Oilers (78-83) and Beaumont Exporters (77-84). The defending champion Houston Buffaloes went from first to worst, tumbling from a 99-61 record in 1951 to 66-95 in 1952.

Fort Worth infielder Billy Hunter was the Texas League Player of the Year. His .285 batting average was the best of his minor league career, he ranked fifth in the league in base hits (174) and was an equally talented defensive player. Hunter made the 1953 American League All-Star team as a rookie shortstop with the St. Louis Browns in the final year before the team became the Baltimore Orioles.

After the 1954 season, Hunter and pitcher Don Larsen went from Baltimore to the New York Yankees in a 16-player trade. Larsen went on to pitch a perfect game against the Brooklyn Dodgers in the 1956 World Series. Hunter later served as manager of the Texas Rangers, posting a 146-108 record with second-place finishes in the American League's Western Division in 1977 and 1978.

Hal Erickson of the Dallas Eagles was the Texas League Pitcher of the Year, posting a 20-14 record with a 2.59 ERA. It was Erickson's third 20-win season in the minors. A 6-foot-5, 230-pound right handed pitcher, Erickson didn't fare so well as a 33-year-old major league rookie with the Detroit Tigers, going 0-1 with a 4.73 ERA in 18 appearances.

Dallas Eagles right-handed pitcher Dave Hoskins became the first African-American player in the Texas League and the former Negro League outfielder made an impressive debut. His 22 victories led the league and his 2.12 earned run average was the fifth-best among all TL pitchers, thanks primarily to throwing a curve ball that was next to impossible to hit. And proving his versatility, Hoskins also posted a .328 batting average and was frequently used in clutch pinch-hitting situations.

During his Negro League career, Hoskins played for the legendary Homestead Grays as well as the Cincinnati Clowns, Chicago American Giants and Louisville Buckeyes. After suffering a skull fracture during his high school baseball career, Hoskins followed the advice of Negro League legend (and future Tulsa Oilers coach) Satchel Paige and switched positions from the outfield to the pitching mound.

Hoskins posted a 9-3 record with a 3.99 ERA for the 1953 Cleveland Indians but spent most of his professional baseball career bouncing between the Double-A and Triple-A leagues along with the Mexican Baseball League.

1953: A Tulsa team that many thought could finish in last place unexpectedly had a winning season and reached the best-of-seven Texas League championship series, only to fall to the regular season champion Dallas Eagles, 4-1.

The Oilers won their semifinal series against the Fort Worth Cats, 4-2, while Dallas was taken to the limit before eliminating the Oklahoma City Indians, 4-3.

Dallas had the best regular season record at 88-66, followed by Tulsa (83-71), Fort Worth (82-72) and Oklahoma City (80-74). Trailing those teams in the standings were the Shreveport Sports (79-75), Houston Buffaloes (72-82), San Antonio Missions (67-87) and Beaumont Exporters (65-89).

Third baseman Chuck Harmon and first baseman Nino Escalera became the first African-Americans to play for the Tulsa Oilers.

Harmon led the team in batting average (.311), base hits (176) and stolen bases (25). He was also a collegiate basketball standout, leading the University of Toledo Rockets to the finals of the 1943 National Invitation Tournament in New York City's Madison Square Garden in his freshman year.

He played just five games for the Negro League's Indianapolis Clowns before catching the eyes of scouts for the Oilers' major league affiliate, the Cincinnati Reds. The following year, Harmon made history again as the Reds' first African-American player.

He was traded to the St. Louis Cardinals in 1956 for Joe Frazier and former Oiler Alex Grammas and finished his baseball career in 1957, splitting time between St. Louis and the Philadelphia Phillies.

Escalera led the Texas League with 19 triples, a league season record that still stands. He batted .305 and led the Oilers in runs scored (95) and was second in stolen bases (17). During the TL semifinals, Escalera hit for the cycle and had six RBIs in a win over Fort Worth.

Regarded by many Latin baseball experts as one of the best first basemen to come from Puerto Rico, Escalera served as a scout for the New York Mets in 1966-81 and is a member of the Puerto Rico Baseball Hall of Fame.

Rookie catcher Ed Bailey struck out more times (104) than any Texas League hitter. Despite that and a .243 batting average, he led the Oilers that year with 88 RBIs and was second on the team in home runs (21). Bailey spent nine of his 14 major league seasons with the Cincinnati Reds, playing on five National League All-Star teams and repeatedly ranked among baseball's best catchers during the 1950s when it came to throwing out would-be base stealers.

Center fielder Ed Barr batted .263 that year with 12 home runs, 75 RBIs and 16 stolen bases. But he also had the dubious honor of being the Texas League's leader in most times hit by a pitch (10). Ironically, Oiler players would lead the league in that category each of the next two years: 11 times by Joe Macko 11 in 1954 and 13 times by Mike Lutz in 1955.

Howie Judson was the ace of Tulsa's pitching staff, posting an 11-0 record, a stingy 1.80 ERA and 86 strikeouts in 90 innings, along with complete games in eight of his 10 starts. But Judson had a losing record the following year when promoted to the parent Cincinnati Reds and never returned to the majors.

No major league exhibitions were played in Tulsa that year but a barnstorming game was played between The House of David and the Harlem Globetrotters baseball team. The House of David won a sloppily-played game, 13-4, before 1,775 fans.

The House of David broke the game open by scoring five runs in the sixth inning and adding four more runs in the ninth. Shortstop Rocky Carlini and center fielder Jerry Ledwidge led the victors with three hits apiece.

The Globetrotters made seven fielding errors and the start of the game was delayed 27 minutes by miscommunications between the Oiler front office staff and the two teams as to who was responsible for providing umpires for the game.

Negro League pitching legend Leroy "Satchel" Paige, who played in the 1953 major league All-Star Game representing the St. Louis Browns, pitched the first three innings for the Globetrotters but gave up three runs. Shortstop Sammy Gee and third baseman Johnny Britton had three hits each for the Globetrotters.

Comic relief was provided by Frank "Bobo" Nickerson, a rubber-faced, loose-limbed man known as "The Screwball of Baseball" who portrayed a base coach for The House of David that night. The spirit of the routines done by Nickerson, Max Patkin and other baseball entertainers of that era continues today with teams in the majors and minors who nowdays use fuzzy, kid-friendly mascots to perform similar skits.

Oiler games were carried on KOME-AM (1300) but Mack Creager returned to the microphone and began a three-year partnership with University of Tulsa announcer Tony George on the baseball broadcasts.

1954: The sizzle the Oilers generated in 1953 turned into a fizzle in this season. Fans stayed away in droves and the Cincinnati Reds went out the door as the Oilers' parent team due to increasing operating costs. The Reds sold the franchise to Tulsa's general manager Grayle Howlett after the season ended.

But this would also be the year that a future Hall of Famer played for Tulsa but never appeared in a home game. He would also be referenced in one of the most popular baseball-related movies ever made.

Tulsa tumbled to a 78-83 record, cursed by having the worst hitting and fielding team in the Texas League. The season attendance of 104,378 was a drop of nearly one-third from the previous year and more than 50 percent from the record set just six years earlier.

The pitching staff was the only saving grace for the Oilers that year. Al MacNeilance was the Texas League's co-leader in shutouts with four. He also had 10 complete games and a 3.52 ERA but was a hard-luck pitcher, posting an 11-10 won-lost record. He was nicknamed "Mr. Peepers" for wearing glasses with thick lenses.

During that season, McNeilance pitched the first 14 innings of a 22-inning victory over Dallas in his first start following an emergency appendectomy. Arm ailments forced a premature retirement but he remained in Tulsa and was a long-time employee of the United States Postal Service.

Bullpen ace Dick Bokelmann appeared in 61 games that season, tops among Texas League pitchers. The Northwestern University alumnus went 10-4 with a sparkling 1.80 ERA in what would be his eighth and final minor league season after spending parts of the previous three seasons with the St. Louis Cardinals.

Frank Robinson played at second base and third base in eight games for the Tulsa Oilers but never played for them in the city of Tulsa.

That's because the Oilers opened the season on the road, then had their entire first homestand of the season rained out and then went back on the road. After going 8-for-30 with just one RBI in those first road games, the 18-year-old Robinson was sent down to the Columbia

(South Carolina) Reds of the class A South Atlantic League while the Oilers were traveling.

That was the only minor league lowlight for Robinson. He was called up to the Cincinnati Reds in 1956 and later played in 14 All-Star Games. He enjoyed a career revival with the Baltimore Orioles, helping them win World Series championships in 1966 and 1970. Robinson became Major League Baseball's first African-American manager with the 1975 Cleveland Indians and he was a 1982 inductee into the Baseball Hall of Fame.

He was also part of one of the most lopsided trades in baseball history when the Reds traded him on December 9, 1965 to the Baltimore Orioles for pitchers Milt Pappas and Jack Baldschun plus outfielder Dick Simpson. Reds executives thought Robinson was washed up but he won the American League Triple Crown with Baltimore in 1966, leading the AL in batting average, home runs and runs batted in.

That former Tulsa Oiler was even name-checked in the 1988 movie, *Bull Durham*. A baseball groupie named Annie Savoy (played by Susan Sarandon) referenced the Frank Robinson-Milt Pappas swap as being a bad trade during her opening monologue.

Oilers baseball broadcasts were in the second year of a three-year run on KOME-AM (1300) with Mack Creager and Tony George calling the action.

The Houston Buffaloes barely missing having the best record in the league but they won the pennant convincingly, defeating the Fort Worth Cats in the playoffs, 4-1. Houston defeated the Oklahoma City Indians and Fort Worth eliminated Shreveport respectively, 4-1.

Shreveport had the best regular season record at 90-71 with Houston in hot pursuit at 89-72, followed by Oklahoma City (87-74) and Fort Worth (81-80). Then came the San Antonio Missions and Tulsa Oilers tied at 78-83 and the Beaumont Exporters (77-84). The defending champion Dallas Eagles had their wings clipped by a 64-97 record and finished in last place.

Shreveport's John Andre was the Texas League Pitcher of the Year, sharing the league lead in victories (21) and posting his fourth and final 20-win season in his minor league career. Andre also led the Texas League in innings pitched (266) and ranked among the top 10 pitchers in complete games (16) and strikeouts (142). His major league career consisted of 22 appearances with the 1955 Chicago Cubs, going 0-1 with a 5.80 ERA.

San Antonio first baseman Frank Kellert was the Texas League Player of the Year, leading the league with 146 runs batted in and finishing second in home runs (41). A graduate of Oklahoma City's Northwest Classen High School, he was a pitcher at what is now Oklahoma State University before switching to first base in the minor leagues. Kellert spent parts of four seasons in the major leagues with four different teams.

1955: The Cleveland Indians would be Tulsa's parent team for one year and the Oilers went through three managers. And the man who broke Babe Ruth's single-season home run record nearly quit baseball due to bad experiences in Tulsa.

Nevertheless, attendance increased by nearly 39,000 fans over the previous year, the Oilers improved their victory total by eight games and barely missed reaching the Texas League playoffs.

The Houston Buffaloes and Tulsa Oilers had tied for the fourth and final playoff spot with 86-75 records but Houston advanced by winning a one-game playoff on September 7th, 2-1.

Manager Dutch Meyer got the heave-ho on May 1st after a 7-17 start. First baseman Joe Macko went 4-0 as a player/interim manager and Hank Schenz, the 1946 Texas League Most Valuable Player as Tulsa's third baseman, finished the year with a 75-58 record.

Macko was Tulsa's power hitter, leading the team with 28 home runs, 38 doubles and 109 RBIs. He would return to Oiler Park as manager of the 1963 Amarillo Gold Sox. Macko later spent 40 years as the equipment manager and clubhouse manager for the Texas Rangers.

Outfielder Rod Graber led the Texas League with 13 triples. He also led the Oilers that year in bases on balls (103) while batting .290. Graber played four games for the 1958 Cleveland Indians and spent 14 years in the minor leagues.

First baseman Lloyd Jenney tied a Texas League record by receiving 18 intentional walks among his league-leading 118 walks. The Texas League season record for intention walks was originally set by Dallas Eagles first baseman Bill White in 1955 and matched by three other players.

Roger Maras was no stranger to Oklahoma, having been recruited from Fargo, North Dakota by University of Oklahoma football coach Bud Wilkinson to play running back for the fabled Sooners. But he spent less than one semester in Norman and returned home to consider his future in baseball.

Maras looked very ordinary in 25 games with the Oilers, batting just .233 with just one home run and nine runs batted in. Schenz was fed up with Maras' poor play and chewed him out in the locker room to the point that Maras wondered if he'd ever make it to the majors. That year, he changed his last name to Maris from Maras to avoid heckling from fans who tried to create rhymes involving the second syllable of his original last name.

After later playing for the Kansas City Athletics, Maris was traded to the New York Yankees and broke Babe Ruth's single-season record with 61 home runs in 1961, albeit in a 162-game season compared to Ruth's 60 home runs in 154 games in 1927. Maris' record would stand for 37 years and he was a two-time winner of the American League Most Valuable Player award and also played in seven World Series.

Al Widmar led Tulsa pitchers in victories with 18. Despite having a 13-30 record over five major league seasons, he would spend 45 years with the Toronto Blue Jays, Philadelphia Phillies, Baltimore Orioles and Milwaukee Brewers as either a minor league manager, major league pitching coach, player scout or a team executive. One of his sons, Tom, pitched for the University of Tulsa and was drafted by the Brewers.

While working as Milwaukee's Director of Player Development, he developed players such Robin Yount, Jim Gantner, Moose Haas and Paul Molitor who later led the Brewers to a World Series championship in 1982.

In 10 seasons as Toronto's pitching coach, Widmar was the mentor that turned Dave Steib, Jimmy Key, David Wells and Jim Clancy into American League All-Stars and he also revived the career of Doyle Alexander. Widmar was the Phillies' coach who helped pitchers Rick Wise, Grant Jackson, Ray Culp and Chris Short achieve stardom.

Oiler baseball broadcasts were in their third and final season on KOME-AM (1300) with Mack Creager and Tony George calling the action.

The Shreveport Sports earned their second Texas League championship in four seasons by defeating the Houston Buffaloes in the best-of-seven championship series, 4-3. Shreveport had eliminated the San Antonio Missions in the semifinals, 4-2, while Houston downed the Dallas Eagles, 4-2.

Dallas posted the best regular season record for the third time in four years, finishing 93-67 while San Antonio went 93-68 with Shreveport at 87-74. Houston and the Tulsa Oilers tied for fourth (86-75). Trailing those teams were the Fort Worth Cats (77-84), Oklahoma City Indians (70-90) and Beaumont Explorers (51-110). The only other Texas League team to have more losses in a year than Beaumont's 110 was the 1914 Austin Senators who finished 31-114.

Dallas also dominated the postseason awards with John Robert "Red" Murff winning Pitcher of the Year honors while catcher Ray Murray won the Player of the Year award.

Murray led the Texas League with a .329 batting average and his 25 home runs were tied for fourth-highest in that category. Three years later, he became a manager in the farm system of the New York/San Francisco Giants. His 1960 Rio Grande Valley Giants had the Texas League's best record that year (85-59).

Murff was the dominant pitcher in all of minor league baseball that year with a 27-11 record along with a sparkling 1.99 ERA. He completed 28 of his 35 starts and pitched 10 shutouts. An arm injury prematurely ended Murff's major league career.

But his baseball legacy reached new heights when as a New York Mets scout, he signed four rookies that would lead the once miserable Mets to the 1969 World Series championship. Three of those players were pitcher Jerry Koosman, infielder Kenny Boswell and catcher Jerry Grote.

That fourth player was a 6-foot-2, 140-pound string bean of a pitcher from tiny Alvin, Texas, that no other team wanted because of his awkward pitching delivery and control problems.

Murff never gave up on Nolan Ryan, who went on to throw seven no-hitters in his 27 major league seasons, set the career record of 5,714 strikeouts, appeared in eight All-Star games, had his jersey number be retired by three different teams and was a 1999 inductee into the Baseball Hall of Fame.

1956: This was a year for familiar faces and familiar places. The Chicago Cubs, Tulsa's parent team for most of the 1940s, returned for a one-season encore affiliation and the Oilers reached the Texas League playoffs for the third time in four years.

The Oilers went 77-77 that year and earned the fourth and final playoff berth. But the Houston Buffaloes romped past Tulsa in the semifinals and the Dallas Eagles in the finals, winning each of their best-of-seven series, 4-1.

The season attendance was 153,612, an increase of nearly 10,000 over the previous year. But the rumbles of discontent between the Tulsa Fair Board and team owner Grayle Howlett were increasing. The Fair Board wanted Howlett to put more money into stadium improvements but Howlett said he didn't have it.

Al Widmar was in his first year as Tulsa's pitcher-manager and also led the team's pitching staff with an 11-11 record and nine complete games. Al Lary and Ernie Groth led the pitchers in strikeouts with 130 and 127, respectively, but their combined win-loss record was a dismal 17-30.

Tulsa outfielder Bob "Butch" Will led the Texas League in doubles with 45. He also led the Oilers that year in base hits (196), runs scored (104) and bases on balls (91). Will later played six seasons with the Chicago Cubs and became a pinch-hitting specialist.

Marvin "Tex" Williams was an outfielder with the Oilers from 1956 through 1958 as well as being a star player in the Negro National League during the 1940s. His best all-around season with Tulsa was in 1956 when he batted .322 with 26 home runs and 111 runs batted in. He also led the Oilers in base hits in 1958 (154).

But Williams could have made baseball history 11 years earlier by being chosen as the first African-American to play major league base-ball instead of Jackie Robinson.

Williams, Robinson and Sam Jethero were three Negro League standouts who were invited to a one-day tryout at Fenway Park on

April 16, 1945. Williams had played first base, third base and outfield for the Philadelphia Stars. Robinson was a shortstop with the Kansas City Monarchs. Jethero was a center fielder for the Cincinnati Buckeyes.

Wendell Smith, a sports writer for a black newspaper, *The Pittsburgh Courier*, was a friend of Red Sox manager and future American League president Joe Cronin and had arranged the tryout. Cronin passed on signing any of those three players so Smith contacted Brooklyn Dodgers general manager Branch Rickey, who had followed Robinson's collegiate sports achievements at UCLA. Rickey signed Robinson to a professional baseball contract on October 23, 1945.

Jethero won the 1945 Negro League batting title and with the 1950 Boston Braves, became the oldest player to win the National League Rookie of the Year award at age 32. Some records, however, show Jethero's age may have been 28 years back then.

Williams never played a game in major league baseball, bouncing around various minor league teams before and after his Tulsa tenure before retiring in 1961 at age 41.

Willard Brown, a 2006 Baseball Hall of Fame inductee and a Negro League star with the Kansas City Monarchs during the 1930s and 1940s, played for the 1956 Oilers in what would be his final season in Organized Baseball. At the age of 41 that year, Brown played for Tulsa, Austin and San Antonio, posting a combined total of 14 home runs and 73 RBIs while batting .299 in 104 games.

More information about Browns' career can be found in the Hall of Fame section of this book.

Major league exhibition games returned to Texas League Park after a four-year absence. Enos Slaughter was 40 years old when the Kansas City Athletics played the Pittsburgh Pirates on April 11th before 1,970 fans, but he played like a 20-year-old with a double and two singles and even started a double play from right field. But the A's didn't have eight other players like him as the Pirates won, 5-3.

Bob Friend pitched a complete game for Pittsburgh and scattering seven base hits. Dale Long hit a home run and drove in four runs. Lou Boudreau was Kansas City's manager. Bobby Bragan, who served as president of the Texas League in 1969-75, was Pittsburgh's skipper. Bragan didn't make it through the game, being ejected after arguing too long and loud about a called third strike. Future Hall of Famer Roberto Clemente suited up for Pittsburgh that day, but didn't play in the game.

Oiler radio broadcasts had an awkward schedule. KTUL-AM (1430), which carried the games in the 1930s and early 1940s, shared broadcast rights with the University of Tulsa radio station, KWGS-FM (89.5). Mack Creager and Karl Janssen were the KTUL announcers with Johnnie Cherblanc and Norm Rennie calling the games on KWGS.

Janssen was one of the pioneers of Tulsa radio during the 1940s and was one of the major movers in the growth of KTUL-AM. His booming voice was frequently featured in productions by Tulsa Little Theater. Cherblanc once was a cheerleader at the University of Tulsa and spent 16 years with TU's athletic booster club and was a high school sports game official before becoming a real estate agent.

The Houston Buffaloes had a 96-58 regular season record and claimed their first Texas League championship since 1951. Trailing Houston were the Dallas Eagles (94-60), Fort Worth Cats (84-70), Tulsa Oilers (77-77), San Antonio Missions (76-78), Austin Senators (72-82), Shreveport Sports (69-85) and Oklahoma City Indians (48-106).

Shreveport's Ken Guettler set the all-time Texas League season records for home runs with 62 and was the unanimous choice as the

Texas League Player of the Year and Rookie of the Year. The previous record was 55 home runs by Clarence Kraft of the 1924 Fort Worth Panthers. He also led the Texas League with 143 RBIs and was one of three men who scored a league-high 115 runs.

While blessed with massive muscular arms and repeatedly leading other minor leagues in home runs, Guettler had significant vision problems that went undiagnosed. They were solved prior to the 1956 season by new eyeglasses with lenses as thick as the bottom of the old soft drink bottles. Incredibly, Guettler was never invited to a major league spring training camp.

Dallas ace Bert Thiel was the Texas League Pitcher of the Year, posting an 18-11 record with a 3.11 ERA, sharing the league lead in complete games (18) and ranking second in innings pitched (249). Thiel pitched 14 years in the minor leagues and later became a scout for the Washington Senators and Atlanta Braves.

Texas League fans were dazzled by the play of San Antonio third baseman Brooks Robinson, whom many baseball historians consider as the best defensive third baseman in baseball history and was a 1983 Baseball Hall of Fame inductee. He led the Texas League in 1956 in fielding percentage while batting .282 with 74 RBIs and lashed 28 doubles.

Robinson spent his entire 23-year major league career with the Baltimore Orioles, winning 16 consecutive Gold Gloves for his defensive excellence and frequently turned what appeared to be certain extra base hits into routine outs. Robinson, who played Little League baseball in Little Rock, Arkansas, was a 15-time All-Star selection and the Most Valuable Player in the 1966 All-Star Game and the 1970 World Series.

1957: The Oilers had their fourth different major league parent club in as many years with the Philadelphia Phillies beginning a two-year relationship with Tulsa. Despite having a losing record, Tulsa reached the Texas League playoffs for the third time in four years.

The Oilers were a hard-luck team from the start of the 1957 season. Six of their first nine home games were rained out and making up those missed games as part of doubleheaders throughout the year took its physical toll on the team.

Tulsa had a 75-79 record and lost their semifinal playoff series with the Dallas Eagles, 4-2. The defending champion Houston Buffaloes squeaked past the San Antonio Missions in the semifinal showdown, 4-3, then defeated Dallas by that same margin to win the pennant.

Reader's Digest Magazine bestowed the title of "America's Most Beautiful City" on Tulsa in a 1957 article. And having the Texas League's best offensive player would be a beautiful sight. But local fans didn't like the merry-go-round of unfamiliar players and season attendance tumbled to 127,465, a decline of nearly 26,000 fans.

There was one familiar face in pitcher-manager Al Widmar, who had a respectable 3.42 ERA but pulling a double shift wore him down and he finished with a 9-12 record.

Earl Mossor and Ron Mrozinski shared the team lead in victories with 11 and Mrozinski, who spent 14 years in the minor leagues, was Tulsa's strikeout king with 130 and also pitched a team-high 11 complete games.

First baseman Lloyd Jenney led the Texas League in bases on balls (116) and batted .266.

Three members of that Oilers squad would have successful careers as coaches or managers: Bobby Winkles, John McNamara and Jim Frey.

Frey was the 1957 Texas League Most Valuable Player and a post-season All-Star Team selection after leading the league in batting average (.336), total hits (198), runs batted in (74), runs scored (102), doubles (50), triples (10), extra base hits (69), stolen bases (21) and on-base percentage (.412).

As a manager, Frey led the Kansas City Royals to their first American League championship in 1980 then his Chicago Cubs won the National League's Eastern Division pennant in 1984, the first post-season appearance by the woeful Cubs since 1945.

Shortstop Bobby Winkles also earned Texas League postseason All-Star honors by leading the league in singles (154) and also batting .279 and stealing 11 bases.

He achieved greater fame in later years as one of the most successful coaches in collegiate baseball history, leading the Arizona State University Sun Devils to the College World Series championship in 1965, 1967 and 1969. Winkles' 11-year coaching record at Arizona State was 524-173. The baseball diamond in the Phoenix suburb of Tempe is named in his honor and he was inducted into the College Baseball Hall of Fame in 2006.

Three of his former ASU players became key contributors to the Oakland Athletics' dynasty during the 1970s: Reggie Jackson, Sal Bando and Rick Monday.

John McNamara batted just .149 in 19 games as a Tulsa Oilers catcher. But he spent 19 years as a major league manager, highlighted by leading the Boston Red Sox to the 1986 American League championship and being honored as the AL's Manager of the Year.

Pitcher Joe Black was the 1952 National League Rookie of the Year with the Brooklyn Dodgers and played four games for the Oilers in a comeback attempt. But Black had no wins or losses in his brief Tulsa tenure. The parent Phillies released Black and he played briefly for the Washington Senators before ending his baseball career.

Black played for Brooklyn from 1952 through 1955. Joining the Dodgers straight from Baltimore's Negro League team, Black led the National League in 1952 with a 15-4 record and 41 games finished. He also saved 15 games and posted a stingy 2.15 earned run average.

The team's radio broadcasts moved to 50,000-watt KRMG (740 AM) with Mack Creager and Hugh Finnerty calling the games. It marked Creager's 10th year of covering Oilers baseball and was the beginning of a hugely-successful five-year pairing with Finnerty.

Dallas had the best regular season record at 102-52. It was also the most victories by any Dallas team during its Texas League tenure. Houston was second at 97-57, followed by San Antonio (76-78) and Tulsa (75-79). Then came the Austin Senators (71-83), Fort Worth Cats (70-84), Oklahoma City Indians (66-88) and Shreveport Sports (59-95).

Dallas Eagles star Tommy Bowers was the Texas League Pitcher of the Year, leading the league in victories (20), innings pitched (250) and finished second in complete games (15). Bowers played seven seasons in the New York/San Francisco Giants farm system but never reached the majors.

First baseman Willie McCovey was a young standout on that Dallas team. The left-handed slugger batted .281 with 11 home runs and 65 RBIs. When he moved up to the parent San Francisco Giants, Willie Mays, Orlando Cepeda and McCovey comprised the heart of the Giants' batting order and became one of the most feared home runs trios in the National League.

McCovey played in the major leagues from 1959 through 1980. He was a six-time All-Star selection, led the National League in home runs three times and twice in RBIs, was the 1969 National League Most Valuable Player and was inducted into the Baseball Hall of Fame in 1986.

The last appearance of the Brooklyn Dodgers in Tulsa was a memorable one as they scored four runs in the ninth inning to beat the Milwaukee Braves, 5-4, before 9,147 fans on April 9th. That was also the largest attendance for an exhibition baseball game in Tulsa to that point in time.

The 1956 World Series champions, managed by Walter Alston, tied the game on Charlie Neal's RBI double. Roy Campanella went 1-for-4 and Gil Hodges hit a home run. Future Dodger Hall of Fame pitchers Don Drysdale and Sandy Koufax suited up but didn't play.

Hank Aaron and Eddie Matthews had the big bats for the Braves. Aaron had three hits and scored two runs while Matthews hit a two-run homer and finished with three RBIs. Warren Spahn pitched six shutout innings for Milwaukee.

1958: On the field, this was not a good year for the Oilers. Pitcher-manager Al Widmar was fired on July 20th following a seven-game losing streak. The team tumbled to seventh place in the eight-team Texas League, finishing with a 71-81 record.

Widmar posted a 45-53 managerial record and a 2-2 pitching record when he was relieved of his command. His replacement as player-manager was catcher Jim Fanning, whose managerial record was slightly better (26-28). Fanning had a .246 batting average that year with three home runs and drove in 23 runs.

Fanning spent parts of three years as the manager of the National League's Montreal Expos, leading them to the National League playoffs in the strike-shortened 1981 season. He previously served as Montreal's general manager from 1969 through 1976.

Relief pitcher Don Erickson had the Texas League's best ERA that year, (2.96) and also led the league in appearances (72). Even though saves were not officially kept that year, Erickson had 32 saves and earned a promotion to the parent Philadelphia Phillies. But the right handed hurler spent the next four years playing for minor league affiliates of the Phillies.

Starting pitcher Norm Camp was the Texas League's co-leader in shutouts with five in the last of his four seasons with the Oilers. Camp that year had a 12-11 record and a 3.78 ERA.

Outfielder Harry Fisher carried the big stick for the Oilers' offense, leading the team in home runs (19) and batting average (.328) and finishing second on the team in runs batted in (65).

Oiler games were carried on KRMG Radio (740 AM) with Mack Creager and Hugh Finnerty describing the action.

Two exhibition games were played in Tulsa that year. An April 10th contest between the Milwaukee Braves and Detroit Tigers was rained out. The next day, Willie Mays and Orlando Cepeda had base hits as the San Francisco Giants won a pitcher's duel with the Cleveland Indians, 2-1, before 5,881 fans. A home run by Gary Geiger, who would be a key player for the Tulsa Oilers 10 years later, accounted for Cleveland's only run. Roger Maris, a member of the 1955 Oilers, went 0-for-3 for the Indians.

The Corpus Christi Giants, who were the Oklahoma City Indians for the previous 23 seasons, produced the first Texas League championship for that southern Texas community, defeating the Austin Senators in the best-of-seven championship series, 4-3. Corpus Christi won its semifinal series with the Houston Buffaloes, 4-1, while Austin advanced after sweeping the Fort Worth Cats, 4-0.

Fort Worth had the best regular season record at 89-64, followed by Houston (79-74), Corpus Christi (77-75) and Austin (77-76). They were followed by the Dallas Rangers (76-77), San Antonio Missions (74-79), Tulsa Oilers (71-81) and Victoria Rosebuds (68-85).

Corpus Christi right fielder Michael Lutz, a Tulsa Oilers earlier in the 1950s, was the 1958 Texas League Player of the Year as he led the league in four offensive categories. Lutz hit 39 home runs with 111 RBIs, scored 114 runs and had 171 hits in addition to a .313 batting average. Surprisingly, Lutz never played in the major leagues and his final minor league season was in 1960.

Joe Kotrany was the fourth consecutive Dallas pitcher to win the Texas League Pitcher of the Year award. The right handed hurler led the Texas League in victories (19), finished with a 2.99 ERA and walked only 47 batters over 244 innings pitched. But Kotrany retired from baseball after the 1959 season.

Tulsa's baseball outlook brightened after the 1958 season, thanks to shrewd moves by Oilers owner Grayle Howlett. With Houston getting a National League expansion franchise in 1962, the St. Louis Cardinals needed a new home for their Texas League affiliate.

Howlett hammered out an agreement with Cardinal executives and Tulsa would be affiliated with St. Louis for 16 years; as a Double-A affiliate in 1959-65 and as a Triple-A affiliate in 1966-76. The Oilers would make 11 postseason appearances and would also win six league championships, thanks to the deep and rich pool of talent provided by the Cardinals' knowledgeable scouting system.

Many "Baby Boomers" considered those years to be the finest years in Tulsa's minor league baseball history. Tulsa fans frequently took chartered bus trips to St. Louis to see their former Oilers heroes playing against National League stars. Another plus for local fans came when the CBS affiliate in Tulsa, KOTV, carried selected Cardinal weekend games. In addition, Cardinal radio broadcasts on KMOX-AM (1120) could be picked up at night in Tulsa.

1959: The Oilers reached the Texas League playoffs for the fifth time during the decade and also won an innovative competition against teams in the Mexican Baseball League.

After the Texas League shrank to six teams with the departure of Houston and Dallas, an agreement was signed with the six-team Mexican League where each team played 36 interleague games as part of the regular season schedule. The arrangement was known as the Pan American Series and lasted through 1961, replacing the Dixie Series which pitted the champions of the Texas League and Double-A Southern League.

The Oilers had the best interleague record of any of team in the Pan American Series (24-11) and was one of four Texas League teams that had a record equal to or better than the 21-15 record of the Mexican League's Mexico City Reds.

Tulsa had a 77-67 overall record that year and earned the third out of four playoff berths. But they were eliminated in the best-of-three semifinals by the eventual playoff champion Austin Senators, 2-1.

Vern Benson began a two-year tenure as the Oilers' manager. He had a track record of success in the St. Louis Cardinals' player development program, taking the Winnipeg Goldeyes to the Class C Northern League championship in 1957.

Bob Blaylock was the ace of Tulsa's pitching staff that year. A graduate of Muldrow High School in southeastern Oklahoma where he pitched four no-hitters, Blaylock finished with a sparkling 10-1 record, a 2.56 ERA and pitched a complete game in seven of his 11 starting assignments. He was also a standout basketball player at Fort Smith (Arkansas) Junior College. Today, that school is the University of Arkansas at Fort Smith and Blaylock was inducted into its Athletic Hall of Fame in 2012.

First baseman Duke Carmel, second baseman Jim McKnight and shortstop Julio Gotay represented the Oilers on the Texas League postseason All-Star Team.

Carmel tied for fourth in the league in home runs (23) and batted .291. Carmel never caught on in the big leagues but gained notoriety by being the subject of humorous statements by New York Yankees pitching legend Whitey Ford in Jim Bouton's controversial 1970 baseball memoir, *Ball Four*.

McKnight ranked second in the Texas League in stolen bases (18) and was fifth in batting average (.332). He played for the Chicago Cubs in 1960-62 and his son, Jeff McKnight, was a utility infielder for the New York Mets and Baltimore Orioles in 1989-94.

Gotay batted .284 with 17 home runs, 64 RBIs and stole 12 bases. He became the St. Louis Cardinals' starting shortstop in 1962 but a sub-par performance led to his being traded after that season for All-Star shortstop Dick Groat.

Oiler games were carried on KRMG Radio (740 AM) with Mack Creager and Hugh Finnerty as the announcers.

Austin won its first Texas League pennant since 1911 when the Senators swept the San Antonio Missions in the championship series, 3-0. Austin defeated Tulsa in its semifinal series, 2-1 while San Antonio swept the Victoria Rosebuds, 2-0.

Victoria had the best regular season record at 86-60, followed by Austin (80-66), Tulsa (77-67) and San Antonio (75-70), the Amarillo Gold Sox (75-71) and Corpus Christi Giants (66-79).

Victoria dominated the postseason honors with Carroll Beringer winning the Texas League Pitcher of the Year award while outfielder Carl Warwick took home Player of the Year honors.

Warwick's 35 home runs and 129 runs scored led the Texas League that year and he ranked second in runs batted in (94) and hits (182).

Beringer led the Texas League that year in victories (19), complete games (18) and had 109 strikeouts against just 22 walks over 196 innings. Beringer spent nine of his 13 minor league seasons in the Texas League but he never played in the majors.

During the season, the Texas League adopted a rule change intended to speed up its games. When a pitcher wanted to intentionally walk a batter, he could wave a hand towards first base instead of throwing four pitches. The end result was that games weren't really played that much faster and the original rule was reinstated the following season.

Billy Williams played left field for the San Antonio Missions, batting .318 with 22 doubles and 79 runs batted in. Ironically, Williams began his professional baseball career in 1956 roughly 95 miles northwest of Tulsa as an 18-year-old outfielder with the Ponca City (Oklahoma) Cubs in the Class D Sooner State League. Fans and opposing players throughout the Texas League marveled at the smooth but powerful batting stroke that Williams displayed.

But Williams encountered such intense racial discrimination that he left the Missions after playing 94 games in a 145-game schedule and seriously considered quitting the sport. Negro League legend Buck O'Neill was the Chicago Cubs scout who signed Williams to a pro contract and finally persuaded Williams not to give up.

Williams joined the Cubs the following year, spend 18 years in the major leagues and was a 1987 inductee into the Baseball Hall of Fame. He won the 1961 National League Rookie of the Year award, formerly held the National League for most consecutive games played, (1,117 from 1963 through 1970) and won the 1972 National League batting championship with a .333 average.

Chapter Seven
The 1960s

Widespread social changes made this decade a turning point in American history. People born after World War II began questioning authority and the rationale behind the Vietnam War. Non-violent protests by African-Americans over racial segregation, unemployment and poverty led to adoption of the Civil Rights Act and Voting Rights Act. Women marched for equal opportunities in employment and salary. Advocates for environmental quality called attention to pollution-related issues.

This was the decade that gave us the predecessor to the Internet (ARPANET), American astronaut Neil Armstrong walking on the moon, a short-lived war in the Middle East, birth control pills, the Beatles and Rolling Stones spearheading an invasion of British rock-and-roll singers, the concert at Woodstock and the creation of the Motown Sound.

There were also the James Bond spy movies, Wal-Mart stores, the Super Bowl to determine a professional football champion and the TV debut of *Sesame Street.* Americans mourned the assassinations of President John Kennedy, Presidential candidate Robert Kennedy and civil rights leader Dr. Martin Luther King.

One of the most successful periods in Tulsa's professional baseball history almost did not happen. A last-minute intervention by a local businessman not only preserved the sport but Tulsa would prosper from a long-standing relationship with the St. Louis Cardinals that became the envy of many observers in minor league baseball.

The Oilers made eight playoff appearances during this decade, seven of those in consecutive years. They won three Texas League championships then moved up to Triple-A competition in 1966 and won the Pacific Coast League title in 1968.

Stan Musial, Bill White, Curt Flood were among the major league baseball stars appearing in exhibition games played in Tulsa. A 1966 exhibition game between the Oilers and St. Louis Cardinals was moved to the University of Tulsa's football stadium and drew the largest crowd ever for a baseball game in Oklahoma.

1960: This would be the best of times and the worst of times for the Oilers. The best of times was winning the Texas League and Pan American Association championships and leading the Texas League in attendance (111,835).

The worst of times was financial problems that took team owner Grayle Howlett within minutes of moving the team to Albuquerque, New Mexico after the season ended. Tulsa businessman A. Ray Smith rode to the rescue in the nick of time, not only saving professional baseball for the city but laying a foundation for future success.

The Oilers capped a late-season surge by sweeping the Victoria Rosebuds, 3-0 in the Texas League championship series. Boston Red Sox legend Johnny "The Needle" Pesky was Victoria's manager. Tulsa won its semifinal series against the San Antonio Missions, 3-1, while Victoria upset the heavily-favored Rio Grande Valley Giants in their semifinal showdown, 3-0.

Dick Hughes was the winning pitcher in the Oilers' 3-2 victory that clinched the Pan American Association championship. The 22-year-old right-hander and University of Arkansas alumnus ranked second in the Texas League that year in strikeouts (166) and shutouts (three). He played four years for the Oilers and had a 16-6 record with the 1967 St. Louis Cardinals.

Tulsa then defeated the Mexico City Tigers, 4-1, in the Pan American Series with a pair of victories over Mexico City pitching ace Luis Tiant laying the foundation for success.

Known for an elaborate pitching delivery along with an effective fastball and curveball, Tiant led the American League in 1968 with a 1.60 ERA, went 21-9 and pitched four consecutive shutouts for the Cleveland Indians. He later joined the Boston Red Sox and pitched two complete games for them in the 1975 World Series against Cincinnati. Tiant was a three-time American League All-Star and won 229 games over 19 major league seasons.

Ted Theim, who never pitched in the major leagues, was the ace of Tulsa's staff. Theim's 12-0 record made him the only pitcher in Texas League history to win at least 10 games and have an undefeated season. He also had a 3.77 ERA and helped his own cause by hitting three home runs and batting .303. By comparison, Theim had a 16-26 record over the next four years, pitching for seven different minor league teams.

Tom Hughes' only victory that season would be Tulsa's first no-hitter in eight years, a 4-0 victory over Rio Grande Valley on August 19th. He had a 65-25 record over the four preceding seasons prior to his no-hitter but went 20-20 over the five subsequent seasons.

Second baseman Harry Watts led the Texas League with 99 RBIs, ranked second in home runs with 26 and batted .263. Third baseman Artie Burnett was the Texas League's co-leader in triples with 11. He also led the Oilers in runs scored (111) and bases on balls (106) while batting .257 with 12 home runs and 68 RBIs.

First baseman Fred Whitfield and right fielder Jim Hickman represented the Oilers on the Texas League's postseason All-Star Team. Whitfield ranked among the Texas League's top 10 hitters in batting average (.310), home runs (22), RBIs (89) and base hits (161). One of his season highlights was getting eight base hits in 10 at-bats when the Oilers swept a doubleheader from Victoria on August 25th. But All-Star Bill White was locked in as the Cardinals' first baseman, so Whitfield was traded to the Cleveland Indians for two players after the 1962 season.

Hickman ranked among the Texas League's top five players that year in batting average (.323) and runs scored (91) and also had 15 home runs and 61 RBIs. He played 13 years in the major leagues and was best known for his times with the New York Mets (1962-66) and Chicago Cubs (1968-73).

Hickman's solo home run accounted for the Mets' only run in the final baseball game played at New York City's venerable Polo Grounds in 1963. He was also the 1970 National League Comeback Player of the Year and his 12th-inning single in that year's All-Star Game led to the memorable collision at home plate between Cleveland Indians catcher Ray Fosse and Cincinnati Reds star Pete Rose, who scored the game-winning run.

Oiler games were carried on KRMG Radio (740 AM) with Mack Creager and Hugh Finnerty describing the action.

The largest crowd in the history of Texas League Park/Oiler Park, 10,023, saw the parent St. Louis Cardinals rout the Oilers, 12-5, in July 28th game. It would also be the last exhibition baseball game in Tulsa for six years. The Cardinals got two hits apiece from Bill White, Julian

Javier and Curt Flood. The Oilers got home runs from Jim Hickman, Artie Burnett and Jim Beauchamp.

Flood and White later played historic roles in the evolution of professional baseball. Flood sued Major League Baseball after refusing to join the Philadelphia Phillies after being traded to them in 1969. His lawsuit claimed that a baseball player is not a piece of property to be sold regardless of the player's wishes and that baseball's reserve clause was unconstitutional because it denied a player the right to try to join another team once his contract expired.

While the U.S. Supreme Court rejected Flood's case by a 5-3 margin, labor arbitrator Peter Seitz issued a ruling a few years later that, for all intent and purposes, nullified baseball's reserve clause and the essence of the Supreme Court's ruling.

Seitz ruled in favor of two pitchers, Andy Messersmith and Dave McNally, who wanted to have the same options that Flood sought in his lawsuit. As a result, the doors of true free agency were opened wide for baseball and other professional sports and the ensuing sky-high player salaries.

After playing 13 major league seasons and being chosen eight times to the National League All-Star team, White was the first African-American to serve as one of the highest-level executives in American professional sports, serving as president of the National League from 1989 through 1994.

The Rio Grande Valley Giants, led by the hitting of Manny Mota and the pitching of future Hall of Famer Gaylord Perry, had the Texas League's best overall record at 85-59. They were followed by the San Antonio Missions (77-68), Tulsa Oilers (76-68), Victoria Rosebuds (77-69), Austin Senators (73-71) and Amarillo Gold Sox (68-78).

Mota batted .307 that year and went on to hit .304 over 20 major league seasons, 13 of those with the Los Angeles Dodgers. In the latter years of his career, Mota became one of the best pinch-hitters in baseball history, producing 150 base hits and a .300 batting average in such situations.

Perry had a 2.82 ERA in 1960 but had a 9-13 won-lost record. That would be an aberration as he won 20 or more games five times as well over his 22-year major league career. He also won the Cy Young Award (the league's best pitcher) as a member of the National League's San Francisco Giants and the American League's Cleveland Indians.

Perry later admitted that he doctored a baseball before throwing it, either with his saliva or by using a foreign substance, to make the ball act differently than a normal pitch. Those actions are against the rules of baseball but they didn't prevent his induction into the Baseball Hall of Fame in 1991.

Rio Grande Valley second baseman Chuck Hiller was the Texas League Player of the Year. He led the Texas League that year in total hits (187) and doubles (47), finished second in stolen bases (17) and fourth in batting average (.334).

Hiller made history in Game 4 of 1962 World Series against New York Yankees as the first National League player to hit a grand slam home run during a World Series game. He later had a long career as a minor league coach and manager.

San Antonio's Jack Curtis was the Texas League Pitcher of the Year. The left-handed hurler led the Texas League with a 19-8 record, 19 complete games, 257 innings pitched and ranked fourth in strikeouts (144). Curtis, however, had a losing record over three major league seasons.

Tom Tresh, a shortstop/left-fielder who would be the 1962 American League Rookie of the Year with the New York Yankees, played six games for the Amarillo Gold Sox late in the season after moving up from the Class A Binghamton (New York) Triplets.

After the season ended, Tulsa came within an eyelash of losing professional baseball yet again. Owner Grayle Howlett had his fill of the deterioration of Texas League Park along with the lack of assistance from city and county leaders.

The Tulsa Fair Board had operated the Tulsa Fairgrounds where Texas League Park was located. An engineering study was authorized to see if the stadium was safe for public use. When that report returned with a resounding "no" and was coupled with the don't-care attitude of local businessmen, the Oilers were all but signed, sealed and delivered to Albuquerque.

It was the bottom of the ninth inning for minor league baseball in Tulsa and defeat seemed to be certain. Then in true baseball fashion, local businessman A. Ray Smith stepped up to the plate and became a hero for the city's sports fans.

Smith operated a petroleum-oriented business called Standard Industries and paid $25,000 to purchase half of Howlett's share of the Oilers franchise for the 1961 season. Smith became the team's sole owner in 1962.

1961: With A. Ray Smith's keen sense of marketing and promotions, this would be the beginning of another golden era of Tulsa professional baseball. The Oilers would average over 200,000 fans per year for each of the first five years of Smith's ownership.

The Oilers' 83 victories were the most since winning 86 games in 1955. The season attendance of 130,443 was an increase of nearly 19,000 over the previous season in which Tulsa was the Texas League champion.

Tulsa reached the Texas League playoffs for the third year in a row but fell in the semifinals to the San Antonio Missions.

George "Whitey" Kurowski was in the first year of his two-year tenure as the Oilers' manager. He played third base for nine years with the St. Louis Cardinals during the 1940s and his all-around play made him that National League's top third baseman during that time and he played in five All-Star Games. The Cardinals defeated the New York Yankees in Game 5 of the 1942 World Series on Kurowski's ninth-inning home run.

Pitcher Harry Fanok led the Texas League with 158 strikeouts and eight complete games. Nicknamed "The Flame Thrower" for an outstanding fastball, Fanok began his minor league career as a third baseman before moving to the mound in 1959. His ERA of 2.24 was the lowest among Oiler pitchers and he finished with a 16-7 record. Fanok saw limited action with the St. Louis Cardinals in 1963 and 1964.

Second baseman Jack Damaska and outfielder Johnny Lewis represented Tulsa on the Texas League's postseason All-Star Team. Damaska was second on the Oilers that year in home runs (19) and RBIs (73) and batted .263.

Born in the same town as the legendary football quarterback Joe Namath (Beaver Falls, Pennsylvania), Damaska didn't have a real future with the St. Louis Cardinals because Julian Javier would be their second baseman throughout the 1960s. Damaska went 1-for-5 in his only major league game and wound up spending 17 years in the minor leagues.

Lewis led Texas League in walks (96), was second in home runs (22) and batted .293. While playing winter baseball in Venezuela after that season, Lewis' wife was killed in a car wreck and he was left to raise their two young sons.

He joined the New York Mets in 1965 and led them in on-base percentage, walks and runs scored and also had the most putouts and assists of any Mets outfielder. Lewis later served as a hitting coach for the Cardinals and the Houston Astros.

Outfielder Doug Clemens led the Texas League with on-base percentage of .443 and his batting average of .342 led the Oilers and was second-highest in the league. But on June 15, 1964, the standout from Syracuse University became part of one of the most lopsided trades in baseball history.

St. Louis traded Clemens, pitcher Bobby Shantz, a three-time All-Star during the 1950s, and pitcher Ernie Broglio to the Chicago Cubs for pitchers Jack Spring, Paul Toth and a talented but inconsistent outfielder named Lou Brock.

Clemens never lived up to his potential, with a nine-year major league batting average of just .229 and left pro baseball four years later. Shantz retired after the 1964 season and Spring played one more major league season. Toth's 18 victories with the 1961 Oilers led the Texas League but he went 8-12 in three years with the Cubs. Broglio won 21 games with St. Louis in 1960 but went 7-19 with a 5.40 ERA over three years with the Cubs.

Brock, on the other hand, stole 50 or more bases in 12 seasons and owned baseball's career stolen base record (938) for 12 years. He blossomed into a six-time National League All-Star, played on two World Series champions and was inducted into the Baseball Hall of Fame in 1985.

Oiler games were carried on KRMG Radio (740 AM) with Mack Creager and Hugh Finnerty describing the action. It was also the final year that professional baseball in Tulsa was carried on a full-time basis by that station.

The San Antonio Missions went through four managers but won their third Texas League championship by sweeping the Austin Senators, 3-0, to end a tumultuous season for the entire league. The Missions defeated Tulsa in the playoff semifinals, 3-1-1, while Austin upset the Amarillo Gold Sox, 3-2.

San Antonio's four managers that year were Ripper Collins (15-15), Harry Craft (12-6), Bobby Adams (15-17) and Rube Walker (32-27).

Amarillo had the league's best overall record at 90-50. They were followed by Tulsa (83-55), San Antonio (74-65), Austin (69-71), the Rio Grande Valley/Victoria Giants (69-71) and the Victoria/Ardmore Rosebuds (57-83).

The Rosebuds moved from Victoria, Texas, to Ardmore, Oklahoma on May 27th after the team's owner Tom O'Connor, Jr., suffered a heart attack and couldn't continue operating the team. But baseball returned to Victoria on June 10th when the Rio Grande Valley Giants also fell upon financial hard times and had to leave Harlingen, Texas. That would also be the last season of Texas League baseball for those two cities, as well.

Austin right-hander Larry Maxie was the Texas League Pitcher of the Year. While his 17 victories and 15 complete games led the league and his 2.08 ERA was nothing to sneeze at, Maxie had control problems as well. He hit more batters (15) than any other Texas League pitcher and also walked 97 batters against 47 strikeouts over 203 innings. Maxie later served as a scout for several major league teams.

A trio of future New York Yankees stars played for Amarillo that year. Infielder Phil Linz led the Texas League with a .349 batting average and was the Texas League Player of the Year. First baseman Joe Pepitone hit 21 home runs, drove in 87 runs and batted .316.

Pitcher Jim Bouton, whose baseball memoir *Ball Four* was published in 1970, was 13-7 and ranked third in the league with 151 strikeouts. Bouton wrote in his book that because of the way Oiler Park's wooden bleachers had been built, there was plenty of what could be called good viewing opportunities for opposing players standing beneath those bleachers unbeknownst to fans.

1962: The 50th actual season of professional baseball in Tulsa was golden, indeed. The Oilers won their second Texas League championship in three years and the fourth in franchise history. Their games were carried by one of America's most powerful radio stations. And the regular season attendance total of 182,895 was the highest in Tulsa professional baseball history since 1950.

The Oilers won the Texas League pennant by defeating the Austin Senators, 3-1. Tulsa beat the Albuquerque Dukes in their playoff series, 3-0, while Austin edged the El Paso Sun Kings, 3-2.

El Paso had the league's best regular season record at 80-60. They were followed by Tulsa (77-63), Albuquerque (70-70), Austin (69-71), the San Antonio Missions (68-72) and Amarillo Gold Sox (56-84).

Tulsa's Gordie Richardson was the Texas League Pitcher of the Year. A hard-throwing lefthander, Richardson went 13-6 that year with a league-leading 3.18 ERA and nine complete games. He also had 153 strikeouts and just 57 walks over 198 innings.

Following the 1964 season, Richardson and outfielder Johnny Lewis were traded to the New York Mets for two players who would have key roles for Tulsa's 1966 Pacific Coast League championship team: infielder Elio Chacon and pitcher Tracy Stallard.

Joining Richardson as Tulsa's representatives on the Texas League's postseason All-Star Team were utility infielder Clyde Stalcup "Bud" Bloomfield and outfielder Joe "Speedo" Patterson.

Bloomfield, who attended the University of Arkansas, was a smooth-fielding third baseman and his .287 batting average that year was the highest of his eight minor league seasons, .287.

Patterson led the Texas League in stolen bases (31) for what would be the first of three consecutive seasons and his .325 batting average was the best of all players who spent the entire season in Tulsa.

Free-swinging first baseman Jeoff Long was a fan favorite, leading the Oilers in home runs (30), RBIs (90), runs scored (88), total bases (235) and walks (91). But the price for that success was also leading the Texas League with 122 strikeouts.

After hitting just one home run over parts of two years with the parent St. Louis Cardinals, his contract was sold to the Chicago White Sox in 1964 to make room for outfielder Mike Shannon, his 1961 Oilers teammate.

Shannon hit 10 home runs, stole 10 bases and batted .254 during his only season in Tulsa. He played nine years with the Cardinals then joined the Cardinals Radio Network in 1972 and has been its play-by-play announcer since the 2002 death of Baseball Hall of Famer Jack Buck.

Shortstop Charles Dallon "Dal" Maxvill batted .348 in just 47 games with Tulsa, earning a quick promotion to the major leagues. He spent 11 of his 14 big-league seasons with the St. Louis Cardinals where he was better known for his defensive skills than his hitting, earning a Gold Glove in 1968 as the National League's best defensive shortstop. Maxvill was part of four World Series championship teams and seven league champions, either as a player, a coach or team executive.

Hunky Mauldin threw a seven-inning no-hitter in Tulsa's 3-0 victory over Amarillo in the first game of an August 31st doubleheader.

Tulsa hosted its first Texas League All-Star Game on July 17th with the South All-Stars defeating the North All-Stars, 2-1, before 3,814 fans at Oiler Park. San Antonio third baseman Don Eaddy of San Antonio had a game-winning home run among his three base hits. Oiler pitcher Gordy Richardson was the North team's starting pitcher.

The final exhibition game in Tulsa between Negro League teams saw the Indianapolis Clowns defeat the New York Stars, 4-2, before 1,227 fans. First baseman James "Nature Boy" Williams was the star player for Indianapolis. Standing 6-foot-2 and weighing at least 220 pounds, Williams was known to have batted without shoes and played with a greatly oversized glove.

Oiler broadcasts moved to another 50,000-watt radio station in Tulsa, KVOO (1170 AM) and the pairing of Len Morton, Mack Creager and Jack Campbell began a nine-year run with some of the most successful teams in Tulsa's professional baseball history.

KVOO had one of the nation's strongest night-time radio signals and could be heard, depending on atmospheric conditions, from the Canadian Rockies to the southern Rio Grande River valley in Texas.

Morton had been the sports director at KVOO Television (Channel 2) in Tulsa since 1956. The TV station was an NBC Network affiliate and also gave Morton opportunities to appear on *The Today Show* as the college football expert in this part of the country. He also served as the play-by-play announcer for radio broadcasts of University of Tulsa football, basketball and baseball games.

Campbell, who began his radio career in 1945, had moved to Tulsa in 1955 and hosted KVOO Radio's "Pleasant Dreams" (an all-night classical music show) and "Sleepwalker's Serenade" (which featured a more contemporary style of music). Campbell later moved into KVOO Radio's newsroom and worked there for 39 years before retiring in 1994.

On the Oiler broadcasts, Campbell was the resident statistician and kept meticulous records of what every Oilers player did during the year. And just like an expert card player, Campbell had an uncanny knack for knowing the perfect statistic to use in the appropriate situation in any sports broadcast.

Former St. Louis Cardinals star and Oklahoma resident Johnny Leonard Roosevelt "Pepper" Martin was the fourth member of the announcing crew. Martin had two roles during the broadcasts: add folksy comments about his playing days and use a fish net to try to catch foul balls that came near the rooftop radio booth.

Nicknamed "The Wild Horse of the Osage" for his aggressive base running style, Martin spent his entire major league career (1928-44) with the St. Louis Cardinals. He was a member of three World Series championship teams, led the National League in stolen bases three times and was a four-time National League All-Star. Martin was also a player-coach for the 1958 Oilers and ended his playing career that year by being a pinch-runner at the age of 54.

What many people might not remember about Pepper Martin was that he also was the manager of two teams that won championships in the Class B Florida International League during the 1950s: the 1950 Miami Sun Sox (affiliated with the Brooklyn Dodgers) and the 1953 Fort Lauderdale Lions (an unaffiliated team). Martin's fiery temper led to him being suspended for part of the 1949 season after choking an umpire and he went into the stands in Lakeland, Florida, to punch a spectator during a 1951 game.

When not involved with baseball, Martin worked as a cattle rancher, a deputy sheriff and director of athletics at the Oklahoma State Penitentiary in McAlester. A heart attack took Martin's life on March 5, 1965.

El Paso shortstop-outfielder Cap Peterson was the Texas League Player of the Year, leading the Texas League with 130 RBIs and 128 runs scored and also batted .335. Peterson was a part-time player for the San Francisco Giants in five of his eight major league seasons. Kidney disease took Peterson's life in 1980 at the age of 37.

Peterson's teammate, outfielder Jesus Alou, made Texas League history by getting at least one base hit in 48 out of 49 games. Alou, who batted .367 during that streak, never batted worse than .324 in his minor league career then spent 15 years in the major leagues.

1963: The Oilers claimed their third Texas League championship in four years and the fifth such crown in Tulsa's professional baseball history. Outfielder Jimmy Beauchamp left an indelible mark on Tulsa's professional baseball history. And the season attendance of 200,557 marked the first time since 1949 that attendance topped 200,000.

Tulsa defeated the San Antonio Bullets, 3-1, in the Texas League championship series. The Oilers had eliminated the Austin Senators in the playoff semifinals, 3-0, while San Antonio ousted the El Paso Sun Kings, 3-2.

San Antonio owned the league's best regular season record at 79-61. They were followed by Austin (75-65), Tulsa (74-66), El Paso (68-72), the Albuquerque Dukes (67-73) and Amarillo Gold Sox (57-83).

Beauchamp was the Texas League Player of the Year and Tulsa's only player named to the Texas League's postseason All-Star team. His .337 batting average was second in the league and his 31 home runs was the most by a Tulsa professional baseball player since Guy Sturdy's 49 home runs back in 1926.

He was also a fan favorite, having been born in Vinita, Oklahoma (about 75 miles northeast of Tulsa) and attending high school in Grove, Oklahoma (about 100 miles northeast of Tulsa).

Beauchamp was a minor league standout, hitting 20 or more home runs four times and stealing 20 or more bases three times over 12 years. But he only hit 14 home runs and batted .231 over 10 major league seasons. When Beauchamp was a member of the 1972 New York Mets, he had to give up his number 24 jersey when Willie Mays joined the Mets in May of that year.

Beauchamp later spent 16 years as a minor league manager and won two International League pennants with the Triple-A affiliates of the Houston Astros and Atlanta Braves. His son, Kash, was the first player chosen by the Toronto Blue Jays in the 1982 amateur draft and also had a long career in the minor leagues, both as a player and manager.

Grover Resinger was in the first year of a two-year stint as the Oilers' manager. Resinger, who never played major league baseball, guided the Billings (Montana) Mustangs to the Class C Pioneer League championship in 1962 after the team finished in last place in 1961. He later served as an assistant coach with the big-league Atlanta Braves, Chicago White Sox, Detroit Tigers and California Angels.

Tulsa's pitching staff had a league-leading ERA of 3.71, the second year in a row that the Oilers led the league in that category. Lefties Gordie Richardson and Tom Hilgendorf gave Tulsa a dynamic duo of pitching. Richardson's 171 strikeouts and 12-8 record led the Oilers with Hilgendorf adding 156 strikeouts, 11 victories and four shutouts.

Hilgendorf became a relief pitcher in the major leagues and spent half of his six-year career with the Cleveland Indians. During a 10-Cent Beer Night game in Cleveland on July 4, 1974 against the Texas Rangers, a near riot broke out with drunken fans throwing metal chairs and other objects onto the field. Hilgendorf sustained a concussion when a metal chair hit him in the head but it didn't stop him from saving a victory for Cleveland the following night.

Oiler radio broadcasts on KVOO (1170 AM) became a five-man crew that year with future major league announcer Skip Caray joining Len Morton, Mack Creager, Jack Campbell and Pepper Martin.

The son of long-time St. Louis Cardinals and Chicago Cubs broadcaster Harry Caray, Skip previously called high school football games on KMOX Radio in St. Louis, which was the Cardinal Radio Network's flagship station. He also told Oklahoma-based media colleagues that he thoroughly enjoyed living in Tulsa, especially when it came to getting around Tulsa since the city's streets had an easy-to-follow alphabetical or numerical pattern.

In 1967, Skip became the radio announcer for the St. Louis Hawks of the National Basketball Association and moved with the team the following year to Atlanta. That opened the door for Skip to handle radio and television broadcasts of Atlanta Braves baseball on the WTBS Superstation, now known as Turner Broadcasting System (TBS) and Turner Network Television (TNT). He also covered college and professional football and ice hockey.

He spent 33 years covering the Atlanta Braves and was equally renowned for equal parts of in-depth baseball knowledge, an easy-on-the-ears announcing cadence and sometimes biting, yet witty comments. His sons, Chip and Josh, followed in the steps of their father and grandfather as baseball announcers.

Albuquerque Dukes pitcher Camilo "The Chief" Estevis was the Texas League Pitcher of the Year. A standout at Pan American College (now the University of Texas-Pan American) in the late 1950s, Estevis led the Texas League with 16 victories and 196 strikeouts. He later played in the Mexican Leagues but never reached the majors.

Austin's Jerry Hummitzsch threw a seven-inning no-hitter against Tulsa in a 2-0 victory on June 7th in the first game of a doubleheader. He was the ace of an Austin pitching staff that had future major leaguers Wade Blasingame, Clay Carroll and Pat House and viewed by many baseball scouts a can't-miss major league prospect.

But Hummitzsch died in an auto accident on May 22, 1964 when he and teammate Walt Hriniak were on an early morning fishing trip. Hriniak, who was thrown through the windshield in the wreck, later became one of the most respected hitting coaches in baseball, counting Boston Red Sox slugger Dwight Evans and Chicago White Sox star Frank Thomas among his pupils.

In an effort to speed up the games, the Texas League instituted a version of the college and professional basketball shot clock and it lasted for two seasons. Pitchers had 20 seconds to throw the ball after receiving it from a catcher when no runners were on base. Failing to do so resulted in a ball being assessed by the home plate umpire. Teams had 90 seconds between innings to change positions. When time ran out, a siren would sound from a system operated by an official sitting in the press box.

The experiment was successful because game times were shortened by an average of 21 minutes and pitchers also issued fewer time-consuming walks than the prior season. While players and managers were supportive of the idea, people selling food and beverages between innings were not pleased, for obvious reasons.

1964: Outfielder Joe "Speedo" Patterson became one of the most beloved players in Tulsa professional baseball history and the Oilers advanced to the Texas League championship series for the fourth time in five years.

Tulsa was defeated by the San Antonio Bullets, 3-1, in the championship finals. The Oilers beat the Albuquerque Dukes in their playoff series, 3-2, while San Antonio beat the El Paso Sun Kings, 3-1.

San Antonio had the league's best regular season record at 85-55. They were followed by Tulsa (79-61), Albuquerque (75-65), El Paso (67-73), the Austin Senators (63-77) and Fort Worth Cats (51-89).

Patterson joined outfielder Bobby Tolan and pitcher Nelson Briles as Tulsa's representatives on the Texas League's postseason All-Star team.

Patterson became the only player to lead the Texas League in stolen bases for three consecutive seasons and his career stolen base percentage of .829 has been a Texas League record for over 50 years. After stealing 31 bases in 1962 and 54 in 1963, Patterson stole 67 bases in 1964, the most by a Texas League player since Bobby Stow swiped 70 bases with the 1915 Fort Worth Panthers.

During his four Texas League seasons in Tulsa, the Oilers won a pair of pennants and reached the championship series two other times. Patterson also led the Texas League in runs scored in 1964 with 116.

Legend has it that Patterson developed a novel idea on how to enhance his speed. He would wear a baseball cap that was at least one size too small so when he took off running, his cap frequently flew off his head to make people think he was faster than he actually was. Patterson played 14 years in the minors but never made it to the big leagues. He was inducted into the Texas League Baseball Hall of Fame in 2012.

Tolan had a .297 batting average in 1964 along with 46 extra base hits and his 34 stolen bases ranked fourth in the Texas League. Tolan played on three National League championship teams before his 27th birthday: the 1967 St. Louis Cardinals and the Cincinnati Reds in 1970 and 1972.

With the 1970 Reds, Tolan's 57 stolen bases led the National League. He was also the National League Comeback Player of the Year in 1972, batting .283 with 171 base hits and 42 stolen bases after missing the entire 1971 season with a serious Achilles tendon injury. He returned to the Texas League for the 1984 and 1985 seasons as manager of the Beaumont Golden Gators, a Double-A affiliate of the San Diego Padres.

Briles went 11-6 with a 2.79 ERA for the Oilers, leading the pitching staff with 132 strikeouts in 25 starts along with seven complete games. He spent 14 years in the major leagues, mostly with the St. Louis Cardinals (1965-70) and Pittsburgh Pirates (1971-73).

His winning percentage of .737 in 1967 (14-5 record) led the National League and he pitched a complete game victory over the Boston Red Sox in Game 3 of the 1967 World Series. Then in the 1971 World Series with the Pittsburgh Pirates, he tossed a two-hit shutout in a Game 5 victory over the Baltimore Orioles and helped his own cause with an RBI single.

Third baseman Roy Majtyka ranked fifth on the Oilers in batting average (.296), runs batted in (54), doubles (21) and base hits (111). Majtyka went on to become just one of 20 men to win 1,800 or more games as a minor league manager. Majtyka won 1,832 games over 27 seasons with nine teams reaching the playoffs and three of them winning league championships.

Tulsa led the Texas League for the third consecutive season with the lowest team earned run average (3.24) and nine of the 20 Oilers pitchers that year had an ERA of 3.00 or lower.

Radio broadcasts on KVOO (1170 AM) reverted to the four-man crew of 1962: Len Morton, Mack Creager, Jack Campbell and Pepper Martin.

Second baseman Joe Morgan was the star of San Antonio's Texas League championship squad and the Texas League's 1964 Player of the Year, leading the league with 42 doubles while batting .323 and driving in 90 runs.

After spending nine years with the parent Houston Astros, Morgan was traded to the Cincinnati Reds in 1972 and played on their 1975 and 1976 World Series championship teams and was the National League's Most Valuable Player in those respective years, as well.

Morgan was a 10-time All-Star selection, stole 40 or more bases nine times in his big-league career, won five Gold Gloves for his defensive skills, enjoyed a long career as the color commentator for ESPN's Major League Baseball telecasts and was a 1990 Baseball Hall of Fame inductee.

San Antonio's Chris Zachary was the Texas League Pitcher of the Year. He was second in the league that year in victories (16), struck out 188 batters in 194 innings and posted a 3.20 ERA. Zachary, who went 10-29 with five major league teams over parts of nine years, pitched for the Oilers during the 1970-71 seasons.

El Paso pitcher Nick DeMatties threw a no-hitter against Tulsa in a 1-0 victory on July 16th. It was the brightest spot in an otherwise lackluster season as he finished 9-12 with a 4.75 ERA and left professional baseball after the 1966 season.

1965: The Texas League split into two divisions and the Tulsa Oilers split for the Triple-A Pacific Coast League after the season ended.

It was a successful farewell as the Oilers played for the Texas League title for the fifth time in six years. But the Albuquerque Dukes would win the first of their two Texas League championships by defeating Tulsa, 3-1.

The Oilers won the Eastern Division with an 81-60 record, followed by the Dallas-Fort Worth Spurs (80-61) and the Austin Senators (70-70). Albuquerque won the Western Division with a 77-63 record, followed by the Amarillo Sonics (60-80) and El Paso Sun Kings (53-87).

Season attendance topped 200,000 for the third consecutive season with 215,423 fans coming to Oiler Park. It was Tulsa's largest regular season attendance total since 1949 but it was also the last time until 1989 when season attendance exceeded 200,000 fans.

Stepping up to Triple-A baseball happened when team owner A. Ray Smith acquired the rights to the Cardinals' Triple-A franchise, which had played in the International League as the Jacksonville (Florida) Suns in 1964 and 1965.

The Pacific Coast League, founded in 1903, had a rich history of minor league success. But astronomical travel costs associated with a league that stretched from Indianapolis, Indiana to Honolulu, Hawaii, forced Tulsa and teams in Oklahoma City, Denver and Indianapolis to join four other teams in recreating the American Association in 1969.

This was Vernon Rapp's only season with the Oilers. He spent 16 years as a minor league catcher and achieved some success as a minor league manager, winning Triple-A American Association titles with the Indianapolis Indians (twice) and Denver Bears (once) in the late 1960s and during the 1970s. But Rapp's heavy-handed managing style didn't set well with major league players and he would be fired by the St. Louis Cardinals and the Cincinnati Reds. His big-league managerial record was 140-300.

Pitcher Larry Jaster, outfielder Walt "No Neck" Williams and catcher Dave Pavlesic were Tulsa's representatives on the Texas League's postseason All-Star Team.

The left-handed Jaster shut out Dallas-Fort Worth for the victory that lifted Tulsa into the playoffs. He led Tulsa pitchers with 14 complete games, five shutouts and a league-leading 219 strikeouts, more than making up for an 11-13 won-lost record.

Jaster was soon promoted to the St. Louis Cardinals and made major league history in 1966 as the first pitcher to throw five consecutive shutouts. All of those shutouts came against the Los Angeles Dodgers, who were the defending World Series champions and won the National League pennant in 1966. Hall of Fame pitcher Grover Cleveland Alexander threw five shutouts in 1916 but those were not in consecutive games.

During Jaster's sensational streak of 45 consecutive scoreless innings, he allowed only 24 base hits (all singles) with 31 strikeouts and held the Dodgers' booming bats to a composite batting average of .157. He even outpitched future Hall of Famer Don Drysdale in consecutive starts. By counting a relief appearance near the end of the 1965 season and his first start against the Dodgers in 1967, Jaster actually held them scoreless for 52 and two-thirds innings.

But Jaster didn't do so well against other teams and throw only two additional shutouts in his big-league career and finished with a 35-33 record. He was chosen by the expansion Montreal Expos in 1969 and threw the first pitch in the history of that franchise, which operates today as the Washington Nationals.

Pavlesic led the league with a .344 batting average and an on-base percentage of .415. He was the last Tulsa professional baseball player to lead a league in batting average and on-base percentage in the same season. Pavlesic played in Tulsa through 1968 but never reached the major leagues and later spent two years as a low-level minor league manager.

Williams led the Texas League with 189 base hits, 144 of those being singles, and scored 106 runs. He also finished in second in batting average (.330) and stole 36 bases.

His "No Neck" nickname came from standing just 5-foot-6 and having a stocky, muscular build. As a baby, his hometown of Brownwood, Texas suffered a major flood and infants were given injections to prevent the spread of typhus. Williams' neck was so thick that the only vein where the injection could be given was in the back of his neck.

Williams played for the Chicago White Sox in 1967-72 and became a fan favorite for his aggressive hitting and defensive skills. He batted a career-high .304 in 1969 and did not make a fielding error during the entire 1971 season. After finishing his playing career with teams in

Japan and Mexico, Williams returned to Tulsa in 1989 as the Drillers' first base coach.

Second baseman Ike Futch set a Texas League season record for the fewest strikeouts (minimum of 130 games played). Futch fanned just five times out of 569 at-bats in 138 games. From May 27th through September 7th, Futch played in 100 consecutive games and batted 418 consecutive times without striking out; both of those statistics are also Texas League season records. He batted .290 that year with 141 of his 165 base hits being singles.

Futch's feat was no fluke because in two previous seasons playing for double-A affiliates of the New York Yankees, he had four strikeouts in 559 at-bats (with a .317 batting average) in 1963 and five strikeouts in 505 at-bats (with a .313 batting average) in 1964.

Outfielder John Kindl had a feast-or-famine year at the plate for the Oilers. He led the team and ranked third in the Texas League in home runs with 21 but his 108 strikeouts was second-highest in the league. Kindl spent five minor league seasons with four different organizations and never reached the major leagues.

With Pepper Martin's unexpected death prior to the start of the season, Oilers radio broadcasts on KVOO (1170 AM) became a three-man operation with Len Morton, Mack Creager and Jack Campbell. That rotation stayed in place through the 1970 season.

In connection with the Oilers joining the Triple-A Pacific Coast League in 1966, the St. Louis Cardinals moved their Texas League affiliate to Little Rock, Arkansas, where it became the Arkansas Travelers and stayed in the Texas League through the 2000 season.

The Cardinals brought their Double-A affiliate back to the Texas League in 2005 when it was relocated to Springfield, Missouri. That team today is known as the Springfield Cardinals.

Amarillo Sonics outfielder Leo Posada was the Texas League Player of the Year. He led the Texas League in home runs (26) and RBIs (107) and batted .305. A member of the Kansas City Athletics in the early 1960s, Posada never returned to the major leagues but a nephew of the Cuban native did very well in the big leagues. Jorge Posada was the New York Yankees' catcher from 1998 through 2010, playing on four World Series championship teams, earning five All-Star selections and is regarded by many baseball historians as one of the best hitting catchers in recent history.

Austin Braves right-hander Ken Nixon was the Texas League Pitcher of the Year, leading the league with 19 victories. Nixon was also among the league's top five pitchers in strikeouts (132) and innings pitched (232) while posting a 3.10 ERA. He played seven years in the minor leagues and never reached the majors.

Chuck Tanner was El Paso's manager in 1965 and 1966 and spent 19 years as a major league manager. He was best known for leading the 1979 Pittsburgh Pirates to a World Series championship. That squad was known for adopting the "We Are Family" hit song as its theme and was led by future Hall of Famer Willie Stargell, who was born in Earlsboro, Oklahoma, and Mike Easler, a member of the 1975-76 Tulsa Oilers.

1966: Tulsa's first season in the Pacific Coast League was special, indeed. The Oilers won the widespread Eastern Division and took the Seattle Angels to the limit in the playoffs before falling, 4-3. But how they got there was an incredible chapter in Tulsa's professional baseball history.

The Oilers, Phoenix Giants and Indianapolis Indians were engaged in a heated battle for the Eastern Division lead from June through August. The Oilers endured a long losing streak but Indianapolis went on a six-game skid and Phoenix got hot and pulled within two games of first place.

Tulsa lost on Saturday, August 20th but Indianapolis dropped a doubleheader that gave the Oilers a half-game lead. The headline in the next day's sports section of the *Tulsa World* would be one of the most memorable in the city's sports history: *Oilers Lose 9th Straight, Pad Lead*.

The Oilers' losing streak reached 10 games and they even wore road uniforms for a home game before they finally snapped out of their funk over the final two weeks of the season.

Tulsa staved off elimination in the championship series with a 2-1 victory at Seattle on September 12th. Barney Schultz, a 40-year-old relief pitcher, picked up the win in relief of Tracy Stallard. But Seattle clinched the series with a 3-1 victory the next day.

Schultz was 2-0 with a 3.24 ERA in 25 appearances with Tulsa. After the season ended, the St. Louis Cardinals briefly activated Schultz to enable him to receive a major league pension.

Stallard had been demoted from St. Louis about two months earlier and had a 3-3 record with a 5.58 ERA in eight games with the Oilers. Long-time baseball fans remember that Stallard was the Boston Red Sox pitcher that gave up Roger Maris' record-setting 61st home run on the final day of the 1961 season.

Tulsa won the Eastern Division with an 85-62 record, followed by Phoenix (81-67), Indianapolis (80-68), the Denver Bears (79-68), San Diego Padres (72-75) and Oklahoma City 89ers (59-89). Seattle won the Western Division with an 83-65 record, followed by the Vancouver Mounties (77-71), Spokane Indians (75-73), Portland Beavers (69-79), Hawaii Islanders (63-84) and Tacoma Cubs (63-85).

The Oilers were an offensive powerhouse, leading the league with a .289 team batting average as well as in base hits and total bases.

Four players were among the top 10 PCL players in batting average. Alex Johnson ranked second (.355), Bobby Tolan was sixth (.333), Walt Williams was seventh (.330) and Dave Ricketts was tenth (.327). Tolan played only 44 games with Tulsa before moving up to the major leagues. Williams led the PCL with 107 runs scored and stole 25 bases.

Charlie Metro was Tulsa's manager that year. For more information about him and his contributions to the game of baseball, please refer back to the 1942 section of this book.

Even though the Oilers stepped up big-time in the level of competition, Tulsa fans stepped away from the turnstiles. The regular season attendance of 158,595 was a drop of nearly 57,000 from the previous year.

Oilers radio broadcasts on KVOO (1170 AM) were handled by Len Morton, Mack Creager and Jack Campbell.

Team owner A. Ray Smith came up with a novel idea resulting in the largest attendance for a baseball game in the state of Oklahoma when the Oilers hosted the parent St. Louis Cardinals on May 5th at Skelly Stadium, the University of Tulsa's football stadium. The Cardinals defeated the Oilers, 5-4, before 18,904 fans in a game that featured some highly unusual ground rules.

With home plate located in the football stadium's southwest corner, the right field foul pole was only 208 feet away so a large screen was placed from that foul pole to nearly the 50-yard line along the east side of the football stadium. Several routine flies cleared that screen and landed in the seats and became ground rule doubles, per the unique rules for that exhibition game.

Future Hall of Famer Lou Brock had two hits, drove in two runs and scored twice for St. Louis. Among the Cardinal legends participating in pre-game ceremonies were Enos Slaughter, Joe Medwick and Stan Musial.

Indianapolis catcher Duane Josephson was the league's Most Valuable Player, batting .324 and driving in 77 runs that season. Josephson made the 1968 All-Star team with the parent Chicago White Sox.

Dallas Green, manager of the 1980 Philadelphia Phillies' World Series champions and who later guided the New York Yankees and New York Mets, went 14-9 that year as a pitcher with the San Diego Padres.

Bob Lemon and Mickey Vernon, each future Hall of Famers and seven-time All-Star selections were the managers of Seattle and Vancouver, respectively.

Don Larsen, who pitched a perfect game for the New York Yankees in Game 5 of the 1956 World Series, played for the Phoenix Giants in a comeback attempt. Larsen went 8-5 with a 2.50 ERA in 35 games that season but went winless with Phoenix in 1967 and with the 1968 Tacoma Cubs before finally retiring from baseball.

1967: The Oilers had a new manager in Warren Spahn, who won more games than any left-handed pitcher in major league history. That was the only bright spot as the team went from first to worst in the Pacific Coast League's Eastern Division.

The parent St. Louis Cardinals were marching towards winning the National League pennant and then defeating the Boston Red Sox in the World Series, so several key players were called up from Tulsa.

Additional complications were a large number of injuries, several newcomers who weren't really ready for Triple-A competition along with a number of disgruntled veterans. The Oilers finished last in the PCL's Eastern Division, made more fielding errors than any team in the PCL, ranked ninth out of 12 teams in hitting and 10th out of 12 teams in pitching.

Things got so bad that Spahn even pitched in three games, trying to boost interest in the team. That experiment ended badly as Spahn had a 0-1 record with a 6.43 ERA. Regular season attendance plummeted to 120,357, a drop of 38,000 from the previous year and over 95,000 lower than in Tulsa's final Texas League season of 1965.

The bright spot on the offense came from first baseman George Kernek, who led Tulsa with 14 home runs and drove in 68 runs while batting .277. The lanky left-handed hitter was a fan favorite, hailing from Holdenville, Oklahoma (about 96 miles south-southwest of Tulsa) and having played collegiately for the University of Oklahoma. Kernek spent parts of two seasons with the St. Louis Cardinals and spent 10 years in the minors.

Hard-throwing left-hander Hal Gilson was Tulsa's best pitcher, posting career highs of 15 victories and 12 complete games. His 141 strikeouts in 34 appearances led the Oilers and ranked seventh in the PCL. But Gilson went 0-2 the following year, his only major league season, splitting time between the St. Louis Cardinals and Houston Astros.

Three future Hall of Famers led the Houston Astros to a 10-3 victory over the defending National League champion Los Angeles Dodgers on April 5th in the first of two exhibition games at Oiler Park that year. Rusty Staub drove in two runs, Eddie Matthews and Joe Morgan had two hits apiece while Bob Aspromonte homered and drove in four runs. Astros pitcher Don Wilson had seven strikeouts over seven innings for the win.

On May 15th, Jose "Coco" Laboy's two-run single in the eighth inning lifted the Oilers to a 5-4 win over a St. Louis Cardinals squad that went on to win the National League pennant. Former Oiler pitching ace Larry Jaster had seven strikeouts in six innings for St. Louis. Lou Brock, who always seemed to play well in Tulsa exhibition games, thrilled a crowd of 4,799 fans with three base hits and kept Oiler pitchers on edge with numerous threats to steal a base.

Despite the lackluster performance on the field, the radio broadcasts on KVOO (1170 AM) were as entertaining as ever, thanks to Len Morton, Mack Creager and Jack Campbell.

The San Diego Padres defeated the Spokane Indians in the playoffs, 4-2. Padres third baseman Rick Joseph was the league's Most Valuable Player, driving in 96 runs while hitting 24 home runs and batting .300.

San Diego, despite having part of the Pacific Ocean nearby, won the Eastern Division and had the league's best record at 85-63. Then came the Indianapolis Indians (76-71), Phoenix Giants (75-72), Oklahoma City 89ers (74-74), Denver Bears (69-76) and Tulsa Oilers (65-79).

Spokane had the Western Division's best record at 80-68. Then came the Portland Beavers (79-69), Vancouver Mounties (77-69), Tacoma Cubs (73-75), Seattle Angels (69-79) and Hawaii Islanders (60-87).

One of the PCL's best players that year was Portland left fielder Lou Piniella. He played for the Beavers in 1966-68 before spending his major league playing career with the Kansas City Royals (1969-73) and the New York Yankees (1974-84). Piniella was the 1969 American League Rookie of the Year and became a successful manager with five major league teams, winning six division championships and the 1990 World Series with the Cincinnati Reds.

Two PCL third basemen later enjoyed successful major league careers. Sal Bando played for Vancouver (.291 batting average) and was a 14-time major league All-Star with the Oakland Athletics and Milwaukee Brewers. Doug Rader played for Oklahoma City (.293 batting average) and won consecutive Gold Glove Awards from 1970 through 1974 for his fielding excellence with the Houston Astros.

1968: This would be the greatest team in Tulsa's professional baseball history since World War II and one of the greatest to ever compete at the Triple-A level. The Oilers won their division by 18 games and routed the Western Division champion Spokane Indians, 4-1, in the Pacific Coast League championship series.

Out of the 29 players on the 1968 Oiler roster, 25 went on to play in the major leagues. They led the PCL in team batting, team fielding and were second in team pitching. Tulsa was an incredible 51-23 at home and 44-30 on the road.

Manager Warren Spahn stated that if the 1968 Tulsa Oilers could have moved intact into the major leagues as an expansion team, that team would have had a winning record.

After a sluggish start to the season, the Oilers got a big lift when veteran outfielder Jim Hicks returned from military service. They proceeded to win 28 out of 33 games and led their division by nearly seven games on Independence Day. Hicks easily won the league's Most Valuable Player award with a .366 batting average and led the league in runs scored (100).

The Oilers had the top four hitters in the league when it came to doubles. Third baseman Jose "Coco" Laboy (who later played for the Montreal Expos) led the league with 44. Shortstop Steve Huntz was next with 35, first baseman Joe Hague had 34 and Hicks had 32. Hicks and Hague each hit 23 home runs, one behind league leader Clarence Jones of Tacoma. Laboy also led the PCL with 100 runs batted in with Hague finishing second (99) and Hicks fourth (85).

Tulsa's five-man pitching rotation was equally excellent. Chuck Taylor led the staff with an 18-7 record and a 2.35 ERA, going the distance in 16 of his 32 starts with five shutouts. He also had 128 strikeouts and just 38 walks over 230 innings. Future major leaguer Mike Torrez went 8-2 with four complete games and struck out 80 batters in 82 innings.

Former major leaguer Pete Mikkelsen had the lowest ERA of any Oilers starter (1.91) along with a 16-4 record. Veteran Dick LeMay was

16-10 with a 3.29 ERA. Sal Campisi went 12-3 with a 3.78 ERA and went 25-6 during his three-year Oiler career.

Tulsa won the Eastern Division with a 95-53 record and was greatly aided by the St. Louis Cardinals having a set roster and not making as many call-ups as in recent years. The San Diego Padres finished second at 76-70, followed by the Phoenix Giants (76-71), Denver Bears (73-72), Indianapolis Indians (66-78) and Oklahoma City 89ers (61-84).

Spokane won the Western Division with an 85-60 record, followed by the Hawaii Islanders (78-69), Portland Beavers (72-72), Seattle Angels (71-76), Tacoma Cubs (65-83) and Vancouver Mounties (58-88).

The 1968 season would also be Tulsa's swan song in the PCL. Budget-busting travel-related expenses were the primary reasons why Tulsa, the Oklahoma City 89ers, Denver Bears and Indianapolis Indians left after the season ended to join the revived and centrally-located American Association. It was also the final PCL season for San Diego and Seattle, who were joining the National and American Leagues, respectively, as expansion teams.

There was one PCL player that had he not been called up to the majors, would have had a better batting average than Tulsa's Hicks. Phoenix outfielder Bobby Bonds was hitting .370 over 60 games when the San Francisco Giants called him up. He would become just the second major league player to hit 300 home runs and steal 300 bases in a career.

His son, Barry Bonds, set major league records for the most home runs in a season (73 in 2001) and career (762). But Barry's legacy was tainted by testimony before a federal grand jury that he never knowingly took performance-enhancing steroids during his career. Barry was convicted in 2011 of obstruction of justice.

Billy Martin and Don Zimmer, two future major league managers, were guiding PCL teams in 1968.

Martin made his managerial debut with the Denver Bears, the top farm team of the Minnesota Twins. He led Denver to a 65-50 finish following an 8-22 start under Johnny Goryl. The former New York Yankees infielder later led the Bronx Bombers to the 1976 and 1977 American League titles, won the 1977 World Series and had a losing record just twice in his 16 seasons as a manager. But Martin paid a high price with his fiery and confrontational personality, factors in his being fired and then rehired four times by the Yankees.

Zimmer was the skipper of the Indianapolis Indians that season. He won 906 games as a major league manager and led the Chicago Cubs to the 1989 National League Eastern Division championship. But his managerial record was blemished in 1978 when his Boston Red Sox team squandered a 14-game lead down the stretch and lost a one-game playoff for the American League pennant to the New York Yankees on Bucky Dent's dramatic home run.

Bo Belinsky was a colorful pitcher who threw a no-hitter in his fourth game as a Los Angeles Angels rookie in 1962. He had a 9-14 record with Hawaii in a comeback attempt. Belinsky never won again the majors, finishing with a 28-51 big-league record and was one of the earliest examples of athletes who squandered talent and golden opportunities in professional sports.

John Richard "Ducky" Schofield, who played for the St. Louis Cardinals three different times during his 14-year major league career, was the hero in the Cardinals' 3-2 exhibition victory over the Oilers on May 27th before 7,011 fans.

Schofield, a member of the Pittsburgh Pirates' 1960 World Series champions, had three hits, drove in the tying run in the top of the ninth inning and later scored the winning run. His son, Dick

Schofield, and grandson Jayson Werth, also played for the Los Angeles Dodgers at different times during their respective careers.

Clay Kirby, who would return to Tulsa later that year, had seven strikeouts in six innings for St. Louis.

Oilers radio broadcasts on KVOO (1170 AM) featured Len Morton, Mack Creager and Jack Campbell describing the action.

1969: There were so many new things about this Oilers season. The American Association, which originally operated from 1902 through 1962, was their new home with eight teams located in the middle of the nation and greatly reduced travel costs.

There was a new position called the designated hitter where another offensive player would bat for a normally weak-hitting pitcher. It was designed to increase scoring in games and, in turn, increase fan interest and attendance. The designated hitter would be adopted by the American League in 1973 and be the scorn of baseball purists for ensuing decades.

Another move designed to help create more offense was the lowering of the pitcher's mound by five inches. And relief pitchers were recognized for their work in pressurized situations late in the game with a new statistic, the save.

In any other season, the Oilers' 79-61 record would be outstanding. The lower pitching mound was no small factor in the Oilers' team batting average of .282, 13 points higher than the previous year. But surprisingly, Tulsa's season attendance total dropped by nearly 15 percent from the previous championship season to 166,023.

The Omaha Royals won the American Association championship with an 85-55 record and many of its players would create a foundation for success by the parent Kansas City Royals during the 1970s. Trailing Omaha and Tulsa in the standings were the Indianapolis

Indians (74-66), Iowa Oaks (62-78), Oklahoma City 89ers (62-78) and Denver Bears (58-82).

Catcher Ted Simmons was the talk of minor league baseball with an amazing blend of offensive and defensive skills. The 19-year-old Simmons batted .317 that year with 16 home runs, 88 RBIs and led Tulsa in base hits (158), doubles (33) and even stole 11 bases. And his laser-accurate throwing arm kept would-be base stealers guessing all season long.

Simmons, an eight-time All-Star selection, finished with 2,472 hits in his 21-year major league career, the most by any catcher until it was broken by someone who, ironically, would play for the Tulsa Drillers, Ivan Rodriguez.

After his playing career ended, Simmons served as a front office executive with the St. Louis Cardinals, Cleveland Indians, Pittsburgh Pirates, San Diego Padres and Seattle Mariners. He joined the Atlanta Braves in late 2015 as a scout.

Sal Campisi and Jerry Reuss shared the league lead in victories with 13 apiece. Reuss was a lanky left-hander who also led the league in strikeouts (151) while Campisi was the league's best relief pitcher with 15 saves and a stingy 1.99 ERA.

Three members of Tulsa's 1968 Pacific Coast League champions helped the St. Louis Cardinals defeat the Oilers, 9-8, before 6,273 fans in a May 5th exhibition game. Joe Hague, Steve Huntz and Jim Hicks combined for seven of the 15 St. Louis base hits. Huntz's two-run home run in the seventh inning proved to be the game-winning hit. Ted Simmons went 2-for-5 and scored twice.

Oilers radio broadcasts on KVOO (1170 AM) featured Len Morton, Mack Creager and Jack Campbell describing the action.

Left-hander Paul Splittorff was Omaha's pitching ace that year, posting a 12-10 record and going the distance in 11 of his 26 starts. He would spend his 15-year big-league career with the Royals, winning 20 games in 1973 and set team pitching records with 166 victories and 392 starts. After retiring from baseball, Splittorff spent nearly 24 years as a color commentator on college baseball and basketball telecasts in the Big 8 and Big 12 Conferences.

Veteran minor league manager Jack McKeon was Omaha's skipper that year. He would serve as a manager or general manager for major league teams over the following five decades: the Kansas City Royals, Oakland Athletics, San Diego Padres, Cincinnati Reds and Florida Marlins. His numerous personnel changes to set the stage for the 1984 San Diego Padres winning the National League pennant earned him the nickname of "Trader Jack." McKeon guided the 2003 Florida Marlins (now known as the Miami Marlins) to a World Series championship.

Indianapolis outfielder Bernie Carbo was the league's Most Valuable Player, batting .359 with 21 home runs and 76 RBIs. The parent Cincinnati Reds made Carbo their first choice in the 1965 amateur draft, ahead of future Hall of Fame catcher and Binger, Oklahoma native Johnny Bench. Carbo was the 1970 National League Rookie of the Year and played a key role for the Boston Red Sox in their dramatic 1975 World Series victory over, ironically, Cincinnati.

Chapter Eight
The 1970s

Americans were weary of war and political scandals during this decade. While the United States pulled its military forces out of the Vietnam conflict in 1973, they were entrapped in international conflict when a group of Americans were taken hostage by a rebellious new regime in Iran. The depth of the Watergate political scandal led to resignations by Vice President Spiro Agnew and President Richard Nixon.

Two world leaders came to the fore during this decade: Pope John Paul II and British Prime Minister Margaret Thatcher. And the music industry was saddened when The Beatles broke up and Elvis Presley died.

It was a decade of new technology with the introduction of pocket calculators, floppy disks for computers, Sony introducing the Walkman portable music device and the founding of a computer software company called Microsoft. The first *Star Wars* movie came out, *M*A*S*H** became a hit television series and the TV miniseries *Roots* captivated audiences.

This was also a decade of sports dominance. The Montreal Canadiens won six Stanley Cup hockey championships, the UCLA Bruins earned five of their 11 collegiate men's basketball titles, the Pittsburgh Steelers won three Super Bowls, and the Oakland Athletics won three consecutive World Series. Swimmer Mark Spitz and gymnast Nadia Comaneci made Olympic history and Arthur Ashe became the first African-American to win the Wimbledon men's singles tennis title.

The Oilers won two championships in the Triple-A American Association but would leave Tulsa after the 1976 season. Two local businessmen stepped in to bring the Texas Rangers' Double-A franchise to town for the 1977 season. That team would be, and is still, known as the Tulsa Drillers.

Catastrophe struck during the first exhibition game under the team's new ownership. A section of the rotting and termite-infested wooden stands behind first base collapsed and many people were injured. Most of the ballpark was demolished shortly afterwards for safety reasons. Attendance totals for Tulsa home baseball games plummeted to a couple of hundred fans per night.

Tulsa voters soundly rejected plans for a tax payer-funded new stadium in 1979 and just like in the late 1950s, it looked like minor league baseball in the city was down to its final out.

There were some bright spots, however. The Drillers reached the 1977 Texas League playoffs. A left-handed pitcher from New Jersey would make Tulsa his home and then embark on a personal journey that led to owning the Drillers, playing a major role in the building of Tulsa's current baseball stadium and being inducted into the Texas League Hall of Fame.

Among the major league stars playing in exhibition games in Tulsa were Lou Brock, Ernie Banks, Billy Williams, Luis Aparicio, Don Kessinger, Cesar Cedeno, Al Oliver, and Gaylord Perry.

1970: The Oilers came within one-half game of reaching the American Association playoffs, a noteworthy achievement considering that 47 different players spent time in Tulsa that year. The revolving door of players didn't set well with local fans as season attendance was 155,786, a drop of nearly 11,000 from the previous year. But this would be a banner year for local baseball fans with three big-league exhibition games played at Oiler Park.

Left-handed pitcher Jerry Reuss was Tulsa's pitching ace during the early part of the season and earned a quick promotion to the St. Louis Cardinals. Reuss went 7-2 with four complete games in 11 starts with the Oilers, posting a stingy 2.12 ERA with 69 strikeouts against 28 walks.

Reuss played high school baseball in St. Louis so joining his hometown big-league team seemed like a dream come true. Reuss spent 22 years in major league baseball, won 220 games and played in two All-Star Games, but his Cardinal tenure lasted just three years.

His longest big-league tenure was with Los Angeles Dodgers from 1979 through 1987. In 1980, Reuss was the National League Comeback Player of the Year and threw a no-hitter against the San Francisco Giants. He finished with an 18-6 record and a 2.51 ERA after going 7-14 the previous year. After retiring, Reuss worked as a radio-TV baseball analyst and developed a sports photography hobby.

Reggie Cleveland was Tulsa's winningest pitcher, posting a 12-8 record with eight complete games and two shutouts. Hailing from Swift Current, Saskatchewan in Canada, he won 10 or more games in eight of his 13 years in the major leagues and was inducted into the Canadian Baseball Hall of Fame in 1986.

Outfielder Luis Melendez was Tulsa's best offensive player that year and ranked among the American Association's top hitters. He led the league with 34 doubles, was the co-leader in base hits (155) and ranked second in runs scored (77) and fourth in RBIs (71) with a .306 batting average. While Melendez played seven of his eight major league seasons with the St. Louis Cardinals, he never fulfilled the potential that he showed in Tulsa.

Melendez later became a successful manager in Puerto Rico's Winter Baseball League, leading the Senadores de San Juan (San Juan Senators) to championships in 1994 and 1995. Some of the future major league stars that Melendez tutored during those years were Roberto Alomar, Carlos Baerga, Carlos Delgado, Edgar Martinez, Bernie Williams and former Tulsa Drillers Juan Gonzalez and Ruben Sierra.

Former major league infielder Jerry Adair batted .299 in 33 games with the Oilers in his bid to return to the major leagues after being released by the Kansas City Royals earlier that year. He spent the following year in Japan's professional leagues before ending his playing career and he later served as an assistant coach on the Oakland Athletics' World Series championship teams from 1972 through 1974.

Adair's hometown was the western Tulsa suburb of Sand Springs and he was a baseball and basketball standout during the 1950s at what is now Oklahoma State University. He batted .438 as a junior shortstop before turning professional and was an All-Big 8 Conference honoree.

Adair spent nine years of his 13 big-league seasons with the Baltimore Orioles but is remembered by long-time Boston Red Sox fans for his defensive wizardry on the 1967 "Impossible Dream" team that won the American League pennant and gave the Red Sox their first World Series appearance since 1946.

The Denver Bears won the Western Division with a 70-69 record with Tulsa finishing 70-70, followed by the Oklahoma City 89ers (68-71) and Wichita Aeros (67-73). The Omaha Royals won the Eastern Division and had the league's best record at 73-65. The Iowa Oaks were next (70-68), followed by the Indianapolis Indians (71-69) and Evansville Triplets (67-71).

This wound up being Tulsa's best season for exhibition games with three being played at Oiler Park. Snow in Chicago forced the Cubs and White Sox to postpone their three exhibition games so they came to Tulsa hoping for a warmer climate. But the first and third games were played in blustery weather better suited for a late December Chicago Bears pro football game and the second game was rained out.

The Cubs won a 13-12 slugfest before 2,160 fans on April 3rd. White Sox pitcher Tommy John was rocked for 12 hits over six innings. The only bright spots were a grand slam home run by Buddy Bradford and former Oiler Walt "No Neck" Williams getting a homer as part of his 2-for-4 effort. Cubs catcher J.C. Martin hit a grand slam home run, Billy Williams drove in three runs while Glenn Beckert, Johnny Callison and Don Kessinger added three hits apiece.

After an April 4th rainout, the Cubs beat the White Sox, 10-8, on April 5th before 3,292 fans. The White Sox built an early lead with former Oklahoma State Cowboys pitcher Joel Horlen scattering five hits over five innings while Bill Melton and John Matias drove in three runs apiece. The Cubs then came alive with middle infielders Glenn Beckert and Don Kessinger combining for four base hits and scoring five runs.

Tulsa shutout the St. Louis Cardinals, 6-0, in a June 4th exhibition game at Oiler Park before 4,685 fans. Cardinal superstars Richie Allen and Lou Brock were held hitless. Jim Campbell had three hits for the Oilers and drove in two runs.

Len Morton and Jack Campbell continued broadcasting Oiler games on KVOO (1170 AM) but this would be the complete-season swan song for local legend Mack Creager. When the season ended, it brought a deep poignancy to his signature sign-off of "I'm rounding third and heading for home." Creager was behind the mike for over 3,000 Oilers baseball broadcasts.

Omaha won its second consecutive American Association championship by defeating the Denver Bears in the finals, 4-1. Omaha then faced the International League champion Syracuse Chiefs in the Junior World Series but lost, 4-1.

Omaha right fielder George Spriggs, at age 33, was the league's Most Valuable Player with a .301 batting average, 11 home runs, 43 runs batted in and 29 stolen bases. Spriggs holds a place in Kansas City's baseball lore as the only person to play for that city's Negro League powerhouse Monarchs and the major league Royals.

Incredibly, Spriggs beat out 20-year-old Iowa Oaks pitcher Vida Blue for the MVP award. Blue went 12-3 with the Oaks with a 2.17 ERA and pitched nine complete games, four of those being shutouts.

Blue was quickly promoted to the Oakland Athletics, where he won the American League Cy Young Award (best pitcher), was a six-time selection to the American League All-Star team, won 20 or more games three times and was one of the aces on the A's pitching staff that won the 1972, 1973 and 1974 World Series.

Wichita first baseman Chris Chambliss won the league's batting title with a .342 average. He would spend 17 years in the major leagues with the Cleveland Indians, New York Yankees and Atlanta Braves.

Oklahoma City had one of minor league baseball's hottest prospects in a 19-year-old outfielder named Cesar Cedeno. He batted .373 in 54 games with the 89ers, adding 14 home runs and 61 RBIs. Cedeno went on to be a three-time National League All-Star and five-time Golden Glove winner in a 12-year career with the parent Houston Astros.

1971: Oiler owner A. Ray Smith asked former general manager Hugh Finnerty to return for one year in the hope of boosting attendance. Finnerty's fan-friendly promotions contributed to the season attendance jumping to 186,414, an increase of roughly 29,000 from the previous year.

That was the only good news that year because the team tumbled into last place in the American Association's Eastern Division. Their 64 victories were also the lowest such total in Tulsa's professional baseball history since 1915.

Things got worse when with a week left in the regular season, the parent St. Louis Cardinals told manager Warren Spahn that his contract would not be renewed for the following year. Spahn immediately quit and outfielder Gary Geiger served as interim manager for the final seven games. Spahn's record of managing in 719 games stood as the Tulsa professional baseball record until it was later broken by Tulsa Drillers manager Bobby Jones.

Bowie Kuhn became the second active Commissioner of Baseball to visit Tulsa when he came to Oiler Park for a ceremony in August of 1971. The visit happened quickly after Kuhn learned of Spahn's resignation. The only other active Commissioner of Baseball to visit Tulsa was the aforementioned November 1920 visit by Kenesaw Mountain Landis.

Fred Rico, a star of the 1969 Omaha Royals' league championship team, was the Oilers' hitting standout. He led the league in base hits and runs scored with 150 and 87, respectively, and also was a co-leader in doubles (31) and second in RBIs (101) while batting .296.

Rico was also the star of the Oilers' 9-2 May 17th exhibition game victory over the St. Louis Cardinals before 5,181 fans at Oiler Park. He had two home runs among his four base hits and he also drove in three runs and stole two bases. Rico's big-league career consisted of only 12 games played the previous year with the Kansas City Royals.

Pitcher Fred Norman went 6-1 in nine games that year and tossed a no-hitter on June 5th in 4-0 victory against the Indianapolis Indians.

Norman later pitched for the Cincinnati Reds' World Series champions in 1975 and 1976.

And speaking of no-hitters, Wichita Aeros pitcher Rich Hand was one walk away from a perfect game in a 3-0 no-hitter against the Oilers on August 19th.

Len Morton and Jack Campbell returned as co-anchors of the Oilers radio broadcasting crew on KVOO-AM (1170).

Rock and roll superstar and Tulsa native Leon Russell performed a concert at Oiler Park on June 23rd. The stage was set up behind home plate and the larger-than-expected audience stretched well into the outfield and down both base lines. Russell was a close friend of Emily Smith, the daughter of Oilers owner A. Ray Smith and the inspiration for Russell's hit song, "Sweet Emily."

The Denver Bears won the American Association playoffs, defeating the Indianapolis Indians, 4-3. The Bears faced the International League champion Rochester Red Wings in the Junior World Series but lost, 4-3.

Denver won the Western Division with a 73-67 record, followed by the Oklahoma City 89ers (71-69), Wichita Aeros (66-74) and Tulsa Oilers (64-76). Indianapolis won the Eastern Division and had the league's best regular season record (84-55), followed by the Iowa Oaks (71-69), Omaha Royals (69-70) and Evansville Triplets (60-78).

Denver outfielder Richie Scheinblum easily won the league's Most Valuable Player award and his .388 batting average was the best in all of Triple-A baseball. He also led the league in RBIs (108), triples (10), shared the league lead in doubles (31) and was second in home runs (25).

Despite making the American League All-Star team in 1972 as a member of the Kansas City Royals, Scheinblum had trouble hitting major league pitching and played briefly for the 1974 Tulsa Oilers before ending his career in Japan's baseball leagues.

A trio of Oklahoma City pitchers finished 1-2-3 in the American Association in strikeouts. James Rodney "J.R." Richard led the league with 202 strikeouts, Scipio Spinks fanned 173 batters and Bill Grief was third with 152. The 89ers' offensive standout was first baseman John Mayberry, who spent 15 years in the majors and was a two-time All-Star with the Kansas City Royals.

Richard played 10 years for the parent Houston Astros and twice led the National League in strikeouts but a series of unfortunate events led to a personal downfall and resurgence. The flame-throwing right-hander suffered a near-fatal stroke on July 30, 1980 and almost died during emergency surgery.

After losing millions of dollars in a divorce and bad financial investments and living for a time beneath a highway bridge, Richard turned his life around and served as a gospel minister in the Houston community.

Wichita third baseman Buddy Bell was another American Association standout. He would spend 18 years in the majors and won six Gold Gloves for his fielding excellence.

Indianapolis Indians pitcher Pedro Borbon would be promoted to the parent Cincinnati Reds and became one of the top relief pitchers on the "Big Red Machine" that dominated the National League from 1970 through 1976 by winning five National League West championships, four National League pennants and the 1975 and 1976 World Series.

1972: The Oilers had the best season attendance total during their entire Triple-A history with 199,080 fans coming to see the games. Even though Tulsa didn't make the playoffs, their 78-62 record was third-best in the American Association that year.

Jim Bibby was the ace of Tulsa's pitching staff, finishing with 13 victories and 208 strikeouts. The only Tulsa Oiler pitchers to have more season strikeouts than Bibby were George Boehler (333 in 1922) and Larry Jaster (219) in 1965.

The stocky Bibby stood 6-foot-5 and the trademark other than his blazing fastball was how profusely he would sweat while pitching. He spent five of his 12 major league seasons with the Pittsburgh Pirates and was a National League All-Star in 1980 at the age of 35 with a 19-6 record and a league-leading .760 winning percentage.

His younger and shorter brother was Henry Bibby, the point guard for UCLA's basketball team that won consecutive collegiate basketball championships from 1970 through 1972. Henry had long careers as an NBA player and assistant coach and earned his own spot in Tulsa sports history. He was the head coach of the 1988-89 Tulsa Fast Breakers, a team that won the Continental Basketball Association championship in its first year of operation.

Catcher Skip Jutze and third baseman Ken Reitz were named to the American Association postseason All-Star Team.

Jutze's .324 batting average ranked third in the league. He was also among the league's top 10 offensive players with 138 base hits and 25 doubles. Jutze spent four of his six major league seasons with the Houston Astros. He finished his big-league career with the 1977 Seattle Mariners and hit the first grand-slam home run in that franchise's history.

Reitz batted .279 with 15 home runs and 66 RBIs but was renowned as one of the best fielding third baseman in all of minor league baseball. He spent eight of 11 major league seasons with the St. Louis Cardinals, had the best fielding percentage of any National League third baseman in 1973 and 1974 and was a 1980 National League All-Star. Reitz turned his life around after dealing with substance abuse issues during his playing career and today does specialty work for Major League Baseball.

Jack Krol began a two-year tenure as Tulsa's manager. He posted a 146-129 record during that period and took the Oilers to the American Association championship in 1973.

Krol spent most of his 12-year minor league playing career in the St. Louis Cardinals' development system but won three league championships and 1,170 games over 17 years as a minor league manager. During the 1980s, Krol was an assistant coach with the National League's San Diego Padres and that franchise created an award in his honor, saluting that organization's top contributor to player development.

A bombshell hit Tulsa sports fans that year when KVOO-AM Radio, the long-time 50,000-watt flagship station for Oiler baseball along with University of Tulsa football and basketball, dropped all of its live sports programming and switched to a 24-hour country music format. KVOO-AM later became one of the nation's most popular AM country music stations. Many years later, the station switched to a politically-oriented news-talk format and changed its call letters to KFAQ-AM.

Oiler radio broadcast rights were picked up by a small FM station in Tulsa's largest suburb. KTBA-FM (92.1) in Broken Arrow was better known for playing free-form rock music but it had a much-weaker signal that KVOO-AM possessed. There was a prior connection to Oiler baseball because station owner Bill Hyden was part of the broadcast crew back in 1947.

Local baseball fans drew some consolation from the fact that familiar voices Len Morton and Jack Campbell were still part of the broadcasts. Morton was also in the first of what would be two seasons as the team's general manager.

The third member of the broadcast crew was Forrest Cameron, who also worked in the team's marketing and public relations departments. Cameron today is the editor-publisher of the *Greater Tulsa Reporter* newspapers, a series of suburban-oriented monthly publications.

The St. Louis Cardinals edged the Oilers, 5-4, in a 10-inning exhibition game on May 1st before 3,594 fans. Utility infielder Marty Martinez, who would serve in 1977 and 1978 as the first manager of the Tulsa Drillers, had a tie-breaking RBI double in the 10th inning. Former Oilers Ed Crosby and Joe Hague led the Cardinals with three hits and two hits, respectively.

Despite going through three managers during the season, the Evansville Triplets won their first American Association championship. They swept the Wichita Aeros in the playoffs, 3-0, and went on to finish fourth in the World Baseball Championship tournament.

Evansville was the top farm club of the Milwaukee Brewers and had joined the league two years earlier. Del Crandall started the year as Evansville's manager before being called up to serve as the Brewers' manager. Former Oiler player-manager Al Widmar went 5-2 as interim manager and Mike Roarke finished the season with a 58-38 mark.

The Triplets won the Eastern Division with an 83-57 record, followed by the Omaha Royals (71-69), Iowa Oaks (62-78) and Indianapolis Indians (61-79). The Wichita Aeros won the Western Division and had the league's best regular season record (87-53), followed by the Tulsa Oilers (78-62), Denver Bears (61-79) and Oklahoma City 89ers (57-83).

One of Evansville's top players was Darrell Porter, a 20-year-old catcher from Oklahoma City's Southeast High School. He only hit .216 for the Triplets but was one of the best defensive catchers in all of minor league baseball, renowned for his skillful handling of pitchers and a rocket-like arm that repeatedly gunned down opposing runners trying to steal a base.

Porter was the Most Valuable Player in the 1972 World Series as a member of the St. Louis Cardinals and was a four-time All-Star selection. But his 17-year big-league career was tarnished by frequent issues involving substance abuse, something which played a role in his death in 2002.

Wichita first baseman Pat Bourque was the league's Most Valuable Player, batting .279 with a minor-league career-high 20 home runs and 87 RBIs. Bourque was a role player for the Oakland Athletics' 1973 World Series champions but only batted .215 over four major league seasons.

Outfielder Jeff Burroughs made a huge impression during his brief time with the Denver Bears. Burroughs' 24 home runs in 84 games would be the best of his minor league career and earned a quick promotion to the parent Texas Rangers. He was the American League's Most Valuable Player in 1974, leading the league with 118 RBIs while batting .301 with 25 home runs.

1973: The Oilers won their first American Association pennant in dramatic style, claiming the Western Division title by one game and then winning the final two playoff games on the road against the Eastern Division champion Iowa Oaks. Tulsa had won the first two playoff games then Iowa took three in a row. The Oilers routed Iowa, 16-0, to tie the series at three wins apiece and then prevailed in Game 7, 4-1.

The Oilers won the Western Division with a 68-67 record, followed by the Wichita Aeros (67-68), Oklahoma City 89ers (61-74) and Denver Bears (61-75). Iowa won the Eastern Division and had the league's best regular season record at 83-53. Trailing Iowa in the

Eastern Division were the Indianapolis Indians (74-62), Evansville Triplets (66-70) and Omaha Royals (62-73).

Tulsa faced the International League champion Pawtucket Red Sox in the Junior World Series but ran out of gas and lost that series, 4-1. Pawtucket was led by future Boston Red Sox standouts Jim Rice, Cecil Cooper and Rick Burleson.

But the late-season heroics didn't result in success at the turnstiles. The season attendance of 135,698 represented a drop of nearly 33 percent from the 1972 total of 199,080.

Outfielder Jimmy Dwyer was Tulsa's lone representative on the American Association All-Star Team, thanks to a league-leading .387 batting average. It was the second-highest season batting average in Tulsa's professional baseball history, surpassed only by Pete Casey's .393 average in 1926.

Dwyer was a prolific hitter at Southern Illinois University where his .413 batting average and All-American selection played key roles in the Salukis finishing in second place at the 1971 NCAA College World Series. He spent 18 years in the major leagues, playing for seven teams and was part of the Baltimore Orioles' 1983 World Series championship team.

Outfielder Arnold Ray "Bake" McBride was a popular player because of his hitting ability and speed on the base paths and in the outfield. McBride batted .315 and stole 27 bases in 60 games with the Oilers in 1972, then batted .289 and stole 23 bases in 58 games in 1973. That earned a quick promotion to the St. Louis Cardinals, where he hit .300 or higher in each of his first four big-league seasons.

McBride was the 1974 National League Rookie of the Year, thanks to a .309 batting average and stealing 30 bases. He became the first Cardinal to win that award since Bill Virdon did it in 1955.

McBride's best major league season was 1976 when he batted .335 and played for the National League in the All-Star Game. He later played for the Philadelphia Phillies' 1980 World Series championship team, batting .309 and driving in a career-high 87 runs.

Bob Forsch, who later starred for the St. Louis Cardinals and Houston Astros, threw a no-hitter in a 5-0 home victory over the Denver Bears on May 25th.

Pitcher Al Hrabosky spent his first five years in the Cardinals' minor league system as a starting pitcher with inconsistent results. He had unimpressive numbers with Tulsa in 1973 (3-6 record, 4.42 ERA).

But becoming a relief pitcher made a night-and-day difference in his baseball career. He spent eight of his 13 major league seasons with the St. Louis Cardinals and led the National League in 1975 by saving 22 victories and had the league's best winning percentage (.813), thanks to a 13-3 record.

Hrabosky was nicknamed "The Mad Hungarian" for his Fu Manchu-style mustache and his routine of psyching himself up before a new batter by turning his back to the batter and slamming the ball into his glove. Today, he serves as a color commentator on Cardinals' regional TV broadcasts.

Two exhibition games were played at Oiler Park that year. Tim McCarver had two hits to lead the St. Louis Cardinals to a 5-3 victory over the Tulsa Oilers before 4,848 fans on June 14th.

Hall of Famer pitchers Bob Feller and Leroy "Satchel" Paige were celebrity managers for an Old-Timers exhibition game on July 8, 1973. The game was played prior to a doubleheader between the Oilers and Evansville Triplets and both teams had star-studded lineups. In a sense, it was a trip back in time to 1946 and 1947 when Feller and Paige led all-star teams in exhibition baseball games around the nation.

Feller's team that day included himself, Paul "Daffy" Dean, Dale Mitchell, Lloyd Waner and Allie Reynolds. Paige's team had Negro League Hall of Famers Ted Page, Bob Boyd and James "Cool Papa" Bell.

Paige had begun a four-year tenure with the Oilers as a part-time pitching coach along with performing a variety of front-office duties. Even though his team lost that day, 3-0, the 67-year-old Paige pitched the whole game. Paige made history in 1971 as the first Negro Leagues player to be inducted into the Baseball Hall of Fame. New York Yankees legend Joe DiMaggio once said that Paige was the best pitcher that he ever faced.

Paige, whose nickname came from carrying luggage as a child at the train station in his hometown of Mobile, Alabama, was the best pitcher in the Negro Baseball Leagues from the 1920s through the 1940s. The lanky right-handed pitcher was renowned for his blazing fastball and durability, pitching countless complete games with little rest in between starting assignments.

In 1948 at the age of 42, Paige became the oldest major league rookie when he joined the Cleveland Indians. He played in two major league All-Star Games and his final game as a player was in 1965, at the age of 59 with the Kansas City Athletics. Coincidentally, a future Tulsa Drillers manager shared the Negro League legends dugout that day.

Oiler radio broadcasts were on their third station in as many seasons, moving to soul/R&B music-oriented KKUL-FM (103.3). Len Morton and Forrest Cameron called the action.

This would also be Len Morton's swan song with the Tulsa Oilers. Morton served as the play-by-play announcer for Oiler baseball for 11 years and later worked as athletic promotions manager for three years at the University of Tulsa and in the sales and marketing operations of what is now the Tulsa office of Cox Cable Television.

Morton virtually always ended his baseball broadcasts with two signature calls. The first was asking fans in the parking lot to honk their car horns to celebrate an Oiler home victory. The other was his trademark farewell of, "Good night, and thanks for sitting in."

Denver designated hitter Cliff Johnson was the American Association's Most Valuable Player, leading the league in home runs (33), runs batted in (117) and runs scored (105) and batted .302. Johnson played for seven major league teams over 15 years and was part of the New York Yankees' 1977 and 1978 World Series champions.

The Omaha Royals finished in the cellar of American Association's Eastern Division despite having a future Hall of Famer as their third baseman. George Brett dazzled fans and major league scouts with his clutch hitting and amazing fielding skills during his final full minor league season, one in which he batted .284.

Brett would have 3,154 base hits during his 21-year career with the parent Kansas City Royals. A 13-time All-Star selection, Brett flirted with history in 1980 when he almost became the first player since Ted Williams to bat at least .400 in a season. (Williams batted .406 with the 1941 Boston Red Sox.) Brett finished with a .390 average, easily winning the 1980 American League Most Valuable Player award and was inducted into the Baseball Hall of Fame in 1999.

Born as Russell Earl O'Dey, Bucky Dent was a shortstop-third baseman with a .295 batting average for the Iowa Oaks that year. He earned baseball fame as a member of the 1978 New York Yankees when his three-run home run at Boston's Fenway Park gave the Yankees a 5-4 victory in a one-game playoff.

Ironically, Dent's home run came off a former Tulsa Oiler pitcher, Mike Torrez. Dent was the Most Valuable Player of the 1978 World Series when the Yankees defeated the Los Angeles Dodgers.

1974: The Oilers won their second consecutive American Association championship in dramatic fashion after being two outs away from losing to the Indianapolis Indians.

Indianapolis held a 3-2 advantage in the best-of-seven series and owned a 4-1 lead in Game 6 with one out in the top of the ninth inning. Tulsa's Joe Lindsey swatted a solo home run then Hector Cruz tied the game with a two-run blast. The Oilers scored four runs in the 15th inning and tied the series with their 8-4 victory. Tulsa then won Game 7, 4-1, with pitcher Mike Thompson scattering three hits and with eight strikeouts.

That made the first year of Ken Boyer's three-year tenure as the Oilers' manager a successful one. The former St. Louis Cardinal was widely regarded as the National League's best third baseman in the late 1950s and early 1960s. He was a seven-time National League All-Star, that league's Most Valuable Player in 1964 and earned five Gold Gloves for outstanding defensive play.

Four Oilers were named to the American Association's postseason All-Star Team: pitcher Ray Bare, catcher Marc Hill, first baseman Keith Hernandez and outfielder Danny Godby.

Bare had the league's lowest ERA (2.34) and led the Oiler pitching staff with a 12-4 won-lost record. Bare spent three of his five major-league seasons with the Detroit Tigers but his overall big-league record was 16-26.

Hernandez, chosen in the 42nd round of the 1971 amateur draft by the St. Louis Cardinals, led the league with a .351 batting average. During his 17-year major league career, Hernandez won 11 Gold Gloves for his defensive skills. He was the co-winner of 1979 National League Most Valuable Player and played for two World Series champions: the 1982 St. Louis Cardinals and the 1986 New York Mets.

Hill was the American Association's Rookie of the Year, tying Hernandez and Ed Kurpiel for Tulsa's home run leadership (14) while batting .278 and driving in 58 RBIs. Known for a strong throwing arm and excellent in-game pitching strategy, Hill spent most of his 14-year major league career with the San Francisco Giants (1975-80) and Chicago White Sox (1981-86).

Godby batted .285, stole 14 bases and his 134 base hits were one fewer than Jimmy Dwyer's team-leading total. But during Godby's tenures with the Cardinals and the Boston Red Sox, there were superstars (Lou Brock in St. Louis and Jim Rice and Fred Lynn in Boston) who kept him from getting a true chance at making the team. After retiring from baseball, Godby returned home to Logan County in West Virginia, where he worked as a school teacher for more than 40 years.

John Denny posted a 9-8 record with a 3.75 ERA and leading Tulsa's pitching staff in strikeouts (79). He won the 1983 Cy Young Award with the National League champion Philadelphia Phillies with his 19 victories and a .760 winning percentage leading all NL pitchers.

Harold "Bucky" Jeffcoat, led the Oilers with seven saves in what would be his final baseball season before pursuing a career in education. After earning a doctorate degree from the University of Kentucky, Jeffcoat served as the president of Texas Wesleyan University in Fort Worth, Texas, and Milliken University in Decatur, Illinois.

Catcher-outfielder Dan Radison played just 40 games with the Oilers that year in what would also be his final minor league season. He had a long career as a college coach and minor league manager, winning three division titles and the 1992 Eastern League championship with the Albany-Colonie Yankees.

Radison holds the distinction of being the only former Tulsa Oiler still wearing a major league baseball uniform, serving as the special assignment coach of the Houston Astros since 2012.

Tulsa defeated the St. Louis Cardinals, 6-3, in a June 13th exhibition game before 4,578 fans at Oiler Park. Keith Hernandez hit a three-run home run while Marc Hill, Jimmy Dwyer and Bob Heise each had two hits for the Oilers.

This would be the first of two seasons that Oiler baseball games were carried by KBJH-FM (98.5). The station was affiliated with American Christian College, a Tulsa-based private Christian college founded by anti-Communist televangelist Billy James Hargis.

Terry Greene handled the play-by-play and was aided by Oilers publicity director Forrest Cameron and local radio announcer Ray Alloway. Greene served as the lead play-by-play announcer for three years. During his time in Tulsa, Greene also worked as a TV news reporter and for an advertising agency. He later held public office and today leads a home construction organization in Illinois.

Surprisingly, Hernandez did not win the 1973 American Association's Most Valuable Player award. It went to Wichita Aeros first baseman Pete LaCock, who batted .327 with 23 home runs and 91 RBIs.

The son of *Hollywood Squares* TV quiz show host Peter Marshall had trouble hitting left-handed pitchers in the major leagues and is known for being the only baseball player who was on a World Series champion one year and played baseball in Japan the following year. LaCock was a platoon player on the 1980 Kansas City Royals then spent 1981 with Japan's Taiyo Whales.

1975: The Evansville Triplets won their second American Association championship in four years but Tulsa third baseman-outfielder Hector Cruz was the brightest star of minor league baseball.

Cruz batted .306 and led the league with 29 home runs and drove in 116 runs, easily winning the Minor League Player of the Year award presented by *The Sporting News* magazine. The only other Tulsa baseball player to win that award was Lou Novikoff in 1939.

Undrafted as an amateur, Cruz hit 20 or more home runs in three of his previous four minor league seasons and showed enough potential that the parent St. Louis Cardinals traded Ken Reitz, a Tulsa Oiler in 1972, to the San Francisco Giants. But Cruz's star burned out quickly as he batted just .225 over nine seasons with four different major league teams.

In the last of his four seasons with the Oilers, shortstop Mick Kelleher set a record for both Tulsa professional baseball history and American Association history for the best fielding percentage at that position (.978). Kelleher was a long-time assistant coach for the New York Yankees and retired from coaching after the 2014 season.

Outfielder Jerry Mumphrey led the American Association with 44 stolen bases, was third in the league in drawing walks (81) and batted .285. He played for the New York Yankees' 1981 American League champions and in the 1984 All-Star Game as a member of the National League's Houston Astros.

The Oilers waited out a 75-minute rain delay and then unleashed a deluge of base hits in an 11-0 victory over the St. Louis Cardinals in a June 5th exhibition game before 4,801 fans. Tulsa's hit parade was led by three hits apiece from Hector Cruz, Wayne Nordhagen and Doug Howard.

Ron Bryant, a 24-game winner with the 1973 San Francisco Giants, was rocked for nine runs over four innings. It turned out that 1975 would be Bryant's final big-league season.

Oiler baseball games on KBJH-FM (98.5) with Terry Greene on play-by-play with Tom Adams handling color commentary provided a little bit of paradise amidst a turbulent year at American Christian College.

The private school founded by Billy James Hargis, a televangelist equally renowned for his anti-Communism views, would close its doors in 1977 and the radio station was sold after *Time* magazine published an investigative story alleging Hargis had sexual affairs with ACC students. The *Tulsa World* and *Tulsa Tribune* declined to publish the allegations and Hargis was later cleared of any wrongdoing by a criminal investigation.

Evansville won the pennant by defeating the Denver Bears in the playoffs, 4-2, and then routing the International League champion Tidewater Tides, 4-1, in the Junior World Series. Tidewater was the top player development team for the New York Mets and Tulsa-born Tides first baseman Brock Pemberton later played for that team.

Evansville won the Eastern Division with a 77-59 record, followed by the Indianapolis Indians (71-64), Omaha Royals (67-69) and Iowa Oaks (56-79). Denver won the Western Division and had the league's best regular season record (81-55), followed by Tulsa (73-63), the Wichita Aeros (68-68) and Oklahoma City 89ers (50-86).

During the final few weeks of that season, the Oilers and the rest of the American Association got a glimpse of an Evansville pitcher who became a national sensation the following year.

Mark "The Bird" Fidyrich was a 20-year-old right-handed pitcher for Evansville, posting a 4-1 record with a sparkling 1.58 ERA in six starts with four of those being shutouts. Fidyrich had curly blond hair along with a lanky build and walk that resembled "Big Bird" who was a star on the popular children's television show, *Sesame Street*.

In his major league debut with the parent Detroit Tigers, Fidyrich held the Cleveland Indians hitless over the first six innings. More adulation came with a nationally televised victory over the powerful New

York Yankees. All the while, Fidyrich drew attention for his quirky antics during a game. Some of those included talking to the baseball, aiming the ball as if were a dart about to be thrown, smoothing out divots on the pitching mound's dirt and shaking the hand of an infield teammate who made a big play.

Fidyrich won the 1976 American League Rookie of the Year award by leading the league with the lowest ERA (2.34) and also posting 24 complete games and 19 victories. His popularity was such that he became the first athlete to appear on the cover of the legendary music/pop culture magazine, *Rolling Stone*.

But numerous arm and shoulder ailments, caused mostly by being overused during his rookie season, resulted in Fidyrich posting a lackluster 10-10 record with Detroit over the ensuing four years.

1976: The United States of America celebrated its 200th birthday with The Bicentennial. But there would be no celebration by Tulsa's sports fans because this was the year that the Oilers, Triple-A baseball and a successful relationship with the St. Louis Cardinals all became history after the season ended.

Long-standing disputes between team owner A. Ray Smith and the Tulsa Fairgrounds Trust Authority over who should pay for sorely needed repairs to the dilapidated wooden stadium was the last straw for Smith. After the conclusion of the baseball season, Smith moved the franchise to New Orleans to play in the Louisiana Superdome in 1977 as the New Orleans Pelicans.

After a one-year financial nightmare in New Orleans, Smith's franchise would be known as the Springfield (Illlinois) Redbirds and the Louisville (Kentucky) Redbirds. Smith sold his stake in the Louisville operation in 1986 and in 1998, the team moved to its current home in Memphis, Tennessee.

Smith had offered to buy the National League's Cincinnati Reds for $25 million in 1985 but was outbid by the controversial Marge Schott. He later served for seven years on the board of directors of the California Angels.

The relationship between the Tulsa Oilers and the St. Louis Cardinals was, arguably, one of the most successful affiliations in minor league baseball history. The Oilers had winning records in 15 out of their 18 seasons as a Cardinal affiliate. They reached the postseason playoffs in 11 of those 15 seasons and won six league championships: three in the Double-A Texas League, one in the Triple-A Pacific Coast League and two in the Triple-A American Association.

Season attendance exceeded 200,000 three times, something that had never happened in Tulsa's professional baseball history and wouldn't happen again until the Tulsa Drillers did so during the 1990s.

As for regular season action, outfielder Mike Easler won the American Association batting championship with a .352 average and led the league's outfielders in assists (16). One of his highlights was hitting nine home runs in a nine-game span, albeit not in consecutive games. His nickname of "Hit Man" was well deserved as he would post a .293 batting average over 14 years in the majors.

Garry Templeton was a 20-year-old shortstop who batted .321 and stole 25 bases with the Oilers and drew even more raves for his defensive play. He would spend five seasons with the St. Louis Cardinals, leading the National League in triples three times and never batted lower than .288 with the Cardinals.

But Templeton's obscene gesture to St. Louis fans near the end of the 1981 season led to his involvement in one of the biggest personnel moves in Cardinals history. He was traded to the San Diego Padres for another shortstop, Ozzie Smith.

Templeton spent 10 years with the Padres but his hitting ability wasn't what it was during his time with the Cardinals. Smith, on the other hand, made 14 of his 15 All-Star appearances as a Cardinal as well as winning 11 of his 13 Gold Glove awards for fielding excellence. Smith's jersey number (1) was retired by the team and he was a 2002 inductee into the Baseball Hall of Fame.

David Hasbach threw a 7-0 inning no-hitter on June 2nd as the Omaha Royals defeated the Oilers, 4-0.

Despite banging out 15 base hits, the parent St. Louis Cardinals held on for a 5-4 victory in a June 10th exhibition game before 4,828 fans at Oiler Park. The game's highlight came when Lou Brock batted right-handed, the opposite of his normal hitting stance, and lashed a triple and scored shortly afterwards. Cardinal catcher Ted Simmons played in right field and went 2-for-2. Another ex-Oiler, Mike Tyson (no relation to the boxing legend), also went 2-for-2 with a home run.

Oiler radio broadcasts marked an ending and a beginning of their own. The games stayed on 98.5 FM but the call letters changed from KBJH-FM to KCFO-FM. That station carried religious programming and later became one of the pioneer radio stations in the development of the Christian pop music movement.

Terry Greene and Tom Adams returned as two of the three announcers. But that other announcer would have a St. Louis Cardinals connection and become a nationally-known play-by-play announcer nearly 40 years later.

The first steps in Bob Carpenter's broadcasting career began that year with Tulsa Oilers baseball. He has been the TV play-by-play announcer for the Washington Nationals since 2006, spent 10 years on radio and television with his hometown St. Louis Cardinals and served as the play-by-play voice for the Texas Rangers, Minnesota Twins and New York Mets.

Carpenter was inducted into the Oklahoma Association of Broadcasters Hall of Fame in 2017. He was also the 2015 co-recipient of the District of Columbia's Sportscaster of the Year award presented by the National Sportswriters and Sportscasters Association.

He also spent 16 years with ESPN covering baseball, college football and college basketball, World Cup soccer and The Masters golf championship. He also covered U.S. Open Tennis, baseball and collegiate sports for other cable networks. What many people forget is that Carpenter was the original host for ESPN's highly-popular college football preview show *College GameDay*.

The Denver Bears won the American Association championship by defeating the Omaha Royals in the playoffs, 4-2. Denver won the Western Division with the league's best overall record, 86-50. They were followed by the Oklahoma City 89ers (72-63), Tulsa Oilers (65-70) and Wichita Aeros (56-79). Omaha won the Eastern Division with a 78-58 record, followed by the Iowa Oaks (68-68), Indianapolis Indians (62-73) and Evansville Triplets (55-81).

Denver first baseman Roger Freed won the league's Most Valuable Player award by hitting 42 home runs with 102 runs batted in. But Freed never had sustained success in the major leagues and became a pinch-hitting specialist, finishing with a .245 batting average and only 22 home runs over eight major-league seasons.

Another member of that Denver team would become one of major league baseball's premier players during the 1980s. Andre Dawson was a 20-year-old outfielder who hit .356 with 20 home runs in just 74 games with the Bears, resulting in a quick promotion to the parent Montreal Expos and winning the 1977 National League Rookie of the Year Award.

Dawson played in the major leagues for 21 years, primarily with Montreal in 1976-86 and the Chicago Cubs in 1987-92. An eight-time

National League All-Star and eight-time Gold Glove winner, Dawson was the 1987 National League Most Valuable Player with the Cubs, hitting 49 home runs with 137 RBIs that year.

1977: Not counting the Texas League suspending operations from 1943 through 1945 due to World War II, it appeared almost certain that Tulsa would not have professional baseball for the first time since 1931.

But acting upon private requests from Tulsa's county commissioners, Sapulpa-based contractor Bill Rollings and Tulsa-based country music superstar Roy Clark stepped up to the plate in January of that year and delivered a game-winning hit for local baseball fans.

After meetings with Texas Rangers co-owners Eddie Chiles and Brad Corbett and other local leaders, the Rangers' Double-A franchise located in Lafayette, Louisiana was purchased and relocated to Tulsa. The team was known as the Lafayette Drillers but a Name-The-Team contest was held for Tulsans to choose a new nickname. They chose to stay with Drillers to continue the link between the oil industry and Tulsa's heritage.

An April 3rd exhibition game between the Rangers and the Houston Astros was to have been the celebration of a new era in Tulsa's professional baseball history. The old wooden stadium previously known as Texas League Park and Oiler Park was renamed Driller Park.

But this would also be the day that antiquated wooden structure died, several fans were hurt and Tulsa's baseball livelihood was seriously injured.

Early morning showers gave way to a sunny afternoon and the game started on time at 1:00 p.m. with about 5,000 people watching the game. About 20 minutes later, a passing shower sent several hundred fans scurrying for cover beneath an overhang behind the first base dugout and just above the Astros' dressing room.

The additional weight suddenly caused a 15-foot wooden section to collapse with a noise that sounded like a clap of thunder. Eighteen people fell approximately 20 feet onto a concrete walkway.

Astros players and paramedics quickly rushed to the scene to pull debris away and treat the injured fans. The game continued despite the loud sirens from emergency responders rushing to the scene. Fortunately, there were no fatalities. Several injury lawsuits arising from the stadium collapse were settled out of court.

The Rangers won the exhibition game, 11-7, but there was a noticeable sadness among the fans and players throughout the rest of that contest. John Ellis was the Rangers' hitting star going 4-for-5 with a home run and Jim Sundberg drove in three runs. Willie Crawford led Houston with four hits, including a home run.

Safety inspectors quickly ruled that all of Driller Park's remaining wooden structure was unsafe for occupancy and it was bulldozed to the ground within the following week. Only the concrete pad for the box seats, a backstop made of chicken wire and the antiquated light towers behind first and third base remained from the original structure built during the 1930s.

Equally ancient and splinter-ridden wooden bleachers once used for stock car races at the Fairgrounds Speedway were hastily installed to provide a semblance of general admission seating. A so-called press box with room for four slender people was built behind first base. Everyone else was at the mercy of the weather since there was no roof on the makeshift baseball stadium.

Despite the distractions, the Drillers had the Eastern Division's best overall record at 66-62. Out of those 62 losses, 32 were by one run which tied the Texas League record set the year before by, ironically, the Lafayette Drillers.

The regular season attendance total of 96,045 was decent for the circumstances. By comparison, the Lafayette Drillers drew 108,357 fans for the 1975 and 1976 seasons, combined.

Following Tulsa in the Eastern Division's overall standings were the Arkansas Travelers (63-67) and the deadlocked Shreveport Captains and Jackson Mets at 62-68. The Western Division champion El Paso Diablos had the league's best season record at 78-52. They were followed by the Midland Cubs (70-60), San Antonio Missions (61-67) and Amarillo Gold Sox (56-74).

Arkansas won the Eastern Division's second half championship and eliminated Tulsa in their playoff series, 2-0. El Paso advanced to the finals by winning both half seasons in the Western Division. And despite finishing four games under .500 in regular season play, Arkansas claimed its first Texas League championship by defeating El Paso Diablos in the best-of-3 finals, 2-0.

Orlando "Marty" Martinez began a two-year tenure as Tulsa's manager. Martinez never hit a home run over seven major leagues seasons with six different teams and was primarily a shortstop, but he played every position, including pitcher, whenever asked by his manager.

After his time with the Drillers, Martinez spent 10 years as an assistant coach with the American League's Seattle Mariners. He played a key role in the development of future Mariner infield standouts Edgar Martinez, Harold Reynolds, Omar Vizquel and Spike Owen.

In a Fan Appreciation Night promotion, Martinez "stepped aside" for the September 1st game against the Jackson Generals to allow Roy Clark to serve as the team's manager. The Drillers won that game, 4-3.

Outfielder Eddie Miller, designated hitter Billy Sample and pitcher Danny Darwin represented the Drillers on the Texas League's postseason All-Star team.

Miller's 80 stolen bases that season are the most in Tulsa's professional baseball history and ranks fourth in Texas League single-season history. A second-round draft pick of the parent Texas Rangers, Miller batted .294 and was second on the team in base hits (110).

On December 8, 1977, Miller wound up with the Atlanta Braves as part of a four-team trade. Notable players involved in that major move were Bert Blyleven, Al Oliver, Tom Grieve and Jon Matlack. Miller's best major league year was 1981 when he stole 23 bases in just 50 games, finishing 10th in the National League.

Sample's batting average was .348, second-highest in the Texas League and he also led the league in triples with 13. His best big-league season was with the 1983 Texas Rangers, ranking fifth in the American League with 44 stolen bases while batting .274 with 43 extra-base hits. After his playing career ended, Sample began a long career as a radio-TV color commentator on radio and authored several newspaper and magazine articles. He wrote, directed and appeared in a 2013 baseball-themed movie, *Reunion 108*.

Darwin was the ace of the Driller staff, posting a 13-4 record, a 2.51 ERA, six complete games, four shutouts (tied with teammate Paul Mirabella for the league lead) and 129 strikeouts in 154 innings. Nicknamed "The Bonham Bullet" for his Texas hometown and a blink-and-you'll-miss-it fastball, Darwin spent 21 years in the major leagues, playing for eight teams. His 2.21 ERA with the 1990 Houston Astros led the National League.

The Jackson Mets threw two nine-inning no-hitters against the Drillers that year, the first time that a Texas League team was on the short end of two nine-inning gems since it happened to the 1915 Shreveport Gassers. The 1940 Tulsa Oilers were on the losing end of two seven-inning no-hitters.

John Pacella severely taxed Tulsa's patience with an April 15th no-hitter in a 3-0 victory. Larry Prewitt tossed the other no-hitter in an 8-1 win on September 1st.

This was the start of a four-year decline in both radio coverage and interest in Tulsa baseball broadcasts. The good news was for the first time since the 1957-61 seasons, baseball games were back on 50,000-watt powerhouse KRMG-AM (740). The bad news was that the only broadcasts involved weekend home games. Jerry Vaughn, a highly popular mid-day disc jockey and the play-by-play voice of Oral Roberts University basketball, was the lone announcer for those few telecasts.

Midland outfielder Karl Pagel was the Texas League Player of the Year, leading the league with 28 home runs and on-base percentage (.451) and was second in RBIs (104). He hit 20 or more home runs five times and batted over .300 four times during his minor league career and was one of the brightest prospects in the Chicago Cubs' organization during the late 1970s. But Pagel did not achieve major league success in brief tenures with the Cubs and, later, the Cleveland Indians.

One of the most pivotal people in modern baseball came through the Texas League that season, playing 13 games for the Arkansas Travelers and then 75 games for the Midland Cubs.

Scott Boras was a decent-hitting, not-so-great defensive outfielder-turned-infielder who retired after three knee surgeries. He earned a law degree from the University of Pacific and become the best-known and, in some quarters, most despised agent representing baseball players in contract negotiations.

The biggest deal that Boras handled was in 1991, getting the Texas Rangers to sign a contract that paid shortstop Alex Rodriguez $252 million over 10 years. Some of the current baseball superstars that Boras represents in contract negotiations are Stephen Strasburg, Jayson Werth, Matt Holliday, Prince Fielder, Jered Weaver and Bryce Harper.

Many people don't know that the loved (or loathed, depending on one's perception) Boras played a significant behind-the-scenes role in the growth of the Tulsa Drillers in the early days of his baseball-oriented business.

New England businessman Went Hubbard contacted Boras in 1986 about purchasing a minor league baseball team after he rejected an offer to become a minority owner of the Boston Red Sox. Hubbard wanted an opportunity to be a hands-on, fan-oriented owner of a minor league franchise.

Boras found three teams in the eastern United States that were for sale and a fourth team out on the midwestern plains that was not for sale. Hubbard would take long weekends to go to the games and visit with fans in different sections of each stadium.

Hubbard would purchase that fourth team, the Tulsa Drillers, from the Texas Rangers and thus began what has arguably been the most successful three decades (and counting) in Tulsa's baseball history.

And what happened to the team formerly known as the Tulsa Oilers? Their only season as the New Orleans Pelicans went badly. Their 57-79 record was the worst of any team in the American Association. On the bright side, the team drew 217,957 fans to the Louisiana Superdome, an increase of 80,000 over its final season in Tulsa.

But if team owner A. Ray Smith fully realized what New Orleans city officials had waiting for him, he might have thought the hassles with the Tulsa officials weren't really that bad. Smith, who operated the Pelicans from Tulsa that year, received no income from parking fees or concession sales and paid a rental fee of $6,000 per game.

And had the team not moved to New Orleans, infielder Tony LaRussa could have ended his minor league playing career with the Tulsa Oilers. LaRussa batted .188 in 50 games with New Orleans in 1977. He had faced the Oilers during the 1970s as a member of the Iowa Oaks (1969-71, 1976), Wichita Aeros (1973) and Denver Bears (1975).

LaRussa would become one of the most successful managers in major league baseball history and a 2014 inductee into the Baseball Hall of Fame. His 2,728 career victories over 33 seasons is the third-highest total in professional baseball history, trailing only Connie Mack (3,731) and John McGraw (2,763).

LaRussa won three American League pennants and the 1989 World Series with the Oakland Athletics then guided the St. Louis Cardinals to three National League pennants and the 2006 and 2011 World Series championships. Midway through the 2014 season, LaRussa was hired by the Arizona Diamondbacks as their Chief Baseball Officer and has worked to rebuild the National League franchise from top to bottom.

1978: The brilliance of Dave Righetti's 13 games in Tulsa was the brightest spot of an otherwise abysmal season, which ended with a 57-78 record. His 5-5 won-lost record was very deceiving because he posted 127 strikeouts in just 13 games (six of those being complete games) and also had a 3.16 ERA.

In a July 16th game against the Midland Cubs, Righetti set a Texas League record which still stands by striking out 21 batters over nine innings. He had scattered five hits over those nine innings and the game was tied, 2-2, when he left. But Midland prevailed in 10 innings, 4-2.

The 6-foot-4 left-handed pitcher from San Jose (California) City College was the Drillers' lone representative on the Texas League postseason All-Star Team. He was the first player chosen by the Texas Rangers in the 1977 amateur draft and the 10th player chosen overall.

The Rangers traded Righetti to the New York Yankees after the season ended as part of a 10-player trade. He proved to be a Yankee Doodle Dandy and spent 11 of his 16 major league seasons wearing the legendary pinstriped home uniform. Righetti tossed a no-hitter against the Boston Red Sox in Yankee Stadium on the Fourth of July in 1983. The following year, he was converted to a relief pitcher and his 224 career saves ranks second in the Yankees' long and proud history.

Since 2000, Righetti has been the pitching coach for the San Francisco Giants, the longest such streak among current major league pitching coaches.

Tulsa baseball fans stayed away in record numbers from the improvised Driller Park. The regular season attendance of 46,098 was the lowest in Tulsa's professional baseball history in 61 years. On a per-game basis, Tulsa's average home attendance was roughly 700 fans. Surprisingly that year, Shreveport drew fewer fans (38,209) and Amarillo's attendance (53,110) wasn't that much better than Tulsa's.

The Drillers performed decently in the first half of the season with a 35-33 record but the bottom fell out in the second half as they went 22-45.

Tulsa had the Texas League's stolen base leader for the second consecutive season in outfielder Greg Jemison. The first choice by the Texas Rangers and 12th overall selection in the 1976 amateur draft, the Seton Hall University product had 65 stolen bases and also batted .263. Jemison had stolen 82 bases the previous year for Tulsa's Class A sister team, the Asheville Tourists. But he never advanced further than Double-A competition and ended his playing career after the 1980 season.

Utility player Marty Scott was the team's leading hitter with a .318 batting average and ranked sixth in the Texas League in that category.

The Houston Astros held off the Texas Rangers for an 11-9 victory at Driller Park on April 2nd before an estimated 3,600 fans in what would be the last visit to Tulsa by any major league baseball team for four years.

The Astros took an early six-run lead but the Rangers rallied to score four runs in the ninth inning before the game ended. Houston's Dave Bergman was the hitting star with three hits and five RBIs. Al Oliver and John Lowenstein each homered for Texas.

Oilers baseball broadcasts were on their sixth radio frequency in eight years, moving over to KXXO-AM (1300). Once again, game coverage was limited to road games played on a weekend with no coverage of home contests. The only consolation for loyal listeners came when Mack Creager, a Tulsa baseball broadcasting legend, was coaxed out of retirement for a one-year encore.

The El Paso Diablos claimed their third Texas League championship by defeating the Jackson Mets in the playoffs, 3-0. For the second straight year, El Paso won both halves in the Western Division and advanced directly to the finals. Jackson won the second half in the Eastern Division and eliminated the first half champion Arkansas Travelers, 2-1, in their divisional series.

Arkansas had the Eastern Division's best overall record at 77-55. They were followed by Jackson (76-58), the Tulsa Drillers (57-78) and Shreveport Captains (55-81). El Paso's overall Western Division record of 80-55 was tops in the league, as well. They were followed by the San Antonio Dodgers (79-57), Midland Cubs (70-65) and Amarillo Gold Sox (44-89).

El Paso outfielder Bobby Clark was the Texas League Player of the Year, leading the league with 31 home runs and 111 RBIs while batting

.316. He later played five years for the California Angels and two years with the Milwaukee Brewers.

1979: This was, in many ways, one of the worst seasons in Tulsa's professional baseball history. The Drillers finished with an overall record of 58-75 and .436 winning percentage.

They finished in last place in the Texas League's Eastern Division in both halves of the season, going 25-35 in the first half and 33-40 in the second. The season attendance total was 48,844, marking the first time since 1914-15 that a Tulsa professional baseball team failed to draw at least 50,000 fans for consecutive seasons.

For only the third time in Tulsa's professional baseball history, there were no radio broadcasts of home or road games during the regular season. The only other times that happened were the bookend seasons to World War II: 1942 and 1946.

But the worst event was a proposal to build a new baseball park being resoundingly rejected by city voters in June of 1979. A $3.7 million bond issue would have built a multi-purpose stadium at Expo Square, seating 9,249 fans with the Drillers being the primary tenants.

Local laws required a 60 per cent approval for passage of a bond issue but the measure was supported by only 47 percent of those casting votes. Opponents back then echoed complaints that still resound today: voters were fed up with the federal and local government and wanted no new taxes.

Despite the threatening storm clouds, there were some rays of sunshine in terms of player performance.

Manager Jim Schaffer earned a place in Tulsa baseball trivia as the first person to be in uniform for both the Tulsa Oilers and the Tulsa Drillers. Schaffer was a catcher for the 1960 Oilers and his 21 home runs for that team. He became a journeyman catcher in the major leagues during the 1960s, spent eight years as a manager in the

Baltimore Orioles' minor league system and 11 years as a major league assistant coach.

Len Whitehouse had Tulsa's third no-hitter of the 1970s in a 2-0, 7-inning victory over the Shreveport Captains in the second game of a June 22nd doubleheader. Whitehouse had a 0-3 record and was within an eyelash of being demoted to a Class A affiliate when he hurled his gem. Despite going 5-7 that year with a 5.65 ERA, Whitehouse was promoted to the Texas Rangers in 1981 and later spent the 1983-85 seasons with the Minnesota Twins.

Steve Nielsen was one of five pitchers tied for the Texas League lead in shutouts with three. He went 8-7 with a 3.64 ERA that season and had a 33-28 record over five minor league seasons and never reached the majors.

Outfielder Riccardo Patrick Emilio "Rick" Lisi was the only Driller named to the Texas League's postseason All-Star Team. His 22 home runs led the Drillers and ranked second in the Texas League. He also batted .306 and led Tulsa in six offensive categories.

This year also marked the beginning of a left-handed pitcher's three-decade journey towards becoming one of the icons of Tulsa's professional baseball history and a member of the Texas League Baseball Hall of Fame.

Chuck Lamson led the Drillers' pitching staff with an 11-8 record and a 3.29 ERA. His 12 complete games tied him with Shreveport's Bob Tufts for the Texas League lead in that category. And on July 11, 1980, Lamson came within one out of pitching a nine-inning no-hitter in a victory over the San Antonio Dodgers.

Lamson was a 6-foot-5 left-hander who played for Gloucester County (New Jersey) Community College and was the Texas Rangers' 10th-round draft pick in the 1977 amateur draft. But arm injuries forced Lamson to end his pitching career after the 1981 season.

His family liked living in Tulsa so much that he stayed with the Drillers, working first in off-season sales at $500 a month plus a 10 per cent commission and also as a groundskeeper. On a nice day, it wouldn't be unusual to find Lamson painting part of an advertising sign on the outfield fence.

Lamson was promoted to Assistant General Manager in 1983 and spent 12 years in that role. Among his responsibilities were marketing, promotions and game day operations, especially being sure that the hot food was hot and the cold beverages were cold for hungry and thirsty fans.

His hard work was rewarded in September 1995 with a promotion to General Manager of the Tulsa Drillers. Lamson would spend nearly 11 years in that role, overseeing all of the franchise's daily operations and building on a long history of fan-friendly activities. The payoff was the Drillers drawing over 300,000 fans in 10 years, the longest such streak in Tulsa's professional baseball history.

In the fall of 2002, Lamson helped negotiate the Drillers' affiliation with the Colorado Rockies after the Texas Rangers pulled out of a 26-year partnership. Lamson purchased the Driller franchise from owner Went Hubbard in June 2006.

While the team's attendance and on-field performance was going well during those years, Lamson faced a major challenge in trying to replace the aging Drillers Stadium at Expo Square. Tulsa was never in danger of totally losing the baseball team, but there was consideration of a new stadium in the southwestern suburb of Jenks. When plans were aired about a possible stadium in downtown Tulsa, a vocal minority objected to the proposed funding methods.

Lamson worked with then-Tulsa mayor Kathy Taylor and other local business leaders to secure financing for construction of the current ONEOK Field. Additional challenges arose with negotiation deadline having to be extended four times before an agreement in principle was reached in August of 2008.

He sold his shares of the Drillers back to Went Hubbard in December of 2010 and started a sports consulting firm along with being co-founder of a technology firm aimed at streamlining sales presentations. Hubbard's sons, Dale and Jeff, served as the team's co-chairmen during Went Hubbard's eventually terminal illness.

Lamson was a three-time honoree as the Texas League's Executive of the Year and the Drillers were three-time winners of the Texas League's Organization of the Year honor. Under Lamson's guidance, the franchise also earned two national awards which saluted long-term stability and community involvement.

The Arkansas Travelers won their second Texas League championship in three seasons by defeating the San Antonio Dodgers in the playoffs, 3-0. Arkansas defeated the Shreveport Captains, 2-0, to win the Eastern Division while San Antonio downed the Midland Cubs for the Western Division title, 2-1.

Arkansas had the best overall record in the Eastern Division and the entire Texas League at 76-57. They were followed by Shreveport (73-62), the Jackson Mets (70-65) and Tulsa Drillers (58-75). Midland had the Western Division's best overall record at 76-59. They were followed by San Antonio (69-62), the El Paso Diablos (61-75) and Amarillo Gold Sox (54-82).

El Paso outfielder Mark Brouhard was the Texas League Player of the Year, posting a .350 batting average (fourth in the league) while leading the league in home runs (28), RBIs (107), base hits (181), total bases (308) and slugging percentage (.596). Brouhard played for the Milwaukee Brewers from 1980 through 1985 but would hit 25 total home runs during that span.

Chapter Nine

The 1980s

R onald Reagan served two terms as President of the United States and became one of the nation's most beloved leaders. Russian Premier Mikhail Gorbachev called for peaceful international relations and the Berlin Wall, long a symbol of Communist oppression, was torn down.

This was the decade that introduced us to personal computers, Rubik's Cube, the Pac-Man video game, Cabbage Patch Kids dolls, Sally Ride becoming the first American female astronaut, singer Michael Jackson's epic album, *Thriller,* the hit movie *E.T.*, the Vietnam Memorial in Washington, DC, the arrival and swift departure of a new version of Coca-Cola, the first all-news cable network (CNN) and a cable channel devoted to music videos, Music Television (MTV).

Pro basketball reached unprecedented popularity with the emergence of a rivalry between Earvin "Magic" Johnson with the Los Angeles Lakers and the Boston Celtics, led by Larry Bird. The Lakers earned five NBA Finals titles while the Celtics took home three championship trophies. Martina Navratilova became a tennis superstar with six Wimbledon women's singles championships.

A new plague called Acquired Immunity Deficiency Syndrome (AIDS) was discovered. The seven-person crew of the space shuttle *Challenger* died when it exploded shortly after its launching in 1986. International terrorism reared its ugly head when a bomb planted on Pan American World Airways Flight 103 exploded over Lockerbie, Scotland, killing 259 New York-bound passengers along with 11 local residents.

Oil prices plummeted to $10 a barrel and dealt devastating blows around the national in general and in Tulsa, in particular. New construction screeched to a halt, thousands of people lost their jobs and local banks and savings institutions were here today and gone tomorrow. Tulsa was able to rebound in part due to a thriving natural gas industry and the growth of customer call centers and other service-oriented businesses.

This was a decade of extreme highs and lows for the Tulsa Drillers. They reached the Texas League playoffs three times and won league championships in 1982 and 1988. The best news came with the building of a privately-funded stadium on the Tulsa State Fairgrounds. Season attendance began a steady upward climb but the 1986 and 1987 finished among the 10 worst teams in Tulsa's professional baseball history.

Some of the future major league standouts wearing a Driller uniform were outfielders Sammy Sosa, Ruben Sierra and Juan Gonzalez along with pitchers Kevin Brown, Ron Darling and Mitch Williams.

1980: The dawn of a new decade brought new beginnings for the Tulsa Drillers. Merrill Eckstein came to town as the team's new General Manager and through his popular promotions, attendance increased for the first time in five years.

Wayne Terwilliger guided the Drillers to a 75-61 record in his only season as a Tulsa manager. While the Drillers did qualify for the Texas

League playoffs, the 75 victories were the most by a Tulsa professional baseball team in six years.

The best news came when a joint effort by Driller co-owners Bill Rollings and Roy Clark, local government officials and a large donation from a Tulsa oil executive led to the start of construction for a new baseball stadium to the east of the decrepit Driller Park.

Clark cashed in a bargaining chip of his own in helping with the private sector fundraising. He co-hosted of the CBS-TV variety show, *Hee Haw*, and got Tulsa's NBC affiliate, KTEW-TV, to donate 90 minutes of air time for a fund-raising telethon on May 20th. Among the *Hee Haw* stars on the telethon were George "Goober" Lindsey, Gordie Tapp, Gunilla Hutton and comedian-actor and native Tulsan Gailard Sartain.

The station's sports director, Jerry Webber, was another mover and shaker behind the telethon. He was heavily involved in local sports both as a broadcaster and as a volunteer coach of school-age teams. Webber saw the new stadium benefitting not only Driller baseball but also baseball and soccer programs for Tulsa-area youth teams.

The telethon raised $106,000 worth of pledges, which was about one-third of the estimated total needed to build a new stadium.

It was bad enough that year playing at a facility better resembling a high school baseball diamond. Making things worse was a summer in which temperatures topped 100 degrees 54 times, one of the hottest summers in time in Tulsa history.

Four Drillers were named to the Texas League postseason All-Star Team: pitcher Jerry Don Gleaton, shortstop Wayne Tolleson, outfielder Mel Barrow and third baseman-first baseman Phil Klimas was picked as the utility player.

This was the first of four seasons when the Drillers had four players earn Texas League postseason All-Star honors. The others were 2004,

2009 and 2013. That total is surpassed only by seven Tulsa Oilers who were so honored back in 1948.

Gleaton led the Drillers with 13 victories and his 138 strikeouts tied for fourth-highest among Texas League pitchers. He had been a collegiate All-American at the University of Texas, the Southwest Conference's Most Valuable Player and the Rangers' first selection (17th overall) in the 1979 amateur draft. Gleaton played in 12 major league seasons, working primarily as a relief pitcher.

Tolleson's 46 stolen bases were second in the league to his team-mate, first baseman Nick Capra who had 55. He also had minor league career highs of 124 hits, 19 doubles and seven triples. Tolleson spent the biggest part of his major league career with the Texas Rangers and New York Yankees. His best Ranger seasons came in 1983 and 1985 when, respectively, he batted .263 with 33 stolen bases and .313 with 21 stolen bases.

Barrow, playing in the third of his four seasons as a Driller, ranked seventh in the league in batting average (.339), stole 20 bases and led Tulsa in home runs (17). Barrow spent 11 years in the Rangers' minor league organization but never played in the majors.

Klimas led the Drillers in base hits (139), doubles (32) and RBIs (84) and ranked second in batting average (.314) and home runs (14).

Catcher Bobby Johnson was the nephew of Chicago Cubs Hall of Fame first baseman Ernie Banks. But when it came to hitting that year, Johnson was very unlike his uncle as he led the Texas League with 106 strikeouts. Despite a .243 batting average, Johnson was second on the Drillers in RBIs with 70 and had 25 doubles among his 41 extra base hits.

The longest game in Tulsa's professional baseball history was played in Jackson, Mississippi, when the Drillers defeated the Jackson Mets, 11-7, in 23 innings on July 7th.

Tulsa scored once in the eighth inning to tie the score, 6-6, and then each team scored once in the 18th. Tulsa put the game away with four runs in the top of the 23rd inning. Driller relief pitcher Dennis Long got the win by giving up one unearned run over the last six innings with four strikeouts and no walks. The game lasted six hours and 39 minutes and the announced attendance was 1,139 fans.

Three future New York Mets played in that game for Jackson: right fielder Darryl Strawberry, left fielder Billy Beane and third baseman Craig Reynolds. Strawberry had a home run among his three hits and drove in two runs.

Baseball was back on the radio but listeners needed a game program to keep up with the changes. Home games were carried in their entirety on KXXO-AM (1300) but reports on road games were phoned in to KELI-AM (1430).

The only constant was that Rob Evans was involved in those radio broadcasts or reports. That would be Evans' only season in Tulsa as he later became the radio play-by-play announcer for the Springfield (Missouri) Cardinals of the Texas League.

The Arkansas Travelers claimed their third Texas League pennant in four years by sweeping the San Antonio Dodgers in the playoffs, 3-0. Arkansas ousted Jackson in the Eastern Division playoffs, 2-0, while San Antonio defeated Amarillo by the same margin the West playoffs.

The Travelers had the best record in the Eastern Division as well as the entire Texas League (81-55) and won the Eastern Division second half championship. Tulsa was second (75-61) while the Jackson Mets (74-62) won the second half title. The Shreveport Captains had the league's worst record (49-87).

After having the Texas League's worst overall record for three years in a row, the Amarillo Gold Sox rebounded to post the Western Division's best record (77-59) and won the Western Division's second half tile. San Antonio (74-62) won the first half championship. The Midland Cubs went through three managers and finished 64-72 followed by the El Paso Diablos at 50-86.

Jackson pitcher Tim Leary was the Texas League Player of the Year. The second overall selection in the 1979 free agent draft out of UCLA where he set a school record with 16 complete games in his career, Leary posted a 15-8 record, a 2.76 ERA and led the league with six shutouts.

He later won the 1988 National League Comeback Player of the Year award by rebounding from a 3-11 season to post a 17-11 record and also batted .269 to help the Los Angeles Dodgers win the 1988 World Series.

1981: This was a very good year for the Drillers, on and off the field. The team finally moved into a modern baseball stadium. They qualified for the Texas League playoffs by winning the Eastern Division's second-half championship. The regular season attendance total of 155,845 was larger than the three previous seasons combined.

Sutton Stadium opened with seating for 4,843 fans. It was located in the northeastern corner of Expo Square and adjacent to the intersection of East 15th Street and South Yale Avenue.

The seating configuration, modeled somewhat after the one used at the Jackson Mets' stadium, consisted of three sections of grandstands connected by a lower level walkway. All of the seats looked down on the playing surface with dugouts built into the dirt beneath the grandstands. Players walked up long flights of stairs to reach their clubhouses. Pitching bullpens were far down the foul lines, near the outfield fences and hidden by large grassy berms.

The stadium had an artificial playing surface except for dirt sliding pits around each of the three bases and the batting circle around home plate. The playing dimensions were 335 feet down the left field foul line, a cozy 349 feet to the left center power alley, 390 feet to straightaway center field, 368 feet to right field and 340 feet down the right field line.

With the wind blowing most often from the south or southwest, fly balls hit to left field or left center frequently got a boost and became home runs. A screen was not in place behind the left field fence during Sutton Stadium's early years. Many times during night games, unsuspecting motorists driving east or west along 15th Street and not listening to a broadcast would be surprised by a hit ball that either bounced off their car's roof or hood or broke a window.

The facility was named in honor of Tulsa oilman Robert B. Sutton, who had anonymously donated $950,000 to bolster the efforts of Driller co-owners Bill Rollings and Roy Clark in general and the 1980 fund-raising telethon in particular. The Tulsa County Commission, after discussing the matter with Sutton, voted to name the new baseball park in his honor.

Sutton was born in El Dorado, Kansas but spent his childhood in the southwestern Tulsa suburb of Sapulpa. He was once ranked by *Forbes* magazine among the world's 400 wealthiest people with most of his earnings coming through oil and gas transactions connected with the oil embargo in the early part of the 1970s.

That same magazine, in a 1986 story, listed Sutton as American's second "poorest" person with $423.1 million worth of debts. Part of that enormous debt was related to legal troubles connected with business transactions.

Major league baseball was on strike for most of the 1981 season but the professional debut of pitcher Ron Darling. The Yale University standout was the top draft choice of the parent Texas Rangers and the ninth pick overall in the 1981 amateur draft.

Darling was a key figure in the Drillers winning the Eastern Division's second half pennant. He spent most of his 13-year major league career with the New York Mets then became a color commentator for the TV networks of the Washington Nationals and the Mets.

Walt Terrell shared the league lead in victories (15) with two Shreveport pitchers: Mark Dempsey and future San Francisco Giants standout Dave Dravecky. A 33rd-round draftee of the Texas Rangers in 1980 out of Morehead (Kentucky) State University, Terrill spent seven of his 11 major league seasons with the Detroit Tigers, winning 15 games in 1985 and 1986 and 17 games in 1987.

Tom Burgess began his two-year tenure as the Drillers' manager. Burgess was no stranger to the city, having served as an assistant coach to manager Warren Spahn on the 1968 Tulsa Oilers' Pacific Coast League championship squad.

A native of London, Ontario, Canada, Burgess was a successful minor league manager, leading four teams to league championships. He also served as an assistant coach for the Canadian National Baseball Team and is a member of the Canadian Baseball Hall of Fame.

Tulsa hosted the Texas League All-Star Game for the second time in its baseball history with the Texas League All-Stars needing a four-run 10th inning to pull out a 9-5 victory over the Drillers before 4,202 fans on July 22nd.

Third baseman Marty Scott played all nine positions in the exhibition contest, finishing with three RBIs and pitching a hitless, shutout inning when he was on the mound. Scott was the only Driller named to the Texas League's 1981 postseason All-Star Team, batting .270 with 38 RBIs.

San Antonio outfielder Dale Holman had three base hits (two singles and a home run) and was the game's Most Valuable Player. Midland outfielder Mel Hall, who later played for the Chicago Cubs, went 1-for-3 and scored three runs. Future Texas Rangers first base-man Pete O'Brien homered for the Drillers, Phil Klimas had three hits and George Wright added two hits.

Driller radio broadcasts returned to 1430 AM, the current home frequency for Drillers games and which carried Tulsa Oilers baseball in 1936-42. Back in the 1960s, the call letters were KELi and it was one of Tulsa's top rock-and-roll stations for two decades. As promotional gimmicks, nearly all of its disc jockeys were given last names of Kelly, a sound-alike for the call letters, and the lower-case letter I was also part of the call letters.

Hal O'Halloran and Dave Ward were the announcers for the 1980 and 1981 seasons. O'Halloran was a radio announcer for the University of Oklahoma Sooner football games in 1954-56 when they was carried on Oklahoma City's WKY-AM Radio. He also worked as sports director at the ABC-TV affiliate in Tulsa and hosted one of Tulsa's earliest sports-talk radio shows.

The Drillers had the best overall record in the ultra-tight Eastern Division at 68-65. After going 32-35 in the first half of the season, they earned a playoff berth by winning the East's second-half title with a 36-30 record. They were followed in the overall standings by Jackson (68-66), the Shreveport Captains (68-67) and Arkansas Travelers (52-80).

San Antonio had the best overall record in Western Division as well as the entire league at 76-57 with Amarillo close behind at 77-59. San Antonio's team batting average was a sizzling .297. They were followed by the El Paso Diablos (65-69) and Midland Cubs (62-73).

The Jackson Mets won their first Texas League championship by sweeping the San Antonio Dodgers in the playoffs, 3-0. Jackson defeated Tulsa to win the Eastern Division, 2-1 while San Antonio beat Amarillo by the same margin to win the Western Division.

Davey Johnson was Jackson's manager and later became the skipper of the parent New York Mets, leading them to the 1986 World Series championship. Johnson later led the Cincinnati Reds, Baltimore Orioles and Washington Nationals to division championships.

A pair of future Los Angeles Dodger standouts played for San Antonio that year. Second baseman Steve Sax ranked second in batting average (.346) and third in base hits (168), easily earning Texas League Player of the Year honors. Sax won the 1982 National League Rookie of the Year award and was a five-time All-Star Game selection.

Reliever Orel Hershiser's 15 saves led the Texas League but he was converted to a starter in the big leagues, where he was a three-time All-Star and the 1988 National League Cy Young Award winner as the league's best pitcher.

Shreveport's Alan Fowlkes was the Texas League Pitcher of the Year, leading the league with 13 complete games, 152 strikeouts and 203 innings pitched en route to a 14-10 record and 2.79 ERA. Despite going 4-2 with the parent San Francisco Giants the following year, control problems doomed his major league career as he gave up 12 home runs in just 85 innings.

A future Hall of Famer blazed a bright trail during his short time in the Texas League. Tony Gwynn batted .462 and drove in 19 runs in just 23 games as the right fielder of the Amarillo Gold Sox. He was promoted to the parent San Diego Padres the following year to begin a 20-year career as one of baseball's best offensive players.

Gwynn posted an amazing .338 batting average during his big-league career with his worst full season batting average being .309 in 1990. He won eight National League batting champions, five Gold Gloves for his defensive skills and was inducted into the Baseball Hall of Fame in 2007. After his playing career ended, Gwynn served as the baseball coach at his alma mater, San Diego State University, where he mentored current Washington Nationals pitching ace Steven Strasburg.

A graduate of Oklahoma City's Millwood High School, outfielder Joe Carter made his professional debut with the Midland Cubs. Carter joined Midland after being named as *The Sporting News* Collegiate Player of the Year after a stellar career at Wichita State University.

Carter was a five-time American League All-Star and earned baseball immortality in the 1993 World Series with the Toronto Blue Jays. He lashed a three-run, walk-off home run against Philadelphia Phillies pitcher (and former Tulsa Driller) Mitch Williams in one of the most dramatic finishes in World Series history.

1982: The Tulsa Drillers won their first Texas League championship by sweeping the El Paso Diablos in the playoffs, 3-0. Tulsa defeated the Jackson Mets to win the Eastern Division, 2-1, while El Paso blanked the Midland Cubs, 2-0, to win the Western Division.

After finishing dead last in the Eastern Division's first half standings (24-43), the Drillers struck a gusher in the second half and went 46-23. The parent Texas Rangers had a helping hand in that second half surge by promoting a large number of talented young players to Tulsa.

All three of the Drillers' Texas League pennant-winning teams (1982, 1988 and 1998) had a common denominator of winning the Eastern Division's second half championship.

Tulsa had the best overall record in the Eastern Division at 70-66 with Jackson close behind at 68-65. They were followed by the Arkansas Travelers (68-68) and Shreveport Captains (62-73). El Paso had the best overall record in Western Division as well as the entire league at 76-60, followed by the Midland Cubs (67-66), San Antonio Dodgers (68-68) and Amarillo Gold Sox (61-74).

Surprisingly, Tulsa's regular season attendance of 128,668 was roughly 27,000 fans lower than the previous year's total.

Outfielder Tommy "Doublemint" Dunbar and pitcher Brad Mengwasser were the Driller representatives on the Texas League's postseason All-Star Team.

Dunbar led the Texas League with 44 doubles and also led the Drillers in seven offensive categories, highlighted by a .323 batting average, 93 runs scored, 16 home runs and 85 RBIs. Dunbar spent parts of three seasons with the Texas Rangers during the 1980s before working for the Cincinnati Reds as a minor league manager and scout.

Mengwasser, who attended Southern Methodist University, was one of three pitchers sharing the Texas League lead in victories with 13. His versatility was shown by having two complete game shutouts along with three saves that year.

Reliever Tom Henke, who led Texas League pitchers in games played (52), had a 2.67 ERA and led the Drillers with 14 saves along with 100 strikeouts in nearly 88 innings.

Nicknamed "The Terminator" for his power-pitching game, Henke never found success within the Texas Rangers system but blossomed after being acquired by the Toronto Blue Jays. Henke played eight of his 14 major league seasons in Toronto, leading the American League in 1987 in saves (34) and games finished (62) as well as being a two-time All-Star selection.

Mike Mason, who played collegiately at Oral Roberts University, led the Drillers in strikeouts (111) and posted a 10-9 record with a 3.89 ERA. Mason spent most of his eight-year major league career with the Texas Rangers and later served as a minor league pitching coach for the Kansas City Royals, Philadelphia Phillies and Chicago Cubs.

Tim Henry threw a no-hitter on August 8th in a 1-0, seven-inning home victory over the Arkansas Travelers. A left-handed pitcher who played collegiately at Texas Wesleyan University, Henry split time between being a starting pitcher and relief pitching roles. Henry went

5-5 that season with a 4.27 ERA but had a 0-4 record with Tulsa the following year and was out of baseball four years later due to an arm injury.

Tulsa hosted the Texas League All-Star Game for the second straight year and the third time in the city's professional baseball history. The Texas League All-Stars faced the Oklahoma City 89ers (the Philadelphia Phillies' Triple-A affiliate back then) and came away with a 10-4 victory before 4,821 fans on July 21st.

Midland's Joe Carter was the offensive standout, finishing with a home run among his three base hits, three runs and two RBIs. Future three-time major league All-Star Julio Franco played for that Oklahoma City team, which would have the American Association's worst record that season (43-91).

The Drillers also prevailed in one of the longest games ever played by a Tulsa professional baseball team. Only July 6th at Smith-Wills Stadium in Jackson, Mississippi, the Drillers needed 23 innings and six hours and 39 minutes to pull out an 11-7 victory over the Jackson Mets. The announced attendance was 1,105 but newspaper estimates had about 200 fans still in the ballpark when the game finally ended.

The parent Texas Rangers visited Sutton Stadium for an August 12th exhibition game and defeated the Drillers, 8-4, before 6,322 fans. It was the largest crowd to see an exhibition baseball game in Tulsa since the 1968 game between the St. Louis Cardinals and Tulsa Oilers drew 7,011 fans to Oiler Park.

Former Driller pitcher Steve Comer tossed a two-hit shutout over five innings for the win. Cliff Johnson and Mike Richardt had three hits apiece for the Rangers. The Drillers got two home runs from Mike Rubel and one round-tripper from Dan Murphy.

Driller games were broadcast on KELI-AM (1430) but this would be a year of transition in that a single person handled all of the radio announcing duties; a format that is still used today.

Jim Roberts began his seven-year tenure as the radio voice of the Drillers and the team's winning Texas League championship in 1982 and 1988 were the bookends of his Tulsa tenure. A veteran freelance announcer, he previously worked for radio stations in Topeka, Kansas and Quincy, Illinois. He also did play-by-play for ESPN, Tulsa Cable Television, University of Kansas football and Oral Roberts University basketball.

Jackson outfielder Darryl Strawberry was the Texas League Player of the Year. The 6-foot-6 left-handed slugger led the league in home runs (34), slugging percentage (.602), walks (100) and finished second in stolen bases (45).

Strawberry played 17 years in the majors and had 10 seasons of 20-plus home runs and three seasons of 100-plus RBIs. He was an eight-time All-Star selection and played on four World Series champions: the 1986 New York Mets and the 1996, 1998 and 1999 New York Yankees.

But Strawberry's big-league baseball career was tarnished by numerous episodes of legal troubles and substance abuse as well as battling colon cancer. He later became a Christian and today serves as an ordained minister as well as working with autism-related charities.

Jackson's Jeff Bittiger, was the Texas League Pitcher of the Year, leading the league with 190 strikeouts and had a 12-5 record and a 2.96 ERA. Making that achievement more special was that Bittiger played third base for most of his youth baseball career.

El Paso slugger Randy Ready led the league in five different offensive categories, highlighted by a .375 batting average. He returned to Texas League as a manager 25 years later and led the San Antonio

Missions to the league championship. He was inducted into the Texas League Baseball Hall of Fame in 2009.

Pam Postema aspired to become the first female umpire in Major League Baseball and her two-year journey through the Texas League ended with a promotion to the Triple-A Pacific Coast League. She spent seven years in the PCL and got to umpire in the 1988 Hall of Fame exhibition game between the New York Yankees and Atlanta Braves.

Many historians felt that Postema's big-league dreams ended shortly after the 1989 death of Baseball Commissioner Bart Giamatti, who was a strong supporter of her efforts. After 13 years of umpiring minor league baseball games, Postema filed a sex discrimination lawsuit against Major League Baseball in 1991. An out-of-court settlement was reached between the two parties and Postema later pursued careers not affiliated with athletics.

1983: There would be three significant developments that year impacting the Tulsa Drillers.

Tulsa baseball fans were immune from the economic devastation caused by the Oil Bust, which lasted from 1982 through 1984. Numerous local energy-related companies either went out of business or relocated to larger cities such as Houston, Texas. A ripple effect was a season attendance of 92,347, a dramatic drop of nearly 63,000 in just the third year of playing in the new Sutton Stadium.

The Tulsa County Commission, which owned Expo Square and the land the ballpark was located on, change the stadium's name to Tulsa County Stadium. The catalyst for the change was the 1982 conviction of Tulsa oilman Robert B. Sutton on two counts of felony business fraud. Sutton, however, was acquitted of 15 other similar charges.

Franchise co-owners Bill Rollings and Roy Clark sold the Drillers back to the parent Texas Rangers. In addition to the impact of the Oil Bust, Sutton's $900,000 donation a few years earlier turned out to be $750,000 short of being fulfilled. Rollings, along with county officials, worked with other private resources to make up for that six-figure shortfall.

The Drillers weren't nearly as talented as they had been in recent years and finished with a 63-73 overall record, going 30-37 in the Eastern Division's first half season and 33-36 in the second half.

Marty Scott, who played in Tulsa for parts of three previous seasons, returned as the Drillers' manager. But Tulsa's overall record matched Midland for the league's worst mark that season and Scott moved on. He later spent nine of his 13 minor league managerial seasons in independent baseball and led the Saint Paul Saints to Northern League championships in 1995 and 1996.

First baseman Kevin Buckley and infielder Steve Buechele provided the only bright spots for the season as the Drillers' representatives on the Texas League's postseason All-Star team.

Buckley hit 32 home runs, the most by a Tulsa baseball player in a post-World War II season since Jim Beauchamp hit 31 homers in 1963 and second-highest in the Texas League that year. It was also the most home runs in Tulsa's professional baseball history since outfielder Joe Munson hit 32 homers back in 1927.

Drama developed when Buckley went nearly a month without hitting a home run. He managed to tie and break Beauchamp's record with home runs in his final two at-bats of the season. Buckley played for the University of Maine team that reached the 1981 College World Series, spent seven years in the minor leagues and played briefly with the 1984 Texas Rangers.

Buechele's award was based on equal parts of offense and defense. He batted .277 with 14 home runs and 62 RBIs that year but drew raves for his slick fielding and rifle-accurate throwing arm. When Buechele played college baseball at Stanford University, his roommate was quarterback John Elway, who became a superstar with the NFL's Denver Broncos and was a 2004 inductee into the Pro Football Hall of Fame.

Buechele spent most of 11-year big-league career with the Texas Rangers. His best major league season was 1991 when he set a major league record for best fielding percentage by a third baseman (.991), making just three errors all year out of 329 fielding chances. He took Ranger minor league affiliates to postseason play in four out of six seasons then was promoted to the major league staff in 2015 to serve as a bench coach.

Mitch Zwolensky was the Texas League leader in complete games (10) while posting a 12-10 record and a 3.33 ERA for the Drillers. He later served as a pitching coach and manager in independent league baseball as well as mentoring former Milwaukee Brewers pitcher Cal Eldred.

Bobby Clark led the Texas League in shutouts with three and had the best of his six minor league seasons. A left-handed pitcher from Southern Illinois University, Clark posted a 12-3 record and a 3.60 ERA along with five complete games.

Driller radio broadcasts moved back to AM 1300 but the station's call letters were KBBJ and descriptive of its musical programming of big bands and jazz.

Beaumont, which last played in the Texas League in 1955 and won league titles back in 1932 and 1938, celebrated its return with a three-game sweep of the Jackson Mets in the championship series.

Beaumont won its divisional series with the El Paso Diablos, 2-1, and Jackson swept its division series with the Arkansas Travelers, 2-0.

What was unusual about the championship series is that the Golden Gators had a .500 record (68-68) during regular season play and Jackson wasn't much better, going 69-67. The Shreveport Captains had the best overall record in the Eastern Division at 72-64. Jackson and the Arkansas Travelers tied for second (69-67) with Tulsa's 63-73 record tied with the Midland Cubs for the league's worst overall mark.

El Paso had the best overall record in Western Division as well as the entire league at 74-62, followed by Beaumont (68-68), the San Antonio Dodgers (66-70) and Midland (63-73). El Paso manager Tony Muser served as manager of the American League's Kansas City Royals in 1997 through 2002 but had losing records in every one of those seasons.

Beaumont's Mark Gillaspie was the Texas League Player of the Year, leading the league in runs batted in (122) and walks (99) while ranking among the league's top five players in three other offensive categories. An outfielder at Mississippi State University, Gillaspie was named to the All-Tournament Team of the 1981 College World Series, but never advanced further than Triple-A over eight minor league seasons.

Two future major leaguers were standouts for Beaumont. First baseman John Kruk had a .341 batting average, the best of his minor league career and also third-highest in the Texas League that season. He also ranked second in the league in doubles (41), tied for second in base hits (170) and led the league in sacrifice flies (13). Kruk was a three-time All-Star in the early 1990s with the Philadelphia Phillies, is a survivor of testicular cancer and works as a baseball analyst for ESPN.

The Golden Gators' shortstop was 19-year-old Oswaldo Jose (Barrios) "Ozzie" Guillen. He was the 1985 American League Rookie of the Year with the Chicago White Sox, where he spent 13 of his 17 major league seasons. Guillen was that team's manager when they won the 2005 World Series. But his brash comments and frequent run-ins with team ownership led to his firing by the White Sox and, later, by the Miami Marlins.

San Antonio pitcher Sid Fernandez became the first man to win the Texas League's pitching Triple Crown and was the Texas League Pitcher of the Year. The left-handed hurler led the league with a 13-4 record, had a 2.82 ERA and 209 strikeouts, the third consecutive season in which he struck out 200 or more batters. He was traded to the New York Mets after the 1983 season and went 16-6 for their 1986 World Series championship team and was also a two-time National League All-Star honoree.

1984: This was the first of 12 years in which Joe Preseren served as general manager of the Tulsa Drillers. Regular season attendance totals increased in 11 of those 12 years, skyrocketing from 124,160 in his rookie season to a total of 344,764 in 1994. The foundation for Preseren's success was family-oriented promotions and keeping his eyes and ears open for what the local baseball fans were saying and thinking.

That was no small feat considering the double whammy of lackluster talent provided more often than not by the parent Texas Rangers and the lingering effects of an economic downturn in Tulsa.

Two other things would be new about the 1984 season. The first was seating capacity at Tulsa County Stadium increasing to 7,500 when bleacher seats were added down the left field line before the start of the season.

Juan "Orlando" Gomez began a two-year tenure as the Drillers' manager. Gomez played 13 years of minor league baseball, mostly in the Oakland Athletics' organization and never reached the major leagues. During the early 1980s when Gomez was a scout for the

Texas Rangers, he convinced future All-Star Ruben Sierra to join the organization.

Gomez posted a 122-149 record with the Drillers and later worked in the player development programs of the Seattle Mariners and Baltimore Orioles.

Steve Kordish threw a no-hitter on May 29th in a 6-0, seven-inning victory over Midland and allowed just one batter to reach base. Kordish was 9-9 that year with the Drillers, ranking second on the team in victories. He was 2-2 in seven games with Tulsa the following year but arm injuries kept him from reaching the major leagues.

Second baseman Greg Tabor was the Drillers' lone representative on the Texas League's postseason All-Star Team. He had a solid season, leading the Drillers in batting average (.299), base hits (138) and doubles (27) and was tied for second in stolen bases (22). Tabor was the Texas Rangers' first selection (10th overall) in the 1981 amateur draft but he had just one base hit in nine pinch-hit appearances with Texas in 1987 and was out of baseball in 1989.

Bob Brower stole 54 bases that year, the most in his eight-year minor league career and became the fourth Driller in eight years to steal 50 or more bases in a season. A former running back on Duke University's football team, Brower played for the Texas Rangers in 1986-88 and with the 1989 New York Yankees.

During Brower's big-league career, Scott Boras was the agent handling his contract negotiations. After Brower's playing career ended, he joined Boras' firm and became a high-ranking executive.

Bob Sebra was Tulsa's best pitcher, posting a 10-5 record and a 3.41 ERA. He would spend six years in the major leagues with five different teams but the former baseball star from the University of Nebraska posted a bigger victory after his baseball career ended.

Sebra never drank alcohol but he contracted Hepatitis C, his liver failed and he would spend several weeks in a coma until receiving a liver transplant. He said that he thinks the disease was contracted by sharing shaving razors with former teammates and taking anti-inflammatory medications. Sebra has since recovered and lives with his family in Ormond Beach, Florida.

Jim Roberts returned as the announcer for Driller radio broadcasts but they moved to KMYZ-FM (104.5), which was transitioning to a classic rock musical format. It was the only season that Drillers baseball was carried by that station.

The Jackson Mets won their second Texas League title during the 1980s by beating the Beaumont Golden Gators, 4-2, in a rematch of the 1983 Texas League championship series. Both teams won their first and second half season titles to advance directly to the championship series.

Jackson's 83-53 record made them the only Eastern Division team to have a winning record that year. Tulsa was a distant second at 62-73, followed by the Arkansas Travelers (62-74) and Shreveport Captains (59-77). Beaumont won the Western Division with a league-best 89-47 record, the most victories by a Texas League team since the Amarillo Gold Sox won 90 in 1961.

Bobby Tolan, an outfielder on the 1964 and 1966 Tulsa Oilers, was the Golden Gators' manager that year. The El Paso Diablos were second at 72-63, followed by the San Antonio Dodgers (64-72) and Midland Cubs (52-84).

Among the Jackson players who later achieved big-league success were outfielder Lenny Dykstra and pitcher Calvin Schiraldi. Dykstra's 53 stolen bases were third-best in the league and he would be a three-time National League All-Star selection. He fell upon hard times after retiring from baseball and was convicted in 2012 of three felony charges related to his filing for bankruptcy.

Schiraldi was the Texas League co-leader in victories (14) and finished second in strikeouts (135), easily winning Texas League Pitcher of the Year honors. The previous year, he capped a stellar career with the University of Texas Longhorns by being named the Most Outstanding Player of the 1983 College World Series. One of his Longhorn teammates was Roger Clemens and many scouts back then considered Schiraldi to be superior in talent to Clemens.

But Schiraldi only had a 32-39 record over eight major league seasons and he retired at the age of 29. He later coached a high school baseball coach and was also inducted into the University of Texas Athletic Hall of Fame.

Outfielder Billy Beane batted .281 and tied for third in the Texas League in doubles (29) and was also tied for fourth in home runs (20) but batted just .219 over six major league seasons. He was touted by New York Mets scouts as a future superstar and was also offered a scholarship by Stanford University to be a backup for quarterback John Elway.

Beane joined the Oakland Athletics' business management team after his retirement and learned an important lesson from general manager Sandy Alderson. There was great value in using sabermetrics (statistics) to build a talented team with a very restrictive budget. The key to success was finding players that had statistical value but were overlooked or released by other teams.

He became Oakland's general manager in 1997 and by using sabermetrics, the A's reached the playoffs several times in the 2000s. His life and baseball knowledge would be the subject of *Moneyball*, a 2003 book by Michael Lewis which became a 2011 movie that earned a Best Actor Oscar nomination for Brad Pitt's portrayal of Beane.

Beaumont first baseman-outfielder Jim Steels was the Texas League Player of the Year, leading the league in stolen bases (35) and finishing third in batting average (.340). Steels didn't do so well in the major leagues but he became a star in the Mexican League. He was that circuit's first player to hit at least 30 home runs and steal at least 30 bases in the same season and batted .336 over five Mexican League seasons.

Shawon Dunston batted .329 in 73 games as the Midland Cubs' shortstop. Dunston played 12 years with the Cubs, was a National League All-Star in 1988 and 1990 and played a key role on the Cubs' 1989 National League Eastern Division championship team.

El Paso outfielder Dale Sveum led the Texas League with 172 hits, 41 doubles and was second in batting average (.329). He spent 12 years in the major leagues and played for five managers who, at some point during their careers, would be named Manager of the Year: Tony LaRussa, Joe Torre, Lou Piniella, Jim Leyland and Gene Lamont. Sveum served as the manager of the 2008 Milwaukee Brewers and the 2012-13 Chicago Cubs.

1985: Outfielder Ruben Sierra was the lone bright spot for the Drillers that year, showcasing the raw ability that resulted in his being chosen four times to play for the American League All-Star team. Sierra led the Drillers and ranked among the Texas League's top 10 hitters in runs batted in (74), runs scored (63), hits (138), doubles (34), triples (8) and stolen bases (22).

Born in Rio Piedras, Puerto Rico, Sierra spent 10 of his 20 major-league seasons with the Texas Rangers, was a four-time American League All-Star selection and also drove in 100 or more runs four times during his big-league career. He was runner-up for the 1989 American League Most Valuable Player award, leading the league with 119 RBIs and 14 triples.

Sierra won the 2001 American League Comeback Player of the Year Award by hitting 23 home runs and batting .291 with the Rangers, noteworthy considering that Sierra missed the entire 1999 season due to personal issues.

Left-hander Mitch Williams had a non-descript season as a Driller starting pitcher, posting a 2-2 record with a 4.64 ERA in six starts. Over 33 innings, he posted more walks (48) than strikeouts (37). But after moving up to the Texas Rangers in 1986, he was converted into a relief pitcher.

Despite a wildness that frequently negated his blazing fastball and sharp-breaking curve ball, he became the bullpen ace of the Chicago Cubs and Philadelphia Phillies. That erratic pitching style earned him the nickname of "Wild Thing" after a similar pitcher played by Charlie Sheen in the 1989 comedy movie, *Major League*.

Williams ranked among the National League's top 10 relief pitchers in saves each season from 1989 through 1993. He played in the 1989 National League All-Star Game as a Cubs representative then posted a career-high 43 saves with the Phillies in 1993.

The Drillers defeated the parent Texas Rangers, 4-3, in an April 15th exhibition game at Tulsa County Stadium. It was the first visit by the Rangers to Tulsa in three years and three more years would pass before it happened again. Ruben Sierra was one of four Drillers to get two hits during the contest. Alan Bannister and former Driller George Wright had two hits each for the Rangers.

Jim Roberts was behind the mike once again as the radio voice of the Tulsa Drillers but the games returned to KELI-AM (1430).

The Jackson Mets won their third and final Texas League title of the 1980s by sweeping the El Paso Diablos in the championship series, 4-0. Jackson swept the Arkansas Travelers in the Eastern Division series, 2-0, while El Paso advanced directly to the finals by winning the Western Division's first and second half titles.

Jackson's 73-63 record was barely better than the Shreveport Captains' 72-64 mark. The Arkansas Travelers won the Eastern Division's first half title but finished with a 64-70 overall record followed by the Tulsa Drillers (60-76). El Paso had the best overall record in Western Division as well as the entire league for the third time in four years, finishing 86-50, followed by the Beaumont Golden Gators (69-67), San Antonio Dodgers (59-75) and Midland Angels (59-77).

Diablos pitcher Juan Nieves was the Texas League Pitcher of the Year, posting an 8-2 record, a 3.52 ERA, two shutouts in five complete games and 91 strikeouts in 120 innings. Nieves was a key part of the parent Milwaukee Brewers' pitching rotation from 1986 through 1988 and threw a no-hitter in 1987 against the Baltimore Orioles. That made him, at age 22, the second youngest pitcher in major league history to throw a no-hitter. Arm injuries shortened his career and he later worked as a pitching coach.

El Paso third baseman-outfielder Billy Jo Robidoux was the Texas League Player of the Year, leading the league in batting average (.342), RBIs (132), runs scored (111), base hits (176), extra base hits (72) and also hit 23 home runs. He was once one of the most promising prospects in the Milwaukee Brewers' farm system, but hit just five home runs over six major league seasons.

Diablos left-handed pitcher Dan Plesac ranked second in the league in victories (12) and third in strikeouts (128). He was called up to the Milwaukee Brewers the following year and converted to a relief pitcher. As the Brewers' bullpen ace, Plesac made 124 saves in his first five seasons and was a three-time American League All-Star selection (1987-89).

Future major league manager Jim Riggleman was in the first of his four seasons as Arkansas' manager. He later served as a major-league manager with the San Diego Padres, Chicago Cubs, Seattle Mariners and Washington Nationals.

1986: This Driller team set new "standards" in Tulsa's professional baseball history. First was the worst winning percentage (.366 based on a 49-85 record). Those 85 losses were the most by any Driller squad and the fifth-highest total by any Tulsa professional baseball team. Their 28-40 record in home games was the worst in Tulsa's professional baseball history and they also failed to score in 18 games.

Nevertheless, the season attendance total of 162,529 was the best by any Tulsa professional baseball team since 1972.

Bill Stearns began his two-year tenure as the Drillers' manager. A former catcher in the New York Yankees' player development system, Stearns ended up with one of the worst managerial records in Tulsa's professional baseball history: a 101-169 record and a .374 winning percentage.

Second baseman Jerry Browne was among the Texas League's best offensive performers. He led the league with 125 singles and ranked second in stolen bases (39) and triples (7). After the 1988 season, Browne was one of three Texas Rangers players traded to the Cleveland Indians for second baseman Julio Franco.

Kirk Killingsworth was the lone bright spot on an otherwise woeful pitching staff, posting a 10-5 record and a 3.77 ERA as a starting pitcher. The former University of Texas standout had been the bullpen ace (9-0 record, 0.80 ERA) on the 1982 Texas Longhorns pitching staff that featured Roger Clemens and Calvin Schiraldi among its starting pitchers and reached the College World Series.

Jim Roberts handed the play-by-play for Driller games on radio but they returned to their flagship station of the 1983 season, KBBJ-AM (1300).

El Paso claimed the fourth of its five Texas League pennants as the Diablos swept the Jackson Mets in the championship series, 4-0. El Paso won the first and second halves of the Western Division while Jackson defeated the Shreveport Captains in the Eastern Division series, 2-1.

The Diablos had the best regular season record at 85-50 en route to winning the Western Division, followed by the San Antonio Dodgers (64-71), Midland Angels (62-71) and Beaumont Golden Gators (60-76). Shreveport had the Eastern Division's best overall record at 80-56, followed by Jackson (72-63), the Arkansas Travelers (67-47) and the Tulsa Drillers (49-85).

Shreveport relief pitcher George Ferran became one of only two men to win the Texas League's pitching Triple Crown (leading the league in victories, lowest earned run average and strikeouts) and easily won Texas League Pitcher of the Year honors. He won 16 games with a 2.29 ERA and 147 strikeouts.

Ferran went 20-2 during two years in Shreveport and was inducted in 2008 into the Texas League Baseball Hall of Fame. But he wasn't as fortunate in three other minor league seasons, posting a combined 17-25 record and never played in the major leagues.

El Paso had the Texas League Player of the Year for the fifth time in 11 years. Infielder Steve Stanicek finished among the Texas League's top five players in seven offensive categories, highlighted by a .343 batting average with 25 home runs and 93 RBIs. He also hit 25 home runs the following season in Triple-A ball but managed just three base hits in 16 major league at-bats.

One of El Paso's best players that year played high school baseball for Tulsa's Bishop Kelley Comets. Catcher Charlie O'Brien had the best offensive season of his minor league career with a .314 batting average, 15 home runs and 75 RBIs. Ironically, O'Brien was a 14th-round draft pick of the Texas Rangers in the 1978 Major League Amateur Draft but he never signed with them.

Primarily a backup catcher known for above average defensive skills, O'Brien played for eight teams during his 15-year major league career with the high point being part of the Atlanta Braves' 1995 World Series champions. He was the personal catcher for Cy Young Award winner Greg Maddux when they were Braves teammates.

Near the end of his career, O'Brien helped develop a catcher's face mask which resembled a protective face mask worn by an ice hockey goalie and is currently used by many catchers. O'Brien's autobiography, *The Cy Young Catcher,* was published in 2015.

Joe Maddon's record over the 1985-86 seasons with the Midland Angels was 121-148 and all six of his minor league managerial seasons resulted in losing records. That turned out to be an aberration for Maddon, who never advanced past Class A competition in four years as a minor league catcher.

After the downtrodden Tampa Bay Devil Rays had Major League Baseball's worst record in 2007, Maddon led them to the 2008 American League championship and AL Manager of the Year honors. He won that award again in 2011 by taking Tampa Bay to the AL Playoffs after being nine games behind in the AL Wild Card playoff race. Maddon posted winning records in six of his nine seasons (2006 through 2014) with Tampa Bay before becoming manager of the Chicago Cubs, starting with the 2015 season.

Sandy Alomar Jr. was renowned for his defensive skills and handling of pitchers as a 20-year catcher in Beaumont that year as well as with the 1987 Wichita Pilots. After he and Carlos Baerga were traded from the San Diego Padres to the Cleveland Indians, Alomar turned into one of baseball's best catchers during the 1990s. He was the 1990 American League Rookie of the Year award and a six-time American League All-Star selection.

1987: These Drillers weren't as bad as the 1986 squad, but not by much. Their winning percentage of .382 is second-worst in Tulsa's professional baseball history. That was worsened by a 16-game losing streak, the longest such skid in Tulsa professional baseball history.

But the best news for Drillers fans and Tulsa's professional baseball history came during the previous December when New Hampshire businessman Went Hubbard purchased the Drillers from Texas Rangers management. Under Hubbard's quiet leadership, Tulsa became one of the elite Double-A franchises in minor league baseball.

The white-haired Hubbard had just retired as the top executive Hubbard Farms, a poultry genetics research firm in Walpole, New Hampshire. He had also worked as a director of a Vermont-based bank holding company and as president of a home for economically and socially-disadvantaged children, also in Vermont.

Unlike some previous team owners in Tulsa's baseball history, Hubbard never drew attention to himself, leaving the day-to-day team operations to general managers Joe Preseren and, later, Chuck Lamson. But he led efforts to increase Drillers Stadium seating to just over 11,000 and convert the playing surface from artificial turf to natural grass.

An example of that came in 1987 when attendance rose for the third year in a row, reaching 170,932. *The Sporting News* magazine honored Preseren as its Minor League Executive of the Year. It was the first time that a Tulsa minor league baseball executive won that award since Oilers general manager Hugh Finnerty did so in 1963.

Hubbard's leadership and influence were lauded when the Drillers twice won the Bob Freitas Award, presented to the nation's best Double-A baseball franchise. His work also led to other awards honoring franchise stability and community involvement. After Hubbard retired in 2006, he was inducted into the Texas League Baseball Hall of Fame.

But there were many nights when he walked around the ballpark with a towel, cleaning the metal seats and fans likely thought it was a retired gentlemen working at a baseball game to earn a little extra spending money. Hubbard preferred meeting fans one-on-one and talking to them about what they liked at the ballpark and seeking their input on what could be improved.

Shortstop Ed Jurak was the only Driller named to the 1987 Texas League postseason All-Star Team. His .347 batting average was the best by a Tulsa professional baseball player in 10 years and ranked third in the Texas League that season. Jurak played for the Boston Red Sox from 1982 through 1985.

Outfielder Jim St. Laurent set a team record for most base hits in a season with 153, a mark that stood for nearly a decade. St. Laurent batted .287 and drove in 70 runs but hit just four home runs. He never reached the major leagues and later became a high school baseball coach in Monadnock, New Hampshire.

While Rick Odekirk and Tommy West led the pitching staff with nine victories apiece, Tulsa's best pitcher was bullpen ace Gary Mielke with a 3-3 record, 2.98 ERA and 15 saves while waking just 10 batters in 28 appearances.

A unique promotion had first baseman Whitney Harry being married at home plate prior to a game. A limousine was parked at second base with a white walkway running from the car and over the pitching mound to the waiting wedding party at home plate. Harry's teammates held wooden bats to create an arch near home plate.

Matrimony was meaningless in helping Harry's on-field performance. He batted .222 with a team-leading 128 strikeouts and he left minor league baseball when the 1987 season ended.

This would be the last of Mike Jirschele's five seasons as a Tulsa Driller. The shortstop-third baseman appeared to have a chance to reach the Texas Rangers during the early 1980s but a severe knee injury prevented that from happening. He joined the Kansas City Royals' player development system the following season; a move that would lead towards a legacy of service within that organization.

Jirschele then spent 14 years as the manager of the Royals' Triple-A affiliate in Omaha, Nebraska, guiding them to seven winning seasons along with Pacific Coast League championships in 2011 and 2013 and the overall Triple-A crown in 2013. He mentored many of the key players on the Royals' 2014 American League championship team and was promoted by the Royals to serve as a bench coaching in 2014.

Jim Roberts handed the radio play-by-play for Drillers games on AM 1300, but the station's call letters were KAKC. The original KAKC was Tulsa's top rock-and-roll and news station during the 1950s and 1960s.

Matt Kinzer of the Arkansas Travelers threw a seven-inning no-hitter against Tulsa in a 10-0 victory in the second game of a June 6th doubleheader.

Despite having just the fifth-best regular season record in the Texas League, the Wichita Pilots pulled one of the biggest upsets in Texas League history by defeating the Jackson Mets to win the championship, 4-2.

The Pilots, who moved from Beaumont after the 1986 season, defeated the defending champion El Paso Diablos in the Western Division playoffs, 2-1, while Jackson advanced by eliminating Shreveport in the Eastern Division series, 2-1.

Shreveport had the best record in the Eastern Division as well as the entire Texas League at 78-57, followed by the Arkansas Travelers (72-63), Jackson (70-66) and the Tulsa Drillers (52-84). El Paso led the Western Division with a 75-59 record, followed by the Midland Angels (75-61), Wichita (69-65) and the San Antonio Dodgers (50-86).

Shreveport's Dennis Cook was the Texas League Pitcher of the Year, striking out 90 batters with just 20 walks over nearly 106 innings. He posted a 9-2 record and his 2.13 ERA was the lowest among the league's starting pitchers.

Cook became a relief pitcher and played for nine teams over a 15-year major league career and was a surprisingly good hitting pitcher, sporting a .264 career batting average. He was part of two National League championship teams: the 1997 Florida Marlins who also won the World Series and the 2000 New York Mets.

He excelled in postseason play, not giving up an earned run over 16 and one-third innings with 16 strikeouts and allowing just five hits.

El Paso's LaVel Freeman and 19-year-old Jackson infielder Gregg Jefferies waged a heated battle for the Texas League's offensive Triple Crown. Freeman led the league in batting average (.395) and home runs (24) and was second in runs batted in (96). His 208 base hits that year were the most by a Texas League Player since Shreveport's Ev Joyner, Jr. had 201 in 1956. Jefferies' 101 RBIs led the league and he finished second in batting average (.367) and in home runs (20) and was the Texas League Player of the Year.

But their major league careers were total opposites. Freeman went hitless in three at-bats with the 1989 Milwaukee Brewers and never returned to the majors after superstar Paul Molitor came off the disabled list. Jefferies was touted by the New York City media as the next

Mickey Mantle but never lived up to that hype while with the Mets. Jefferies played for six major league teams with his best seasons coming in 1993 and 1994 with the St. Louis Cardinals, hitting .320 and .342 respectively, and being a National League All-Star selection in both years.

One of the brightest stars on the 1987 Wichita Pilots was shortstop Roberto Alomar, who batted .319 with 43 stolen bases, 12 home runs, 41 doubles, 68 RBIs. The following year, he switched to second base and began a 17-year big-league career in which he played in 12 Major League All-Star Games and won 10 Gold Gloves for his defensive skills, the most Gold Gloves ever won by a second baseman.

While Alomar was a 2011 inductee into the Baseball Hall of Fame, his legacy was tarnished in a September 27, 1996 game between Alomar's Baltimore Orioles and the Toronto Blue Jays. Alomar spit in the face of home plate umpire John Hirschbeck after being ejected from the game after arguing over a called third strike. Alomar apologized after the incident.

Midland Angels bullpen ace Bryan Harvey ranked second in the league with 20 saves. Harvey moved up to the California Angels and his 46 saves in 1991 led the American League. As a member of the expansion Florida Marlins in 1993, he posted 45 saves along with a 1.70 ERA.

1988: Jim Skaalen's only season as manager of the Tulsa Drillers was a resounding success, to say the least. The team went from the outhouse to the penthouse that year, claiming their third Texas League pennant since rejoining the league and the seventh Texas League title in Tulsa's professional baseball history.

The Drillers edged the El Paso Diablos in the championship series, 4-2, but their march to claiming the Texas League pennant was remarkable in that four of their six playoff victories came in road games.

They reached the playoffs by winning the Eastern Division's second-half pennant by one-half game over the Arkansas Travelers. Then they eliminated Shreveport to win the Eastern Division crown, 2-0. El Paso had defeated the San Antonio Missions, 2-0, to win the Western Division series.

Shreveport had the best record in the Eastern Division at 74-62, followed by Tulsa (71-65), the Arkansas Travelers (67-69) and Jackson Mets (61-75). El Paso had the Western Division's best record at 74-60, followed by San Antonio (73-60), the Midland Angels (61-74) and Wichita Pilots (60-76).

Pitching was the strongest point of that Driller team. Wilson was the ace of the staff, posting a 15-7 with a 3.16 ERA, three shutouts and ranked third in the league in strikeouts (132). He was part of a post-season trade with the Chicago Cubs that brought Raphael Palmiero and Jamie Moyer to the parent Texas Rangers. But Wilson didn't fare so well in six major league seasons, winning just 13 games over that span.

Brown, the fourth overall pick in the 1986 amateur baseball draft out of Georgia Tech, had a 12-10 record and was seventh in strikeouts (118). Considering that Brown was 1-11 with three different minor league teams the year before, his Tulsa performance was outstanding.

Brown won 211 games over 19 major league seasons and was a six-time All-Star selection. His 21 wins with the 1992 Texas Rangers led the American League and he twice led the National League in the lowest earned run average: a sparkling 1.89 ERA with the 1996 Florida Marlins and a 2.58 ERA with the 2000 Los Angeles Dodgers.

It was with the Dodgers that Brown made baseball history as the first player to earn a contract paying over $100 million. His 1988 contract was a seven-year deal worth $105 million.

One of Brown's Tulsa teammates, Kenny Rogers, was a 38th-round pick in the 1982 amateur draft. He had a 4-6 record in 1988 and was 5-14 during his Driller career. But Rogers would win 219 games over 20 major league seasons. The highlight was pitching the 14th perfect game in major league baseball history in the Texas Rangers' 4-0 win over the California Angels on July 28, 1994.

Relief pitcher Rick Raether had a streak of 39 consecutive innings without allowing an earned run and finished with 16 saves, a 4-1 record and a stingy 0.96 ERA. The sidearm-throwing right-hander played for the University of Miami's 1985 College World Series champions and was later inducted into that school's Athletic Hall of Fame. Surprisingly, Raether never made it to the majors and quit pro baseball after the 1989 season, citing broken promises from Texas Rangers officials.

Krueter batted .265 that year and did a fine job working with the Driller pitchers on in-game strategy. He spent 16 years in the majors with his best season coming with the 1993 Detroit Tigers, ranking fourth in fielding assists by American League catchers (69).

After his playing career ended, Krueter spent four years as the University of Southern California baseball coach after his father-in-law, Mike Gillespie, retired. Those Trojans have more College World Series championships than any other team (12) but they never participated in that hallowed event during Krueter's four years there, posting a 111-117 record. Krueter later worked for a baseball-related business in south Florida.

Left fielder Kevin Reimer led the Texas League with 11 triples while leading the Drillers with a .302 batting average along with 147 base hits, 30 doubles and 21 home runs. His best major league season was 1991 when he hit 20 home runs for the parent Texas Rangers.

Paul Postier became the first of four men who once played high school baseball in the Tulsa area and later played for the Drillers.

Postier graduated from Tulsa's Edison High School and played for the Drillers in 1988-90 and 1992. He was a solid defensive utility infielder but never reached the major leagues.

The season attendance of 188,375 was Tulsa's highest total in 15 years. Postseason honors included Jim Skaalen winning the Texas League Manager of the Year award along with pitchers Kevin Brown and Steve Wilson being chosen to the league's postseason All-Star team, as was catcher Chad Krueter.

Skaalen, who had been an infielder in the Baltimore Orioles' minor league system, later worked as a manager in player development programs for four other teams as well along with being a baseball scout.

Tulsa County Stadium underwent remodeling prior to the 1988 season. Additional seating behind home plate increased the capacity to 8,193 and a larger and more functional press box was added, as well.

An April 25th exhibition game drew 4,257 fans to see the Texas Rangers rout the Tulsa Drillers, 9-1. Steve Kemp drove in four runs and was one of three Rangers to hit a home run. The Drillers didn't help their own cause as they made five fielding errors.

The 1988 United States Olympic baseball team defeated South Korea's national team, 7-3, in a pre-Olympic exhibition game that drew 7,560 fans to Tulsa County Stadium. Left-handed pitcher Jim Abbott, who overcame a birth defect involving one arm but would go on play big-league baseball, struck out eight batters over six innings. Other future major leaguers on Team USA that night were Robin Ventura, a former Oklahoma State standout, Tino Martinez and pitchers Andy Benes and Ben McDonald.

Jim Roberts handed the play-by-play for Drillers games on radio on KAKC-AM (1300). With the team's management deciding to change announcers prior to the 1989 season, this would be Roberts' final season covering the Drillers.

Midland third baseman Jeff Manto was the Texas League Player of the Year, finishing second in the league in home runs (24) and RBIs (101) while batting .301. That more than made up for a sub-par fielding performance as he committed 32 errors that year. Manto hit .276 over 16 minor league seasons and was formerly a hitting coach for the Chicago White Sox.

Jackson's Blaine Beatty was the Texas League Pitcher of the Year, leading the league with 16 victories, 12 complete games and five shutouts in addition to posting a 2.46 ERA and walking just 34 batters over 208 innings. While arm problems derailed a promising major league career, Beatty became a minor league pitching instructor and helped develop younger pitchers that have played key roles in the Baltimore Orioles' recent resurgence.

The El Paso Diablos team that faced the Drillers for the Texas League championship had two hot-hitting players who latter starred for the Milwaukee Brewers and had long major league careers: 19-year-old shortstop Garry Sheffield and left fielder Greg Vaughn.

Sheffield batted .314 in just 77 games and added 19 home runs and 65 RBIs. He played in nine All-Star Games during his 22-year big-league career but his sometimes temperamental nature drew as much attention as his playing abilities.

Vaughn led the Texas League in home runs (28) and runs batted in (105). He played in four Major League All-Star Games and hit 20 or more home runs in eight of his 15 major league season, capped by hitting 50 homers for the 1998 San Diego Padres.

1989: While the Drillers missed the Texas League playoffs, their 73-63 overall record was the second-highest in franchise history. The Drillers seemed to have the Eastern Division's first half championship and the accompanying playoff berth in the bag, but it slipped through their fingers as they lost nine of their final 13 games.

The regular season attendance of 218,755 fans was Tulsa's largest in 24 years and marked the sixth consecutive season in which season attendance had risen.

This was also a year in which local baseball fans saw glimpses of brilliance from four future major league stars: outfielder Sammy Sosa and Juan Gonzalez, pitcher Wilson Alvarez and third baseman Dean Palmer.

Sosa's Driller debut was a memorable one. His inside-the-park home run down the right field line was a key play in a 6-4 win over the Arkansas Travelers before 13,988 fans on April 12th, the largest crowd at Drillers Stadium to that date.

Born in San Pedro de Macoris in the Dominican Republic, Sosa batted .297 in 66 games with the Drillers, hitting seven home runs, driving in 31 runs, stealing 15 bases and drawing raves for his fielding and throwing skills. Sosa and pitcher Wilson Alvarez were two of three players traded by the Texas Rangers to the Chicago White Sox on July 29th of that year for veteran outfielder Harold Baines.

Sosa drew lots of attention, both good and bad, for his 18-year baseball career after leaving Tulsa. He became one of the National League's most feared hitters when he played for the Chicago Cubs from 1992 through 2004. His 609 career home runs ranks eighth in Major League Baseball history and are the most hit by any for-eign-born Major League Baseball player.

Sosa and St. Louis Cardinals first baseman Mark McGwire capti-vated baseball fans around the world in 1998 with their memorable chase of the single-season home run record of 61 set by Roger Maris with the 1961 New York Yankees. Sosa finished with 66 home runs in 1998 while McGwire hit 70 homers.

(As mentioned earlier in this book, that same Roger Maris hit just one home run in 25 games with the 1955 Tulsa Oilers.)

In 2009, newspaper articles claimed that Sosa was one of several players that used illegal performance-enhancing drugs during the 2003 season. The specific drug was never identified and Sosa denied ever using those substances.

Despite a 2-2 record in seven starts with the Drillers, Alvarez demonstrated good control by allowing just 16 bases on balls over 48 innings. He pitched a no-hitter against the Baltimore Orioles in his Chicago White Sox debut on August 11, 1991. Alvarez spent seven of his 14 big-league seasons with the White Sox and played in the 1994 All-Star Game. He was inducted into the Caribbean Baseball Hall of Fame in 2010.

Palmer and Gonzalez were the Driller representatives on the Texas League's postseason All-Star Team.

Palmer's 25 home runs made him the first Tulsa player to lead a league in home runs since Hector Cruz's 29 home runs with the 1975 Tulsa Oilers led the Triple-A American Association. He also led the Texas League in extra-base hits with 62. Palmer went on to hit 20 or more home runs during seven of his 14 major league seasons.

Gonzalez was a 19-year-old outfielder who led the Drillers with a .293 batting average and 147 hits. Quickly promoted to the parent Texas Rangers for his powerful hitting stroke, "Juan Gone" was the American League's Most Valuable Player in 1996 and 1998. During his 17-year major league career, Gonzalez hit 40 or more home runs five times and drove in 100 or more runs eight times.

Today, Gonzalez is active in community work in his native Puerto Rico and also served as an assistant coach on the Puerto Rican National Team during international baseball tournaments.

Tommy Thompson was in the first of his two seasons as the Drillers' manager. He posted a 141-131 record during that time and became the second Driller manager to post consecutive winning seasons. The first was Tom Burgess who had a 138-131 record in 1981-82.

The parent Texas Rangers defeated the Tulsa Drillers, 5-3, on August 14th before the largest crowd to see an exhibition game at Tulsa County Stadium (8,664). The Rangers rocked Driller pitchers for 14 hits, led by three hits from Cecil Espy and a two-run homer from ex-Driller Jeff Kunkel.

Jamie Moyer, who played for the Drillers as part of an injury rehabilitation assignment that season, was their starting pitcher and took the loss. Moyer's big-league career spanned four decades and in 2012 at the age of 47, he won a game playing for the Colorado Rockies, who would later become the Drillers' parent team.

Shreveport Captains pitchers Larry Carter and Scott Gay combined to throw one of the most unique no-hitters in the professional baseball history in a 9-0, seven-inning victory over the Drillers on August 20th. Carter pitched no-hit ball for the first three innings but was thrown out of the game after participating in a bench-clearing brawl. Gay came in from the bullpen and completed the rare gem.

Bruce Howard began a seven-year stint as the radio voice of the Drillers. Howard previously worked as a broadcaster for the Triple-A Nashville (Tennessee) Sounds. During his time with the Drillers, Howard was also the radio voice for Tulsa's Continental Basketball Association teams, the Tulsa Fast Breakers and Tulsa Zone, and University of Tulsa football and basketball.

In 1995, Howard was named as the Director of Sports Broadcasting at the University of Tulsa, a position he still holds. Howard has actually been the Golden Hurricane's play-by-play announcer on football and basketball games since 1993 and also hosts radio call-in shows.

Hank Aaron, who formerly held baseball's career home run record, came to Tulsa County Stadium on June 15th to lead an instructional clinic for young baseball players. After eager encouragement from the kids in attendance, the 55-year-old Aaron stepped to the plate for a brief batting practice session and lashed several drives within a few feet of the outfield fence.

The Arkansas Travelers won their first Texas League championship since 1980 by defeating the Wichita Wranglers in the championship series, 4-3. Arkansas swept the Shreveport Captains, 2-0, in the Eastern Division playoffs while Wichita advanced directly to the finals by the winning the first and second half titles in the Western Division.

Arkansas had the Eastern Division's best overall record at 79-56, followed by Shreveport (75-61), the Tulsa Drillers (73-63) and Jackson Mets (61-74). Wichita led the Western Division with a 73-63 record followed by the Midland Angels (70-66), El Paso Diablos (63-73) and the San Antonio Missions (49-87).

Traveler center fielder Ray Lankford was the Texas League Player of the Year, leading the league with 158 base hits while batting .317 with 11 home runs, 98 RBIs and 38 stolen bases. Blessed with a rare combination of power and speed, Lankford quickly moved up to the parent St. Louis Cardinals and was one of their top players from 1990 through 2001. He had five seasons in which he hit 20 or more home runs and also stole 20 or more bases, the only player in franchise history to achieve such a feat.

Wichita pitcher Andy Benes, the first player chosen in the 1988 amateur draft, was the Texas League Pitcher of the Year, striking out 115 batters in just 16 games. The Evansville University standout had an 8-4 record, a 2.16 ERA and three shutouts in five complete games.

Benes won 15 on more games three times during his 14-year major league career. Pitching for the San Diego Padres, he was a National League All-Star in 1993 and led the National League in 1994 with 189 strikeouts despite a hard-luck 6-14 record that year.

Rod Beck had a 7-3 record in 14 starts with the Shreveport Captains. But the parent San Francisco Giants turned Beck into a relief pitcher in 1991 and he became one of the National League's most feared bullpen aces during the 1990s.

He was a three-time All-Star and made 30 or more saves five times, highlighted by 51 saves in 70 chances with the 1998 Chicago Cubs. Near the end of his 13-year career, Beck battled drug-related problems and died in 2007 at age 38, three years after his final big-league game.

Chapter Ten

The 1990s

Use of the internet and e-mail skyrocketed as technical programs once thought to be impossible to understand became much easier to use. South African civil rights leader Nelson Mandela was released from prison and later elected as that nation's president.

This was the decade that brought a male enhancement drug called Viagra, Caller ID for telephones, the Iraq war, the Euro as the common currency for European nations and the first cloned sheep. Golfer Tiger Woods won his first Masters championship and an auto accident took the life of Britain's Princess Diana. *Titantic* won 11 Academy Awards and became the first movie to earn over $1 billion. Fox Television debuted what would become the longest-running animated comedy series, *The Simpsons*.

President Bill Clinton was impeached by Congress on charges related to an extramarital affair with a White House intern. But the second step of removing him from office failed and he became the first Democrat President since Franklin Roosevelt to win re-election. Pro football legend O.J. Simpson was acquitted of two murders in a controversial court case but his legacy was forever tarnished by subsequent events.

Musical horizons broadened like never before. Nirvana and Pearl Jam led a hard-driving new form of music called grunge rock while Green Day fueled a revival of punk rock. Mariah Carey, Whitney Houston and Britney Spears were top-selling female vocalists. Hip hop and rap soared in popularity, led by Dr. Dre, The Notorious B.I.G., Tupac Shakur, and Queen Latifah.

Oklahoma native Garth Brooks was the biggest star in country music, breaking records left and right for sales of both records and concert tickets. All five of his concerts at Tulsa's Drillers Stadium were sellouts.

Terrorism struck in America's heartland with the 1995 bombing of the Oklahoma City Federal Building led by Timothy McVeigh, a Gulf War veteran and militia movement sympathizer. The bombing killed 168 people, injured over 680 others and caused over $650 million in damage. The Oklahoma City bombing was America's most destructive terrorism event prior to the terrorist attacks on September 11, 2001.

The Tulsa Drillers made four trips to the Texas League playoffs and took home the championship trophy in 1998. Bobby Jones became the winningest manager in Tulsa's professional baseball history during this decade. A local high school teacher honed his craft at Driller games as a nerdy character that would become the current Clown Prince of Baseball.

Finally, there was arguably the greatest player in Tulsa Driller history. He only spent 50 games with the team but catcher Ivan "Pudge" Rodriguez dazzled local baseball fans with the all-around skills that catapulted him to superstardom in the major leagues.

1990: The Drillers came close to claiming a playoff berth and finished with a 68-68 record. Their home field was renamed Drillers

Stadium prior to the start of the season. But the biggest success story involved the team's management.

For the second time in three years, general manager Joe Preseren was chosen by *The Sporting News* magazine as its Minor League Executive of the Year. The season attendance was 226,461 fans, the largest in Tulsa's professional baseball history to that point in time.

That feat was even more remarkable when considering that seven home games were rained out prior to May 19th. By comparison, the Drillers had a combined total of four home rainouts in the 1988 and 1989 seasons.

Tulsa hosted the Texas League All-Star Game for the fourth time in its professional baseball history and for the third time in 10 years. The West All-Stars took a 4-0 victory over the East All-Stars before 4,291 fans at Drillers Stadium.

Wichita pitcher Ricky Bones was the game's Most Valuable Player, pitching a perfect game over the first three innings. The five pitchers who followed Bones scattered three hits over the following six innings. Bones spent five of his 11 major league seasons with the Milwaukee Brewers and played in the 1994 All-Star Game. He has been the bullpen coach of the New York Mets since 2011 and was the pitching coach for the Puerto Rico National Team that placed second in the 2013 World Baseball Championship.

San Antonio first baseman Eric Karros was the offensive star of the game, leading a 14-hit attack with a first-inning home run among his three hits. Karros played 12 of his 14 major league seasons with the Los Angeles Dodgers and was the 1992 National League Rookie of the Year.

Driller pitcher Steve Allen found nothing funny about pitching in the eighth inning for the East, being rocked for three runs and five hits.

Catcher Bill Haselman was Tulsa's lone representative on the Texas League postseason All-Star Team. His batting average of .319, 80 RBIs and 39 doubles led the Drillers and he finished among the Texas League's top 10 offensive players in five different categories. Haselman was the Texas Rangers' first selection (23rd overall) in the 1987 amateur draft out of UCLA, where he was also the Bruins' quarterback.

Haselman's 13-year major league career was split between the Texas Rangers, Boston Red Sox and Seattle Mariners. Two of his biggest thrills came with the Red Sox. He was the catcher when Roger Clemens had 20 strikeouts against the 1996 Detroit Tigers and in his first year as an assistant coach, was part of Terry Francona's staff that led the Red Sox to victory in the 2004 World Series.

First baseman Rob Maurer hit 21 home runs, tops for Tulsa and second-highest in the Texas League. Outfielder Kevin Belcher led the Drillers in stolen bases with 29. Eric McCray was Tulsa's best pitcher, ranking fifth in the Texas League in strikeouts (98) despite an 8-7 record and 4.21 ERA.

Bruce Howard was in his second year as the Drillers' radio announcer on KAKC-AM (1300).

Despite finishing with a losing regular season record, Shreveport earned its first Texas League title since 1955 as the Captains defeated the San Antonio Missions in the championship series, 4-2. Shreveport swept the Jackson Mets, 2-0, in the Eastern Division playoffs while San Antonio defeated the El Paso Diablos, 2-1, in the Western Division playoffs.

Jackson had the Eastern Division's best overall record at 73-62, followed by the Tulsa Drillers (68-68), Shreveport (65-68), and the Arkansas Travelers (56-80). The Drillers came within a half-game of a playoff berth during the first half of the season. Shreveport won the

Eastern Division's first half tile with a 34-31 mark followed by Jackson at 35-32 and Tulsa at 34-32.

San Antonio led the Western Division with a 78-56 record followed by El Paso (77-58), the Wichita Wranglers (67-68) and Midland Angels (56-80).

Jackson pitcher Anthony Young was the Texas League Pitcher of the Year, leading the league with minor league career bests of a 15-3 won-lost record and a 1.65 ERA. He was one of prime prospects in the New York Mets player development system during the early 1990s and was a 2014 inductee into the Texas League Hall of Fame.

But instead of finding fame, Young found infamy just over two years. He lost 27 consecutive games over two seasons (May 6, 1992 through July 24, 1993), breaking the major league record of 23 consecutive losses set by Cliff Curtis with the National League's 1910 Boston Doves and 1911 Boston Rustlers.

Young lost 14 consecutive games as a starter before changing to a relief pitcher, hoping that a scenery change would work wonders. But despite converting 12 consecutive save opportunities as a reliever, he lost another 13 games in a row. Shortly after his bad-luck streak ended, he made a guest appearance on NBC Television's *Tonight Show with Jay Leno*.

San Antonio outfielder Henry Rodriguez was the Texas League Player of the Year, leading the league with 28 home runs and 109 RBIs while batting .291. After being traded from the parent Los Angeles Dodgers, Rodriguez hit 20-plus home runs twice with the Montreal Expos two additional times with the Chicago Cubs. He was a 1995 National League All-Star honoree with career highs of 36 home runs and 103 RBIs, things that lessened the sting of also leading the National League that season with 160 strikeouts.

1991: The Drillers set a season attendance record for the second year in a row, despite having a 58-78 overall record. They drew 260,864 fans for 60 home dates, which ranked third in the Texas League behind the El Paso Diablos (273,438 for 67 home games) and the Arkansas Travelers (265,268).

The highlight of this season was Ivan Rodriguez playing catcher for the Drillers. He only spent 50 games with the team but showed fans of all ages the skills that would lead many long-time baseball observers to proclaim Rodriguez to be one of the greatest defensive catchers in professional baseball history.

Rodriguez batted .274 with three home runs and 28 RBIs but the 19-year-old catcher put on amazing displays for Texas League fans with a cannon-like throwing arm that caught runners trying to steal a base nearly 60 percent of the time. He also demonstrated a maturity beyond his years in working with pitchers. What Rodriguez did in just 50 games was more than enough to secure a spot as Tulsa's representative on the 1991 Texas League All-Star Team.

The Drillers had planned a promotional event between games of a June 20th doubleheader with the Shreveport Captains where Rodriguez and his fiancée, Maribel Rivera, were supposed to be married. The wedding bells were delayed when one day before the wedding, Rodriguez was called up to the Texas Rangers to replace injured catcher Geno Petralli. The couple was married in a civil ceremony on June 21st but divorced in 2005. Their oldest son, Dereck, was an outfielder in the Minnesota Twins' player development program.

Nicknamed "Pudge" as a salute to his mentor with the same nickname, Carlton Fisk, Rodriguez caught major league base runners stealing nearly 46 per cent of the time, a rate which was tops among active major league catchers when he retired in 2011 and is still third highest among all catchers who played 20 or more major league seasons.

Rodriguez spent 13 of his 21 major league seasons with the Texas Rangers, was a 14-time All-Star selection, won 13 Gold Gloves as best the best defensive player at his position, won seven Silver Sluggers as the best offensive player at his position, won the 1999 American League Most Valuable Player Award and was a key player on the Florida Marlins' 2003 World Series champions.

After Rodriguez moved on, Rick Wrona played 27 games at catcher for the Drillers. Despite batting just .159, he made history as part of the first father-son duo to play professional baseball in Tulsa. His father, Walt Wrona, starred for the Tulsa Oilers in the late 1940s and early 1950s. Rick Wrona later spent parts of six seasons with four major league teams.

Three Tulsa Drillers were part of a no-hitter on April 18th in a 2-0 win against the Arkansas Travelers. Cedric Shaw pitched the first seven innings with Everett Cunningham pitching the eighth inning and Barry Manuel the ninth inning.

Shaw's share of the pitching gem had some blemishes. He walked six Arkansas batters and shortstop Ozzie Hernandez made a spectacular defensive play to end the seventh inning. A left-handed pitcher who attended Grambling State University in Louisiana, Shaw covered his flaws by picking three runners off base.

Shaw had a 9-8 record and ranked sixth among Texas League pitchers in strikeouts (111). But he never reached the major leagues and was out of baseball four years later. Cunningham left professional baseball later that year and later became an executive with a health services company.

Manuel, who led the Texas League that year with 25 saves, would spend parts of five seasons with four major league teams before working for a Christian school in Opelousas, Louisiana.

Shortstop Cris Colon had the Drillers' hottest bat when the season ended, finishing with a 17-game hitting streak and a .392 batting average in just 20 games after being promoted from Class A Charlotte. A nephew of Chico Carrasquel, a four-time American League All-Star shortstop with the Chicago White Sox during the 1950s, Colon's future looked very bright. But he batted just .167 (6-for-36) in 14 games with the 1992 Texas Rangers and wound up spending 16 years in the minor leagues.

Second baseman Jeff Frye, who played collegiately at Southeastern Oklahoma State University in Durant, had 152 base hits that year, one shy of the Drillers' single-season record and tied for fifth-highest in the Texas League. He later spent four of his eight major league seasons with the Boston Red Sox.

In an April 11th exhibition game at Drillers Stadium, Tulsa overcame a five-run deficit and pulled out an 8-6 victory over the parent Texas Rangers. Ozzie Hernandez scored the go-ahead run in the sixth inning and Trey McCoy's eighth-inning home run capped the comeback. The Rangers did bring 14 of their best offensive players for the game but the mainstays of their pitching staff did not make the trip.

The game drew 9,110 spectators, the largest crowd to see the Texas Rangers play in Tulsa and the largest to see an exhibition game in a baseball-only stadium in Tulsa since a 1960 game between the Tulsa Oilers and St. Louis Cardinals drew 10,023 fans.

George W. Bush was a co-owner of the Texas Rangers prior to serving as governor of the state of Texas and spending eight years as the 43rd President of the United States. Bush visited with Drillers owner Went Hubbard before the game began.

Wichita Wranglers pitcher Kerry Knox authored the first no-hitter at Drillers Stadium in 14 years in his 1-0 victory in the second game of a May 17th doubleheader. A left-handed pitcher who broke the Fort Worth Brewer High School season strikeout record set by Texas Rangers phenom David Clyde, Knox set down the final 13 Drillers that he faced.

But there was plenty of drama before the final out of Knox's gem. After taking a first-pitch strike, outfielder Donald Harris was ejected after a lengthy argument with the home plate umpire. Pinch-hitter Paco Burgos then flied out to end the game. Ironically, Knox would pitch for the Drillers in 1995, posting a 2-2 record over five games before playing for Texas-based independent teams and then retiring from baseball.

During the year, team executives aggressively pursued buying a Triple-A franchise with the hope of moving it to Tulsa prior to the 1993 season. An opening developed when Denver had a Triple-A franchise needing to be relocated due to the Colorado Rockies joining the National League as an expansion team. Those dreams went up in smoke when the Triple-A Alliance awarded franchises to Charlotte, North Carolina and Ottawa, Ontario, Canada.

Bruce Howard was in his third year as the Drillers' radio announcer on KAKC-AM (1300).

After the season ended, Drillers Stadium underwent a multi-million dollar renovation. New general admission seats were added to fill in the gaps between the three grandstands along with an updated main entrance, new concession stands and a sorely needed upgrade of the executive offices and ticket booths.

Fernando Valenzuela's road back to the major league came through Tulsa on July 24th as a pitcher for the Midland Angels. The former Los Angeles Dodgers All-Star was rocked for four runs and eight hits over five innings in Tulsa's 4-2 victory. Jeff Frye's two-run triple was the key hit as the Drillers scored all four runs in the second inning.

That game drew over 11,000 fans, the fourth-largest home crowd in Tulsa baseball history to that point. Valenzuela returned to the majors in 1993 and pitched five more years before retiring but he was a shadow of the pitcher that created Fernandomania.

The Shreveport Captains won their second straight Texas League title by defeating the El Paso Diablos in the championship series, 4-2. Shreveport advanced directly to the finals by winning the Eastern Division's first and second half championships. El Paso defeated the Midland Angels in the Western Division playoffs, 2-0.

Shreveport had the Eastern Division's best overall record at 86-50, followed by the Jackson Generals (70-66), Tulsa Drillers (58-78) and Arkansas Travelers (49-87). El Paso led the Western Division with an 81-55 record followed by the Wichita Wranglers (71-64), Midland (67-68) and the San Antonio Missions (61-75).

Shreveport pitcher Paul McClellan was the Texas League Pitcher of the Year, leading the league with a winning percentage of .917 while going 11-1 in just 14 games and allowing just 30 walks over nearly 95 innings. But McClellan didn't fare so well after moving up to the parent San Francisco Giants, going 3-7 over parts of two years prior to bouncing between minor league and independent teams before ending his career.

El Paso first baseman John Jaha was the Texas League Player of the Year, leading the league with 30 home runs, 134 RBIs, 71 extra base hits, 121 runs scored and also ranking sixth in batting average (.344). He spent seven years with the parent Milwaukee Brewers, highlighted by 34 home runs and 118 RBIs in 1996. After joining the Oakland Athletics as a free agent in 1999, Jaha was an American League All-Star selection with a career-high 35 home runs along with 111 RBIs and drawing 101 walks.

1992: The Drillers reached the Texas League playoffs for the first time in four years by winning the Eastern Division's second half title over the Shreveport Captains. But Shreveport, the East's first half champion, eliminated Tulsa by sweeping the two-game divisional playoff. The Wichita Wranglers won their Western Division playoff against the El Paso Diablos, 2-1, and went on to a four-game sweep of Shreveport in the championship series.

Shreveport and Tulsa deadlocked for the best record in the Eastern Division at 77-59, followed by the Jackson Generals (61-74) and Arkansas Travelers (59-73). El Paso led the Western Division with a 73-63 overall record followed Wichita (70-66), the Midland Angels (61-72) and San Antonio Missions (62-74).

Local baseball fans showed their enthusiasm for the Drillers' success with a season attendance total of 290,393, a jump of nearly 30,000 over the 1991 total. It was the ninth consecutive season in which attendance increased.

For Driller manager Bobby Jones, success was sweet in comparison to his 58-78 debut with Tulsa the year before. He would become the winningest manager in Tulsa's professional baseball history with 485 victories. He spent seven full seasons with the Drillers (1991-92 and 1995-99), taking them to the Texas League playoffs four times and winning the pennant in 1998.

Jones' major league career wasn't all that much. He was a 36th-round draft pick of the Washington Senators back in 1967 and spent parts of nine seasons with the Texas Rangers and California Angels. But he clearly found his calling as a minor league manager in the Rangers' player development system.

Counting his experiences in Tulsa, Oklahoma City and elsewhere, Jones won 1,656 games as a minor league manager and guided his teams to 12 postseason appearances. Jones was an assistant coach with the Rangers in 2001 and 2006 and returned to that position starting with the 2014 season.

Left-hander Dan Smith was the Texas League Pitcher of the Year, posting an 11-7 record, leading the league with a 2.52 ERA and three shutouts and also finished among the league's top 10 pitchers in strikeouts and complete games. The 6-foot-5 lefthander out of Creighton University was the first choice of the parent Texas Rangers in the 1990 amateur draft.

On June 13th, Smith came within one pitch of the only nine-inning, complete game no-hitter by a Drillers pitcher in a 4-0 win over the Arkansas Travelers. Arkansas' Steve Fanning faced a 1-2 count with two outs in the bottom of the ninth inning.

Smith, Tulsa catcher Pete Kuld, the Driller dugout and a majority of the 6,459 fans in attendance thought that the next pitch was strike three and the no-hitter was finished. Home plate umpire Jim Wheeler ruled otherwise, saying the pitch was a ball. Fanning singled on the next pitch to end the no-hit bid. After Fanning reached first base, Wheeler ejected Kuld and manager Bobby Jones after a heated argument.

Smith spent parts of two seasons with the Texas Rangers and finished with a 53-73 record in 11 years of minor league baseball.

Joining Smith as Tulsa's representatives on the Texas League postseason All-Star Team were second baseman Jon Shave and designated hitter Jose Oliva.

Shave, who played collegiately at Mississippi State University, led Tulsa in base hits (130), shared the team lead in runs scored (57), ranked second in batting average (.287) and was an above-average defensive player. He played 11 years in the minors and parts of three seasons with the Texas Rangers and Minnesota Twins.

Oliva didn't have transportation to get to Tulsa after spring training ended in 1992 so former Driller slugger Sammy Sosa, a long-time friend, purchased a car for him. Oliva led Tulsa that year with 75 RBIs and 28 doubles and batted .270. He also led all Texas Rangers minor leaguers in a dubious category: most strikeouts (130).

After the season ended, Oliva was traded to the Atlanta Braves for pitchers Charlie Leibrandt and Pat Gomez. He played in China and the Dominican Republic winter baseball circuit then had an offer to join the Seattle Mariners organization. However, Oliva died in a one-car accident in Santo Domingo on December 22, 1997.

Robb Nen finished a three-year career as a Drillers starting pitcher with a 2-9 record and Texas Rangers executives gave up on the 32nd-round draft pick who was the son of former Washington Senators first baseman Dick Nen.

The Rangers sent him to the Florida Marlins as part of a three-player trade in 1993. When the Marlins moved Nen to the bullpen, his baseball life was reborn. He became a three-time National League All-Star and posted 40 or more saves in four of his final five big-league seasons, highlighted by a league-leading 45 saves in 2001.

Nen played for the Marlins from 1994 through 1997 and was part of their 1997 World Series championship team. Then he played for the San Francisco Giants from 1998 through 2002 and contributed to the Giants' 2002 National League championship team.

El Paso outfielder Troy O'Leary was the Texas League Player of the Year and the second of four Diablos to claim that award during the 1990s. O'Leary led the league with a .334 batting average, 169 base hits and 92 runs scored and also ranked among the top 10 players in doubles and stolen bases. He spent seven of his 11 major league seasons with the Boston Red Sox. O'Leary later proposed a reality TV series with a baseball theme but was turned down by numerous networks.

A 2016 Baseball Hall of Fame inductee would play the first 31 games of that season for San Antonio before being promoted to the Los Angeles Dodgers that season. That was the prelude for a 16-year major league career, playing in 12 Major League All-Star Games, winning 10 consecutive Silver Slugger Awards for hitting excellence, batting .300 or higher in 10 seasons and being regarded by baseball historians as the best offensive catcher in baseball history.

Mike Piazza did quite well, considering that he was chosen by the Dodgers in the 62nd round of the 1988 amateur draft.

Piazza batted .377 in just 31 games with the Missions, hitting seven home runs and with 21 RBIs. He would win the 1992 National League Rookie of the Year award, leading Dodger regulars in batting average (.318), home runs (35), runs batted in (112), base hits (174) and runs scored (81).

His major league career consisted of seven seasons with the Dodgers, eight seasons with the New York Mets and short tenures with the Florida (now Miami) Marlins, San Diego Padres and Oakland Athletics. The Mets would retire Piazza's jersey number (31) in honor of his achievements with that team.

From 1991 through 2002, Double-A baseball teams from the Eastern, Southern and Texas Leagues would play an all-star exhibition game with two teams comprised of American League Double-A affiliates and National League Double-A affiliates. The most famous player from this contest was Jim Thome, a five-time major league all-star and one of just eight players with 600 or more home runs in his big-league career.

The second such contest was played in Charlotte, North Carolina on July 13, 1992 with 4,009 fans looking on and the American League affiliates pulled out a 4-3 victory over the National League affiliates. Driller second baseman Jon Shave had a two-run double in the seventh inning to win the Texas League Star of Star Awards. He would be the first of two Drillers to win that award, the other one being pitcher Spike Lundberg in the 2000 contest.

Bruce Howard was in his fourth year as the Drillers' radio announcer on KAKC-AM (1300).

1993: For the first time in Tulsa's professional baseball history, season attendance topped the 300,000 mark with 325,135 fans coming to Drillers Stadium.

Left fielder Rusty Greer was the breakout star of the Drillers that year. He ranked among the Texas League's top 10 hitters in batting average (.291), home runs (15), base hits (138), triples (6) and runs scored (76). He spent all nine of his major league seasons with the Texas Rangers and was an outstanding hitter, batting .300 or higher in five of those nine seasons. In 2007, Greer was inducted into the Texas Rangers Hall of Fame.

First baseman Homer "Trey" McCoy lived up to his first name by leading the Texas League that year with 29 home runs, 59 extra-base hits, 95 RBIs, being hit by a pitch 19 times and also batted .293. A standout at Virginia Tech University, McCoy played nine years for minor league affiliates of the Texas Rangers and New York Mets and was a 2007 inductee into Virginia Tech's Athletic Hall of Fame.

Former Texas Rangers outfielder Oddibe McDowell played 34 games with the Drillers in his attempt to return to the major leagues. He was the Rangers' first pick in the 1984 amateur draft and the Golden Spikes Award winner (best college baseball player) while at Arizona State University and was a 2011 inductee into the College Baseball Hall of Fame. McDowell batted .342 with the Drillers and had eight home runs, 31 RBIs and scored 26 runs. He spent the 1994 season with the Rangers before retiring.

Rick Helling was the ace of Tulsa's pitching staff, leading all Texas League pitchers in strikeouts (180) and his 12 victories was third-highest in the league. The Texas Rangers' first draft choice (22nd overall) out of Stanford University in the 1992 amateur draft, he demonstrated great control of his pitches, allowing just 46 walks over 177.1 innings.

Helling spent eight of his 12 major league seasons with the Texas Rangers with the highlight being an American League-leading 20 victories in 1998 when the Rangers claimed their second American League Western Division championship. The only other Ranger pitchers to win 20 or more games in a season are former Driller Kevin Brown and veteran Ferguson Jenkins.

Former major league catcher Stan Cliburn began his two-year tenure as the Drillers' manager after Bobby Jones was promoted to Triple-A Oklahoma City. Cliburn played 14 years of minor league baseball and spent part of the 1980 season with the California Angels. He had a 129-142 record in two years in Tulsa but would spend 24 years as a minor league manager, winning three league championships and sharing a fourth.

The artificial turf was ripped out of Tulsa County Stadium prior to the start of the season and natural grass along with a dirt infield was installed, much to the delight of those who played on it during Tulsa's frequently torrid summers.

Bruce Howard was in his fifth year as the Drillers' radio announcer on KAKC-AM (1300).

The Drillers had a chance to reach the playoffs during the Eastern Division's second half schedule but the Shreveport Captains grabbed the berth with a 37-31 record while Tulsa went 35-32.

Jackson won the fourth of its five Texas League championships by sweeping the El Paso Diablos in the championship series, 3-0. The Generals defeated the Shreveport Captains in the Eastern Division playoffs, 3-1, while El Paso eliminated the Wichita Wranglers in the Western Division playoffs, 3-1.

The Generals had the Eastern Division's best overall record at 73-62, followed by the Arkansas Travelers (67-69), Tulsa Drillers (66-69) and Shreveport Captains (66-70). El Paso led the Western Division with a 76-59 record followed by the Wichita Wranglers (68-68, Midland Angels (67-68) and San Antonio Missions (58-76).

Jackson first baseman Roberto Petagine was the Texas League Player of the Year, finishing third in the league in batting average (.334), second in on-base percentage (.442) along with having 15 home runs and 90 RBIs. He was part of an 11-player trade between the Houston Astros and San Diego Padres after the 1994 season ended. The stars of that trade were Ken Caminiti and Andujar Cedeno going to San Diego in exchange for Pedro Martinez and Derek Bell.

Not quite good enough for the major league baseball in the United States, Petagine became one of the top players in Japan's Central League from 1999 through 2003 with the Yakult Swallows. In his first five Japanese seasons, his batting average was never lower than .316, he never hit fewer than 34 home runs in a season and, according to media reports, he increased his salary ten-fold.

San Antonio's Ben Van Ryn was the Texas League Pitcher of the Year, leading the league with a 14-4 record and had the lowest ERA among starting pitchers (2.21). The first player picked by the Montreal Expos in the 1990 amateur draft, the 6-foot-5 left-hander had 144 strikeouts over 134 innings, second only to the 188 strikeouts by Driller ace Rick Helling. Van Ryn spent 10 years in the minors and made brief appearances with four major league teams.

1994: The largest crowd in Drillers Stadium baseball history, 16,780, saw Tulsa take a 6-4 victory over the Jackson Generals in the season opener. A portion of right field was roped off and nearly 2,000 fans chose to sit there and special ground rules were used that night but were never really a factor. The single-season attendance of 344,764 was the largest in Tulsa's professional baseball history to that point in time.

But success at the ticket window didn't translate to success on the field. With the Texas Rangers not providing much in terms of talented players, Tulsa's 63-73 record was the worst in the Texas League's Eastern Division and they also finished in last place in the first and second half standings, as well. In addition, no Tulsa player was chosen for the Texas League's postseason All-Star Team.

There were bright spots in the play of shortstop Rich Aurilia and outfielder Desi Wilson. Aurilia only batted .234 but more than made up for his hitting problems with smooth and steady defensive work. The 6-foot-7 Wilson led the Texas League with 109 singles and also led the Drillers with a .288 batting average.

After the season ended, the Texas Rangers chose Aurilia and Wilson as the minor leaguer players to be traded to the San Francisco Giants for veteran pitcher John Burkett.

Aurilia spent 12 of his 16 major league seasons with the San Francisco Giants and was involved in postseason playoff action in three of those years. In 2001, he led the National League in base hits (201) and played in the All-Star Game. Wilson spent part of 1996 with the San Francisco Giants but played 17 years in American professional baseball.

Another Tulsa outfielder, Terrell Lowery, ranked second in the Texas League in stolen bases (33) and was tied for fourth in total base hits (142) while batting .286. Lowery was an outstanding point guard on Loyola Marymount's University's basketball team and in his junior year, became the only player in NCAA history to finish among the nation's top five players in points and assists in the same season. Lowery didn't fare so well in big-league baseball, spending parts of four seasons with three teams.

Lance Schuermann was the only Tulsa pitcher to reach double figures in victories, posting a 10-11 record and ranked sixth in the Texas League in strikeouts (124).

That record-setting Opening Night was also a historic event for a Syracuse University graduate who eventually worked his way up the corporate ladder to become the current general manager of the Drillers.

Mike Melega served as a food and beverage intern that season and that Opening Night overflow crowd was his "first day on the job." Needless to say, his jaw probably dropped and his eyes bugged out upon seeing the large number of cars trying to enter the parking lots and the equally large number of hungry and thirsty fans standing in line to enter the ballpark.

Melega willingly did what some people considered as grunt work with wrapping hot dogs and rolling beer kegs all part of his nightly duties. But Melega's hard work and dedication to providing fans with an enjoyable experience helped him follow in the footsteps of Chuck Lamson and eventually serve as the Drillers' general manager.

Bruce Howard was in his sixth year as the Drillers' radio announcer on KAKC-AM (1300).

Kevin Gallaher and Jamie Daspit of the Jackson Generals teamed up for a rain-shortened, seven-inning no-hitter in a 1-0 victory over Tulsa on April 10th at Drillers Stadium. Gallaher struck out nine batters over six innings and retired 11 consecutive Drillers before heavy rain forced a 69-minute delay prior to the seventh inning. Daspit pitched in the seventh before another cloudburst forced the game to be called off. None of the four Drillers who reached base in the game made it to second.

El Paso earned its fifth and final Texas League championship with a four-game sweep of the Jackson Generals in the championship series. The Diablos advanced directly to the finals by winning the Western Division's first and second half titles. The Generals defeated the Shreveport Captains in the Eastern Division playoffs, 3-2.

Jackson had the Eastern Division's best overall record at 74-61, followed by the Shreveport Captains (73-63), Arkansas Travelers (68-67) and Tulsa Drillers (63-73). El Paso led the Western Division with an 88-48 record followed by the San Antonio Missions (62-74), Midland Angels (61-75) and Wichita Wranglers (54-82).

El Paso also dominated the Texas League's postseason honors with Tim Unroe winning the Texas League Player of the Year and Sid Roberson taking the Pitcher of the Year award.

Unroe led the league with 103 RBIs and 242 total bases while hitting .310 with 15 home runs and 14 stolen bases. He would be another player whose star shone brightly in the minors and then dimmed in the major leagues, hitting just two home runs over three years with the Milwaukee Brewers.

Roberson led the league with a 15-8 record and eight complete games along with a 2.83 ERA. While he was a two-time NAIA All-American at the University of North Florida with a 36-6 record and still holds the school's career records for strikeouts and complete games, Two rotator cuff surgeries cut short a promising career and Roberson returned to Jacksonville, Florida to work in the financial sector.

Tim Ireland was El Paso's manager that year and he would return to the Texas League finals three times during the 2000s: as the manager of the 2002 Tulsa Drillers and as the skipper of the 2003 and 2004 Frisco Roughriders.

1995: Bobby Jones returned as the Drillers' manager, hoping to rekindle the magic that produced a Texas League championship in 1992. But this would not be a year for pulling a rabbit out of a black top hat...or a baseball cap, for that matter.

The Drillers posted a league-worst 52-83 record and were horrible in the first half of that year, posting a 21-46 record. By comparison, the fewest victories in any half of a season in Texas League history were 19 in the second half of the 1979 season by the Amarillo Gold Sox. The Drillers also ranked dead last in the Texas League in seven hitting categories and seven pitching categories.

While season attendance topped 300,000 for the third year in a row, that sub-par performance was no small factor in the first decline in Tulsa's season attendance total since 1983. A total of 321,662 fans came to Drillers Stadium, even in spite of additional seating which increased the ballpark's capacity to 11,009.

After the season ended, general manager Joe Preseren resigned to accept a job in Frederick, Maryland as part of the Baltimore Orioles' player development program. During his 12 years in Tulsa, he was a two-time winner of the Texas League Executive of the Year Award (1987 and 1990), a two-time winner of the Double-A Minor League Baseball Executive of the Year award from *The Sporting News Magazine.* More importantly, season attendance nearly quadrupled under Preseren's family-friendly promotions.

On the field, Johnny Monell was the only Tulsa player to bat higher than .300, finishing at .306. Monell spent all 15 of his professional baseball seasons in the minor leagues or Mexican leagues but his son, Johnny Monell, Jr., played for the San Francisco Giants in 2013.

Hanley Frias led Tulsa with 14 stolen bases and later spent three of his four major league seasons with the Arizona Diamondbacks. Second baseman Alex Smith had a team-leading 16 home runs.

Julio Santana was, by default, the ace of Tulsa's pitching staff, posting a 6-4 record with a 3.15 ERA with three complete games in 15 starts. The nephew of former major leaguer Rico Carty, Santana pitched for six different teams over seven major-league seasons and played one year of baseball in Japan.

For the second year in a row, the Tulsa Drillers had no players chosen for the Texas League's postseason All-Star Team. But it was the last time that would happen.

Bruce Howard was in his seventh and final season as the Drillers' radio announcer on KAKC-AM (1300). Howard was hired by the University of Tulsa in June 1995 to be its Director of Sports Broadcasting and had done TU football and basketball broadcasts the previous two years.

Shreveport won its seventh and final Texas League championship by defeating the Midland Angels in the championship series, 4-1. Shreveport advanced directly to the finals by winning the Eastern Division's first and second half titles. Midland held off the Wichita Wranglers in the Western Division playoffs, 3-2.

Shreveport had the Eastern Division's best overall record at 88-47, followed by the Arkansas Travelers (70-65), Jackson Generals (62-73) and Tulsa Drillers (52-83). Wichita led the Western Division with a 72-64 record followed by the El Paso Diablos (68-68), Midland Angels (66-70) and San Antonio Missions (64-72).

Wichita outfielder Johnny Damon was the Texas League Player of the Year, ranking among the league's top five players in batting average (.343), on-base percentage (.434), stolen bases (26), runs scored (83) and base hits (145). The top draft choice in the 1992 amateur draft by the Kansas City Royals, he later starred for the Boston Red Sox and New York Yankees.

Damon was an American League All-Star in 2002 and 2005 and played on World Series championship teams in 2004 (Boston Red Sox) and 2009 (New York Yankees). He finished with a .284 career batting average over 18 seasons, ranked among the AL's top 10 base stealers eight times and among the top five outfielders in defensive putouts four times.

Shreveport right-hander Steve Bourgeois was the Texas League Pitcher of the Year in 1995, going 12-3 and posting the third-lowest earned run average among starting pitchers (2.85). Despite his minor league success, Bourgeois went 1-3 over 15 games with the parent San Francisco Giants and spent most of the 2000s playing for independent teams and in Mexican baseball.

1996: The Drillers reached the Texas League playoffs for the first time in four years, going from the league's worst record in 1995 to Eastern Division champions in 1996. Season attendance at Drillers Stadium rebounded from a one-year slump with 343,196 fans coming to watch the action, an increase of nearly 22,000 over the previous season.

The taste of success was very sweet but the Drillers' trip to the playoffs was turbulent, to say the least.

In the first half of the season, Tulsa needed to win just one of its final three games to clinch a playoff berth but could not get the job done. In the second half of the season, starting pitchers Juan Castillo, Jeff Davis and Dave Geeve suffered season-ending injuries and out-fielder Mark Little went on the disabled list for the final four weeks of play. Nevertheless, the Drillers rallied from three-and-a-half games out of first place with two weeks left to play and punched their ticket to the playoffs.

The Jackson Generals upset the Drillers in the Eastern Division playoffs, 3-1, and then swept the Wichita Wranglers in four games to win the league title. It would be Jackson's fifth and final Texas League championship. Ironically, both Jackson and Wichita finished regular season play with identical 70-70 records. Wichita had reached the finals by defeating the El Paso Diablos in the Western Division playoffs, 3-1.

Tulsa owned the Eastern Division's best overall record at 75-64, followed by the Shreveport Captains (73-66), Jackson Generals (70-70) and Arkansas Travelers (67-73). El Paso led the Western Division with a 76-63 record followed by the Wichita Wranglers (70-70), San Antonio Missions (69-70) and Midland Angels (58-82).

First baseman Charles Lee "Bubba" Smith hit a Texas League-leading 32 home runs, tying the franchise's single-season home run record set by Kevin Buckley in 1983 and easily winning Texas League Player of the Year honors. The 6-foot-6, 255-pounder also led the league with 94 RBIs, finished third in base hits (150) and also batted .292.

A 26th-round draft pick of the Seattle Mariners in 1991, Smith never advanced further than Triple-A competition and later played in Korea and Mexico and for independent teams in the United States.

Shortstop Hanley Frias led the Texas League with 12 triples while batting .287.

Right-handed pitcher Jonathan Johnson led Texas League pitchers with 13 victories and six complete games along with a 3.56 ERA. Johnson was a two-time All-American and pitched 16 scoreless innings to lead the Florida State University Seminoles to their first Atlantic Coast Conference baseball title in 1995.

Shortly afterwards, the Texas Rangers made him their first draft pick and the seventh overall selection in the 1995 amateur baseball draft. But Johnson was converted to a relief pitcher in the majors and didn't fare so well, posting a 2-4 record and a 6.63 ERA with three major league teams over six seasons.

After retiring from baseball, Johnson became an ordained minister and is one of the leaders of Honoring the Father Ministries, a sports-related Christian organization serving youth in Latin America. R.A. Dickey, who pitched for the 1999 Tulsa Drillers and won the 2012 National League Cy Young Award with the New York Mets, has also been involved with that ministry.

The Drillers introduced a kid-friendly mascot prior to the start of the season. The fact that it happened the day after Groundhog Day wasn't lost on many members of the local media.

The mascot was a large blue-colored bull named Hornsby, in a roundabout tribute to baseball Hall of Famer Rogers Hornsby. The Drillers' website said that Hornsby found his way to Tulsa from the plains of western Oklahoma. Then Hornsby became a student of David Raymond, the man who was the original mascot of the Philadelphia Phillies, the Phillie Phanatic.

Mark Neely began what would be a 13-year career as the radio announcer for Tulsa Drillers baseball games on KQLL-AM Radio (1430). The only other radio announcer to cover more games than Neely was Mack Creager who spent 23 complete seasons with the Tulsa Oilers.

A 1986 graduate of the University of Kansas, Neely previously called minor league baseball games on the radio in Boise, Idaho; Springfield, Illinois; Louisville, Kentucky and Salem, Virginia.

He would also serve as the radio voice of Tulsa Oilers minor league hockey, Oral Roberts University men's and women's basketball and University of Tulsa women's basketball. His work caught the ears of TV executives and work in major league baseball, college football and college basketball quickly followed, highlighted by appearances on ESPN and the Big Ten Conference's cable TV network.

During his time in Tulsa, Neely created an ironman streak that baseball legends Lou Gehrig and Cal Ripken Jr. would have appreciated. He once handled the play-by-play duties in 1,270 consecutive broadcasts of various sports. It was broken in July of 2000 when he was a sideline reporter for ESPN at the Double-A All-Star Baseball Game.

Shreveport pitcher Keith Foulke was the Texas League Pitcher of the Year, posting a 12-3 record and also finishing second in strikeouts (129) and second in lowest ERA by a starting pitcher (2.76). In his only season with the Oakland Athletics (2003), Foulke led the American League in saves (43) and games finished (67).

But his star shone brightest during the Boston Red Sox's march to the 2004 World Series championship, their first such triumph since 1918. Foulke pitched in 11 of their 14 postseason contests, allowing just one run and scattering seven hits over 14 innings and also won one game and saved three other victories.

1997: After a horrible first half of the season (23-44), the Drillers barely missed reaching the playoffs for the second year in a row. They went 38-34 in the second half but Shreveport, which won the Eastern Division's first half title, advanced to the playoffs by going 39-32 in the second half. Tulsa held a three-game lead over Shreveport with two weeks remaining, then lost six of its final eight games with five of those being one-run losses.

A 19-8 slugfest with the Shreveport Captains on June 19th was a memorable contest. The Drillers trailed, 6-1, when they came to bat in the bottom of the fifth inning. When the smoke cleared, they held an 18-8 lead after six innings.

Dan Collier and Fernando Tatis were the Texas League's top two players when it came to hitting home runs. Collier led the league with 26 and Tatis was close behind with 24.

Collier, who played the previous six years in the Boston Red Sox's minor league system, became the first Texas League player to hit a home run in seven consecutive games and just the fourth player in minor league baseball to achieve that feat. By comparison, the major league record for home runs in consecutive games is eight, shared by Dale Long, Don Mattingly and Ken Griffey, Jr.

Collier's 26 home runs marked the only time in Texas League history that any Tulsa baseball player led the league in home runs in consecutive seasons. But that would be Collier's final season in minor league baseball due to shoulder surgery complications that left him unable to throw a baseball for over two years.

Had Tatis not been promoted to the parent Texas Rangers in late July of that year, he would have likely broken the Driller franchise record for most home runs in a season and also made a serious run at being just the third player in Tulsa professional baseball history to hit 40 or more home runs in a season.

He once missed pre-game batting practice to pick up his late-arriving fiancée at the Tulsa airport. He more than apologized a few hours later by becoming the first Driller to hit three home runs in a game. In 102 games with the Drillers, Tatis also batted .314, drove in 61 runs and stole 17 bases.

Tatis was later traded to the St. Louis Cardinals and on April 23, 1999, he became the first major leaguer to hit two grand slam home runs in one inning. Both of those came off Los Angeles Dodgers pitcher Chan Ho Park. That was also his best major league season with 34 home runs, 107 RBIs and 21 stolen bases.

Second baseman Edwin Diaz set a Texas League record by striking out six times in a 5-4, 10-inning loss at Jackson on August 28, 1997. But he was a respectable hitter with Tulsa that year, batting .275 and hitting 15 home runs. Diaz had 20 or more doubles in nine of his 13 minor league seasons.

Driller baseball was carried on KQLL-AM (1430) with Mark Neely handling all of the announcing duties.

San Antonio won its first Texas League championship since defeating the Tulsa Oilers in the 1964 finals. The Missions, who won the first and second half Western Division titles, defeated Shreveport in the finals, 4-3.

For the second time in three years, El Paso swept the Texas League Player of the Year and Pitcher of the Year honors, with Mike Kinkade and Steve Woodard being the respective winners.

Kinkade's .385 batting average was the fifth-highest in Texas League history and the highest since Danny Clark hit .399 with the 1925 San Antonio Bears. Kinkade also led the league in RBIs (109), base hits (180), on-base percentage (.455), runs scored (112).

While Kincaide batted just .256 over parts of six years with three major league teams, he was a member of the United States' gold medal-winning baseball team in the 2000 Summer Olympics in Sydney, Australia. Kinkade scored the tying run in Team USA's comeback victory over Korea in the Olympic semifinals.

Woodard struck out 95 batters and walked only 27 while posting a 14-3 record and 3.17 ERA and leading the league with six complete games. He moved up to the parent Milwaukee Brewers the following year and was voted as the team's best rookie player with 135 strikeouts and 33 walks while going 10-12 that year. Woodard played seven years in the major leagues and finished with a 32-36 record.

Country music superstar and Oklahoma native Garth Brooks drew 80,000 fans for five sellout concerts at Drillers Stadium on July 17th through 21st, the largest attendance for any non-baseball event in the stadium's history. In additional to the existing 10,800 baseball seats, bleachers were added to seat 5,200 more fans.

A six-story stage was built over second base and a combination of rails and porous plastic coverings allowed the infield and outfield grasses to still get water and sunlight. Concession stands were created in the team dugouts and beyond the box seats stretching behind first base and third base. Portable restrooms added a "crowning" touch to the stadium design, stretching from foul pole to foul pole.

A sudden and severe thunderstorm hit the stadium about an hour before the start of the July 20th concert. Approximately 20,000 Tulsa residents lost electrical service but there were no injuries and the concert proceeded after a brief delay.

Besides being a javelin thrower for Oklahoma State University's track and field team in 1980-83, baseball is a part of Brooks' athletic background. He attended the 2000 New York Mets' spring training camp as a third baseman-outfielder to benefit one of his charitable programs.

Brooks was a 2012 inductee into the Country Music Hall of Fame and today lives with his wife, award-winning singer/author Trisha Yearwood, and his daughters at a rural home northeast of Tulsa.

1998: To call this edition of the Tulsa Drillers the best in the franchise's history would be an understatement. They set a franchise record of 78 victories in one season and claimed their third (and what's proven to be their most recent) Texas League championship. It was also the eighth Texas League title won by a Tulsa professional baseball team.

Tulsa claimed its first league championship in 10 years by defeating the Wichita Wranglers in the finals, 4-3. Ironically, the Drillers won the pennant on September 12th, which was also the 30th anniversary of the 1968 Tulsa Oilers' clinching of the Triple-A Pacific Coast League championship.

The Drillers swept the Arkansas Travelers in three games to win the Eastern Division playoffs. Wichita advanced by defeating the San Antonio Missions in the Western Division playoffs, 3-2.

The Arkansas Travelers actually had the Eastern Division's best overall record at 80-60, followed by the Tulsa Drillers (78-62), Jackson Generals (70-70) and the Shreveport Captains (57-83). Wichita had the Western Division's best record at 75-65, followed by the El Paso Diablos (69-71), San Antonio Missions (67-73) and Midland Angels (64-76).

The Drillers made one of the greatest turnarounds in the Texas League's split season history. After tumbling to a 28-40 record in the first half, the Drillers were hotter than summertime in Oklahoma during the second half and finished 50-22. That was the first time that a second half champion had won 50 or more games in the Texas League since the 1932 Dallas Steers had 56 wins.

Those 78 victories were also the most by a Tulsa professional baseball team since the 1972 Triple-A Tulsa Oilers went 78-62.

Outfielder Ruben Mateo's 27-game hitting streak, which ran from June 16th to July 14th, was the longest in Tulsa's professional baseball history. He finished with a .309 batting average, led the Drillers with 18 home runs and was second on the team in base hits (134), doubles (32), runs scored (79), RBIs (75), and stolen bases (18). Mateo spent three of his six major league seasons with the Texas Rangers.

Another factor in Tulsa's success was a helping hand lent by the expansion Arizona Diamondbacks. The Diamondbacks didn't have enough players to fill a Double-A team of their own that year but the Texas Rangers allowed them to send some of those players to Tulsa.

One of those players was second baseman Ernest Lee (Junior) Spivey, a graduate of Oklahoma City's Frederick A. Douglass High School. Despite being a 36th-round draft choice of the Diamondbacks, Spivey batted .311 in just 34 games with the Drillers and would be a member of the Diamondbacks' 2001 World Series champions that defeated the New York Yankees. Spivey also played for the National League in the 2002 Major League All-Star Game.

Another Diamondback prospect was outfielder Jason Conti, a 32nd-round draft choice who wound up making the Texas League's postseason All-Star Team. He led the Texas League in runs scored (125) and ranked second in base hits (167) and triples (12) while batting .315. Conti was also very talented as a defensive player and had a strong throwing arm. He also set a Texas League single-game record on May 27th by reaching first base twice on interference by the catcher.

Shortstop Kelly Dransfeldt drove in 112 runs, which was the most by any middle infield in minor league baseball that year. He also had eight RBIs in the championship series against Wichita along with four postseason home runs and drew raves from fans and scouts alike for his excellent fielding skills.

The parent Texas Rangers once viewed Dransfeldt, a collegiate standout at the University of Michigan, as their future shortstop. That is, until they decided to sign Alex Rodriguez to a $252 million contract. Dransfeldt eventually played 51 major league games with the Rangers and Chicago White Sox over parts of four seasons.

Driller baseball was carried on KQLL-AM (1430) with Mark Neely handling all of the announcing duties.

Despite Tulsa's championship campaign, Arkansas swept the Texas League Player of the Year and Pitcher of the Year awards with outfielder Tyrone Horne and Jose Jimenez being the respective winners.

Horne led the Texas League with 37 home runs and 139 RBIs while batting .312. He was a 44th-round draft pick of the Montreal Expos in 1989 and bounced between several minor league teams until landing with the Travelers and making professional baseball history during the Travelers' 13-4 victory at San Antonio on July 27th.

That night, Horne did something that no major league or minor league baseball player had ever done before or since: hitting for the cycle in home runs. He hit a two-run home run in the first inning, belted a grand slam in the second inning, added a solo home run in the fifth inning and capped the night with a three-run shot in the sixth.

Horne himself never made it to the Baseball Hall of Fame, much less the major leagues as a neck injury ended his 13-year minor league career in 2001 but his bat is on display in Cooperstown.

Jimenez led the league in victories with 15 and posted a 3.11 ERA. As a St. Louis Cardinals rookie, he threw a no-hitter against the Arizona Diamondbacks on June 25, 1999 and outpitched 2015 Baseball Hall of Fame inductee Randy Johnson. But Jimenez went 5-14 that year and would be traded to the Colorado Rockies. Jimenez then became the Rockies' top relief pitcher from 2000 through 2003 with a career-best 41 saves in 2002.

Adrian Beltre, a 2004 inductee into the National Baseball Hall of Fame, was a 19-year-old third baseman for the San Antonio Missions when he faced the Drillers that season. Beltre had a .321 batting average over 64 games with 13 home runs and 56 runs batted in.

Beltre played for four teams in his major league career: the Los Angeles Dodgers (1998-2004), Seattle Mariners (2005-09), Boston

Red Sox (2010) and the Texas Rangers (2011-18). He appeared in four All-Star Games and won five Gold Gloves for his defensive skills.

1999: The Tulsa Drillers and Wichita Wranglers collided in the Texas League finals for the second straight year, but the Wranglers wrought revenge with a four-game sweep. It would be Wichita's second and final Texas League pennant.

The Drillers had defeated the Shreveport Captains in the Eastern Division playoffs, 3-1, while Wichita advanced by winning the Western Division's first and second half titles.

Tulsa had the best overall record in the Eastern Division at 74-66, followed by Shreveport (71-69), the Jackson Generals (68-72) and Arkansas Travelers (59-81). Wichita had the Western Division's best overall record at 83-57, followed by the Midland RockHounds (74-66), San Antonio Missions (67-73) and El Paso Diablos (64-76).

It was the Drillers' third playoff appearance in four years; a feat that had not happened in Tulsa professional baseball since a span from 1965 through 1968. Back then, the Oilers reached the Double-A Texas League playoffs in 1965, then qualified for the Triple-A Pacific Coast League playoffs in 1966 and 1968.

Tulsa clinched the second half Eastern Division title on the final day of the regular season in a victory at Jackson. Right fielder Juan Piniella, who struck out more times that year (120) than any other Driller, hit a grand slam home run to win the game and clinch the playoff berth. Piniella played nine years in the minor leagues but never reached the majors.

A key to Tulsa's second half success was leftfielder, Cliff Brumbaugh, who had 20 home runs and 57 RBIs coming down the stretch. By contrast, Brumbaugh hit just five home runs with 32 RBIs during the first half schedule. He later played in the minor league systems of the Colorado Rockies and Chicago White Sox before finishing his baseball career playing for teams in South Korea, Japan and Mexico.

R.A. Dickey, the 2012 National League Cy Young award winner with the New York Mets, was the biggest success story among Driller pitchers that year. What made Dickey's success more remarkable is that after the Texas Rangers made the University of Tennessee stand-out their first selection (and the 18th overall) in the 1996 amateur draft, doctors discovered Dickey's throwing arm did not have an important tendon in his throwing elbow. That meant his baseball career was one pitch away from ending on countless occasions.

Because that missing arm tendon didn't provide the power and velocity that most pitchers have, the knuckleball was adopted as the go-to pitch. Dickey had a 6-7 record, a 4.55 ERA and 10 saves with the Drillers but his strikeouts-to-walks ratio improved dramatically after being moved from the bullpen into the starting rotation. That move also laid the foundation for success in the major leagues.

Dickey's 2012 campaign with the New York Mets was the finest of his big-league career. He led the National League in strikeouts (230), innings pitched (233.2), games started (33), complete games (five) and shutouts (three) as well as being the National League's starting pitcher in the All-Star Game. But a dispute over a new contract led the Mets to include Dickey in a seven-player trade with the Toronto Blue Jays the week before Christmas 2012.

Dickey has worked with former Tulsa Driller pitcher-turned-minister Jonathan Johnson on foreign mission trips combining religion and sports activities and also helped in the construction of Latin American churches. Dickey also took part in a 2011 postseason fund-raising climb of Africa's Mount Kilimanjaro despite threats by the Mets that his contract could be voided.

In an autobiography published prior to the 2012 season, Dickey said that he was a victim of sexual abuse during his childhood and also how surprised he had been by the widespread use of illegal steroids when he joined the Rangers in 2001.

Tulsa hosted the Texas League All-Star Game for the fifth time and drew a crowd of 9,374 fans to Drillers Stadium despite a temperature of 96 degrees when the game began. It was the largest attendance for a Texas League All-Star Game played on American soil since 1966 when 10,434 saw the game at Arlington Stadium.

El Paso catcher Rod Barajas was the game's Most Valuable Player, ripping a two-run home run in the fourth inning to lift the West All-Stars to a 4-0 victory over the East All-Stars. Six Drillers played in the game and manager Bobby Jones was a coach for the East team.

Tulsa pitchers R.A. Dickey and Corey Lee threw one scoreless inning apiece while second baseman Tom Sergio and third baseman Mike Lamb each had a base hit.

Lamb led the Texas League that year with 176 base hits (a Tulsa Driller season record) and 51 doubles. That latter total was the most by a Texas League player since Herb Conyers had 52 doubles with the 1949 Oklahoma City Indians. Lamb played for five major league teams from 2000 through 2010.

The season attendance total of 351,929 fans was the highest in Tulsa's professional baseball history to that point in time.

Driller baseball was carried on KQLL-AM (1430) with Mark Neely handling all of the announcing duties.

Baseball fans would notice what the winners of the 1999 Texas League postseason player awards did in the major leagues over ensuing years, but in a negative light. Both honorees were named in the Mitchell Report, which claimed that there was widespread use of illegal performance-enhancing substances and would also lead to the current and stricter program of drug testing.

Midland third baseman Adam Piatt was the Texas League Player of the Year, leading the league with 39 home runs, 135 RBIs, 90 extra base hits, 128 runs scored and also batted .345.

Piatt's testimony in the Mitchell Report stated that during his time with the 2000-03 Oakland Athletics, he not only used illegal substances but also sold them to teammate Miguel Tejada, who would win the American League Most Valuable Player award in 2002. Piatt publicly apologized for his wrong-doings and later entered a career in financial investments.

San Antonio's Eric Gagne, who once pitched for Seminole (Oklahoma) Junior College, was the Texas League Pitcher of the Year. A hard-throwing right-hander, he led the league with 185 strikeouts in 26 games and went 12-4 with a 2.63 ERA.

Gagne appeared to be a lock for a spot in the starting pitching rotation of the parent Los Angeles Dodgers until manager Jim Tracy made him the team's bullpen ace in 2002. The rest was baseball history. He was major league baseball's best relief pitcher from 2002 through 2004 with 52, 55 and 45 saves in those respective All-Star seasons along with 365 strikeouts and just 58 walks over that three-year span. In 2003, he became the second Canadian-born pitcher to win the National League's Cy Young Award (former Chicago Cubs ace Ferguson Jenkins was the other person).

Gagne's name appeared in the Mitchell Report as a player who was accused of using illegal substances while he played for the Dodgers. Gagne later admitted to using human growth hormone (HGH) in trying to recover from a knee injury but added that HGH probably shortened his baseball career by five years.

Chapter Eleven

The 2000s

The start of the 21st century brought life-changing events. Apple, Inc., unveiled the iPod, which changed the way people listened to music and its iPhone forever changed how people communicate with each other. Social media grew by leaps and bounds thanks to the introduction of Facebook and Twitter. The fantasy-themed novel series of *Harry Potter* and *Twilight* captured the imagination of readers around the world and a series of hit movies soon followed.

There were two historic presidential elections. George W. Bush lost the 2000 popular vote to Democrat Al Gore but the Republican former governor of Texas won the election by carrying the Electoral College. Barack Obama, a Democrat U.S. Senator from Illinois, in 2008 became the first African-American to be elected as President.

The Boston Red Sox won their first World Series in 86 years but baseball received a black eye when the Mitchell Report documented widespread abuse of performance enhancing drugs throughout the sport. Golfer Tiger Woods completed a unique Grand Slam by winning the U.S. and British Opens and the PGA Championship in 2000 then opened 2001 with a victory in The Masters. American Olympian swimmer Michael Phelps made history by winning eight gold medals in the 2008 Summer Games in Beijing, China.

Tragedies of unprecedented proportions struck throughout the world. Over 2,900 people were killed on September 11, 2001 when Islamic terrorists hijacked and then crashed commercial jetliners in Boston, New York City, and Washington, D.C. A 2004 mega-earthquake in the Indian Ocean created a gigantic tidal wave and related flooding that killed over 230,000 people in the countries of Indonesia, India, Thailand and Sri Lanka. Over 1,800 people died and $108 billion worth of damage occurred in 2005 when Hurricane Katrina, the third-strong hurricane ever recorded, crashed ashore near New Orleans, Louisiana.

Two Oklahoma-based singers began their music careers with respective victories on the Fox reality TV show *American Idol*. Checotah native Carrie Underwood won in 2005 and became a country music superstar. David Cook, who performed in a Tulsa-based rock band, won in 2008 and went on to a successful performing career.

The Tulsa Drillers reached the Texas League playoffs five times, highlighted by a trip to the championship finals in 2002 but came up short each time. They also had six different managers over a five-year period. Nevertheless, attendance kept increasing and topped the 300,000 mark.

Pitcher Jeff Francis was the best pitcher in minor league baseball during a magical 2004 season. Shortstop Troy Tulowitzki became arguably the best-known Tulsa Driller to wear a Colorado Rockies uniform. Center fielder Dexter Fowler showcased the tools that earned a quick promotion to the major leagues.

A 26-year affiliation between the Tulsa Drillers and Texas Rangers ended after the 2002 season. That void was quickly filled by a partnership with the Colorado Rockies. It would also be the end of the line for the aging Drillers Stadium at Expo Square with construction beginning on ONEOK Field in downtown Tulsa.

Bobby Jones became the winningest manager in Tulsa professional baseball history, finishing with 486 career victories before moving up within the Rangers' organization. In 2007, first base coach Scott Coolbaugh died after being hit in the head by a foul ball during a game in Little Rock, Arkansas.

2000: This was a disappointing season with the Drillers missing the playoffs, going through three managers and beginning what would be a four-year decline in season attendance. But Carlos Pena was a power-hitting first baseman who used his time in Tulsa as a cornerstone in building his big-league career.

Pena was the Texas Rangers' first pick and the 10th overall selection in the 1998 amateur draft after playing for Northeastern University in Boston, Massachusetts. He received the highest signing bonus ever paid to that point in time by the Texas Rangers and proved he was worth every penny as Tulsa rallied for a 9-7 season-opening win over the Shreveport Captains. The first of Pena's two home runs sparked Tulsa's rally from a 7-2 deficit and his grand slam in the seventh inning proved to be the game-winning hit.

Pena put on a tantalizing power display, leading the Texas League in runs scored with 117, ranked second in base hits (158) and RBIs (105), shared third place for most home runs (28) while batting .299. But with sluggers like Rafael Palmeiro, Ruben Sierra and Andres Galarraga already on the Texas Rangers' roster, find fame and fortune in the American League had to happen somewhere else.

He found it with the Tampa Bay Rays, starting by winning the 2007 American League Comeback Player of the Year with a career-high 46 home runs and 121 RBIs. A Gold Glove award for defensive excellence followed with Tampa Bay's 2008 American League champions. Despite missing most of the final month of the 2009 season with a broken hand, he hit 39 home runs and tied New York Yankees slugger Mark Teixeira for the AL's home run leadership. Pena would hit 20 or more home runs in six of his 14 major-league seasons.

Right fielder Craig Monroe etched his name in Tulsa baseball history by hitting three home runs and driving in nine runs during a 17-2 victory over Shreveport on April 8th at Drillers Stadium. Monroe's nine RBIs tied a single game record set by Tulsa Oiler Wally Post on September 1, 1950 and his three homers made him the third Tulsa professional baseball player to achieve that feat.

Monroe batted .282 with 20 home runs, 89 RBIs and scored 89 runs. He would spend six of his nine major league seasons with the Detroit Tigers (2002-07) and later worked as a studio analyst for the Tigers' TV network.

Manager Bobby Jones joined the Rangers as an assistant coach on May 8th. Moe Hill went 4-5 as Tulsa's interim manager and James Byrd was named manager for the rest of the season on May 17th and finished the season with a 50-50 record.

Pitcher Spike Lundberg was the winning pitcher in the Double-A Association All-Star Game and was also named the Texas League's Star of Stars in that event. Lundberg, who moved from the bullpen into the starting rotation that year, finished 14-7 and won his final nine starting assignments. His earned run average of 3.05 was the third-best among Texas League starting pitchers. After playing 13 years in the minors, Lundberg worked for baseball player agent Scott Boras before working as a baseball scout.

Season attendance was 334,207, a drop of nearly 17,000 from the record-setting attendance total of the previous year.

Driller baseball was carried on KQLL-AM (1430) with Mark Neely calling the game action.

The Round Rock Express won a Texas League championship in their first year of existence, defeating the Wichita Wranglers in the finals, 4-1. The franchise had operated as the Jackson Generals for the previous 10 years. Round Rock defeated the El Paso Diablos in the Western Division playoffs, 3-2, while Wichita eliminated the Shreveport Captains, 3-1.

Round Rock is located just north of Austin, the capital of Texas. Two owners of the Round Rock franchise were Hall of Fame pitcher Nolan Ryan and his son, Reid, and the "Express" was derived from Nolan Ryan's nickname during his distinguished career.

Wichita had the Eastern Division's best overall record at 76-61, followed by the Arkansas Travelers (68-71), Tulsa Drillers (64-76) and Shreveport Captains (58-81). Round Rock led the Western Division with an 83-57 record followed by the El Paso Diablos (74-66), Midland RockHounds (70-69) and San Antonio Missions (64-76).

Round Rock second baseman Keith Ginter was the Texas League Player of the Year, batting .333 with 26 home runs, 92 RBIs and finishing among the league's best hitters in four offensive categories. Ginter, an All-American at Texas Tech University and one of that school's top players during the 1990s, spent six years in the majors.

Arkansas pitcher Bud Smith was the Texas League Pitcher of the Year and was also named as Player of the Year for all of Double-A baseball. He had a 12-1 record with a 2.32 ERA and 102 strikeouts in nearly 109 innings. Shortly after moving up to the parent St. Louis Cardinals in 2001, he became the 18th major league rookie pitcher since 1900 to throw a no-hitter, weaving a 4-0 masterpiece against the San Diego Padres on September 3, 2001.

Smith was sent to the Philadelphia Phillies in 2002 as part of a trade that brought Scott Rolen to the Cardinals. Phillies fans hoped Smith would fill the shoes of Curt Schilling as the team's power pitcher. But arm problems related to being overworked in the minors kept Smith from going higher than the Triple-A level.

2001: The Drillers came within two games of making the Texas League playoffs but the story of this season was a hot-hitting and history making third baseman named Hank Blalock.

On June 26th, Blalock became the first Driller to hit for the cycle (a single, double, triple and home run in one game) in a victory over the Midland RockHounds. Two days later, he repeated that feat and became the first minor leaguer in baseball's "modern era" to hit for the cycle twice in a single season.

That June 28th contest had a different kind of drama for the talented youngster. The game was in the 10th inning when Blalock tumbled to the ground after lightning struck near the ballpark. After settling his nerves during a lengthy rain delay, Blalock belted a two-run homer in the 11th inning to win the game.

Blalock was promoted to the big leagues in 2002 and joined multi-millionaire shortstop Alex Rodriguez on the left side of the Rangers' infield. He also played for the American League in the 2003 and 2004 All-Star Games, hitting 61 home runs and driving in 200 runs over those two years. But a series of injuries over nine major-league seasons kept Blalock from living up to the lofty expectations others held for him.

Kevin Mench tied a Texas League record by belting two doubles in the same inning (fourth) of a 10-6 home victory over the Arkansas Travelers on August 8th. Mench, who spent five of his eight major league seasons with the Rangers, was the subject of an urban legend where his 8-1/4 cap size was reportedly the largest of anyone in the history of major league baseball.

Left-handed pitcher Andy Pratt threw the first no-hitter by a Drillers pitcher in 10 years in a 1-0, seven-inning victory over the

Arkansas Travelers in the first game of an April 13th doubleheader in Little Rock. Pratt, who struck out 11 batters and allowed just two walks, had not posted a victory over his last 10 starts of the previous season.

Pratt had an 8-10 record that year and ranked eighth among Texas League pitchers in strikeouts (132). Pratt's major league career consisted of one game with the 2002 Atlanta Braves and four games with the 2004 Chicago Cubs.

Colby Lewis led Tulsa pitchers with 10 victories and ranked fourth among Texas League pitchers in strikeouts (162). Unfortunately, he also led the league's pitchers in wild pitches (16) and hitting batters with a pitch (16). Lewis spent six of his eight major league seasons with the Rangers and pitched for their 2010 and 2011 American League championship teams.

Paul Carey posed a 69-70 in his only season as the Tulsa Drillers' manager. Carey was a two-time All-American at Stanford University and the Most Outstanding Player in the 1987 College World Series. His walk-off grand-slam home run capped a furious rally by the Cardinal in the championship game against Louisiana State University and future major league pitcher Ben McDonald. But success as a minor league manager was a different story as all five seasons spent with Ranger affiliates produced just one winning season.

Mark Neely once again was the radio voice for Tulsa Drillers baseball and the games were still carried on AM 1430. But on New Year's Day, the station's call letters changed to KTBZ-AM with a new nickname of "The Buzz." Driller games are still carried on "The Buzz", making it the longest continuous broadcast affiliation in Tulsa's professional baseball history.

The Arkansas Travelers were crowned as Texas League champions for the fifth time in team history and earned their first pennant since

1989 as they defeated the Round Rock Express in the championship series, 2-0. That best-of-seven series was cut short due to the aftermath of terrorist attacks on the United States on September 11th.

Arkansas defeated the Wichita Wranglers, 3-1, in the Eastern Division playoffs. The Drillers made a late-season run to try reaching the playoffs, but Wichita prevailed with a 43-27 second half record to Tulsa's 41-29 mark. Round Rock edged the San Antonio Missions, 3-2, in the Western Division playoffs.

Wichita had the Eastern Division's best overall record at 76-61, followed by the Arkansas Travelers (68-71), Tulsa Drillers (64-76) and Shreveport Captains (58-81). Round Rock led the Western Division with an 83-57 record followed by the El Paso Diablos (74-66), Midland RockHounds (70-69) and San Antonio Missions (64-76).

Round Rock won both postseason honors with outfielder Jason Lane winning the Texas League Player of the Year award and Tim Redding taking the Pitcher of the Year award.

Lane led the league with 124 RBIs and 103 runs scored while batting .316 with 38 home runs and 14 stolen bases. He played for the University of Southern California's 1998 College World Series champions and hit a grand slam home run in the title game. Lane's best major league season was in 2005 with 26 home runs and 76 RBIs for the Houston Astros' National League champions.

Redding went 10-2 with a 2.18 ERA along with 113 strikeouts and only 25 walks in 14 games. It was his third consecutive minor league season with over 100 strikeouts. His best major league seasons were in 2003 with the Houston Astros (a 3.68 ERA despite a 10-14 record) and with the 2008 Washington Nationals (10-11).

2002: The month of September was one of the most memorable in Tulsa Drillers history. They came within one game of winning the Texas League championship, ended a 26-year association with the

Texas Rangers and began their current relationship with the Colorado Rockies.

San Antonio claimed its seventh Texas League title by defeating Tulsa in the best-of-seven finals, 4-3. San Antonio eliminated the Round Rock Express in the Western Division playoffs, 3-2, for the chance to face Tulsa in the championship series. The Missions had a marvelous season, rebounding from being the Texas League's worst overall team in the first half (25-45) to finish 43-27 in the second half.

Right-handed pitcher Rafael Soriano had a season-high 14 strike-outs in San Antonio's 4-1 victory in the Missions' triumph over the Drillers. Soriano later became a relief pitcher and has posted 40 or more saves three times in his career, highlighted by an American League-leading 45 saves with the Tampa Bay Rays in 2010.

The first game of that Tulsa-San Antonio showdown was one of the most memorable in Texas League championship history. Driller pitchers Ben Kozlowski and Keith Stamler combined on a nine-inning no-hitter but the game went into extra innings. Adrian Myers, who played for the Drillers in 1999, ended the no-hitter with a two-out RBI single in the 10th inning and the Missions went on to win, 3-2.

Tulsa swept the Wichita Wranglers in three games to win the Eastern Division playoffs and allowed the Wranglers to score just three combined runs. Shortstop Drew Meyer, who had played in the College World Series with the University of South Carolina just three months prior, scored the winning run in the Drillers' last two triumphs.

What made Tulsa's sweep of Wichita more satisfying was that the Drillers had ended the regular season with a nine-game losing streak, the longest such skid by any Driller team in 15 years.

Earlier in the year, the Drillers endured a nightmarish 19-2 loss at Wichita on May 22nd in which the Wranglers rewrote part of the

Texas League's record book. The Wranglers set seven offensive team records in a single inning: most runs in a third inning (14), most consecutive players scoring a run (14), most hits in an inning (13), most players with two hits in an inning (5), most batters reaching first base (16), most consecutive batters reaching first base (16) and most singles (7).

And to top it all off, Wichita's Harris became just the sixth Texas League player to bat three times in a single inning. All three of Harris' hits in that inning were home runs. The teams played a late-morning game the next day and Tulsa won that contest, 5-2.

Wichita had the Eastern Division's best overall record at 80-59, followed by Tulsa (72-67), the Shreveport Swamp Dragons (60-79), and Arkansas Travelers (51-89). The El Paso Diablos actually had the Western Division's best record at 76-62 record, followed by the Midland RockHounds (75-64), Round Rock (75-65) and San Antonio (68-72).

Tim Ireland, who took the El Paso Diablos to the Texas League title in 1994, was Tulsa's manager in 2002. When the Rangers moved their Double-A affiliate to Frisco, Texas, for the 2003 season, Ireland stayed with the Rangers' player development program and took the Frisco RoughRiders to two consecutive playoff appearances and a Texas League title in 2004.

Ireland's major league playing career consisted of 11 games with the 1981-82 Kansas City Royals. But in 10 complete seasons as a minor league manager, Ireland's teams made six playoff appearances and won three league championships. Inexplicably, he was replaced in the first year of his two attempts in managing at the Triple-A level.

First baseman Mark Teixeira, the Rangers' first round draft pick and fifth overall selection in the 2001 amateur draft, was impressive in just 48 games with the Drillers. The Georgia Tech University product batted .316 and hit 10 home runs with 28 runs batted in. Teixeria quickly moved up to the majors leagues and has played for the New York Yankees since 2009. He has been a two-time American League All-Star and earned three of his five Gold Glove awards for defensive excellence as a Yankee.

Travis Hughes was Tulsa's pitching ace, posting a 9-7 record with a 3.52 ERA and ranked second in the Texas League in strikeouts (137). The 6-foot-5 right-hander's big-league experience came with the 2005 and 2006 Washington Nationals.

Relief pitcher Greg Runser led the Texas League with 25 saves, something made more remarkable by his 1-4 record and having more walks (29) than strikeouts (25). Following his stay in Tulsa, Runser played for four independent teams in as many years.

Arkansas Travelers pitcher Hatuey Mendoza threw a nine-inning no-hitter at Drillers Stadium in a 3-0 victory on May 13th. What made the feat more remarkable was that he was a last-minute substitute for scheduled starter Tony Milo, who developed elbow problems. Mendoza retired the last 24 Drillers that he faced and allowed just two batters (one hit batsman and one walk) to reach base. Prior to the no-hitter, Mendoza's minor league career record was 25-52 with a 5.92 ERA.

Driller games were broadcast on KTBZ-AM (1430, "The Buzz") with Mark Neely calling the action.

El Paso third baseman Chad Tracy was the Texas League Player of the Year, leading the league in batting average (.344), doubles (39) and base hits (177). He earned Pacific Coast League MVP honors the following year before spending six years with the Arizona Diamondbacks and topped 20 home runs in 2005 and 2006. Tracy later played for the Washington Nationals as a pinch-hitting specialist and played a key role on their 2012 National League Eastern Division championship team.

Kirk Saarloos of Round Rock was the Texas League Pitcher of the Year, posting a 10-1 record, 1.40 ERA and 82 strikeouts in just 13 appearances. On June 11, 2003, he was part of baseball history as one of a major league-record six Houston Astros pitchers who combined to throw a no-hitter at Yankee Stadium against the New York Yankees. Saarloos later worked as a collegiate pitching coach.

On September 26th, an agreement was reached between the Drillers, Texas Rangers and Colorado Rockies regarding Tulsa's Double-A baseball affiliation. The Drillers were allowed to end a four-year contract with the Rangers two years earlier than planned and then they signed a contract to serve as the Rockies' Double-A affiliate.

The Rangers had announced plans back in 2000 to build a stadium for its Double-A franchise in Frisco, Texas, which is about 35 miles northeast of Rangers Stadium in Arlington, Texas. The Rangers had purchased the former Shreveport Captains franchise and moved it to Frisco.

During a 26-year affiliation with the Texas Rangers, the Tulsa Drillers reached the Texas League playoffs nine times and claimed championships in 1982, 1988 and 1998. The Drillers' last appearance in a Texas League championship series would be in 2002.

The Colorado Rockies had longed for a Double-A affiliate in the Texas League ever since their inception. Their previous Double-A affiliate had been the Carolina Mudcats and played in Zebulon, North Carolina.

Many baseball observers, including some in Tulsa, had questions about the wisdom of the move back then. The Rockies had their hands full with declining attendance as well as being on the financial hook for huge contracts to players who had seen better days.

But through good times and bad, the Rockies showed a commitment to player development with an increased emphasis beginning when players were promoted to Tulsa. The Drillers made seven Texas League postseason appearances during their 12-year affiliation with the Rockies but they reached the championship series only once during that time.

2003: The Drillers had the best overall record in the Texas League's Eastern Division but they missed reaching the playoffs on a tiebreaker. After going 34-34 in the first half of the season, Tulsa made a furious finish by winning 13 of its last 20 games for a 40-30 second half record. The Wichita Wranglers got the playoff berth because of its better season record in head-to-head games with Tulsa.

Tulsa's 74-64 overall record was the sixth-best in franchise history to that point in time. But it also marked the seventh time in 15 previous seasons that they lost a half-season in which it led during that half-season's final week.

The Drillers had a local attraction with former Oklahoma State University star outfielder Matt Holliday playing for them. He was a seventh-round draft pick of the Colorado Rockies in the 1998 amateur draft as well as a high-school football star at Stillwater High School with 68 career touchdown passes, 35 of those coming in his junior year.

Holliday was likely guilty of trying too hard when playing in Tulsa and his .253 batting average and hitting only 12 home runs were evidence of that. But an adjustment to his batting stance led to a better second half of the season and his 72 runs batted in ranked sixth in the Texas League.

He moved up to the major leagues to stay in 2004 and spent most of his big-league career with the Rockies and St. Louis Cardinals with a one-year stint with the Oakland Athletics sandwiched in between.

With the 2007 Rockies, he led the National League in batting average (.340), runs batted in (137), doubles (50) and total base hits (216).

Holliday is a six-time National League All-Star (three times each with the Rockies and Cardinals) and played on the Rockies' 2007 NL championship teams and for the Cardinals' NL title teams in 2011 and 2013.

His father, Tom, spent 26 years as an assistant coach and then head coach at Oklahoma State. During that time, the Cowboys made 11 appearances in the College World Series and 155 players would play in the major leagues. Tom is currently the pitching coach at Auburn University. Tom's other son and Matt's brother, Josh, has been OSU's head baseball coach since the 2013 season.

Outfielder Cory Sullivan and pitcher Chin-Hui Tsao were Texas League leaders that year. Sullivan led the league with 167 base hits then missed the entire 2004 season due to injuries. He spent four of his six major league seasons with the Colorado Rockies.

Tsao had the league's best earned run average (2.46) while posting an 11-4 record with 125 strikeouts and just 26 walks in 18 starts. He also pitched for Chinese Taipei in the 2004 and 2008 Summer Olympic Games. Tsao became the first Taiwanese pitcher to play in the major leagues and the Rockies viewed him as their ace relief pitcher in 2005 but shoulder injuries ended his big-league career in 2007.

Tsao returned to Taiwan and the Chinese Professional Baseball League and in 2009 became entangled in a gambling-related controversy reminiscent of the 1919 Black Sox game-fixing scandal. While he was never indicted on criminal charges, he was among several players and coaches who were released.

Ironically, Tsao launched a comeback attempt in 2015 in the Los Angeles Dodgers player development program. The first game in that journey was an appearance with the Drillers in their season opener at ONEOK Field.

First baseman Andy Tracy led the Drillers with 25 home runs and also batted .299. After spending parts of five seasons in the major leagues, he served as the minor-league hitting coordinator of the Philadelphia Phillies.

Right fielder Brad Hawpe had a team-high 68 runs batted in and hit .277. He played for the Colorado Rockies from 2004 through 2010 and was chosen to the 2009 National League All-Star team.

Justin Huisman was the bullpen ace with 26 saves, a 1.75 earned run average and a 7-2 record. He was a collegiate standout with the University of Mississippi Rebels, where he broke the school pitching records for most saves in a season and a career. He later became a coach in the small-college baseball ranks.

A blemish on the 2003 season was a total attendance of 273,155, down largely due to a warmer-than-normal Oklahoma summer and an ongoing downturn in the local economy and related job market. That attendance total was Tulsa's lowest since drawing 260,864 in 1991.

It was also former big-league catcher Marv Foley's only season as the Drillers' manager. In 15 full seasons as a minor league manager, Foley had 10 winning seasons, took eight teams to postseason playoffs and won four league championships, three of those at the Triple-A level.

The Colorado Rockies' first visit to Tulsa was a winning one as they defeated the Drillers, 8-1, in a March 30th exhibition game that drew 8,189 fans. Darren Oliver, who pitched for the Drillers in 1992 and 1993 when they were affiliated with the Texas Rangers, allowed six hits over five scoreless innings to earn the victory.

Tulsa pitcher Scott Elarton, who won 17 games with the 2000 Houston Astros but was on the comeback trail from major shoulder surgery, took the loss by allowing six runs in four-plus innings. Major league veterans Todd Helton, the Rockies' first baseman, and out-fielder Larry Walker, were hitless in that game.

Driller games were broadcast on KTBZ-AM (1430, "The Buzz") with Mark Neely calling the action.

The San Antonio Missions successfully defended their Texas League championship, defeating the Frisco RoughRiders in the finals, 4-1. San Antonio advanced directly to the finals by winning the first and second half titles in the Western Division. A franchise previously operating as the Shreveport Captains, Frisco won the Eastern Division playoffs against the Wichita Wranglers, 3-0.

Tulsa (74-64) was followed in the Eastern Division by Frisco (73-67), Wichita (71-69) and the Arkansas Travelers (70-70). San Antonio led the Western Division with an 88-51 record followed by the Midland RockHounds (69-70), El Paso Diablos (67-73) and Round Rock Express (46-94).

San Antonio third baseman Justin Leone was the Texas League Player of the Year. He led the league in extra base hits with 66, 38 of those being doubles and 21 others being home runs and also batted .288 with 92 RBIs. Leone was a promising prospect in the Seattle Mariners organization but he never fully recovered from a broken hand late in the 2004 season.

Missions ace Travis Blackley was the Texas League Pitcher of the Year with a league-leading 17 victories, the most by a Texas League pitcher since Jeff Reardon won 17 games for the 1978 Jackson Mets. Born in Melbourne, Australia, the hard-throwing lefthander also finished fourth in strikeouts (144) and posted a 2.61 ERA. Blackley never fully regained his effectiveness after missing the entire 2005 season due to a shoulder injury and subsequent surgery.

2004: The Drillers reached the Texas League playoffs for the second time in three years, thanks to winning the Eastern Division's first-half championship but did not have enough to reach the championship finals.

The Drillers had a 38-31 record in the first half but slumped to a 33-37 mark in the second half when many of their star players were promoted to Triple-A Colorado Springs. Then they were swept in three games in the Eastern Division playoffs by the eventual Texas League champion Frisco RoughRiders.

Nevertheless, Tulsa had the TL's top-ranked pitching staff that year, leading the league in five different pitching categories highlighted by the most shutouts (15) and lowest team earned run average (3.67).

Tulsa swept the Player of the Year and Pitcher of the Year awards for the first time since rejoining the Texas League in 1977. Ryan Shealy took the Player of the Year honor while Jeff Francis claimed the Pitcher of the Year award.

Arguably the most complete pitcher in Tulsa Drillers history, the left-handed Francis was also named as the 2004 Minor League Baseball Player of the Year by *Baseball America* magazine and by *USA Today Sports Weekly*. Francis went 13-1 with a league-leading 1.98 ERA with 147 strikeouts and just 22 walks in 17 appearances.

The ninth overall selection in the 2002 amateur draft, the 6-foot-5 Canadian native's best season with the Rockies was in 2007 with a 17-9 record and 165 strikeouts in 34 appearances. Arm injuries developed in 2008 and despite returning to Tulsa twice for rehabilitation assignments in, Francis never regained the form that once made him a can't-miss prospect.

Shealy, the Drillers' first baseman, led the Texas League with 29 home runs. 64 extra-base hits and 99 RBIs while batting .318. A season highlight was belting back-to-back three-run home runs in Tulsa's 11-3 victory at El Paso on May 8th. He also hit a pair of doubles in that game and finished with five hits in six at-bats.

Standing 6-foot-5 just like Francis, he never got a real chance to move up to the Rockies due to the presence of perennial National League All-Star first baseman Todd Helton. The former University of Florida standout never fully recovered from an elbow injury sustained when then-Rockies manager Clint Hurdle tried to convert Shealy into an outfielder.

A Driller led the Texas League in base hits for the second year in a row. Shortstop Danny Sandoval had 169 hits and also led the team in batting average (.319), doubles (37) and stolen bases (22).

Bullpen ace Ryan Speier posted 37 saves in 61 games, tops among Texas League pitchers and won the 2004 Minor League Baseball's Rolaids Relief Pitcher Award. Those 37 saves (27 of those being consecutive) along with finishing 58 games each set Texas League season records. He was also 3-1 that year with a 2.04 ERA. He played for the Rockies' 2007 National League championship team before briefly returning to his alma mater, Radford University, as an assistant coach.

Tom Runnells was the Drillers' fourth manager in as many years but his two-year Tulsa tenure was successful. Tulsa reached the Texas League playoffs in both of those years and his 146 victories were the most in the first two seasons by any Driller skipper. He later managed the Rockies' Triple-A affiliate in Colorado Springs and has been a bench coach with the National League team since 2009.

Season attendance rebounded from a four-year slump with 320,733 fans coming to Drillers Stadium.

Driller games were broadcast on KTBZ-AM (1430, "The Buzz") with Mark Neely calling the action.

The Frisco RoughRiders won their second straight Texas League title by defeating the Round Rock Express in the best-of-seven finals, 4-1. Round Rock advanced directly to the finals by winning the first and second half titles in the Western Division.

Frisco had the Eastern Division's best overall record at 81-59, followed by the Wichita Wranglers (73-66), Tulsa Drillers (71-68) and Arkansas Travelers (59-80). Round Rock led the Western Division with an 86-54 record followed by the Midland RockHounds (72-68), San Antonio Missions (66-72) and El Paso Diablos (48-89).

Midland RockHounds outfielder Nelson Cruz was one of the top prospects in the Oakland Athletics' player development program that year, batting .314 with 14 home runs in just 67 games. Cruz was later a two-time American League All-Star with the Texas Rangers. But in August of 2013, he served a 50-game suspension for his involvement with a health clinic in Miami, Florida that sold performance enhancing drugs to several current baseball players.

Felix Hernandez was an 18-year-old pitcher for the San Antonio Missions that year, posting a 5-1 record in 10 games with a 3.30 ERA. Nicknamed "King Felix," he joined the parent Seattle Mariners the following year, became a perennial American League All-Star and won the 2010 American League Cy Young Award as that league's best pitcher. Hernandez pitched the 23rd perfect game in major league baseball history in a 1-0 home victory over the Tampa Bay Rays on August 15, 2012.

2005: The Drillers reached the Texas League playoffs in consecutive seasons for the third time in franchise history, thanks to winning the Eastern Division's first half championship. Their 75 overall victories were the second-highest total in franchise history. But once again, promotions of the top players in the Colorado Rockies' player development program left a shorthanded squad when the postseason rolled around.

Tulsa was 43-27 in the first half but went from the penthouse to the outhouse in the second half, tumbling to a 32-38 record. The

Drillers were then swept in three games by the Arkansas Travelers in the Eastern Division playoffs.

Midland won its first outright Texas League championship by defeating Arkansas in the championship series, 3-1. The RockHounds had defeated the San Antonio Missions in the Western Division playoffs, 3-2.

Tulsa had the Eastern Division's best overall record at 75-65, followed by Arkansas (71-69), the Springfield Cardinals (70-70) and Wichita Wranglers (68-72). Midland led the Western Division with a 78-62 overall record followed by San Antonio (76-64), the Corpus Christi Hooks (64-76) and Frisco RoughRiders (58-82).

Driller fans responded well to the team's success with season attendance totaling 335,018. That was an increase of nearly 15,000 from the previous year and nearly 62,000 from two years earlier.

Once again, pitching was a strong point of the team, leading the Texas League in complete games (8) and fewest walks allowed (352). Jon Asahina and Sandy Nin shared the Texas League lead in complete games with four.

Asahina went 12-10 that year in what would be his best minor league season, sharing the team lead in victories with Zack Parker. Nin went 10-6 that year with 80 strikeouts and just 16 walks over 129 innings.

Reliever P.J. Bevis became the third Driller in four years to lead the Texas League in saves. The Australian-born right-hander made a career-high 21 saves in 39 relief appearances, despite going 0-5 with a 4.26 ERA.

Outfielder Ryan Spilborghs led Tulsa with a .341 batting average in 71 games and also had 23 doubles and drove in 54 runs. He played for the Colorado Rockies in 2005-11.

Center fielder Tony Miller was the team leader in home runs (18), stolen bases (26) and runs scored (120) while batting .280. A standout baseball and football player at the University of Toledo, his 87 bases on balls ranked second in the Texas League.

Driller games were broadcast on KTBZ-AM (1430, "The Buzz") with Mark Neely calling the action.

Midland outfielder Andre Ethier was the Texas League Player of the Year, leading the league in runs scored (104), was second in base hits (161) and batted .319 with 18 home runs and 80 RBIs. He was one of the brightest prospects in the Oakland Athletics' farm system but was traded after that season to the Los Angeles Dodgers for outfielder Milton Bradley and infielder Antonio Perez.

He became a two-time National League All-Star after joining the Dodgers and in 2009, posted career highs of 31 home runs and 106 RBIs. His four walk-off home runs (hit on what proved to be the final pitch of a game) tied the major league record for most walk-off homers in a season. His 30-game hitting streak in 2011 became the second-longest in Dodger history.

Corpus Christi's Jason Hirsh was the Texas League Pitcher of the Year, leading the league with 165 strikeouts in 29 games and having the lowest ERA among starting pitchers with 20-plus starts (2.87) along with a 13-8 record.

A 6-foot-8, 250-pound right-hander from California Lutheran University, Hirsh was the Pacific Coast League's Pitcher of the Year in 2006 with a 2.10 ERA and held his opponents to a .196 batting average. Arm problems kept Hirsh from realizing his full potential and he retired after a few more minor league seasons.

2006: Same song, third verse for the Drillers. They won the Texas League Eastern Division's first-half championship and a related play-off berth, they had a losing record in the second half of the season when their best players were promoted and then lost in the first round of the playoffs.

The only difference was manager Stu Cole starting his three-year tenure as Tulsa's manager. Prior to joining the Drillers, Cole produced winning records in four of his five years with the Rockies' Class-A affiliates. Cole was a second baseman-shortstop whose big-league career consisted of one base hit in seven at-bats for the 1991 Kansas City Royals.

Another noteworthy change was general manager Chuck Lamson's promotion to team president in June.

Having several of the top prospects in the Rockies' player development system, such as shortstop Troy Tulowitzki and pitcher Ubaldo Jiminez, laid the foundation for early success. But when they moved up to either Triple-A Colorado Springs or to the major leagues, Tulsa's championship dreams left with them.

Tulowitzki batted .291 and was third on the team in doubles (34). But the parent Colorado Rockies inexplicably called him up to the majors on August 30th, just a few days before Tulsa's playoff schedule began and with the Rockies being eliminated from National League playoff contention several weeks earlier.

During his career with the Rockies, Tulowitzki has batted .300 or higher four times, was runner-up for the 2007 National League Rookie of the Year award, been a four-time National League All-Star and earned two Gold Gloves for defensive excellence.

Jiminez went 9-2 with a 2.45 ERA in just 13 games with 86 strikeouts and just 40 walks. He played for the Colorado Rockies from 2006 through 2011 and was a National League All-Star in 2010 when his winning percentage of .704 led that league.

The 2006 season opener was a special one for Tulsa, having rallied from an 8-2 deficit in the seventh inning to pull out a 9-8 win over the

Wichita Wranglers in 16 innings. Jordan Czarniecki's two home runs sparked a rally which resulted in Tulsa tying the game with five runs in the ninth inning. Alvin Colvina, a defensive replacement in the 14th inning, hit a game-winning homer in the 16th.

Right fielder Seth Smith led the Texas League with 46 doubles that year and also led the Drillers with 154 base hits. He finished with a .294 batting average along with 15 home runs and 71 RBIs. He played baseball at the University of Mississippi and was also the backup quarterback to future New York Giants superstar Eli Manning on the Rebels' football team.

First baseman Joe Koshansky led the Texas League and set a Driller franchise record with 109 runs batted in, the second of three years in which he had triple-digit RBI seasons. The 2004 Atlantic Coast Conference Player of the Year at the University of Virginia, Koshansky played five years in the Rockies player development program.

Catcher Chris Iannetta was another offensive standout, batting .321 with 11 home runs and 26 RBIs in just 44 games before his promotion to Triple-A. His defensive skills improved when he played for the Colorado Rockies from 2006 through 2011 and his 82 assists in 2011 was tops among National League catchers. Iannetta has played for the Los Angeles Angels of Anaheim since the 2012 season.

Juan Morillo was one of five players tied for the Texas League lead in victories with 12. His 132 strikeouts led the Drillers and ranked third in the Texas League. But Morillo had no wins or losses in six brief appearances with the parent Colorado Rockies through 2008. He later played in the minor league systems of the Minnesota Twins and Philadelphia Phillies and in the Mexican League.

Another starting pitcher, Marc Kaiser, was the third consecutive Driller to lead the Texas League in complete games with four. Kaiser, who played collegiately for the University of Arizona Wildcats, was 10-10 with a 4.15 ERA that year but never advanced past Triple-A.

Manuel Corpas emerged as the bullpen ace with 19 saves, a 0.98 ERA and 35 strikeouts and just four walks in 36.2 innings. His best major league season was with the Rockies' 2007 National League championship team when he saved 19 victories and had a stingy 2.08 earned run average in 78 games.

Relief pitcher Josh Newman appeared in 62 games, tops among Texas League pitchers, and posted a 9-5 record and a 3.16 ERA. A graduate of Ohio State University, Newman still ranks among the Buckeyes' top 10 pitchers in career victories, innings pitched and strikeouts. After his professional career ended, Newman served as an assistant baseball coach at Ohio State and Marshall University.

The season attendance total was 333,763. While that was a drop of about 2,000 fans from the previous year, it also marked the beginning of what would be a four-year decline in season attendance for Driller games. That decline would be heavily influenced by a downturn in the local economy and employment figures coupled with increasingly hot summer temperatures.

The Corpus Christi Hooks won their first Texas League championship by defeating the Wichita Wranglers in the championship series, 3-1. Corpus Christi swept the Midland RockHounds in three games to win the Southern Division playoffs while Wichita beat the Tulsa Drillers in the Northern Division playoffs, 3-1.

Driller games were broadcast on KTBZ-AM (1430, "The Buzz") with Mark Neely calling the action.

Wichita had the Northern Division's best overall record at 77-62, followed by Tulsa (75-64), the Springfield Cardinals (66-72) and Arkansas Travelers (51-87). Midland led the Southern Division with a 78-61 record followed by Corpus Christi (76-63), the Frisco RoughRiders (72-68) and San Antonio Missions (60-78).

Corpus Christi's only other Texas League pennant came in 1958 when the Corpus Christi Giants defeated the Austin Senators in the finals, 4-3. One of the stars of that team was pitcher Eddie Fisher, who played baseball at the University of Oklahoma and became of the best relief pitchers in the American League during the mid-1960s.

Wichita third baseman Alex Gordon was the Texas League Player of the Year, pulling off one of the best overall offensive seasons in the last 20 years. Winner of the 2005 Dick Howser Trophy as college baseball's Player of the Year with the University of Nebraska Cornhuskers, Gordon led the Texas League in slugging percentage (.588), walks (72), runs scored (111) and total bases (286) and also ranked third in batting average (.325), home runs (29) and RBIs (101). He also won *Baseball America Magazine's* Minor League Player of the Year award.

After a rocky first four seasons with the parent Kansas City Royals, Gordon became a two-time American League All-Star while earning four Gold Glove awards for defensive excellence. His 51 doubles in 2012 led the American League.

Corpus Christi claimed the Texas League Pitcher of the Year award for the second consecutive season. Right-hander Matt Albers had the lowest earned run average (2.17) among TL starting pitchers and finished with a 10-2 record. The parent Houston Astros sent Albers to the Baltimore Orioles on December 12, 2007 as part of a trade for slugger Miguel Tejada and Albers became a middle reliever.

2007: The Drillers reached the playoffs for the fourth year in a row, the second-longest streak of playoff appearances in Tulsa's professional baseball history. But it also marked the third time during that span that they failed to win a single playoff game.

Tulsa went 69-69 and made the postseason playoffs as the Eastern Division's wild card entry because the Springfield Cardinals won the first and second-half season championship and Tulsa had the second-best season record. But Springfield swept the three-game series with Tulsa to advance to the Texas League finals.

The Drillers led the Eastern Division for most of the season but injuries to three pitchers and the big-league promotion of Franklin Morales (who would join the Boston Red Sox in 2011) dashed Tulsa's dreams of achieving greater things.

Morales set a Texas League record by hitting three batters in the third inning of 7-4, 10-inning loss to the San Antonio Missions in the first game of a home season-opening doubleheader on April 6th. Morales took the loss but, surprisingly, didn't walk a batter and struck out six.

Third baseman Christian Colonel led the Texas League with 163 base hits and 47 doubles. He also led Tulsa in runs scored (78), home runs (17) and RBIs (84) and was the Colorado Rockies' Minor League Player of the Year. Colonel has been out of professional baseball since 2011 and later operated a baseball training facility in Pocatello, Idaho.

Second baseman Corey Wimberly led the Texas League with 36 stolen bases. He was the Pioneer Rookie League batting champion in 2005 when he batted .381 and also stole 36 bases. Prior to turning professional, Wimberly played at Alcorn State University, a historical black college, where his .462 batting average and .606 on-base percentage was the best among all Division I baseball players.

Relief pitcher Steve Register led all minor league pitchers in saves with 37. It was his first full season coming out of the bullpen after going 4-10 with a 5.57 ERA as a Tulsa starter the year before. Register was Colorado's third-round draft pick out of Auburn University in the 2004 amateur draft but played briefly for the Rockies and

Philadelphia Phillies before ending his professional career after the 2010 season.

The season attendance of 296,017 marked the fourth consecutive season of declining attendance and was just the second time in 15 years that the Drillers failed to draw more than 300,000 fans in one year.

Mark Neely was once again the announcer for Driller games on KTBZ-AM (1430, "The Buzz"). But on July 22nd in North Little Rock, Arkansas during a game between the Drillers and Arkansas Travelers, he covered one of the most somber events in recent professional baseball history.

The Travelers were leading in the ninth inning, 7-3, when Tulsa's Tino Sanchez was batting. A line drive off the bat of Sanchez struck Driller first base coach Mike Coolbaugh just below his left ear. He did not see the ball coming because he was coaching a runner at first base. The blow ruptured the left vertebral artery and caused a fatal brain hemorrhage.

Despite receiving immediate and intensive medical assistance on the field, Coolbaugh died about an hour after being hit. It was the first in-game death caused by a baseball since Ray Chapman of the Cleveland Indians died after being hit in the head by a pitch during a 1920 game against the New York Yankees.

Texas League president Bill Valentine, who happened to be in attendance that night, suspended play shortly afterwards and declared the contest to be a complete game. The two teams did not play the following night.

Coolbaugh was 35 years old. He was survived by his wife, Mandy, sons Joseph and Jacob and a daughter, Anne, who was born just over three months after his death. Sanchez would leave professional baseball after the 2007 season.

The Colorado Rockies pledged to give Mandy Coolbaugh a full share of their playoff winnings after qualifying for the 2007 National League playoffs. Because the Rockies reached the 2007 World Series, that share was worth more than $230,000.

Mike Coolbaugh's life was the subject of a 2009 book by Sports Illustrated writer and author Scott L. Price, entitled, *Heart of the Game: Life, Death and Mercy in Minor League America.*

Starting with the 2008 season, major league general managers required all base coaches to wear batting helmets. Minor League Baseball created the Mike Coolbaugh Award, which is presented annually to a minor league coach showing excellence as an on-field mentor to younger players.

Sanchez, who spent 11 years in the Rockies' player development system and never reached the majors, walked away from professional baseball after the 2007 season.

The San Antonio Missions claimed their third Texas League crown during the 2000s by defeating the Springfield Cardinals in the championship series, 3-1. San Antonio swept the Frisco RoughRiders in three games to win the Southern Division playoffs and Springfield had swept Tulsa in three games to win the Northern Division.

Springfield had the Northern Division's best overall record at 73-63, followed by Tulsa (69-69), the Arkansas Travelers (65-75) and Wichita Wranglers (56-84). Frisco led the Southern Division with an 85-55 with San Antonio second at 73-66, followed by the Midland RockHounds (67-70) and Corpus Christi Hooks (67-73).

San Antonio swept the Texas League postseason awards with Chase Headly named the Player of the Year and Josh Geer taking Pitcher of the Year honors.

Headly hit .330 with 20 home runs, 78 RBIs and finished among the TL's top five hitters in eight offensive categories. He was quickly promoted to the parent San Diego Padres and he was the 2012 National League leader in RBIs (115). After being traded to the New York Yankees during the 2014, he has been the Bronx Bombers' regular third baseman.

Geer led the league with a 16-6 record and his 3.20 ERA was the second lowest among starting pitchers making at least 20 appearances. The Rice University alumnus was also named as the San Diego Padres' Minor League Pitcher of the Year. But after two so-so seasons with the Padres, he earned a much more important title: cancer survivor.

Geer was diagnosed with Stage III melanoma, a form of skin cancer, after his first two Triple-A games in 2011. He missed the rest of that season following cancer surgery and related treatments but has been cancer free ever since. In 2013, he had an 8-5 record in 34 appearances with San Antonio and was the winning pitcher in the game that clinched the Texas League championship for the Missions.

2008: The overall season record of 58-82 would not be fondly remembered. Only three other teams in franchise history won fewer games than the 2008 Tulsa Drillers. The weak link was a youthful pitching staff that ranked either last or next-to-last in the Texas League in five different categories.

However, two players from that Driller team would be part of baseball history eight years later, helping the Chicago Cubs win the 2016 National League pennant and play in their first World Series since 1945.

The bright spots were found in hitting. The Drillers' team batting average of .279 led the Texas League, the first time that a Tulsa team had done so since the 1953 Tulsa Oilers batted .268. A trio of Drillers ranked among the TL's top 10 players in batting average: left fielder Matt Miller batted .344, center fielder Dexter Fowler batted .335 and third baseman Tony Blanco batted .323.

Miller would have won the batting championship but league officials invoked an infrequently-used rule regarding plate appearances. Midland's Jesus Guzman, who was four at-bats shy of qualifying under the normal rules, was awarded the championship with a .364 batting average.

Fowler had an impressive debut by hitting home runs in his first two at-bats. He would be the Texas League's co-leader in triples with nine and added 20 stolen bases. He played six seasons for the Rockies before spending 2014 with the Houston Astros and then joining the Chicago Cubs for the 2015 and representing that team in the 2016 All-Star Game.

Fowler and relief pitcher Pedro Strop contributed to the 2016 Chicago Cubs winning the National League championship and making their first World Series appearance since 1945. Strop served mostly as a middle relief pitcher with the Cubs, paving the way for bullpen aces Hector Rondon and Aroldis Chapman.

Strop started the 2008 Driller season as the top relief pitcher and saved three victories in his first seven games while posting a 2.57 ERA. But an arm injury derailed his season and he would be released by the Colorado Rockies. He played for the Texas Rangers in 2009-11, the Baltimore Orioles in 2011-13 and with the Cubs from mid-2013 to the present.

Corey Wimberly won the Texas League stolen base championship for the second year in a row and ranked seventh among all minor league baseball players with 59 steals. He was on track to break Eddie Miller's franchise record of 80 stolen bases set in 1977 but a hand/wrist injury sidelined him for 16 games late in the season. Despite his talent, Wimberly never reached the major leagues.

Another offensive standout was outfielder Eric Young who stole 46 bases and batted .290 for the Drillers. He spent slightly more than four unremarkable seasons with the Colorado Rockies but blossomed after being traded to the New York Mets early in the 2013 season. Young's 46 total stolen bases led the National League that year and he later played for the Atlanta Braves.

Brandon Hynick was the only Tulsa pitcher and one of just six in the league to win 10 or more games. He posted a 10-7 record in 27 starts but also allowed a league-leading 27 home runs. Hynick returned to the Texas League in 2013 with the Arkansas Travelers, posting a 12-5 record in what would be his final professional season.

Despite the awful record, Tulsa's season attendance of 297,409 was actually a slight increase (about 1,400 fans) over the previous season. More importantly, it would be the last time that the Tulsa Drillers would fail to draw 300,000 fans in one year.

This would be the final season for Mark Neely announcing Driller games KTBZ-AM (1430, "The Buzz"). He left Tulsa because a dream held by countless minor league baseball players throughout the years finally came true for him: a promotion to the major leagues.

He signed a three-year contract to be play-by-play announcer for the San Diego Padres' TV network and his family relocated to southern California. But in the second year of Neely's contract, the team's management unexpectedly brought in sports broadcasting legend Dick Enberg to do the play-by-play and Neely's appearances on Padres TV games would be sharply reduced.

Despite the disappointing turn of events, Neely fulfilled his contract then he and his family relocated to the Kansas City metropolitan area. He resumed working with ESPN and other TV sports outlets, focusing on collegiate sports and other baseball-related activities.

The Arkansas Travelers won their fifth Texas League championship and first since 1989 by defeating the Frisco RoughRiders in the finals, 3-2. Arkansas swept the Northwest Arkansas Naturals in three games to win the Northern Division playoffs while Frisco used a three-game sweep of the San Antonio Missions to win the Southern Division playoffs.

Springfield had the Northern Division's best overall record at 76-64, followed by the Northwest Arkansas Naturals (75-65), Arkansas (62-78) and the Tulsa Drillers (58-82). Frisco led the Southern Division with an 84-56 record followed by the Midland Rock-Hounds and San Antonio Missions tied at 75-65 and the Corpus Christi Hooks (55-85).

Northwest Arkansas first baseman Kila Ka'aihue was the Texas League Player of the Year, leading the league with 26 home runs, batted .314 and after being promoted to Triple-A Omaha, his 104 total walks that year was the most of any minor leaguer.

After spending 10 years in the Kansas City Royals' minor league system, the Hawai'i-born hitter was the Royals' 2011 Opening Day first baseman. A hitting slump led to him being cut by the Royals then attempting comebacks through the minor league systems of the Oakland Athletics, Arizona Diamondbacks and Washington Nationals.

Midland's Vin Mazzaro was the Texas League Pitcher of the Year, leading the league in victories (12), lowest ERA (1.90) and lowest opponent batting average (.229). The parent Oakland Athletics traded Mazzaro to the Kansas City Royals after the 2010 season and in a game against the Cleveland Indians on May 16, 2011, he would take a place in baseball infamy.

Mazzaro came out of the bullpen and gave up 14 runs in two-and-one-third innings of a 19-1 loss to the Indians. That not only set a franchise record for the most runs allowed by any pitcher in a game, it also made him the first major league pitcher since 1900 to give up that many runs and not last three innings.

He was sent back to Triple-A Omaha the next day and released by the Royals after the 2012 season. He rebounded nicely in 2013 after being acquired by the Pittsburgh Pirates, posting an 8-2 record as a middle reliever as the Pirates earned both their first winning season and first National League playoff appearance since 1992.

2009: This was the final season for Drillers Stadium but hosting a playoff series was not to be. Tulsa's 74-66 overall record was tops in the Texas League North Division but the Drillers missed winning the first half and second half championships by one game.

Attendance for the final season at Drillers Stadium was 316,365, an increase of nearly 20,000 from the previous year. A lavish farewell to the stadium was staged in October when a helicopter transported home plate to the new ONEOK Field.

Stu Cole started the season as Tulsa's manager but was promoted to Triple-A Colorado Springs as part of the fallout from the Colorado Rockies' firing of manger Clint Hurdle. Rockies roving instructor Ron Gideon was named as Cole's replacement. Cole had a 24-22 record through May 29th of that year and finished with a 226-219 record during his time in Tulsa. Gideon went 50-44 as Cole's replacement.

Pitcher Samuel Deduno became the third player to win the Texas League's pitching Triple Crown (most victories, lowest earned run average and most strikeouts) and easily won the Pitcher of the Year Award. Previous TL Triple Crown pitchers were San Antonio's Sid Fernandez in 1983 and Shreveport's George Ferran in 1986.

The hard-throwing right-hander had a 12-4 record with a 2.57 ERA and a league-leading 123 strikeouts over 133 innings. But Deduno missed the 2008 season with a career-threatening elbow injury and was released by two major league teams before joining the Minnesota Twins in 2012. He joined the Houston Astros in 2014.

Deduno starred in the 2013 World Baseball Classic, leading his native Dominican Republic to the championship after defeating the United States and Puerto Rico in consecutive starts. He posted a 0.69 ERA over 13 innings in the WBC with 17 strikeouts against just five bases on balls.

Venezuelan-born right-handed pitcher Jhoulys Chacin had an 8-6 record for the Drillers that year. Chacin became a fixture in the Colorado Rockies' starting rotation in 2010, posting a career-high 150 strikeouts in 2011 and won a career-best 14 games in 2013. But the Rockies released him prior to the 2015 season.

Andrew Johnston led the Texas League with a career-high 31 saves while posting a 2-4 record and a 3.69 ERA. A 6-foot-5 right-handed pitcher who played collegiately at the University of Missouri, Johnston played eight years in the Rockies organization before switching to independent teams in 2012.

Outfielder Cole Garner was Tulsa's best all-around hitter, leading regular players with a .288 batting average and also had 16 home runs, 64 runs batted in and 13 stolen bases. After leaving the Colorado Rockies organization in 2011, Garner played for minor league affiliates of the New York Yankees and Milwaukee Brewers.

Right fielder Ryan Harvey carried the big stick in Tulsa's offense. His 23 home runs led the team and ranked third in the Texas League and his 82 RBIs led the team and ranked eighth in the TL. He was the sixth overall selection and first pick of the Chicago Cubs in the 2003 Major League Baseball amateur draft but never advanced past Double-A competition due to his all-or-nothing hitting style.

Daniel Mayora represented Tulsa in the 2009 Texas League All-Star Game but became the sixth player tie the TL single-game record for errors by a shortstop (three) in an 8-6 road loss to the Northwest Arkansas Naturals.

Better known as the son of rock music star Todd Rundgren ("Hello, It's Me" and "Bang on the Drum All Day"), Rex Rundgren played second base and shortstop for the Drillers. He batted .238 with 15 doubles, one home run and 24 RBIs. Rundgren also had the dubious distinction of hitting into 21 double plays that year, tops on the Drillers and second-highest among all Texas League players. All 12 of his professional baseball seasons were spent in the minor leagues.

Dennis Higgins became the radio voice of the Tulsa Drillers on KTZB-AM (1430) and continues to serve in that capacity today. He was no stranger to the Drillers' microphone, being an audio pinch-hitter when Mark Neely had ESPN-related schedule conflicts from 2005 through 2007.

Higgins lives in Tulsa during the baseball season and in Wichita, Kansas during the offseason. He previously worked in minor league baseball for the Wichita Wranglers, Fresno Grizzlies and Eugene Emeralds. During the baseball offseason, he is the radio play-by-play announcer for Butler County (Kansas) Community College football and basketball games. The Butler Grizzlies have won six National Junior College Athletic Association football championships.

The Midland RockHounds hoisted the Texas League championship pennant for the second time in four years by defeating the Northwest Arkansas Naturals in the championship series, 3-1. Midland defeated the San Antonio Missions in the Southern Division playoffs, 3-1, while Northwest Arkansas used a three-game sweep of the Springfield Cardinals to win the Northern Division playoffs.

Tulsa had the Northern Division's best overall record at 74-64. Northwest Arkansas was next at 73-67, followed by the Springfield Cardinals (71-69) and Arkansas Travelers (61-79). Midland led the Southern Division with a 78-62 record followed by the Frisco

Roughriders (72-68), San Antonio (70-70) and the Corpus Christi Hooks (61-79).

Midland first baseman Chris Carter was the Texas League Player of the Year, leading the league in runs scored (108) while batting .337 with 24 home runs and 101 RBIs. Carter was the Minor League Player of the Year in the Oakland Athletics' organization that year as well as the previous year when he was the Class A California League's Rookie of the Year.

Carter's best major league season was 2014 with the Houston Astros when his 37 home runs ranked second in the American League.

Chapter Twelve
The 2010s

Technology took another giant step forward with the development of electronic tablets and readers. The most prominent of these new inventions were Apple's iPad and the Kindle book reader from Amazon. More and more, movies were shot in three-dimensional photography, greatly enhancing the film-watching experience.

Printed books and newspapers were being passed over in favor of self-published electronic books (eBooks) and reading newspaper stories on the Internet, smartphones or electronic tablets.

The United States began a slow but steady recovery from The Great Recession in the late 2000s. Barack Obama was elected to a second term as President of the United States. A controversial new program of government-backed health insurance coverage made its debut. Controversy related to the White House reached new heights (or lows, depending on one's viewpoint) with the 2018 election of New York City billionaire and political novice Donald Trump as Obama's successor.

America began scaling back its military presence in terrorism-related conflicts in Iraq and Afghanistan. A major triumph came in 2011 when a highly-trained group of soldiers snuck past enemy lines and killed Islamic terrorism mastermind Osama Bin Laden in his home in

Pakistan. But terrorists groups would reorganize and resurface with a series of grisly attacks throughout the world, most notably in Paris, France and in San Bernardino, California.

The Tulsa-based QuikTrip convenience store chain maintained its presence in Forbes magazine's list of 100 Best Companies to Work For. The Folds of Honor Foundation, which supports families of American soldiers severely wounded or killed in the line of duty, increased its national presence through a wide variety of activities.

The merger between American Airlines and US Airways had a ripple effect on Tulsa's economy. While increased aircraft maintenance work was expected at American's maintenance base at Tulsa International Airport, a significant number of jobs were lost when accounting operations were transferred to Dallas or Phoenix.

The Tulsa Drillers claimed their fourth Texas League championship and their first since 1998 by defeating the San Antonio Missions in 2018. Tulsa also reached the championship series in 2014 and 2017 and also qualified for the TL Playoffs in 2012, 2013 and 2014.

Counting playoff games, the 2014 season drew the largest season attendance in Tulsa's professional baseball history: 415,403.

The team's leadership group was honored by the Texas League in 2013 for outstanding baseball and community-oriented achievement.

The Los Angeles Dodgers, one of the most iconic names in all of professional sports, signed a player development contract with the Drillers that started with the 2015 season. Many local sports historians likened the news about the Dodgers to the 1959 events in which the St. Louis Cardinals became the parent club for the Tulsa Oilers.

Outdoor professional soccer returned to Tulsa when Driller management was awarded a United Soccer League franchise that began play in 2015. In honor of the Tulsa Roughnecks from the North

American Soccer League, the new team was named the Tulsa Rough-necks FC and played its home matches at ONEOK Field.

2010: The single-season attendance record for Tulsa professional baseball was resoundingly shattered during the first year at the new ONEOK Field in downtown Tulsa. A total of 408,183 fans came to see the Drillers with 12 of those games being sellouts. The average game attendance of 6,185 fans ranked 25th out of all 176 minor league baseball teams and was higher than 11 Triple-A franchises.

ONEOK Field, located in downtown Tulsa, has 6,333 fixed seats fans and a listed seating capacity of 7,833 but that is frequently exceeded with people sitting on abundant grassy berms beyond the outfield fences which also feature recreational activities for younger children.

ONEOK Field serves as the eastern anchor of The Brady District, an expanse of new business, hotels, residences, night clubs and restaurants on the north perimeter of downtown Tulsa. It is also adjacent to what once was the Greenwood District, also known back in the 1920s as "Black Wall Street" for its large number of successful African-American businesses.

Sidewalk plaques with the names of business destroyed in the horrific 1921 Tulsa Race Riot can be found on either side of Brady Street, which runs just beyond the center and right field fences. The John Hope Franklin Reconciliation Monument is located within walking distance from ONEOK Field's main ticket office.

Despite its downtown location, abundant parking exists within a short walk from any direction from the stadium. Thanks to Interstate 244 running just north of the stadium and access to other major highways located close by, driving to and from ONEOK Field is easy.

The project's total cost was roughly $60 million with just over $39 million spent on stadium construction. Nearly $30 million was raised through private donations, another $25 million came from a revenue bond and the remaining $5 million came from the Drillers signing a long-term lease.

The Drillers unveiled new uniforms prior to Opening Day. Home uniforms were white with blue trim with a script "Drillers" on the jersey's front and the player's last name on the jersey back. The road uniforms were light gray with a script "Tulsa" on the front. The Drillers' cap, which had the letter T but with an oil derrick comprising most of that letter and an illustration of oil flowing out of the top, was unchanged except for the cap becoming royal blue.

Unfortunately, the team's on-field performance didn't have the "wow" factor that accompanied the new stadium. The Drillers finished 69-70 and missed the playoffs for the third straight season. Tulsa stumbled to a 29-40 record in the first half of the season but their 40-30 mark in the second half was the second-best in the Texas League.

The players spending time on Tulsa's injured list could have arguably contended for the league championship had they been a team of their own, and healthy. Shortstop Hector Gomez, one of the Colorado Rockies' brightest prospects, played in just nine games. Pitching phenom Christian Frederich missed nearly a third of the season.

Pitchers Sean Jarrett and Craig Baker were sidelined for three months apiece while utilityman Jeff Kindle and infielder Daniel Mayora each sat out for two months. Catcher Wilin Rosario led Tulsa with 19 home runs but missed the final months of the season due to injury.

On the brighter side, Bruce Billings was the ace of the pitching staff with a team-leading 11-6 record and 3.28 ERA. He set a Tulsa professional baseball record with 38 consecutive scoreless innings during a stretch in May through June. But several Colorado Rockies executives felt Billings' chances in the big leagues would be better as a reliever. He moved to the bullpen and finished with 101 strikeouts and 44 walks over nearly 110 innings. That did not translate to big-league success as he pitched in just 11 total innings for three different major league teams.

Fellow reliever Stu Pomeranz, whose brother Drew would play briefly for Tulsa in 2011, had a league-leading 18 saves. The 6-foot-7 Pomeranz played in the minor league systems of the St. Louis Cardinals, Los Angeles Dodgers and Baltimore Orioles.

Left fielder Anthony Jackson's 33 stolen bases ranked second in the Texas League. Right fielder Bronson Sardinha, a former first-round draft choice of the New York Yankees, had the best batting average (.299) of anyone playing more than half of the season in Tulsa. After missing the first 50 games with injuries, center fielder Charlie Blackmon batted .297, hit 11 home runs, drove in 55 runs and stole 19 bases. Second baseman Jason Van Kooten had a team-high 58 RBIs.

Arkansas Travelers pitcher Ryan Brazier threw a nine-inning, no-hitter against the Drillers in a 4-0 victory in Little Rock on April 29th, the first such no-hitter in the Texas League in eight years. Brazier walked two batters but neither of them went further than first base.

Driller games were carried on KTBZ-AM (1430 "The Buzz") with Dennis Higgins calling the game action.

The Northwest Arkansas Naturals claimed their first Texas League championship by defeating the Midland RockHounds, 3-1, in a rematch of the 2009 Texas League championship series. Northwest Arkansas held off the Springfield Cardinals to win the Northern Division playoffs, 3-2, while Midland beat Frisco, 3-1, in the Southern Division playoffs.

Northwest Arkansas had the Northern Division's best overall record at 86-54 followed by the Springfield Cardinals (76-64), Tulsa Drillers (69-70) and Arkansas Travelers (55-85). Frisco led the Southern Division with a 72-67 record followed by the Midland Rock-

Hounds (70-70), San Antonio Missions (68-72) and the Corpus Christi Hooks (63-77).

Mike "Moose" Moustakas of Northwest Arkansas was the Texas League Player of the Year, winning the award despite playing in just 66 out of 140 games. The Kansas City Royals' first selection (and second overall) in the 2007 MLB amateur draft led the league in batting average (.347) and slugging percentage (.687) while adding 21 home runs and 76 RBIs.

Moustakas played for the Kansas City Royals from 2011 through 2017 and has been with the Milwaukee Brewers since 2018. He has appeared in three MLB All-Stars Games, most recently in 2019.

Frisco's Blake Beavan was the Texas League Pitcher of the Year, also winning a postseason award despite playing roughly half of the season. The 6-foot-7 right-hander was 10-5 with a 2.78 ERA in 17 games with 68 strikeouts and just 12 walks.

He was among several minor league players traded by the parent Texas Rangers to the Seattle Mariners midway through the 2010 in exchange for 2008 American League Cy Young Award winner and four-time All-Star Cliff Lee. His best Seattle season came in 2012 when he posted an 11-11 record.

2011: The sting of missing the Texas League playoffs for the fourth straight year was soothed somewhat by several outstanding individual performances.

Attendance for the second season at ONEOK Field dropped to 366,291, a decline of over 42,000. Nevertheless, that was the second-largest season attendance total to that point in Tulsa's professional baseball history.

That figure was more remarkable when considering the fact that Tulsa endured one of its hottest summers on record. How hot was it, you ask? The temperature for the first pitch of an August 13th game was 113 degrees.

Duane Espy, a long-time major-league hitting coach, made his debut as a Tulsa manager. The Drillers had their third losing record in four years, going 68-72 for the year (33-37 in the first half, 35-35 in the second half).

When the parent Colorado Rockies traded standout pitcher Ubaldo Jimenez to the Cleveland Indians late in the season, three young and talented pitchers were acquired and assigned to Tulsa: Drew Pomeranz, Alex White and Joe Gardner.

Tulsa was 54-66 when that transaction was made and proceeded to win 13 of its next 15 games to move into contention for a Northern Division playoff berth entering the final weekend of the season. A season-ending injury to Pomeranz, regarded as one of the best prospects in all of minor league baseball, coupled with Driller relievers blowing 18 saves during the year proved too much to overcome.

Center fielder Tim Wheeler was the offensive standout for the Drillers, setting the franchise single-season home run record as well as leading the Texas League with 33 home runs. In addition to batting .287, driving in 86 runs and stealing 21 bases, Wheeler also led the league in five offensive categories: runs scored (105), total hits (161), extra base hits (67), at-bats (561) and total bases (300).

Catcher Willin Rosario hit 21 home runs and was chosen to the Texas League's postseason All-Star Team as well as being called up to the Rockies in September.

Pomeranz, White and Juan Nicasio also moved up to the big leagues. Nicasio (5-1, 2.22 ERA in nine starts) had the Texas League's lowest ERA when he was promoted and was doing well for Colorado before his season ended after sustaining a head injury after being hit by a line drive. Ironically, the Rockies traded Nicasio to the Drillers' new parent team, the Los Angeles Dodgers, following the 2014 season.

Pomeranz never tasted success with the Colorado Rockies, going 4-14 over three seasons before being traded after the 2013 season to the Oakland Athletics. White spent two seasons with the Rockies but lingering arm problems led to his being released then attempting a comeback with the Houston Astros minor league system.

Rob Scahill's 12 victories were tops for Tulsa and second-highest in the Texas League. Steven Dodson (10-2, 3.47 ERA) and Joe Torres (3-1, 2.28 ERA) also had fine seasons. Cory Riordan and Christian Frederich were expected to anchor Tulsa's pitching staff but each endured nightmarish seasons. Despite having the lowest walk ratio among league pitchers, Riordan went 1-12 with a 5.37 ERA and gave up 21 home runs while Frederich went 6-10 with a 5.00 ERA and allowed 20 home runs.

The Drillers held the parent Colorado Rockies hitless for the first eight innings, and then held on for a 5-3 preseason exhibition victory on March 29th before 7,516 fans. Friedrich pitched a six-inning no-hitter and was credited with the victory. Colorado scored three runs in the bottom of the ninth inning and had runners at first and third base when Ryan Spilborghs grounded out to end the game.

Scott Beerer had four hits and an RBI to lead the Drillers and Rosario had a home run among his three hits. Ben Paulsen and Mike Daniel also homered for the Drillers.

After a rare instance of two foul balls flying onto the Interstate 244 highway that runs behind the third base line, a screen measuring 110 feet tall by 160 feet wide was installed prior to the start of the season to prevent possible auto accidents.

The highway was undergoing reconstruction of its eastbound traffic lanes at that time. One foul ball bounced into the traffic-carrying westbound lanes but did not hit any passing cars. The other foul ball was stopped by a concrete median. Since the screen was installed, there is no known record of other foul balls reaching that highway.

Driller games were carried on KTBZ-AM (1430 "The Buzz") with Dennis Higgins calling the game action.

The San Antonio Missions won their fourth Texas League championship in 10 years with a three-game sweep of the Arkansas Travelers. Arkansas defeated the Northwest Arkansas Naturals, 3-1, to win the Northern Division playoffs while San Antonio beat Midland beat the Frisco RoughRiders, 3-1, in the Southern Division playoffs.

San Antonio's home victory in Game 2 of the championship series was one for the ages. After 20 innings and six hours and three minutes of competition, San Antonio earned a 5-4 victory. The temperature for the game's first pitch was 98 degrees. The score was tied, 3-3, after nine innings and each team scored once in the 14th inning, Sawyer Carroll lashed a two-out RBI single to end the marathon contest.

Northwest Arkansas had the Northern Division's best overall record at 73-64 followed by the Arkansas Travelers (68-69), Tulsa Drillers (68-72) and Springfield Cardinals (62-78).

San Antonio's 94-46 record led the Southern Division and was the best season record by a Texas League team since the legendary 1957 Dallas Eagles, led by slugger Willie McCovey, went 102-52. The Frisco RoughRiders (79-61) were second followed by the Midland RockHounds (63-77) and Corpus Christi Hooks (50-90).

Springfield first baseman Matt Adams was the Texas League Player of the Year. A 23rd-round 2009 draft choice of the St. Louis Cardinals, he led the league with 100 RBIs and finished second in home runs (32) while batting .300. Adams currently plays for the St. Louis Cardinals.

Arkansas' Matt Shoemaker was the Texas League Pitcher of the Year, leading the Texas League in victories (12) and lowest ERA (2.2

1). In 2014 with the Los Angeles Angels of Anaheim, Shoemaker led American League pitchers with a .800 winning percentage, thanks to a 16-4 record and finished second in voting for the American League Rookie of the Year.

One of the Texas League's brightest young stars that year (or in most recent years, for that matter) was Arkansas outfielder Mike Trout, who batted .326 and ranked among the circuit's best hitters in four categories.

Nicknamed "The Millville Meteor", Trout has played on the American League's All-Star Team every year since 2012. He was the AL Rookie of the Year in 2012, won the AL's Most Valuable Player in 2014 and 2016 and finished second in that award's voting four other times.

2012: Tulsa reached the Texas League playoffs for the first time in five years with a 75-64 record. But it was the same old story in that early-season promotions of the Colorado Rockies' most talented prospects left the Drillers shorthanded for postseason play.

The Drillers took the Springfield Cardinals to the limit in the best-of-five Northern Division playoffs before falling, 3-2. The Frisco RoughRiders swept the Corpus Christi Hooks in three games to win the Southern Division playoffs. Springfield won its first Texas League championship by defeating Frisco in the finals, 3-1.

Springfield had the Northern Division's best overall record at 77-61 followed Tulsa (75-64), the Arkansas Travelers (62-78) and Northwest Arkansas Naturals (58-81). Corpus Christi led the Southern Division with an 81-59 record, followed by Frisco (80-60), the Midland Rock-Hounds (64-74) and San Antonio Missions (60-80).

Driller general manager Mike Melega was presented with the 2012 Bill Valentine Executive of the Year Award, which recognizes excellence by an executive of a Texas League team. It was the first time that

Melega received the award and the sixth time that a Driller executive was chosen.

Tulsa's season attendance of 372,624 was one of the five highest totals in the city's professional baseball history.

The Drillers had the Texas League's top pitching staff with the lowest ERA (3.36), the most saves (39) and fewest walks allowed (329 over 140 games). That helped overcome an anemic offense that ranked seventh in the eight-time league.

Left-handed pitcher Edwar Cabrera led all minor league pitchers in strikeouts during 2011 (217) and was quite impressive during his short stay in Tulsa. He was 8-4 in 15 games with the Drillers, posting a 2.94 ERA and had 82 strikeouts and just 23 walks. Cabrera took a no-hitter into the sixth inning and finished with a one-hit shutout win over the Northwest Arkansas Naturals on June 11th.

Many baseball observers felt that had Cabrera stayed in Tulsa instead of being promoted to the Rockies, the Drillers had a strong chance to win the Texas League title. Cabrera lost both of his games with the Rockies that year and has been attempting a comeback through the Texas Rangers' minor league system.

Josh Outman came within one pitch of a nine-inning no-hitter on August 30th in a 9-1 road victory over the Springfield Cardinals. Oscar Taveras, one of the most talented players in the St. Louis Cardinals' player development system, spoiled the gem with a two-out, two-strike bloop single into centerfield. Outman had nine strikeouts and five walks en route to his second victory of the year.

Reliever Josh Sullivan appeared in 60 games, tops among Texas League pitchers. An Auburn University product, Sullivan was the Rockies' fifth-round selection in the 2005 amateur draft. He made 17 saves that year while posting a 1-2 record and a 2.76 ERA.

Parker Frazier led Texas League pitchers in innings pitched (167) and was also the hard-luck co-leader in losses (14). A graduate of Tulsa's Bishop Kelly High School, Frazier and Harry Perkowski (263 innings with the 1948 Tulsa Oilers) are the only Tulsa professional baseball players to lead the Texas League in innings pitched.

Frazier also pitched for minor league affiliates of the Cincinnati Reds and Chicago White Sox. His father is George Frazier, a 10-year major league pitcher and long-time Tulsa resident who was the color commentator on the Colorado Rockies TV network from 1998 through 2015.

Tyler Chatwood set a Tulsa professional baseball record and tied a Texas League record when he threw four wild pitches during the fifth inning of a 6-2 home loss to the Arkansas Travelers on July 29th. Ironically, Chatwood struck out the side in that same inning but one of those strikeouts came on a wild pitch and the batter reached first base.

Second baseman-shortstop Josh Rutledge was Tulsa's only player with a batting average higher than .300. He batted .306 with 13 home runs and 14 stolen bases.

In the first Texas League All-Star Game played at ONEOK Field, the only thing hotter than the action on the field was a record-setting 105-degree temperature when the game began. Nevertheless, 8,047 fans saw the North All-Stars, managed by Tulsa skipper Duane Espy, walk away with a 3-1 victory over the South All-Stars.

Oscar Taveras was the game's Most Valuable Player, going 3-for-4 with a fourth-inning, two-run home run and was a triple shy of hitting for the cycle. Driller third baseman Nolan Arenado had an RBI double in the fourth and robbed Corpus Christi's Jose Martinez of an extra-base hit with a spectacular defensive play in the first inning.

The North used eight pitchers, three of them being Tulsa Drillers, to hold the South to three hits. Dan Houston was the North starter and pitched two perfect innings. Lefthander Nick Schmidt would earn the victory with a three-up, three-down fourth inning. Drillers bullpen ace Coty Woods escaped a ninth-inning jam and picked up the save.

Former American League Most Valuable Player and five-time All-Star Jason Giambi played three games with the Drillers as part of an injury rehabilitation assignment. The first baseman-outfielder had three hits in seven at-bats and drove in one run.

Giambi spent eight of his 20 major league seasons with the Oakland Athletics and hit 30 or more home runs eight times. He was the AL's MVP in 2000 with career highs of 43 home runs and 137 runs batted in and also led the league with 137 bases on balls. During the 2005 Congressional hearings on the illegal use of steroids in major league baseball, Giambi testified that he had used steroids in the past.

Driller games were carried on KTBZ-AM (1430 "The Buzz") with Dennis Higgins calling the game action.

Springfield outfielder Oscar Taveras won the Texas League Player of the Year award, leading the league in batting average (.321) and doubles (47) while ranking second in home runs and RBIs (23 and 94, respectively), base hits (153) and slugging percentage (.572). He batted .320 over six minor league seasons and the St. Louis Cardinals envisioned him as their everyday right fielder, starting in 2015.

But on October 26, 2014, Taveras and his girlfriend were killed in a drunk-driving accident near his hometown of Puerto Plata in the Dominican Republic. Taveras was 22 years old.

Barret Loux of the Frisco Roughriders was the Texas League Pitcher of the Year, leading the league in victories (14) and winning percentage (.933 on a 14-1 won-lost record) and also posted a 3.47 ERA.

The 6-foot-5 right-hander from Texas A&M University was the sixth overall pick in the 2010 amateur draft by the Arizona Diamondbacks but he left professional baseball after the 2013 season.

2013: For the sixth time since becoming an affiliate of the Colorado Rockies, the Drillers qualified for the Texas League playoffs but saw their dreams of a league championship fizzle with a first-round loss. Nevertheless, there were many causes for celebration.

The Drillers received the 2013 Texas League Organization of the Year award, honoring the league's most successful operation. Aided by more seasonable summertime temperatures and the early on-field success, the total attendance of 393,600 was the second-highest regular season total in Tulsa's professional baseball history.

Tulsa's season attendance ranked fifth among the 30 teams playing Double-A baseball. ONEOK Field also had 14 sellouts for 69 home games, the largest total in Tulsa's professional baseball history to that point in time.

ONEOK Field also hosted the fourth consecutive sellout in one of college baseball's top rivalries, the Bedlam Series between the Oklahoma State University Cowboys and the University of Oklahoma Sooners. Oklahoma State won that game, 4-3.

The animal rights advocacy group People for the Ethical Treatment of Animals (PETA) named ONEOK Field's vegetarian menu selections as the best in all of minor league baseball.

Tulsa ranked among the league's best teams in pitching and defense but aside from outfielder Kyle Parker's superb season, their progress was hindered by a below-average offense. Tulsa finished last in the Texas League in team batting average (.245) and runs scored (544).

The Drillers led the Texas League in turning the largest number of double plays along with the best team fielding percentage (.980). One of Tulsa's top defensive players was center fielder Delta Cleary Jr., who made just one fielding error in 116 games, an achievement that more than made up for a lowly .207 batting average.

Parker was Tulsa's best all-around hitter with 23 home runs, 74 RBIs and a .288 batting average. A baseball and football standout at Clemson University, he ranked among the Texas League's top 10 hitters in five offensive categories. But Parker hit just .192 with just one RBI and 14 strikeouts in 18 games with the Rockies in 2014.

He and Bergman were two of four Drillers named to the Texas League's postseason All-Star Team. The others were shortstop Cristhian Adames and utility infielder Angelys Nina.

Nina led the Drillers in stolen bases (19), ranked second in base hits (125) and had a .980 fielding percentage. Adames had a .973 fielding percentage and lead the team in sacrifice hits (17).

First baseman Kiel Rollings led the Drillers and ranked fourth in the Texas League in both home runs (24) and runs batted in (84) prior to a season-ending injury.

Their team ERA of 3.67 was third-lowest among the eight teams in the Texas League. Christian Bergman was the ace of Tulsa's pitching staff with a 3.37 ERA and 111 strikeouts against just 23 walks in 27 starts along with an 8-7 record.

Eddie Butler showed why he was one of the Colorado Rockies' best pitching prospects with outstanding performances at three levels of minor league baseball. In just six starts with the Drillers, Butler posted a 0.65 earned run average with 25 strikeouts against just six walks over 27.2 innings.

Right-hander Chad Bettis posted a 3.71 ERA in 12 starts with Tulsa and was quickly promoted to the Rockies, quite an achievement considering that he missed all of the 2012 season and two months of the 2013 season with injuries.

Two-time National League All-Star pitcher Roy Oswalt had a 3-2 record plus a 2.16 ERA in five games with the Drillers in an injury rehabilitation assignment. He tossed eight-and-one-third shutout innings in the game that clinched the Northern Division's first-half championship for Tulsa. Oswalt was eventually returned to the Colorado Rockies but had a 0-6 record plus an 8.63 ERA in nine appearances and retired when the season ended.

The Drillers were part of an innovative program created by the Colorado Rockies for their minor league affiliates. Each minor league level had a Development Supervisor, frequently a former manager, to serve as the equivalent of a business firm's chief executive officer and worked in conjunction with the team's field manager. The Development Supervisor's goal was to better develop players for major league careers while the field manager and assistant coaches handled the daily game preparations.

Tulsa's field manager for the 2011-12 seasons, Duane Espy, was promoted to serve as the Drillers' Development Supervisor and hitting coach Kevin Riggs replaced Espy as the field manager.

This would be Riggs' first managerial experience after serving as a hitting coach in the Rockies' minor league organization for six years. He also became the first person to never have served as a minor league manager prior to joining the Drillers.

Tulsa won the Northern Division's first half championship with a 34-34 record and finished with a 68-70 overall record. But they were swept in three games by the Arkansas Travelers in the North Division playoffs. The San Antonio Missions won the Western Division playoffs by upsetting the Corpus Christi Hooks, who had the Texas League's best overall record. The Missions then edged the Travelers in the finals for the second time in three seasons, 3-2.

After slumping midway through the first half-season, the Drillers earned a championship and playoff berth by winning 11 of their final 15 games for a one-game edge over the Springfield Cardinals and a one-and-a-half game margin over Arkansas.

Springfield was scheduled to host Tulsa in the final two games of the first half-season but both games were not played because the Springfield ground crew inexplicably failed to cover the field prior to a heavy thunderstorm and the diamond was rendered unplayable for those two games.

Arkansas had the Northern Division's best overall record that year (73-66), followed by Tulsa (68-70), Springfield (64-74) and Northwest Arkansas (59-81). The Corpus Christi Hooks won the Southern Division title with an 83-57 record, followed by San Antonio (78-61), the Frisco RoughRiders (70-70) and Midland RockHounds (62-78).

Driller games were carried on KTBZ-AM (1430 "The Buzz") with Dennis Higgins calling the game action.

Corpus Christi swept the individual postseason awards with center fielder George Springer named as the Texas League Player of the Year and David Martinez earning Pitcher of the Year honors.

In just over two months of action with the Hooks, Springer had a .297 batting average with 19 home runs, drove in 55 runs and stole 23 bases in just 73 games. When Springer's Double-A and Triple-A numbers were combined, he came close to being just the fifth player in minor league baseball history to hit 40 home runs and steal 40 bases in the same season. He finished with 37 home runs, 45 stolen bases, drove in 108 runs and batted .303.

Springer joined the Astros in 2014 and went on to become a two-time American League All-Star and was the Most Valuable Player in the 2017 World Series. He batted .379 and hit five home runs as the

Astros claimed their first World Series championship by defeating the Los Angeles Dodgers in seven games.

Martinez posted a 14-2 record along with a league-leading 2.02 ERA and was the only Texas League pitcher to win 10 or more games in 2013. He also had 86 strikeouts and just 20 walks in 18 starting appearances. Martinez spent parts of the 2013 and 2014 seasons with the Astros.

2014: This was a pivotal season in the history of the Drillers franchise. They came within one victory of winning their first Texas League championship since 1998 and drew the largest single-season attendance total in Tulsa's professional baseball history. A 12-year affiliation with the Colorado Rockies ended then the Drillers became the Double-A affiliate of one of baseball's most popular teams, the Los Angeles Dodgers.

The Drillers won two of the first three games against the Midland Rockhounds in the best-of-five Texas League championship series. But the Rockhounds rallied to win the final two games in the TLCS and claimed their third league championship in 10 years.

Tulsa won the Northern Division championship in the first half of the season then won three out of four games against the second-half champion Arkansas Travelers in the best-of-five TL Divisional Series. Second baseman Taylor Featherston led the Drillers with a .467 batting average against the Travelers and in the series-clinching victory, went 4-for-4 with a home run and drove in five runs.

Midland and Tulsa split the first two TLCS games played at ONEOK Field then the teams moved to Midland's Security Bank Ballpark for the final three games. In Game 3, Tulsa first baseman Will Swanner broke a 2-2 tie in the 11th inning with a three-run home run that gave the Drillers a 5-2 victory. Swanner went 2-for-4 in that contest and drove in all five of Tulsa's runs.

Being one game away from elimination must have jolted Midland's offense from its slumber as the RockHounds won Games 4 and 5, outscoring the Drillers by a 14-4 margin. Nate Long was the winning pitcher in Game 5, scattering six hits over five and two-thirds scoreless innings.

Despite the outcome, the playoff performance by the 2014 Drillers was the franchise's best postseason record as an affiliate of the Colorado Rockies. Tulsa went 5-4 in 2014 playoff games compared to a combined 3-18 mark over six previous playoff seasons.

Arkansas had the Northern Division's best overall record in 2014 at 75-65, followed by Tulsa (71-68), Springfield (68-72) and Northwest Arkansas (53-87). The Frisco RoughRiders won the Southern Division with the league's best overall record, 80-59, then came Midland (77-63), San Antonio (68-72) and Corpus Christi (67-73).

Tulsa's 39 road victories ranked second in the league to Arkansas' 40. The Drillers' 22 road victories in the first half of the season led the league. But the Drillers' 32-37 home record was a disappointment, considering that they drew a franchise-record 18 sellout crowds to ONEOK Field.

Anchored by a strong pitching staff, Tulsa went 38-31 in the first half of the season to win their seventh first-half division championship. The Drillers' team earned run average of 3.21 was the second-lowest among all Texas League teams. The second half of the season was a different story. Six Drillers were on the injured list at one point, a key factor in the team tumbling to a 16-20 home record.

Dan Winkler had the lowest ERA among Texas League starting pitchers during the first half of the season with a stingy 1.41 mark and allowed just 33 hits over 70 innings. Reliever Scott Oberg produced saves in all 15 of his opportunities, a key factor in the Drillers' posting a 33-0 first-half record when leading a game entering the ninth inning.

But Winkler and Oberg suffered arm injuries in mid-June and the Rockies' top pitching prospect, former Oklahoma Sooner Jon Gray, missed his last two regular season starts and all playoff games with arm problems.

Pitcher Tyler Anderson, second baseman Taylor Fetherston and shortstop Cristhian Adames were named to the 2014 Texas League postseason All-Star Team with Anderson adding the Pitcher of the Year award to his honors.

Anderson's 1.98 ERA led the league and matched the Driller franchise record for lowest ERA in a season set by Jeff Francis in 2004, the year he also earned Texas League Pitcher of the Year honors.

The Colorado Rockies' first selection in the 2011 amateur draft out of the University of Oregon, Anderson finished with a 7-4 won-lost record with 106 strikeouts and allowed just 40 walks in 118.1 innings pitched. The left-handed pitcher was lethal over his last 10 regular season starts, posting a 4-1 record with a stingy 1.01 ERA.

Featherson led the league in total bases (218) and extra-base hits (53) and ranked among the Texas League's top five hitters in six offensive categories as well has hitting 16 home runs and driving in 57 runs. He was a key player for the 2010 Texas Christian University Horned Frogs baseball team that reached the semifinals of the College World Series.

For Adames, it was the second year in a row to be honored as the Texas League's best shortstop. He batted .276 in just over a half-season with Tulsa and then hit .338 in 38 games with Triple-A Colorado Springs prior to a brief tenure with the Rockies in July 2014. The Dominican Republic native had joined the Rockies' organization as an undrafted free agent.

Catcher Ryan Casteel led the Drillers a .280 batting average that was sixth-highest in the Texas League. His numbers were more remarkable considering that he suffered a fractured cheekbone on July 11th sliding into second base but returned to action just eight days later. Relief pitchers Cole White and Scott Oberg combined for 31 saves.

As a team, the Drillers' offense led the league in total bases and their .252 team batting average was third-highest. Tulsa's 11 pitching shutouts tied San Antonio for second place.

With four playoff games added in, the Drillers total home attendance of 415,403 was the largest in Tulsa's professional baseball history. The Drillers' regular season attendance of 403,732 was the second highest total in franchise history, surpassed only by the 408,183 total in the 2010 debut season of ONEOK Field. There were also 18 sellout games, the most in Tulsa professional baseball history.

The Drillers drew an average of 6,211 fans per home game, putting them in fourth place among the 30 Double-A baseball teams and also better than 13 teams on the Triple-A level. Among the Triple-A cities that drew fewer baseball fans than Tulsa in 2014 were New Orleans, Nashville, Memphis, Oklahoma City, Omaha and Colorado Springs.

The Drillers also made history by becoming just the third franchise to win the Texas League's Organization of the Year honor in consecutive seasons. The award salutes the franchise that embodied the highest levels of success on and off the field as well as professionalism and community involvement. The Round Rock Express won the award in 2000 and 2001 and the Springfield Cardinals claimed the award in 2006, 2007 and 2008.

Springfield Cardinals catcher Cody Stanley hit a two-run home run in the fourth inning and was the game's Most Valuable Player as the North All-Stars defeated the South All-Stars, 3-1, in the Texas League All-Star Game on June 24th in North Little Rock, Arkansas.

Eleven Drillers were selected to play in that game and seven participated, the most from any team. Outfielder Brian Humphries, shortstop Cristhian Adames and designated hitter Harold Riggins started for the North. Reserve players were Driller pitchers Jon Gray, Dan Winkler, Eddie Butler, Scott Oberg and Kraig Sitton, catcher Dustin Garneau and infielder Taylor Featherston. Winkler and Oberg did not play due to injuries while Butler and Garneau were promoted to Triple-A Colorado Springs in days prior to the game.

Gray pitched in the fifth inning and needed just 13 pitches, 10 of those being strikes, to retire the three batters he faced. Sitton pitched in the seventh inning and retired the side in order. Adames and Humphries each went 1-for-3 in their hitting appearances.

The 2013 National League batting champion, Colorado Rockies right fielder Michael Cuddyer, played three games with the Drillers as part of an injury rehabilitation assignment in mid-August. He had missed a couple of months of play while recovering from a broken left shoulder socket.

Cuddyer, who spent the his first 11 big-league seasons with the Minnesota Twins prior to joining the Rockies in 2012, had two base hits in 11 at-bats with the Drillers and scored two runs. Shortly after leaving Tulsa and rejoining the Rockies, Cuddyer became the first major league baseball player during the 2014 season to hit for the cycle; getting a single, double, triple and home run during one game.

Driller games were carried on KTBZ-AM (1430 "The Buzz") with Dennis Higgins calling the game action.

Arkansas Travelers second baseman Alex Yarbrough, another top prospect in the St. Louis Cardinals' player development program, was the Texas League Player of the Year. He led the league in runs batted in (77) base hits (155) and doubles (38). In 2013, the graduate of the

University of Mississippi ranked third among all minor league hitters, regardless of classification, in total base hits.

Tulsa's player development contract with the Colorado Rockies ended after the Texas League Championship series and the Rockies' Double-A operations were transferred to New Britain, Connecticut. New Haven was the home of the Rockies' first Double-A team from 1994 through 1998 but team officials have indicated the franchise might move to a new stadium in Hartford, Connecticut in 2016.

2015: A new era of Tulsa's minor league baseball history began with the Drillers becoming the Double-A affiliate of one of baseball's most prestigious franchises, the Los Angeles Dodgers. With the Dodgers also moving their Triple-A franchise from Albuquerque, New Mexico to Oklahoma City, their top two minor league teams were roughly 100 miles apart.

In a nod to the Dodgers' heritage, the Drillers primary jersey colors became blue and white and an alternate game jersey was created with their nickname written in the legendary Dodgers script on the front of the jersey.

The Dodgers' previous Double-A team was the Chattanooga (Tennessee) Lookouts, who reached the 2014 Southern League Championship Series despite a 61-77 regular season record. A late rally in the second half of the season, coupled with timely hitting and pitching, lifted the Lookouts into the Southern League playoffs.

The Dodgers have a long heritage of developing their own minor league players, as evidenced by Hall of Famers such as Jackie Robinson, Sandy Koufax, Duke Snider, Don Drysdale, Steve Garvey, Roy Campanella and many others. That system also developed consecutive National League Rookies of the Year from 1992 through 1996.

But in recent years, the focus in Los Angeles shifted to big-money major-league players and the Dodgers' player development system slipped from the lofty level it once enjoyed. During an introductory news conference at ONEOK Field, Dodgers President and Chief Executive Officer Stan Kasten said the team's new ownership group had made the rebuilding of its player development programs a high priority.

Two of the brightest stars in the Dodgers organization played for the 2015 Drillers; shortstop Cory Seager and left-handed pitcher Julio Urias.

Seager became the first player in the new affiliation to begin a season with the Tulsa Drillers and finish the season with the Los Angeles Dodgers. The Dodgers' first selection in the 2012 amateur draft and younger brother of Seattle Mariners All-Star Kyle Seager had a team-leading .375 batting average in just 20 games with Tulsa before being promoted to Triple-A Oklahoma City. His combined 2015 minor league hitting totals were a .293 batting average with 18 home runs and 76 runs batted in.

Playing in 27 games with Los Angeles, Seager batted .337 with four home runs and 17 runs batted in. Then he made Dodger baseball history in the 2015 National League Division series against the New York Mets as the youngest position player (21 years and 165 days old) to start a postseason game in franchise history.

A teenager when he played for the Drillers, Urias was reminiscent of other power-pitcher Dodger lefties from recent years. Over parts of the 2013 and 2014 minor league seasons, the Mexican native posted 176 strikeouts against just 53 walks in 142 innings.

While Urias missed most of the month of June due to surgery to remove a benign mass from his left eye, his left arm was fine and dandy. He posted 46 strikeouts and just nine walks over 36 innings and opposing teams batted just .194 against him.

New manager Razor Shines brought a legacy of success as a minor league skipper with his teams reaching the postseason playoffs in six out of 10 previous seasons.

Despite the hubbub about the affiliation with the Dodgers, the Drillers' 2015 season was not what local baseball fans hoped for, as evidenced by a last-place finish in the Texas League's North Division and a 29-39 record in home games.

Pitching was not the problem because Tulsa led the Texas League in fewest base hits allowed (507) and was a co-leader or ranked second in three other pitching categories.

The Drillers endured a power outage when it came to hitting. They finished last overall in runs scored (248), runs batted in (226) and on-base percentage (.300) and their team batting average of .239 ranked seventh in the eight-team league.

Season and single-game attendance figures dropped slightly when compared to previous seasons, mostly due to the second-heaviest May rainfall in the city's history (14.77 inches) along with the team's sub-par performance.

The Drillers' 2015 season attendance was 380,759 and the average attendance for home games was 5,858. Both of those totals were the second highest in the Texas League but the season total was roughly 23,000 lower than in 2014 and the per-game average was 353 lower than in 2014.

The Midland RockHounds became the first Texas League team in 12 years to win consecutive championships, posting a three-game sweep of the Northwest Arkansas Naturals in the Texas League Championship Series. Midland defeated the Corpus Christi Hooks, 3-1, to win the Southern Division playoffs while Northwest Arkansas posted a three-game sweep of the Arkansas Travelers to win the Northern Division playoffs.

Parker Frazier, a Tulsa Driller in 2012 and 2013 and Bishop Kelley High School alumnus, pitched the first complete game shutout of his professional baseball career to clinch the pennant for Midland. He scattered three hits while striking out nine batters and did not allow a runner to go past second base in the finale.

Given that Frazier was playing for his fourth team and second big-league organization in 2015 as well as battling through a back injury during postseason play, the victory was even sweeter.

Arkansas had the Northern Division's best overall record at 71-68 followed by Northwest Arkansas (69-70), the Springfield Cardinals (64-76) and Tulsa Drillers (62-77). Corpus Christi's 89-51 record led the Southern Division. Midland (83-57) was second followed by the Frisco RoughRiders (60-79) and San Antonio Missions (60-80).

Northwest Arkansas' quest to reach the 2015 Texas League play-offs were dealt a crushing blow when outfielder Mike Bianucci drew an 80-game suspension for violating the minor league baseball rules against using performance enhancing substances. Bianucci had been chosen to play in the Texas League All-Star Game and his 12 home runs tied him for second place in that category.

Midland shortstop Chad Pinder was the Texas League Player of the Year. In addition to leading the TL with 86 runs batted in and ranking second in batting average (.318), he also hit 15 home runs and had an on-base percentage of .360 in 111 games. Pinder was ranked as the seventh-highest prospect in the Oakland Athletics' player development system.

Arkansas' Nate Smith was the Texas League Pitcher of the Year. The lanky left-hander played in only 17 games for the Travelers before earning a promotion to Triple-A Salt Lake City but his TL performances were outstanding. Smith posted an 8-4 won-lost record with a 2.48 earned run average and held opposing hitters to a .218 batting average. In just under 102 innings, Smith posted 81 strikeouts against just 28 walks.

The Texas League joined the other Double-A and Triple-A leagues by implementing a 20-second pitch clock identical to the one used in 1963 and 1964. Just like back then, pitchers had 20 seconds to throw the ball after getting it from the catcher or the umpire would call a ball. Two pitch clocks were located behind home plate with the other in the outfield.

Other rules intended to speed up the game required hitters to keep one foot in the batter's box during the entire at-bat and time limits were imposed on pitching changes.

Driller games were carried on KTBZ-AM (1430 "The Buzz") with Dennis Higgins calling the game action.

ONEOK Field was named as the Texas League's best baseball stadium and ranked third among all Double-A ballparks in a 2015 survey published by *Baseball America* magazine.

The *Baseball America* rankings came from a survey of over 100 minor league baseball executives, league observers and print and electronic media representatives from all levels of minor league baseball.

Three Tulsa Driller pitchers appeared in the 2015 Texas League All-Star Game on June 30th at Whataburger Field in Corpus Christi, Texas. The North All-Stars defeated the South All-Stars, 9-4, with Northwest Arkansas star Jorge Bonfacio winning Most Valuable Player honors for a tie-breaking two-run home run in the eighth inning that gave the North the lead for keeps.

The Driller honorees were pitchers Chris Anderson, Jeremy Horst and Jeremy Kehrt and Shines was named as the manager for the TL North All-Stars.

However, no Tulsa Drillers were chosen for the 2015 Texas League Postseason All-Star Team.

After the season ended, the Dodgers made wholesale changes within its minor league structure. Shines' contract as Drillers manager was terminated and, surprisingly, Damon Berryhill was fired as manager of the Triple-A Oklahoma City Dodgers after taking that team to the Pacific Coast League's best record (86-58) and a playoff berth.

2016: The sting of squandering two opportunities to reach the Texas League playoffs was soothed by outstanding performances by a trio of Driller standouts selected to the Texas League postseason All-Star team. One member of that trio, Chase DeJong, earned the TL Pitcher of the Year award in his Double-A baseball debut.

Another bright spot came off the diamond when the parent Los Angeles Dodgers extended their Double-A affiliation with the Tulsa Drillers at least through the end of the 2018 season.

After losing 17 of 25 games to open the season, the Drillers caught fire and set a franchise record for most consecutive victories, winning 10 in a row from May 28th through June 8th. That surge placed them on the cusp of clinching the Northern Division's first-half championship and an automatic berth in the Texas League playoffs.

But Tulsa lost its final four games in the first half schedule, opening the door for the Springfield Cardinals to clinch that playoff berth with their own five-game winning streak.

Then Tulsa reeled off seven wins in an eight-game span and was a game out of first place in the second half standings prior to an August 21st game at the Frisco RoughRiders. Left fielder Jacob Scavuzzo would be lost for the rest of the season with an injured shoulder in that contest and the Drillers would lose 11 of their final 14 games.

DeJong earned the TL Pitcher of the Year award by posting a league-leading 14 victories and coming within one win of matching the Drillers' franchise record for the most pitching victories in a season. He also came within three outs of throwing Tulsa's first no-hitter in 15 years during the first game of a doubleheader in Little Rock against the Arkansas Travelers on July 22nd.

He also led Texas League pitchers in winning percentage (.737), lowest opponent batting average (.207) and walks/hits-to-innings pitched ratio, or WHIP (1.02). He also ranked third among TL pitchers in strikeouts (125) and fourth in innings pitched (141.2).

DeJong became the fifth Driller and seventh Tulsa pitcher to receive the Texas League Pitcher of the Year award. He would later play in the major leagues for the Seattle Mariners and Minnesota Twins.

Second baseman Willie Calhoun and centerfielder Alex Verdugo joined DeJong as the Drillers' representatives on the TL postseason All-Star team.

Calhoun, likened by some baseball scouts to Boston Red Sox star Dustin Pedroia for his baseball skills, led the Texas League in runs batted in (88) and total bases (232). He also finished second in the TL in home runs (270, runs scored (74) and slugging percentage (.486).

Verdugo finished fourth in the TL in base hits (130) and ninth in batting average (.277). He also hit 12 home runs and drove in 61 runs for the Drillers.

Cody Bellinger, who would become an All-Star first baseman for the Los Angeles Dodgers, missed the first month of the season with an inflamed nerve in his right hip but came on strong to finish third in the Texas League in home runs with 23. Bellinger also drove in 65 runs and batted .263 in 114 games with Tulsa.

Arguably the unsung hero and heart of the 2016 Drillers was shortstop Drew Maggi, whose .299 batting average was the best of his seven years in minor league baseball and his defensive play earned a spot in the Texas League All-Star Game. With Maggi in the lineup, the Drillers had a 51-42 record. Playing without him, Tulsa went 25-44.

Five other Drillers were promoted to the Dodgers during their march to the 2016 National League Western Division championship. They were outfielders Andrew Toles and Enrique "Kike" Hernandez along with pitchers Brock Stewart, Grant Dayton and Carlos Frias.

Toles batted .314 and stole 13 bases in 43 games with Tulsa. That led to a quick promotion to Triple-A Oklahoma City and a subsequent call-up to the Dodgers.

Despite a 3-4 record, Stewart was the Drillers' power pitcher early in the season. The Illinois State University product posted 65 strikeouts against only 11 walks in 59.1 innings pitched along with a stingy 1.37 ERA.

Dayton was Tulsa's best relief pitcher early in the season with 28 strikeouts against just three bases on balls over 15.2 innings. He posted a 3-0 record with a 2.30 ERA in 12 appearances.

Frias and Hernadez played briefly for the Drillers as part of their minor league injury rehabilitation assignments.

A total of 18 Drillers earned promotions to Triple-A Oklahoma City during 2016.

Ryan Garko, who never served as a minor league manager and had been out of professional baseball since 2013, was Tulsa's manager that year. Garko spent nearly four of his five major league seasons with the Cleveland Indians and also played briefly for the San Francisco Giants and Texas Rangers.

Garko was the catcher for Stanford University's baseball teams that reached the College World Series finals in 2001 and 2003. He won the 2003 Johnny Bench Award as the best catcher in Division I collegiate baseball and was named to the College World Series Legends Team in 2010.

Future MLB All-Stars who joined Darko on that collegiate dream team are Barry Bonds, Dave Winfield, Sal Bando, Fred Lynn, Robin Ventura, Bob Horner, Will Clark and Nomar Garciaparra.

While Tulsa's season and average game attendance totals were the second-highest in the Texas League and among the best teams in all of Double-A baseball, those respective numbers declined for the second year in a row. Season attendance was 366,734, a drop of just over 14,000 fans from 2015. The average game attendance of 5,393 was 465 fans fewer then the previous season.

Driller games were carried on KTBZ-AM (1430 "The Buzz") with Dennis Higgins calling the game action. The 2016 season marked the 12th consecutive season that Driller games were carried on "The Buzz" and the 31st consecutive season of the Drillers' partnership with iHeart Media, which was previously known as Clear Channel Radio.

As for regular season action, the Springfield Cardinals had the Northern Division's best overall record at 75-65 followed by Tulsa (68-71), the Arkansas Travelers (67-73) and the Northwest Arkansas Naturals (65-75). Northwest Arkansas would back into its playoff berth by being the only Northern Division team to have a winning record (36-34) during the second half schedule.

For the second year in a row, the Corpus Christi Hooks had the best overall record in both the Southern Division and the entire Texas League. The Hooks went 85-55, followed by Midland (78-62), the Frisco RoughRiders (63-76) and the San Antonio Missions (58-82).

Midland defeated Northwest Arkansas, 3-1, to win the best-of-five TL Championship Series and its third consecutive Texas League championship. The RockHounds upset Corpus Christi, 3-1, in the Southern Division playoffs while the Naturals ousted Springfield, 3-1, in the Northern Division playoffs.

Midland third baseman Matt Chapman was the Texas League Player of the Year. Chapman led the TL in home runs (29), runs scored (78), extra-base hits (59) and slugging percentage (.521) and finished second in runs batted in (83) and total bases (228).

Chapman was the Oakland Athletics' first-round draft choice in the 2014 amateur draft after playing collegiate baseball for California State University-Fullerton. He joined the A's in 2018 and was the winner of the American League Platinum Glove for third baseman, presented to the league's best defensive player at a specific position.

Nine Drillers were on the Northern Division roster for the Texas League All-Star Game on June 28th in Springfield, Missouri. Joining DeJong, Calhoun, Maggi and Verdugo were catcher Paul Hoenecke, outfielder Jacob Scavuzzo and pitchers Jordan Schafer, Caleb Dirks and Scott Barlow.

The Southern Division All-Stars won the contest, 8-5, before 7,832 fans with Frisco RoughRiders center fielder Ryan Cordell being chosen as the game's Most Valuable Player. Cordell went 3-for-5, hit a home run and drove in four runs.

The Driller All-Star pitchers accounted for six of the 14 strikeouts by the North's pitching staff while allowing just two runs and five hits over two and two-thirds innings.

Verdugo went 3-for-5 with a double. Maggi went 1-for-3, drew a walk and scored two runs. Calhoun drove in one run with a sacrifice fly. Scavuzzo went 1-for-4 while Hoenecke went hitless in two at-bats.

Shortstop Alex Bregman, who would play for the Houston Astros and win the 2018 Major League Baseball All-Star Game Most Valuable Player award, was a member of the 2016 Corpus Christi Hooks. In 62 games with Corpus Christi, Bregman had a .297 batting average (second-highest among regular players) with 14 home runs and 46 runs batted in.

2017: Scott Hennessey turned in one of the greatest managerial seasons in Tulsa's professional baseball history, rallying the Drillers from a break-even record two-thirds of the way through the season to win the Texas League's Northern Division and coming within one game of their first Texas League championship since 1998.

When manager Ryan Garko unexpectedly resigned in late July to become head baseball coach at the University of the Pacific in Stockton, California, Tulsa had a 50-50 record. In his resignation, Garko cited a need to be closer to his family and a chance to reunite with Pacific athletic director Ted Leland, who was also the athletic director when Garko played college baseball at Stanford University.

Hennessey had been a scout in the Dodgers organization for a decade and took the Drillers job on an interim basis. Prior to joining the Dodgers as a scout, Hennessey's coaching experience consisted of coaching two different high schools in the Jacksonville, Florida area and serving as an assistant coach in 1997 and 1998 on the Cowley County (KS) Junior College teams that won the National Junior College Athletic Association World Series championships.

With Hennessey at the helm, the Drillers closed the season by posting a 27-13 record and winning the Texas League's North Division second-half season championship.

Even more impressive was the Drillers posting an 18-2 record in home games under Hennessey, highlighted by 15 consecutive victories from July 27th through August 30th.That broke the Tulsa professional baseball record set by the 1968 Tulsa Oilers.

In the Texas League playoffs, Tulsa rallied from a 2-1 series deficit to defeat the Northwest Arkansas Naturals for the North Division championship. In Game 4, Tulsa rallied from a 4-0 deficit to post a 16-8 victory and set a franchise playoff record for most runs scored in a postseason game. The Midland RockHounds performed a similar feat to claim the South Division championship in a series with the San Antonio Missions.

Pitcher Dennis Santana was Tulsa's postseason pitching ace, going 13 innings without giving up an earned run. The highlight was his work in Game 5 against Northwest Arkansas, scattering three hits over seven scoreless innings along with 11 strikeouts.

Ironically, Santana made his Driller debut in Hennessey's first game as the team's interim manager.

The Drillers won the first two games of the championship series in Midland. Then Tulsa's booming bats went silent and Midland won the next three games at ONEOK Field. In the winner-take-all Game 5, Midland scored in the first inning and held on for a 1-0 victory.

The turning point of the 2017 Texas League championship series came early in Game 3 when the Drillers loaded the bases twice with one out but failed to score. Midland escaped with a 2-0 victory in Game 3 then posted a 6-3 triumph in Game 4.

Midland won its fourth consecutive Texas League championship and became the first team to achieve that feat since the Fort Worth Cats won six pennants in a row from 1920 through 1925.

Tulsa and Springfield shared the Northern Division's best over-all record that year (77-63) but the Drillers advanced to the playoffs by winning its regular season series with the Cardinals. They were followed by Northwest Arkansas (67-73) and Arkansas (65-75). San Antonio won the Southern Division title with a 78-62 record followed by Corpus Christi and Midland (67-71) and the Frisco RoughRiders (60-80).

Drillers third baseman Matt Beaty was the Texas League Player of the Year and only the third Driller to win that honor. He posted a .326 batting average and ended the regular season with a 13-game hitting streak.

Beaty also hit 15 home runs with 69 RBIs, was the Texas League co-leader in doubles (31), ranked second in slugging percentage (.505) and third in total base hits (143). Beaty provided an offensive spark in the playoffs with a .357 batting average over 10 games.

In addition to a 6-3 won-lost record, Scott Barlow led Texas League pitchers with the lowest earned run average (2.10) and lowest opponent batting average (.192) for pitchers with at least 100 innings. He also had 124 strikeouts and allowed only 37 walks over 107.1 innings.

Former Oklahoma Sooner pitcher Corey Copping was the Drillers' bullpen ace, finishing second among relief pitchers in saves (18) and leading the Texas League in games pitched (49).

A trio of Drillers would rank among the Texas League's top 11 players in batting average. In addition to Beaty's league-leading .326, shortstop Erick Mejia finished eighth in batting average (.289) and was third in the league in stolen bases (25). Outfielder Tim Locastro ranked 11th with a .285 average and added 22 stolen bases.

Locastro also earned a place in infamy when it came to baseball history in Tulsa and the Texas League. He was hit by a pitch 26 times before moving up on August 1st to Triiple-A Oklahoma City. That set a Tulsa season record and was one plunking shy of matching the Texas League record of 27 set in 1916 by Ed Miller of the Galveston Pirates.

Despite a lackluster .237 batting average, left fielder Jacob Scavuzzo belted three home runs in a June 21st game at Springfield; becoming the first Driller to achieve that feat since 2002.

Three players from that Drillers team would make their major league debuts later that year with the Dodgers: catcher Kyle Farmer, starting pitcher Walker Buehler and relief pitcher Edward Paredes. Buehler, blessed with a fastball clocked at nearly 100 miles per hour, would become part of the Dodgers' starting pitching rotation in 2018.

Attendance at ONEOK Field increased slightly from the previous year. In 67 home games, the Drillers drew 374,976 fans; an increase of roughly 8,000 from 2016 and ranked second to the Frisco RoughRiders. The average per game attendance was 5,597; up nearly 200 per game from 2016.

And speaking of revolving turnstiles or doors, the 2017 Drillers set a Tulsa professional baseball record of using 72 players in a season. The old record was 69 in 2015 which was Tulsa's first season in the Dodgers' organization.

Driller game broadcasts were carried on KTBZ-AM (1430 "The Buzz") for the 13th consecutive season with Dennis Higgins once again calling the game action.

A seven-run fourth inning gave the South All-Stars a 10-3 victory over the North All-Stars in the Texas League All-Star Game played in Frisco, Texas.

Four Tulsa Drillers participated in that game: third baseman Edward Rios, catcher Paul Hoenecke and pitchers Edward Paredes and Corey Copping.

Midland left fielder B.J. Boyd was the game's Most Valuable Player, getting three hits in four at-bats, scoring two runs and driving in three runs. Two of his hits came during that fourth-inning scoring outburst.

Rios had tied the game, 3-3, with a solo home run in the top of the third inning. Boyd opened the fourth inning with a single to center field off Parades and would score the first of the South's seven runs.

Paredes would give up four runs and allowed three hits and a walk while retiring just one batter. Hoenecke had a single in two at-bats while Copping retired all three batters he faced in the eighth inning.

Texas League president Tom Kayser retired in 2017 after 25 years of service in that position; the longest presidential tenure in TL history.

Under Kayser's leadership, Texas League annual attendance totals rose from 1.7 million fans in his first year to 2.8 million fans in his final season and seven franchises have played in new stadiums since 2002.

Tim Purpura, a longtime minor league baseball executive, was chosen by the Texas League Board of Directors to replace Kayser. Purpura spent 11 years with the Houston Astros' player development program and his work bore fruit when the Astros reached the National League playoffs six times over a nine-year span.

Purpura served as the Astros' general manger from 2005 through 2007 with the highlight coming in 2005 when that franchise won its only National League pennant. He later served in the Texas Rangers' player development program from 2011 through 2013.

2018: After 20 years of frustration, the Tulsa Drillers finally won the Texas League championship by sweeping the San Antonio Missions in the best-of-five TL Finals. It ended the longest period between championship pennants among the league's teams.

But the Drillers' road to the title wasn't easy by any means. After being down two games to one in the best-of-five North Division championship series against the Arkansas Travelers, Tulsa rallied for a pair of 5-3 victories and advanced to face the upstart San Antonio Missions, who overcame a 2-0 series deficit and eliminated the heavily-favored and talent-laden Corpus Christi Hooks. Outfielder Yordan Alvarez, who would earn a quick promotion to the Houston Astros and become of the team's brightest young stars, was the spark plug for Corpus Christi's early success.

Shortstop Gavin Lux was one of Tulsa's heroes in the Arkansas series, hitting safely in every game and going 9-for-21 (.429 batting average) at the plate. In Game Five, pitcher Mitchell White took a no-hitter into the fourth inning and retired the side in order four times.

The first two games of the TL Finals were played at ONEOK Field in Tulsa. The Drillers won the first game in 10 innings, 3-2, after Lux reached base on a fielder's choice and later scored the winning run on catcher Keibert Ruiz's one-out single to left field.

Game Two saw San Antonio jump to an early 5-1 lead, aided by two doubles and two runs batted in by Josh Naylor. But Tulsa would rally again and pulled out a 6-5 victory.

Driller relief pitchers Andre Scrubb ,Yadier Alvarez and Karch Kowalczyk set the stage for the rally by combining to pitch five score-less innings while scattering three hits and striking out five batters.

Then in the bottom of the ninth inning, Lux scored the tying run on Ruiz's RBI single then Drew Jackson scored the game-winning run on a wild pitch by San Antonio reliever Dauris Valdez.

The series shifted to San Antonio's Nelson Wolff Stadium for Game Three. After a 48-minute rain delay to start the game, Lux belted the game's first pitch over the right centerfield fence for a solo home run. In the seventh inning, D.J. Peters and Jacob Scavuzzo would hit back-to-back home runs and the Drillers coasted to a 5-2 victory.

Dustin May was the winning pitcher in the title-clinching victory, scattering seven hits over five innings and not walking a batter. And Driller relief pitchers came through in the clutch by not allowing the Missions to score during their times on the pitching mound. Shea Spitzbarth was the bullpen playoff ace posting a 0.50 ERA over 6.2 innings in four games with eight strikeouts and no walks.

Lux batted .324 in just 28 regular season games but his .424 batting average in eight playoff games was the sparkplug in the Drillers' drive for the Texas League championship. He was a first-team selection for the 2018 all-minor league all-star team chosen by *Baseball America*.

Ruiz was another postseason Driller standout with a .333 batting average and repeatedly snuffed out opponent rallies by throwing out runners trying to steal a base.

Third baseman Connor Joe batted .304 with 11 home runs early in the season before being promoted to Triple A Oklahoma City.

Pitcher Caleb Ferguson posted a 3-0 record and a sparkling 1.38 earned run average in just eight starts before being promoted to the Los Angeles Dodgers. After being moved to the bullpen in the big leagues, Ferguson finished that year with a 7-2 record in 29 appearances and allowed just one base runner over six postseason appearances.

Peters and Scavuzzo finished first and second, respectively, in the Texas League's home run rankings with 29 and 24. Peters tied for second in the TL in runs scored (79) while Scavuzzo finished third in RBIs with 79.

An inspirational story involved Drillers left-handed pitcher Devin Smeltzer and his two-pronged quest to reach the major leagues after being diagnosed with abdominal cancer at the age of nine. He posted a 5-5 record with the Drillers before being traded to the Minnesota Twins midway through the 2018 season. Then on May 28, 2019, Smeltzer pitched six shutout innings in his MLB debut in a 5-3 Twins victory over the Milwauikee Brewers.

Tulsa had the North Division's best overall record in 2018 (74-65) followed by Arkansas (71-68), Northwest Arkansas (70-70) and Springfield (60-79). Corpus Christi easily won the South Division title with a league-best 82-56 record followed by the San Antonio Missions (71-67) and Frisco RoughRiders (60-80).

Arguably, the turning point in Drillers' season was a stretch from July 5th through the 18th when they won 11 of 12 games and started the streak in style by winning six in a row at ONEOK Field.

Arkansas first baseman Joey Curletta, a Drillers outfielder in 2016, was the 2018 Texas League Player of the Year. Curletta led Texas League hitters in runs batted in (94) and walks (81), finished third in home runs (23) and batted .282 for the season. It was the first time that an Arkansas Traveler led the Texas League in RBIs since Mike Napoli did so with 99 back in 2005.

San Antonio's Logan Allen was the 2018 Texas League Pitcher of the Year, posting a career-high 10 victories (tied for third in the TL) in 19 starts. Allen, who would join the Cleveland Indians the following season, posted a 10-6 record with a 2.75 ERA along with 125 strikeouts and just 38 walks in 121 innings. Allen and relief pitcher Jason Jester combined for the Texas League's only no-hitter in 2018. Ironically, the Tulsa Drillers were on the losing end of that May 31st contest.

San Antonio had a 19-year-old shortstop, Fernando Tatis Jr., who would have a breakout season with the 2020 San Diego Padres. The son of a 1997 Tulsa Drillers third baseman batted .286 with 16 home runs in 88 games with the Missions that season. However, his defense left something to be desired as evidence by a team-leading 13 fielding errors.

Driller game broadcasts were carried on KTBZ-AM (1430 "The Buzz") for the 14th consecutive season with Dennis Higgins handling the play-by-play.

Tulsa's season attendance was 350,396 with an average per game attendance of 5,230. Both numbers were the second highest in the Texas League but the total attendance was 24,580 fans lower than the previous season.

2019: What was poised to be the finest season in Tulsa Drillers franchise history and, arguably, one of the five greatest in the city's professional baseball history was spoiled by a complete collapse in the final inning of the final game of the Texas League Finals.

The expansion Amarillo Sod Poodles (loving called the Soddies by their fans) erupted for seven runs in the top of the ninth inning and stole an 8-3 victory from the Drillers in the winner-take-all Game Five of the championship series at ONEOK Field.

Amarillo rejoined the Texas League in 2019 when the San Diego Padres moved their Double-A franchise from San Antonio to the Texas Panhandle city. The new team's quirky nickname of Sod Poodles (supposedly an Old West nickname for a prairie dog) was chosen by a vote of local baseball fans.

On the bright side, the Drillers' 78-61 regular season record was the best in franchise history as was winning a third consecutive Texas League division championship. There was also a noteworthy increase in attendance plus ONEOK Field hosted the 2019 Texas League All-Star Game,

In addition, the ace of the Los Angeles Dodgers pitching staff played at ONEOK Field in an injury rehab assignment and the 2019 Minor League Player of the Year also wore a Drillers uniform.

Four Driller pitchers combined to throw a no-hitter against the Arkansas Travelers on April 14th but Tulsa came out on the short end of a 1-0 decision.

The Arkansas Travelers had the best overall regular season record in the North Division as well as the entire league at 81-57 followed by the Drillers (78-61), Springfield Cardinals (60-80) and Northwest Arkansas Naturals (60-80). Midland won the South Division title with a 73-66 record followed by Amarillo (72-66), the Frisco RoughRiders (68-71) and Corpus Christi Hooks (66-73).

The Drillers also had the Texas League's best record in home games (43-27) and went 22-10 to end the second half of the regular season.

Second baseman Gavin Lux was the 2019 Minor League Baseball Player of the Year and his first half heroics led to a quick promotion to Triple-A Oklahoma City and then his big league debut came on September 2 against the Colorado Rockies.

In just 64 games with the Drillers, Lux ranked among the Texas League's top five hitters in batting average (.313), base hits (81), home runs (13), slugging percentage (.521) and on-base percentage (.375). When his Oklahoma City totals were added in, Lux had a .347 batting average with 26 home runs and 76 runs batted in before joining the Dodgers.

Dustin May was Tulsa's early-season pitching ace and quickly earned a promotion to the parent Dodgers, as well. In his 15 starts with the Drillers, he led the Texas League in starting appearances and his 86 strikeouts were among the TL's top five pitchers when he was promoted to Triple-A Oklahoma City. May's farewell appearance was memorable, setting a career high and ONEOK Field record by striking out 14 batters.

Second half standouts included catcher-third baseman Connor Wong, shortstop Jeter Downs and starting pitcher Edwin Uceta.

Wong batted .349 with 31 runs batted in over 40 games, highlighted by a streak in which he had three base hits six times over a span of seven games. Then he hit safely in all 10 postseason games and drove in 11 runs.

Downs batted .347 over 22 regular and postseason games and all nine of his home runs came against Amarillo.

Uceta, a slender right-handed pitcher from the Dominican Republic, led Driller starting pitchers with seven victories; all of them coming over his last nine starting appearances. He posted a stingy 1.55 earned run average over his last 15 games and then allowed one run over 10 innings in the North Division playoff series against Arkansas.

Right fielder Cody Thomas led Tulsa as well as all Texas League hitters in home runs with 23. He also paced the Drillers in runs batted in (76) and triples (6). Thomas competed against future pro football star Baker Mayfield in 2015 for the Oklahoma Sooners' starting quarterback position then chose to focus on his baseball career.

The Drillers hosted the 2019 Texas League All-Star Game on June 25th at ONEOK Field. It was the second time ONEOK Field hosted that midseason showcase and the seventh time that Tulsa would host that event.

Two members of the Midland RockHounds led the South Division All-Stars to a 4-1 victory over the North Division All-Stars before 7,449 fans. Midland center fielder Luis Barrera was the game's Most Valuable Player with three base hits. Ironically, a severe shoulder injury two games afterwards sidelined him for the rest of the season. Catcher Collin Theroux, who played collegiately at Oklahoma State University, added a two-run home run.

Tulsa outfielder Chris Parmalee defeated teammate Cody Thomas in a slugfest to win the Home Run Derby contest prior to the All-Star Game.

Springfield Cardinals center fielder Dylan Carlson was the 2019 Texas League Player of the Year. A first-round draft choice of the St. Louis Cardinals in 2016, he ranked second in the Texas League in home runs (21) and runs scored (81) while posting a .281 batting average and stealing 18 bases. Out of his 117 base hits that season, 51 went for extra bases.

Arkansas right-hander Darren McCaughan was the 2019 Texas League Pitcher of the Year. McCaughan struck out 89 batters and allowed just 13 walks over 102.2 innings and posted a 7-5 record with a 2.89 ERA in 17 starts. But after earning a promotion to the Seattle

Mariners' Triple-A affiliate in Tacoma, he went 0-6 with a hideous 8.06 ERA.

Driller game broadcasts were carried on KTBZ-AM (1430 "The Buzz") for the 15th consecutive season with Dennis Higgins handling the play-by-play.

Tulsa's season attendance was 374,501 with an average per game attendance of 5,507. The season attendance was an increase of just over 24,000 from the previous year.

Chapter Thirteen

The 2020s

The dawning of a new decade brought events that no one in Tulsa ever dreamed could possibly happen.

First and foremost was a global tragedy with a significant local impact. The deadly novel coronavirus, more commonly known as Covid-19, along with various strains of that disease ravaged every nation on the face of the earth beginning in 2020. The Centers for Disease Control and Prevention (CDC), a federal health agency, reported that over 20 million Americans contracted Covid-19 that year.

Data compiled by the World Health Organization showed 264,808 Americans dying from Covid-19 in 2020. In the state of Oklahoma, there were 290,936 confirmed cases with 2,489 deaths during that period.

Glimmers of hope became brighter with the creation of various Covid-19 vaccines along with heightened and proactive efforts related to disease prevention such as the wearing of masks or face shields, increased sanitation measures and people staying six feet apart, more popularly known as social distancing.

Face-to-face meetings for such events as school classes, church worship services and public meetings were frequently staged by video conferencing. While live concerts and sporting events and crowded movie theaters and restaurants were abandoned for a period of time, drive-in theaters once fondly regarded as a relic of days gone by enjoyed a resurgence of popularity because people watched movies in a safe environment.

On a much lower priority level, no minor league professional baseball games were played in Tulsa or anywhere else in the United States in 2020. Locally, it marked the first time since the end of World War II in 1945 that professional baseball games were not played locally.

A deeply divided and tumultuous nation turned out in record-setting numbers for the 2020 presidential election. In a hard-fought contest, former Vice President Joe Biden defeated incumbent Donald Trump in both the popular vote and the Constitutionally-ordained Electoral College.

On January 6, 2021 following a protest rally in Washington, DC with Trump's keynote speech that featured false claims about the election results and proceedings, many armed supporters invaded the United States Capitol building while Congress was in session. Five people were killed, 140 others were injured and members of Congress were ushered to safety from the failed attempt to overturn the president election results.

A collegiate version of Tulsa Drillers baseball participated in the 2020 Texas Collegiate League and reached the championship finals. The professional version of the Tulsa Drillers returned in 2021 but the Texas League, whose origin dated back to 1888, ceased to exist and was replaced by the Double-A Central League when Major League Baseball reorganized the professional minor leagues.

The Los Angeles Dodgers won the 2020 World Series and the following year, extended their working relationship with the Tulsa Drillers through the end of the 2030 baseball season.

The Collective Bargaining Agreement between MLB team owners and the players union expired after the 2021 MLB season. The owners implemented their lockout late in 2021 and while it stretched into the spring of 2022, minor league teams like the Tulsa Drillers weren't serious affected.

(A lockout is where owners tell players that they can't come to work until a new contract is agreed upon. A strike is where players tell owners that they won't come to work until a new contract is agreed upon.)

The players' union wanted shorter time frames in reaching salary arbitration and free agency, along with better salaries for players with lesser MLB experience and a larger share of the money created by lucrative TV contracts.

Owners, who have prevailed in the most recent CBA negotiations, wanted the postseason expanded from 10 to up to 14 teams but refused to increase player salaries accordingly. The owners also wanted to implement a universal designated hitter (both teams using the DH instead of just the American League) along with other rule changes.

2020: The sixth season of the affiliation between the Los Angeles Dodgers and Tulsa Drillers dawned with bright promise. But the rapid global spread of the deadly coronavirus brought baseball, professional sports and life as we know it to a screeching halt.

Nevertheless, baseball games were played at ONEOK Field in downtown Tulsa that summer and seeds planted in Tulsa in previous years by the Los Angeles Dodgers produced a bountiful harvest for baseball fans.

After several months of speculation, Major League Baseball announced on June 30th that it would not provide players to its affiliated minor league teams for the 2020 season. While the big league teams would go on to play a drastically reduced schedule later that year and the Dodgers' season would open on July 23rd, it meant no professional minor league baseball games would be played throughout the United States.

Thanks to creative thinking by the management of the Tulsa Drillers and other Texas League teams, there would be baseball games played in their stadiums.

The Texas Collegiate League, created in 2003 to provide minor-league level experiences for talented collegiate baseball players, stepped in to fill the gap. The TCL received a boost when one of America's most popular summer collegiate baseball programs, the Cape Cod League, cancelled its 2020 season due to the Covid-19 pandemic.

Teams in the TCL's North Division were the Tulsa Drillers, Amarillo Sod Squad, Amarillo Sod Dogs, Frisco RoughRiders and Texarkana Twins. South Division teams were the Acadiana (Youngsville, Louisiana) Cane Cutters, Brazos Valley (Bryan/College Station, Texas) Bombers, Round Rock Hairy Men, San Antonio Flying Chanclas and Victoria Generals.

The Muscogee (Creek) Nation was a presenting partner with the TCL Drillers and the two organizations honored the history of the city of Tulsa and that Native American tribe with a unique game jersey.

When that tribe founded the area where the city of Tulsa is today, it was originally referred to as Tallahassee, which would later be shortened to the spellings of Talasi and then Tvlse.

So instead of the traditional blue and white color scheme from the Dodgers affiliation, the TCL Drillers jerseys were red with a light blue trim around a white band on the edges. And instead of the word "Tulsa" on the front on the jersey, the city's name was spelled "Tvlse" in script lettering.

That team's roster had nine players who spent their high school baseball days playing for teams in state of Oklahoma; four of those came from the metropolitan Tulsa area.

TCL Drillers manager Tom Holliday was no stranger to local collegiate baseball followers. He was on Oklahoma State University's staff (as pitching coach from 1978-96 then as head coach in 1997-2003) when the Cowboys made 11 appearances in the College World Series and finished as national runner-up three times.

Holliday later served on the staffs at the University of Texas, North Carolina State University and Auburn University. One son, Matt, became a seven-time All-Star player during his 15-year MLB career. Another son, Josh, has been OSU's head baseball coach since 2013.

The Amarillo Sod Squad had the North Division's best regular season record at 22-11, followed by Tulsa (19-15), Frisco (16-14), Amarillo Sod Dogs (15-15) and Texarkana (4-26 with a season-ending 16-game losing streak). Brazos Valley topped the South Division with a 22-11 record, followed by Round Rock (16-13), San Antonio (16-14), Acadiana (15-14) and Victoria (9-21)

Tulsa defeated the Amarillo Sod Squad in the best-of-three North Division playoffs while Brazos Valley swept San Antonio in the South Division playoffs. Then on August 8th, Brazos Valley defeated Tulsa in the TCL Championship Game, 13-2, winning the TCL pennant for the third consecutive season and the seventh time in eight years.

The TCL Drillers pitching staff had the league's second-lowest earned run average (3.27) but the team's composite .225 batting average ranked next to last in the 10-team league. Tulsa posted an 11-4 record in home games and went 5-7 on the road. Had the team not lost eight of 11 games that were decided by one run, the TCL Drillers would have easily posted a better regular season record.

Many local sports observers wondered how many fans in Tulsa would turn out to watch collegiate players instead of professional players. Surprisingly, the TCL Drillers drew 25,069 fans for 16 games with an average attendance of 1,567 per game. By comparison, that per game average wasn't that far removed from typical home crowd totals for early week Texas League games.

Bryce Osmond, a right-handed pitcher who attended Jenks High School and Oklahoma State University, led TCL pitchers in strikeouts with 36 over 22.3 innings while allowing just nine base hits all year. Teammate Riley Boyd, who played collegiately at Western Kentucky, was the TCL co-leader in pitching wins with four.

Pitcher Matt Merrill and Garret Crowley along with outfielder Cabe Cabbiness were named to the TCL North Division Postseason All-Star Team in voting by managers of TCL teams.

Merrill, who played for the University of Science and Arts Oklahoma, averaged two strikeouts per inning in his five appearances. Crowley, a left-handed pitcher from Fordham University, posted a 3-0 won-lost record over games along with 31 strikeouts over 21.1 innings. Cabbiness, who played high school baseball at Bixby and collegiately at Oklahoma State, had a .293 batting average with four home runs and 21 RBIs.

After that baseball season ended, Drillers leadership created new opportunities to serve the local community through the performing arts and the 2020 presidential election.

ONEOK Field was the venue for performances by the Tulsa Community College Signature Symphony, the Tulsa Symphony Orchestra and the Tulsa Opera's presentation of *Rigoletto*, one of the renowned operas by composer Giuseppe Verdi.

During the first weekend of November, the concourse at ONEOK Field served as Tulsa County's exclusive site for early voting in the

2020 presidential election. Working with the Tulsa County Election Board and blessed with good weather and swiftly moving lines, just over 15,000 voters cast their ballots.

Even though there was not a Texas League baseball season, that organization named the Drillers and the Amarillo Sod Poodles as co-recipients of the TL Organization of the Year Award. For the Drillers it was the fourth time in eight years that they received the honor and the seventh time overall in the franchise's history.

The Los Angeles Dodgers became World Series champions for the first time in 32 years by defeating the Tampa Bay Rays in six games and 15 former Tulsa Drillers played roles in that quest for baseball supremacy.

Heading that list was shortstop Corey Seager (2015), who was named the Most Valuable Player of both the World Series and the National League Championship Series. Seager hit .328 during the postseason along with a team-leading eight home runs and 20 runs batted in.

On the pitching side, Julio Urias (2015) closed out the title-clinching win by weaving 2.1 perfect innings of relief pitching and striking out four of the seven batters he faced to claim the save in Game 6. Urias was on the mound when the Los Angeles Dodgers won the 2020 World Series and followed that feat by leading National League pitchers with 20 victories in 2021.

Offensively, former Drillers combined to hit 18 home runs in the Dodgers' 18 playoff games. In addition to Seager's eight home runs, contributing to the home run parade were Cody Bellinger (2017) with four and two each from Kiki Hernandez (2016), Edwin Rios (2016-17) and Will Smith (2017-18).

Former Driller pitchers claimed all four World Series wins. All-Star Clayton Kershaw, who made an eventful injury rehabilitation start at

ONEOK Field in 2019, went 2-0 with a 2.31 ERA and 14 strikeouts in 11.2 innings.

Victor Gonzalez (2019 Drillers) picked up the World Series-clinching victory in Game 6 by striking out three of the four batters he faced. Walker Buehler (2017 Drillers) got the Game 3 win, striking out 10 batters over six innings and became the first World Series pitcher to ever strike out 10 batters in a start of six innings or less.

Other former Drillers who appeared in postseason games included pitchers Pedro Baez (2018), Tony Gonsolin (2018), Dustin May (2018-19) as well as infielders Matt Beaty (2017) and Gavin Lux (2018-19). In addition, catcher Keibert Ruiz (2018-19) was on the Dodgers' initial playoff roster and current Drillers manager Scott Hennessey was with the Dodgers throughout their playoff run.

The triumph marked the first time in the 40-plus years of Tulsa Drillers baseball that the club's major league affiliate has won a World Series title. For Tulsa professional baseball, it marked the first World Series win for a MLB affiliate since the St. Louis Cardinals defeated the Boston Red Sox in 1967 when the Tulsa Oilers were the Cardinals' Triple-A affiliate.

2021: Changes galore were in store for this baseball season in Tulsa: a new league, new team ownership, and a new structure for all of minor league baseball. The best news came in the form of actual minor league baseball games, albeit it in a shortened season and the return of a familiar face.

Major League Baseball took over the operation of minor league baseball teams from the Florida-based National Association of Professional Baseball leagues; the organization that had governed minor league baseball since 1901.

There would be 120 teams playing in four classification levels in 11 geographically-oriented leagues. By comparison, there had been 160 teams in 15 leagues. Each MLB team would have four minor league affiliates.

For the Los Angeles Dodgers, there were no changes. The Oklahoma City Dodgers remained as the team's Triple-A affiliate, the Tulsa Drillers were the Double-A partner, the Great Lakes (Midland, Michigan) Loons, were the High-A affiliate and the Rancho Cucamonga (California) Quakes were the Low-A affiliate.

And as part of that minor league realignment and the related Player Development License (PDL), the Drillers and Dodgers extended their baseball affiliation through the end of the 2030 season.

That 16-year affiliation is the second longest in Drillers history, surpassed only by the 26-year partnership with the Texas Rangers from 1977 through 2002. The Tulsa Oilers were affiliated with the St. Louis Cardinals at the Double-A or Triple-A levels for 18 seasons (1959-76).

Other noteworthy changes included greatly improved player accommodations and conditioning facilities at minor league ballparks, weekly salary raises from $350 to $600 for Tulsa Drillers players and minor league teams being within an average of 200 miles from their parent club; a significant cost savings for all involved parties.

The Texas League, founded in 1888, went out of operation for one season and was rebranded as the Double-A Central League. The Wichita Wind Surge and the San Antonio Missions, two franchises scheduled to operate at the Triple-A level in the Pacific Coast League prior to the pandemic, were shifted to the Double-A Central League to create a 10-team league.

Ironically, both of those cities had a long history with Tulsa and the Texas League. Wichita was in the Texas League from 1983 until 2007 at which time the team was relocated to Springdale, Arkansas and became the Northwest Arkansas Naturals. The Wichita Pilots were the 1987 TL champions while the Wichita Wranglers claimed the TL pennant in 1992 and 1999.

San Antonio's Texas League heritage dates back to 1888. Playing as the Bronchos, Bullets or Missions, San Antonio won 13 TL championships between 1897 and 2013, tied with Dallas and Fort Worth for the second-highest championship total behind the 16 won by Houston between 1889 and 1957.

The Tulsa Drillers played in the North Division along with Wichita (Minnesota Twins affiliate), the Northwest Arkansas Naturals (Kansas City Royals), Springfield Cardinals (St. Louis Cardinals), and Arkansas Travelers (Seattle Mariners).

South Division teams were San Antonio (San Diego Padres), the Amarillo Sod Poodles (Arizona Diamondbacks), Frisco RoughRiders (Texas Rangers), Midland RockHounds (Oakland Athletics) and Corpus Christi Hooks (Houston Astros).

The Drillers played an unbalanced schedule of 120 games, a format designed to reduce travel-related expenses and accommodate health concerns related to the Covid-19 pandemic. Each team would play a six-game weekly series with Mondays being the designated off days.

Tulsa played home-and-home series against all four of its North Division rivals but would only face Amarillo and Midland from the South Division that season. A quirk of the schedule saw the Drillers playing 30 of their 120 games against Wichita.

Scott Hennessey returned as the Drillers manager and was assisted by pitching coach Dave Borkowski, hitting coach Brett Pill, performance coach Noah Huff, bench coach Chris Gutierrez, athletic trainer Yuya Mukaihara and video associate Danny-David Linahan.

While the Drillers posted their fourth consecutive winning season in Double-A baseball and had numerous individual standouts, a series of hard-luck events left them two games short of another playoff appearance.

A six-game losing streak June 12-18 dug the Drillers into a hole that they couldn't climb out of. Tulsa was outscored by a 29-13 margin during that slump. Equally painful were losses to Wichita on July 17th and August 15th; two games in which the Drillers squandered six-run leads.

Had the Drillers finished their season-ending road trip with a 7-5 record, they would have advanced to the playoffs. However, they went 5-7 and the pain was worsened by losing three consecutive contests to Springfield, which had the league's worst overall record.

Wichita had the best overall regular season record in the North Division as well as the entire league at 69-51. Chasing the Wind Surge were the Northwest Arkansas Naturals (64-55), Arkansas Travelers (64-56), Tulsa Drillers (63-57) and Springfield Cardinals (45-75). Frisco had the best record in the South Division at 64-55, followed by Midland (59-60), Amarillo (59-61), San Antonio (57-63) and Corpus Christi Hooks (54-65).

The Naturals, who barely qualified for the playoffs, would sweep Wichita in three games to claim their first Double-A baseball championship since winning the Texas League title in 2010.

Three Drillers were named to the Double-A Central League's postseason All-Star team: designated hitter Ryan Noda, third baseman Miguel Vargas and second baseman Michael Busch.

Vargas etched his name in Tulsa baseball history by becoming the second Driller in 44 years to win a league batting championship. He batted .321 and added 16 home runs and 60 RBIs.

Noda's 29 home runs, the fifth-highest season total in Drillers history, led the league and he ranked second in RBIs with 78. He was the third consecutive Driller to be the league's home run king, following in the footsteps of D.J. Peters in 2018 and Cody Thomas in 2019.

Busch, regarded as the Dodgers' top prospect on the Drillers 2021 roster, overcame an injury-riddled start to the season to lead the league in runs scored (84) and extra base hits (48). He also batted .267 with 20 home runs and 67 RBIs.

Outfielder Donovan Casey finished third in the league with a .296 batting average in just 73 games with the Drillers. He came to Tulsa as part of the trade in late July that brought pitcher Max Scherzer and second baseman Trae Turner from the Washington Nationals to the Los Angeles Dodgers.

First baseman Justin Yurchak batted .383 in just 30 games after being promoted from Single-A Great Lakes. When his Single-A numbers were included Yurchak's .365 batting average was the best among full-season minor league baseball players.

Relief pitchers Guillermo Zuniga and Justin Hagenman each won seven games, one shy of leading the league. Mark Washington was the Drillers' top relief pitcher with a 2.00 ERA and a 6-1 record plus 65 strikeouts in 63 innings.

The relief pitching trio of Andre Jackson, Darien Nunez and Justin Bruihl went from the Drillers' opening day roster to making their major league debuts with the Dodgers. A notable feat considering those three pitchers had never played at a higher level than Class A prior to 2021.

Busch and Jackson were chosen to play for the National League team in the 2021 All-Star Futures Game which was part of the 2021 MLB All-Star festivities at Coors Field in Denver, Colorado.

A franchise record 23 runs were scored in the Drillers' 23-8 July 25th victory over Northwest Arkansas. Miguel Vargas had a career-high eight RBIs in addition to scoring four runs along with a home run among his three base hits.

Tulsa ranked second in attendance among Double-A Central teams with 300,270 fans coming to ONEOK Field, a commendable feat considering early-season restrictions related to the Covid-19 pandemic. A sellout crowd of 8,361 on June 25th was the Drillers' largest single-game attendance since the 2018 season opener. And the attendance of just over 5,000 fans for their season opener against Amarillo was the largest such attendance in all of minor league baseball.

Tulsa businessman Arlo DeKraai acquired a minority ownership stake in the team and pledged to keep the team from relocating elsewhere. It was also announced that Dale and Jeff Hubbard would remain as the team's majority owners and long-time general manager Mike Melega also would be retained in that role.

DeKraai is no stranger to Drillers baseball, having been chairman of the construction committee during the building of ONEOK Field and later serving as chairman of the Tulsa Stadium Trust, which owns the ballpark.

And nearly 40 years earlier when the Drillers played at Sutton Stadium/Drillers Stadium in midtown Tulsa, DeKraai said that when the weather was nice he and his family would often walk six blocks from their home to that ballpark.

The left field concourse at ONEOK Field was the site for a large mural saluting the life and legacy of Jackie Robinson, the former Brooklyn Dodgers star who broke baseball's racial barrier in 1947. The project was a partnership between the Drillers and the Greenwood Chamber of Commerce, which has an exterior wall facing into the ballpark.

Selected Driller home games were carried on MILB.TV, an internet-based video service operated by Minor League Baseball. MILB.TV mostly carried games played by Triple-A teams but the Drillers were one of the few Double-A and Single-A teams to be featured by the service. The video feed included the radio play-by-play from veteran announcer Dennis Higgins.

For the first time since 2002, a number of Driller home games were broadcast over a Tulsa-area television station. KRSU-TV (Channel 35), a public television station owned by Rogers State University in nearby Claremore, carried over 20 games on Friday and Saturday nights.

Northwest Arkansas catcher M.J. Melendez was the Double-A Central League's Most Valuable Player, hitting 28 home runs and leading the league in that category for most of the season prior to his promotion to Triple-A Omaha.

When his 13 home runs with Omaha were included, Melendez became the first catcher to win the Joe Bauman Award, presented to the player hitting the most home runs in minor league baseball. Melendez mashed four home runs in his six games at ONEOK Field.

Frisco RoughRiders pitcher Cole Winn was the league's Pitcher of the Year, posting a stingy 2.31 earned run average with 97 strikeouts over 78 innings while allowing only 26 walks and 38 base hits. Winn was the 15th overall selection in the 2018 MLB Amateur Draft.

Ramon Borrego was the league's Manager of the Year for guiding the Wichita Wind Surge to a 69-51 record and a spot in the championship finals in their inaugural season. Borrego has spent 24 years in the Minnesota Twins organization, the last 12 years managing minor league teams. He has also coached baseball teams in Venezuela and the Dominican Republic.

Shortstop Bobby Witt Jr., the top prospect in the Kansas City Royals organization, was honored by *Baseball America* magazine as the 2021 Minor League Player of the Year for his hitting and fielding achievements; first with the Naturals and then with the Triple-A Omaha Storm Chasers.

Witt made his MLB debut in 2022 with the Royals and led the team in runs batted in, doubles and triples.

The son of former Oklahoma Sooners and 16-year MLB pitcher Bobby Witt, he led all minor league hitters in combined extra base hits (72) and was second in runs scored (99), fourth in home runs (33) and RBIs (97) while stealing 29 bases and posting a .290 batting average.

2022: The ending of Tulsa's 2022 baseball season left a bitter taste with Drillers fans and players but there were several positive events during this campaign.

The Drillers posted their fifth consecutive winning season under manager Scott Hennessey and reached the playoffs for the fourth time in five years under his leadership. And the Double-A Central League name was benched for good and the Texas League name was reinstated.

Three of the top four prospects in the Los Angeles Dodgers organization opened the season with the Drillers and the team enjoyed a high level of experience, thanks to having 22 players, including 14 pitchers, returning from the 2021 Driller squad. That talented trio consisted of starting pitcher Bobby Miller, second baseman Michael Busch and right fielder Andy Pages.

The 6-foot-5 Miller, whose spring training fastball was consistently clocked at 98 miles per hour, was the pitching ace for the 2019 University of Louisville Cardinals who advanced to the semifinals of that year's College World Series. Miller was the first player chosen by the Dodgers in the 2020 amateur draft and in his 2021 professional debut with two Dodger affiliates, Miller struck out 70 batters while allowing just 13 walks over 56 innings.

Busch, thought to be the Dodgers' middle infield anchor of the future, overcame an injury-riddled start to the 2021 season to lead the league in runs scored (84) and extra base hits (48). He also batted .267 with 20 home runs and 67 RBIs and was named to the 2021 postseason Double-A Central League All-Star team. Prior to the 2024 season, Busch was traded to the Chicago Cubs in moves related to signing of free agent superstar Shonei Ohtani.

Pages, who signed with the Dodgers in 2017 after defecting from Cuba, won the 2021 Most Valuable Player award in the High A Central League with the Great Lakes Loons. Pages led that league with 31 home runs and 88 runs batted in. Pages was arguably considered to be Cuba's premier outfield prospect.

Tulsa won the TL North Division's first half championship and kept winning in spite of the Dodgers' promoting several key players to Triple-A Oklahoma City.

The Drillers clinched the first-half championship by winning six out of seven games in a showdown with the Wichita Wind Surge. Five of those six victories were decided by one run. Left-handed pitcher Andrew Heaney, sent to Tulsa by the Dodgers for an injury rehabilitation starting assignment, played a key role in the series with a strong performance.

However, the turning point of the 2022 season came on August 14th when top pitchers Bobby Miller and Gavin Stone were promoted to OKC. The Drillers' overall record on that date was 59-49 and they would go 10-22 the rest of the season due to injuries to outfielders Ryan Ward and Johnny DeLuca as well as catcher Carson Taylor plus third baseman Kody Hoese.

And Wichita got its revenge against Tulsa by winning eight of the final nine meetings,

Despite his injury absence, Ward hit 28 home runs to lead the Drillers and would likely have broken the franchise's single-season home run record of 33 set by Tim Wheeler in 2011.

Outfielder James Outman was easily the Drillers' best offensive player in the first half of the season, as shown by batting .295 with 16 home runs and 45 RBIs in just 68 games. A total of 34 of his 77 base hits went for extra bases. After being promoted to Triple-A Oklahoma City, he belted another 15 round-trippers. Then Outman smashed a two-run homer in his first major league at-bat on July 31st against the Colorado Rockies in Denver.

Left-handed pitcher Alec Gamboa posted an 11-4 record, the most victories by a Drillers hurler since 14 by Chase DeJong when he earned TL Pitcher of the Year honors in 2016.

Gavin Stone, rated as the number three pitching prospect in the Los Angeles Dodgers player development program, won the 2022 Branch Rickey Award as the organization's top minor league pitcher. While in Tulsa, Stone struck out 107 batters with just 30 walks over 14 appearances and posted a stingy 1.60 ERA. He also led all full-season minor league pitchers with a 1.48 ERA over 25 starts

Tulsa tied a franchise record for runs scored in a 23-7 triumph at Northwest Arkansas.

Left-handed pitcher John Rooney led all minor league pitchers with 17 pickoffs of baserunners; something that soothed the sting of a 4-7 record and a 6.15 ERA.

Despite hitting a league-leading 196 home runs, the Drillers placed dead last in the TL in runs scored and they also gave up a team-record 240 stolen bases; which was the most of any team in Double-A or Triple-A baseball.

The Frisco Roughriders claimed their first Texas League championship since 2004 with a two-game sweep of Wichita in the champi-onship since 2004 with a two-game sweep of Wichita in the championship series. Ironically, Frisco pitching coach Jeff Andrews served as Tulsa's pitching coach when the Drillers won the 1988 Texas League pennant.

Frisco manager Jared Goedert was the Texas League's 2022 Manager of the Year. Goedert's 138 victories over two seasons as Frisco's manager are fourth-highest in franchise history.

Right fielder Moises Gomez of the Springfield Cardinals was the Texas League's 2022 Player of the Year. Gomez led minor league hitters with 39 home runs, 23 of those coming when he started the season with Springfield. The parent St. Louis Cardinals picked him up from the Tampa Bay Rays organization before the season started. Surprisingly, Gomez hit only 19 total home runs over five previous minor league seasons and was highly prone to strikeouts.

Taylor Dollard of the Arkansas Travelers was the Texas League's 2022 Pitcher of the Year, leading the league in victories (16) and lowest earned run average (2.25). In only his second season of minor league baseball, the right-handed pitcher posted 131 strikeouts over 144 innings while allowing just 31 walks.

Driller game broadcasts were carried on KTBZ-AM (1430 "The Buzz") for the 17th consecutive season with Dennis Higgins handling the play-by-play for his 13th season. The Drillers' mobile app had a link to allow fans to hear the broadcasts on their cell phone or portable electronic device.

Prior to Opening Day, the Drillers joined with a group led by local baseball historian Wayne McCombs to honor Tulsa's baseball heritage with the dedication of a privately funded and home plate-shaped monument at Expo Square where the Drillers and Tulsa Oilers played home games from 1934 through 1980.

The monument is embedded in a parking lot in the northeastern section of Expo Square. But it also has batter's boxes on either side so fans can step up to the plate and take a trip down memory lane and imagine themselves ready to belt a home run for their hometown heroes.

2023: The Los Angeles Dodgers provided the Tulsa Drillers with several players that would contribute to a minor league championship team. Too bad that championship would be won at Triple-A Oklahoma City instead of at Tulsa's ONEOK Field.

For the first eight weeks of the season, the Drillers were arguably the best team in all of minor league baseball, thanks to having eight of the top prospects in the Los Angeles Dodgers on their roster. Outfielder Jonny DeLuca and starting pitchers and starting pitchers Emmet Sheehan and Kyle Hurt from that group wound up contributing to the Dodgers winning the National League Western Division championship.

Boosted by winning 12 out of 13 games between April 30th and May 13th, Tulsa coasted to a 37-19 record and took a commanding hold on the Texas League North Division lead and a potential playoff berth as the first half of the season drew to a close. But hampered by the Dodgers promoting several players to Triple-A Oklahoma City and an overall lack of talent from players promoted from the Great Lakes Loons of the High-A Midwest League, the Drillers stumbled by losing nine of the final 13 games on the first half schedule. Despite a 41-28 record, they finished four games behind the first half TL North champion Arkansas Travelers.

What was most shocking was seeing Tulsa entering the final series of the first half schedule against the Northwest Arkansas Naturals with the Drillers having a 24-9 home record while the Naturals were an anemic 7-23 in road games. The Drillers proceeded to lose five of those six games and they scored just 18 runs over 54 innings.

The second half of the season would be one of the worst in Drillers history, both on and off the field.

Manager Scott Hennessey missed nearly all of the second half of the season while on a medical leave of absence. Hennessey was diagnosed with Stage 3 curable squamous cell carcinoma in his neck and underwent a rigorous series of chemotherapy and radiation treatments. His in-game strategy and baseball teaching skills were sorely missed.

Tulsa's 24-45 record in the second half of the season was the worst among all Texas League teams. Pitching problems were highly prevalent in those final three months as Driller pitchers gave up a league leading 410 runs. Hitting was a headache as well with Tulsa's 332 runs scored in the second half schedule ranking next to last in the league.

Catcher Diego Cartaya was hyped as being the Dodgers' best minor league prospect entering the 2023 season. But despite belting 19 home runs and adding 57 runs batted in, Cartaya batted just .189 before his season ended due to a back injury.

Before moving up to Triple A Oklahoma City and eventually the Dodgers, outfielder Jonny DeLuca batted .279 over 32 games with 18 of his 34 base hits going for extra bases. After the 2023 season ended, DeLuca and 2021 Driller pitcher Ryan Pepiot were traded by the Dodgers to the Tampa Bay Rays for that team's pitching ace, Tyler Glasnow, and other considerations.

Sheehan won three of his four decisions after joining the Dodgers late in the season. While with the Drillers, he posted a 4-1 won-lost record with 88 strikeouts against 23 walks in 10 starts. Sheehan's 1.86 earned run average was the best among Tulsa's starting pitchers and he was the only Tulsa Driller named to the 2023 Texas League postseason All-Star Team.

Kyle Hurt led Tulsa's pitchers in strikeouts with 110 against just 33 walks in 19 games before eventually moving up to the Dodgers. Considering that Hurt posted a horrific 9.29 ERA on the 2022 Drillers, the improvement by the former University of Southern California hurler was amazing.

Left-handed relief pitcher Alec Gamboa pulled off the rare feat of leading Driller pitchers in victories for two consecutive seasons. After posting an 11-4 record in 2022, Gamboa went 7-0 over 14 appearances in 2023 and added a sparkling 2.25 earned run average.

Shortstop-outfielder Austin Gauthier had Tulsa's best batting average at .293 and was one of the few players that moved up from the Dodgers' Class A teams to be productive with the Drillers in 2023. Center fielder Jose Ramos, who played for Panama in the 2023 World Baseball Classic was second on the Drillers in home runs (19) and RBIs (68).

Other offensive standouts were first baseman Imanol Vargas who ranked fourth in the Texas League in RBIs (90), fifth in home runs (22) and tied for third in doubles (29). Second baseman Jorge Vivas led the team in base hits (113), stolen bases (21) and was second in the Texas League in times hit by a pitch (24).

In terms of team hitting for the 138-game season, the Drillers ranked third in home runs (164) but last in the Texas League in batting average (.240), stolen bases (101) and next to last in base hits (1,102) as well as on-base percentage (.332). Team defense wasn't a forte of this team, as shown by opponents stealing a league-high 265 bases and Tulsa's 119 fielding errors were just four shy of being the league's worst.

Team pitching, on the other hand, had a few bright spots with Tulsa leading the league in strikeouts (1,379), fewest hits allowed (1,037) and combined shutouts (10).

And the 2023 Drillers achieved something they had not done since the 1999 season at the now-defunct Drillers Stadium at Expo Square.

They led the Texas League in total attendance by drawing 356,002 fans. That was 562 more fans that the runner-up Amarillo Sod Poodles.

Aided by several former Tulsa Drillers, the Oklahoma City Dodgers claimed the 2023 Pacific Coast League pennant by sweeping the best-of-three championship series from the Round Rock Express, the Triple-A affiliate of the 2023 World Series champion Texas Rangers. First baseman Michael Busch, a member of the 2021 and 2022 Drillers, was OKC's offensive star that season, posting a .322 batting average while swatting 27 home runs. On January 11, 2024, Busch would be traded to the Chicago Cubs for two minor league players.

The Arkansas Travelers posted the Texas League North Division's best overall record at 73-65, followed by the Springfield Cardinals (72-66), Tulsa Drillers (65-73), Wichita Wind Surge (64-73) and Northwest Arkansas Naturals (64-74). Amarillo had the TL South Division's best overall record at (77-61), followed by a three-way tie between the Corpus Christi Hooks, Midland RockHounds and San Antonio Missions at 70-68 and the Frisco RoughRiders at 64-73.

Arkansas defeated the Springfield Cardinals, 2-1, in the best-of-three Texas League North Division playoffs and Amarillo did likewise to San Antonio in the TL South Division playoffs. Amarillo claimed its second Texas League championship since 2019 by defeating Arkansas, 2-1, in the best-of-three Texas League championship series.

Second baseman Thomas Saggese won the Texas League Most Valuable Player award for leading the league in batting average (.318), base hits (158), runs batted in (107). Even more impressive was the fact that he played for the Frisco RoughRiders and Springfield Cardinals, switching teams because he was part of the trade that sent pitcher Jordan Montgomery from the St. Louis Cardinals to the Texas Rangers. Saggese batted .313 with 15 home runs for Frisco, then batted .331 with 10 more home runs playing for Springfield.

Rhett Kouba from the Corpus Christi Hooks was the Texas League Pitcher of the Year. Born in Woodward, Oklahoma, the sixth-ranked prospect in the Houston Astros organization struck out 118 batters in 110 innings while allowing just 23 walks and holding opponents to a .228 batting average.

Mike Freeman of the Arkansas Travelers was the Texas League Manager of the Year. In his first managerial season, Arkansas won the Texas League North Division championship and held the best record in all of Double-A baseball for most of the season. Freeman was the first Travelers manager to win the award since Chris Maloney in 1998.

2024: Completely from his cancer treatments, Drillers manager Scott Hennessey returned for his seventh season as the team's manager. He started the season with 376 career victories. Bobby Jones is the record holder with 509 wins over the 1991-92 and 1995-2000 seasons.

Diamond Baseball Holdings became the majority owner of the Tulsa Drillers prior to the start of the season. The team's previous ownership team of Jeff and Dale Hubbard and Arlo DeKraai became minority owners and General Manager Mike Melega was retained as well.

DBH owns 32 of the 120 teams in Minor League Baseball and has a track record of retaining a local team's executive staff while heavily investing in local advertising and fan promotions. Its evolution was related to Major League Baseball taking over the organized minor leagues in 2020. Long-time baseball observers, however, have voice concerned that DBH could eliminate many of the lower-level minor league teams which, in turn, would eliminate opportunities for minor league players.

Six of the top 30 prospects in the Los Angeles Dodgers minor league system started this season in Tulsa. Topping that list was catcher Dalton Rushing, the Dodgers' top-ranked major league prospect. The left-handed hitting catcher was a college standout at the University of Louisville before belting 23 home runs in 117 minor league games prior to the 2024 season. Many professional scouts have said once Rushing gets a better understanding of calling pitches in the professional game, he could quickly move up to the big leagues. Rushing had an awkward experience in 2023 playing for the High-A Great Lakes Loons, missing several games due to a concussion after hitting his head while making a backswing.

Former Oklahoma State University pitcher Justin Wrobleski is regarded as one of the Dodgers' promising pitching prospects. Wrobleski was named to the 2023 Midwest League All-Star team after posting 109 strikeouts in just over 102 innings along with a 2.90 earned run average.

Many of the other Texas League teams had players with very bright major league prospects. The defending TL champion Amarillo Sod Poodles had third baseman Ivan Melendez, arguably the top prospect in the Arizona Diamondbacks player development program. Playing for the University of Texas Longhorns in 2021, he hit 32 home runs, led all Division 1 college baseball teams in total bases and slugging percentage and won the Golden Spikes Award which represents America's best amateur baseball player.

Arkansas Travelers catcher-designated hitter Harrison "Harry" Ford is the top catcher prospect in the Seattle Mariners organization and scouts have likened his overall baseball skills to those of Houston Astros Hall of Famer Craig Biggio. A highly disciplined hitter, Ford ranked third among all minor league baseball players in 2023 in drawing bases on balls (103).

Corpus Christi Hooks centerfielder Kenedy Corona is quickly moving up in the Houston Astros organization. Hailing from Maracaibo, Venezuela, Corona became just the second player in Corpus Christi's lengthy baseball history to hit 20 home runs and steal 20 bases in the same season.

Frisco RoughRiders first baseman Abimelec Ortiz was the Texas Rangers' Minor League Player of the Year in 2023. Playing for two Class A teams, Ortiz ranked fourth among all minor league players in total home runs (33).

Midland RockHounds shortstop Jacob Wilson is the top prospect in the Oakland Athletics player development program as well as being the sixth overall selection in the 2023 MLB Amateur Draft. Before turning professional in 2023, Wilson struck out only five times all year at Grand Canyon University and drew raves for his defensive range and throwing arm.

Northwest Arkansas Naturals third baseman Cayden Wallace is ranked third in the Kansas City Royals minor league system. More of a contact hitter with a good eye for hitting into the outfield gaps, Wallace led the 2022 University of Arkansas Razorbacks to the semifinals of the College World Series.

San Antonio Missions pitcher Robby Snelling is the San Diego Padres' top minor league pitching prospect. A former two-sport standout (football and baseball) from the University of Arizona, Snelling posted an 11-3 won-lost record and a stingy combined 1.82 earned run average in his 2023 minor league season, along with 118 strikeouts and just 34 walks over 103.2 innings.

Springfield Cardinals right-handed pitcher Markevian "Tink" Hence is the top pitching prospect in the St. Louis Cardinals minor league system, though several scouts have split opinions on if his best MLB role would be as a starting pitcher or a flame-throwing relief pitcher. Despite a 4-6 won-lost record in 2023, the Pine Bluff, Arkansas native struck out 99 batters over 96 innings.

Wichita Wind Surge center fielder Emmanuel Rodriguez from the Dominican Republic is the third-ranked minor league prospect in the Minnesota Twins organization. An uncanny ability to reach base by drawing walks (just over 20 per cent of the time in 2023) and above-average base-stealing skills have helped atone for a disappointing .242 minor league career batting average.

Chapter Fourteen

National Baseball Hall of Fame and Tulsa

Eight players from the days of the Tulsa Oilers and one player from the Tulsa Drillers are enshrined in the National Baseball Hall of Fame in Cooperstown, New York. Here are their stories:

Ivan "Pudge" Rodriguez: 2017 Inductee, catcher for the 1991 Tulsa Drillers

The only Tulsa Driller alumnus to be enshrined in Cooperstown, Rodriguez spent 13 of his 21 major league seasons with the Texas Rangers, was a 14-time All-Star selection and won 13 Gold Gloves as best the best defensive player at his position.

Rodriguez also won seven Silver Sluggers as the best offensive player at his position, won the 1999 American League Most Valuable Player Award and played a pivotal role on the Florida Marlins' 2003 World Series championship team.

He is just the second catcher in baseball history to be elected for induction to the Baseball Hall of Fame on the first ballot. The other catcher to achieve that honor was Cincinnati Reds legend Johnny Bench, who grew up in the western Oklahoma town of Binger.

Rodriguez played for Texas from 1991 through 2002 then returned to the Rangers for the 2009 season. The other MLB teams he played for were the Florida Marlins (2003), Detroit Tigers (2004-08), New York Yankees (2008), Houston Astros (2009) and Washington Nationals (2010-11).

Nicknamed "Pudge" as a salute to his mentor, Carlton Fisk, along with being short and having a stocky build as a rookie, Rodriguez caught major league base runners stealing nearly 46 per cent of the time, a rate which was tops among active major league catchers when he retired in 2011.

All told, Rodriguez caught 661 runners who tried to steal a base on him along with throwing out 88 runners who were just standing next to a base and not trying to steal. Those latter two totals are major league career records.

As a 19-year-old with the 1991 Tulsa Drillers, Rodriguez dazzled Texas League fans of all ages in just 50 games with the skills that would lead many long-time baseball observers to proclaim him to be one of the greatest defensive catchers in professional baseball history.

Rodriguez batted .274 with three home runs and 28 RBIs while in Tulsa and displayed a cannon-like throwing arm that caught runners trying to steal a base nearly 60 percent of the time. He also demonstrated a maturity beyond his years in working with pitchers and was a near-unanimous choice for a spot on the 1991 Texas League Postseason All-Star Team.

Incredibly, Rodriguez started out as a pitcher and third baseman at the age of seven in Puerto Rico's Little League program. He threw seven no-hitters in his Little League career, including two in a single day. But periodic pitching wildness (once hitting three batters in a row to load the bases) led to his conversion to catcher by the age of 14.

James Laurie "Deacon" White: 2013 Inductee, manager of the 1908 Tulsa Oilers.

White spent 20 years playing major league baseball as a durable catcher and third baseman. White led the National League in runs batted in during its first two years, had an impressive career batting average of .303 and seldom missed a game.

Equally impressive was that White was a barehanded catcher prior to switching to third base. He also participated in creating the chest protector that is worn by catches and was the first catcher to move closer to the batter than those who played before. The legend is that White learned the game of baseball from a Union soldier near the end of the Civil War in 1865.

White's nickname of Deacon was well deserved, given his passion for studying the Holy Bible, faithful attendance at Sunday church services and choosing not to gamble, drink alcoholic beverages or smoke cigarettes or cigars; the latter three being highly common habits of baseball players back then.

When White was inducted into the Baseball Hall of Fame in 2013, it was noteworthy because he was the only player inducted that year.

Modern superstars Barry Bonds and Roger Clemens and others were thought to be certain first-ballot inductees that year but they and other plays felt a strong and bitter backlash from voters over their involvement in a long-running scandal about using performance-enhancing drugs. That backlash was so strong that many baseball experts think that Bonds and Clemens may never reach the Baseball Hall of Fame.

Willard Brown: 2006 Inductee, outfielder for the 1956 Tulsa Oilers.

This power-hitting outfielder was a star for the Negro League's Kansas City Monarchs from 1937 through 1946. Nicknamed "Home Run" Brown for his towering round-trippers, the right-handed hitting Brown played for six Monarch teams that won Negro League pennants and played eight times in its East-West All-Star game.

Brown was also a standout during various stops in the Puerto Rican league where he earned the nickname "Ese Hombre" (That Man) for his baseball feats. He batted .400 or higher in two seasons and his career batting average of .350 is still the best in that league's history. Brown's career totals for home runs (101) and RBIs (473) are among the top 10 totals of players who have come through that renowned circuit.

Baseball historian Bill James likened Brown's all-around baseball skills from that era to that of more recent All-Star outfielders such as Andre Dawson or Juan Gonzalez.

But the 1956 Texas League and a brief stint as a Tulsa Oiler would be Brown's last hurrah in Organized Baseball. The Oilers were one of three teams that he played for that year; the Austin Senators and San Antonio Missions being the others. As a member of the 1956 Tulsa Oilers, Brown's .299 batting average was tops among everyday players. He also ranked second on the Oilers in home runs (14) and runs batted in (73) and third in doubles.

Brown played briefly for the woeful 1947 St. Louis Browns and became the first African-American player to hit a home run in the American League; lashing an inside-the-park homer against Detroit Tigers pitching ace Hal Newhouser. It would also be Brown's only home run in a 21-game career with St. Louis; a tenure shortened by difficulty adjusting the big-league skill set of that era and aggravated by numerous racist encounters with fans and teammates.

Negro League historians have been universal in praise for Brown's baseball skills. Monarchs teammate Buck O'Neill said Brown was so fast that he often stole second base and never had to slide. But many of those same people raised questions about his inconsistent effort.

One story claims that Brown belted a home run on a pitched that bounced in front of home plate. Another tale claimed Brown skimmed through a copy of *Reader's Digest Magazine* while playing in the Kansas City outfield. Yet another story said that Brown frequently played all-out when big crowds appeared for Sunday games but slacked off many other times and especially when the weather even looked slightly bad.

While Brown was among the 5,000 American soldiers that traveled across the English Channel during the World War II invasion of Normandy in 1944, he never served on a field of combat. His primary duties as a member of the Quartermaster Corps focused on transporting ammunition and guarding prisoners.

Frank Robinson: 1982 Inductee, infielder for the 1954 Tulsa Oilers.

This player holds a unique place in Tulsa's baseball history, having played at second base and third base in eight games for the 1954 Tulsa Oilers but never playing for them within the city of Tulsa.

The 1954 Oilers opened the season on the road, had their entire first homestand of the season rained out and then went back on the road. After going 8-for-30 with just one run batted in during those first road games, the 18-year-old Robinson was sent down to the Columbia (South Carolina) Reds of the Class A South Atlantic League while the Oilers were traveling.

That was the only minor league lowlight of his career.

Robinson was called up to the Cincinnati Reds in 1956 and later played in 14 All-Star Games. He enjoyed a career revival with the

Baltimore Orioles, helping them win World Series championships in 1966 and 1970.

He was also part of one of the most lopsided trades in baseball history when the Reds traded him on December 9, 1965 to the Baltimore Orioles for pitchers Milt Pappas and Jack Baldschun plus outfielder Dick Simpson. Reds executives thought Robinson was washed up but he proved them wrong by winning the American League Triple Crown (leading a league in batting average, home runs and runs batted in) with Baltimore in 1966.

That former Tulsa Oiler was even name-checked in the 1988 movie, *Bull Durham*. A baseball groupie named Annie Savoy (played by Susan Sarandon) referenced the Frank Robinson-Milt Pappas swap as being a bad trade during her opening monologue.

Robinson became Major League Baseball's first African-American manager with the 1975 Cleveland Indians. He also served as manager of the San Francisco Giants, Baltimore Orioles, Montreal Expos and Washington Nationals. Today, Robinson serves as a Senior Advisor to the Commissioner of Baseball.

Warren Spahn: 1973 Inductee, manager of the 1967-71 Tulsa Oilers.

The greatest left-handed pitcher in baseball history, Spahn's five seasons as Tulsa's manager resulted in 373 Triple-A victories and the 1968 Oilers won the Pacific Coast League championship. That 1968 team posted a 95-53 record and Spahn expressed the opinion that had those 1968 Oilers stayed intact and played as a major league expansion team, they would have had a winning record.

From the mid-1940s through the early 1960s, Spahn spent 20 of his 21 big-league seasons with the Boston/Milwaukee Braves and his 363 victories are the most by any left-handed pitcher in the sport's history. He played in 14 All-Star Games, won 20 or more games 13 times, led the National League eight times in most victories, four times in most strikeouts, innings pitched and shutouts and three times in lowest earned run average.

Spahn was also the National League's 1957 Cy Young Award winner when he was the pitching ace for the Milwaukee Braves' World Series championship team.

Since 1999, the Oklahoma Sports Hall of Fame has presented the Warren Spahn Award in honor of that season's best left-handed pitcher. Multiple winners of that award are Randy Johnson and Clayton Kershaw (4 each), CC Sabathia (3) and Johan Santana (2). Former Tulsa Bishop Kelley pitcher Dallas Keuchel was the 2015 recipient when he played for the Houston Astros.

Jake "Eagle Eye" Beckley: 1971 Inductee, manager of the 1907 Tulsa Oilers.

Beckley was a first baseman who batted .300 or higher in 13 of his 19 years in the major leagues (1888-1907), playing for the Pittsburgh Pirates, New York Giants, Cincinnati Reds and St. Louis Cardinals.

His hitting achievements were more remarkable considering that those first four years came during the so-called Deadball Era when pitchers dominated baseball.

Beckley owns the professional baseball record for most career putouts by a first baseman (23,709), ranked second all-time in games played at first base (2,376) as well as having 2,930 career base hits.

To say that Beckley was somewhat eccentric during his playing days would be putting it mildly. One of his stunts was trying to bunt by using the baseball bat's handle to hit the ball, a tactic that is now illegal. Sometimes when Beckley got on a hitting streak, he'd sometimes yell "Chickazoola!" at opposing pitchers.

Beckley later became a player-manager for three minor league teams, was an umpire in the Federal League in 1913 and one of the first baseball coaches for William Jewell College in Liberty, Missouri. Fortunately, Beckley's 37-59 managerial record with the Tulsa Oilers had no bearing on his induction into the Baseball Hall of Fame.

Leroy "Satchel" Paige: 1971 Inductee; assistant coach for 1973-76 Tulsa Oilers.

The top pitcher during the heyday of Negro League baseball served as a bullpen coach for the Oilers but actually spent more time in marketing and public relations in behalf of the team, thanks to a long-standing friendship with team owner A. Ray Smith.

Paige's Negro League career lasted from 1927 through 1947, starting with the Birmingham Black Barons, followed by a stint with the Pittsburgh Crawfords and ending with the 1940-47 Kansas City Monarchs. Despite pitching just three or four innings per game, Paige would win 103 games and, even more impressively, struck out 1,231 batters while allowing just 253 bases on balls.

Paige finally reached the major leagues at the age of 41 with the 1948 Cleveland Indians and contributed to their World Series championship team that season. He played for Cleveland in 1949 then played for the St. Louis Browns from 1951 through 1953. At the age of 49 with the Philadelphia Phillies' Triple-A team, the Miami Marlins, Paige posted an 11-4 record with a 1.86 earned run average

Jesse "Pop" Haines: 1970 Inductee, pitcher for 1919 Tulsa Oilers.

Haines' best pitch was the knuckleball but he posted an unimpressive 5-9 record in 14 appearances with the 1919 Oilers. But his baseball life changed forever after taking a train ride later that year to join the Kansas City Blues of the American Association, where he posted a 21-5 won-lost record along with a stingy 2.11 earned run average.

That earned a promotion to the St. Louis Cardinals the following year and 18 years of success ensued. Haines was a member of three of the Cardinals' World Series champions (1926, 1931 and 1934), won 20 or more games three times and twice led National League pitchers in shutouts.

Haines' 208 complete games during his Cardinals career is the second highest total in the history of that storied franchise. Bob Gibson owns the St. Louis career record with 255 complete games.

Jay "Dizzy" Dean: 1953 Inductee, pitcher for 1940 Tulsa Oilers.

The hard-throwing and highly talkative right-handed pitcher was a four-time National League All-Star and won 134 games over seven seasons with the St. Louis Cardinals. His best season came in 1934, highlighted by a 30-7 record with 195 strikeouts.

But a toe injury that Dean sustained in the 1937 All-Star Game wreaked havoc with his pitching motion and ensuing poor performances led to his being traded to the Chicago Cubs prior to the 1938 season.

The Cubs sent Dean to Tulsa during the 1940 season in an attempt to change his pitching delivery and once again capture lightning in a bottle. He posted a respectable 8-8 record with a 3.17 earned run average and only walked 19 batters over 142 innings while with the Oilers.

But "Ol' Diz" would win just 16 games over four seasons with the Cubs and his best baseball days were clearly behind him.

Dean later served as an announcer for major league baseball television broadcasts with most Baby Boomers remembering his work with legendary Brooklyn Dodgers infielder Pee Wee Reese on the CBS Saturday Game of the Week. Dean's insights were often interwoven with his homespun humor and frequently fractured English.

Chapter Fifteen

Black Baseball Teams in Tulsa

Tulsa's first black baseball team took the field in 1908 and over the years, those teams would be known as either the Tulsa Colts, Tulsa White Sox, Tulsa Heart Breakers, Tulsa Black (or Colored) Oilers, Tulsa Blue Jays or, most famously, the T-Town Clowns.

Games were played against low-level professional teams or semi-professional and independent teams in Oklahoma, Texas, Arkansas, Missouri, Kansas or Louisiana.

While newspaper articles and detailed internet research would be hard to find for those teams, what was discovered for this book was interesting and showed the universal love for the game of baseball.

Starting around 1910, black baseball teams in Oklahoma as well as other states became a *de facto* player development program for the Negro American League and Negro National League teams that were primarily located in the eastern and central sections of the United States.

The closest Negro League teams to Oklahoma were the Kansas City Monarchs and the Dallas Black Giants. Kansas City's star players were pitcher Leroy "Satchel" Paige, center fielder James "Cool Papa" Bell, first baseman-manager Buck O'Neill and second baseman Jackie Robinson. The best-known Dallas player was future Chicago Cubs All-Star infielder Ernie Banks.

Tulsa's black baseball teams had their share of interesting people, as well.

Freeman L. Martin was a local attorney who also served as president of Tulsa's Negro Chamber of Commerce and co-owned the Tulsa Colored Oilers baseball team in 1913. After an embarrassing loss to a team from Oklahoma City on April 25th, Martin was so incensed that he fired everyone on his team then went out and purchased the contracts of the players and manager from that Oklahoma City team.

The Tulsa Colts won the Oklahoma Colored Baseball League championship in 1916, posting an 11-5 record and defeating Oklahoma City in the finals.

The Texas Colored League, which operated during the 1919-21 and 1923-26 seasons, showed Tulsa had an unnamed baseball team for the 1920 season and the Tulsa Black Oilers played in that circuit during the 1923 season.

In 1929, the Texas Colored League was revived and rebranded as the Texas-Oklahoma-Louisiana League, or the TOL for short. Original plans called for teams to play 50 games in each half of the season.

Quincy Gilmore, a former secretary of the Negro National League, organized the new league for teams in Tulsa and Oklahoma City along with Shreveport, Louisiana and Texas teams located in Dallas, Houston, San Antonio, Wichita Falls and Fort Worth.

Frank Drake was listed as the manager of the Tulsa Black Oilers in 1929.

While the TOL's mission was noble, two major events led to the league's demise: the beginnings of poverty and unemployment related to the Great Depression along with flooding related to a widespread rainstorm during late May in central and southern Texas.

During the 1930s, the Kansas City Monarchs frequently played exhibition games against local teams in Oklahoma City on a Saturday then take a train to Tulsa or to Muskogee for a Sunday game before heading back home.

The spirit of those barnstorming baseball teams, as well as some of their misadventures, was vividly captured in the 1976 movie *The Bingo Long Traveling All-Stars and Motor Kings*, which starred James Earl Jones, Richard Pryor and Billy Dee Williams.

When World War II escalated during the 1940s, black men and white men teamed up to help the United States in the grueling battle against Nazi Germany as well as Japan. But during those times in the trenches, black men who played baseball would ask their white baseball-loving counterparts this question:

If we're required to stand close to each other and fight enemies of our nation and our freedoms, why can't we be permitted to stand close to each other and throw a baseball back and forth and just play a game of catch?

Sylvester Nichols played second base for the T-Town Clowns, arguably the best known organization among Tulsa's independent black baseball teams. He was a lifelong Tulsan who graduated from Booker T. Washington High School then played for the Clowns from 1946 through 1952 and then the Tulsa Blue Jays through 1955.

During his T-Town Clowns tenure, Nichols received an offer to play professionally for a minor league team in Canada. But after thinking about his new bride coupled with having a decent-paying job with a Tulsa aviation firm, Nichols turned it down.

It's believed that the T-Town Clowns were modeled after the Negro League powerhouse Indianapolis Clowns; the latter team signing Hank Aaron to his first professional baseball contract.

Legend has it that the rivalry between the T-Town Clowns and a central Oklahoma black baseball team, the Guthrie Black Spiders, had all of the passion and animosity of the modern rivalry between the New York Yankees and Boston Red Sox.

While the Tulsa Black Oilers would play games at Texas League Park on the Tulsa State Fairgrounds, the T-Town Clowns' home field was Virgin Street Park, located in the 2000 block of East Virgin Street which is east of the current Booker T. Washington High School and north of downtown Tulsa.

The ballpark was built by local businessman Alfonzo Williams and Nichols was the first player he signed to a contract.

During its heyday, the area around Virgin Street Park was a thriving business district during the daytime thanks to a popular general store and a locally owned gas station and auto repair shop.

And like the song goes, everything gets hotter when the sun goes down. Also in close proximity to Virgin Street Park were the Eagle Bar and Rose Room nightclub; the latter being a popular jazz/R&B venue for nationally-known musicians like Ike and Tina Turner, Ray Charles, Count Basie and others.

The nightclub's owners did their part to keep things safe for the customers, requiring anyone carrying guns to check them at the front door along with any coats.

After U.S. Highway 75 was rerouted in north Tulsa, the highway took out all of what used to be left field and center field. There are no bleachers or markers on that property anymore, just memories.

When Jackie Robinson joined the Brooklyn Dodgers in 1947 and broke through the color barrier of Major League Baseball along with the proliferation of baseball games on television, it hastened the demise of black baseball leagues. Whatever teams were still playing, the T-Town Clowns included, became the equivalent of industrial teams.

Nevertheless, some of the remaining Negro League teams would play exhibition games in Tulsa through 1962 and several notable athletes were featured in those contests.

Reece "Goose" Tatum, a 2011 inductee into the Naismith Basketball Hall of Fame whose jersey number 50 was retired by the Harlem Globetrotters, played first base for the Indianapolis Clowns during a 5-3 loss to the Kansas City Monarchs before 3,000 fans at Texas League Park on April 20, 1947. Tatum also played baseball for the Negro League teams in Louisville, Memphis and Birmingham.

Catcher Elston Howard, who would become a 12-time American League All-Star and played for six World Series championship teams, played for the Monarchs in 1950 exhibition games in Tulsa against Indianapolis, the Philadelphia Stars and Memphis Red Sox.

Chapter Sixteen

High School Baseball History

Twenty-four public and private high schools in the metropolitan Tulsa area have won 94 state baseball championships in various enrollment classifications since 1947. A number of those alumni went on to play collegiate and/or minor league baseball with a select few reaching the major leagues.

Suburban schools account for 53 of those pennants with 32 earned by teams from the Tulsa Public Schools and nine others from metropolitan private schools. Of those 53 state titles won by suburban teams, 15 have been won since 2010.

The Owasso Rams are the powerhouse team of metropolitan Tulsa high school baseball, thanks to a legacy of success created by head coach Larry Turner for over 40 years.

Turner has led Owasso to 12 of its 14 state baseball champions (nine of those since 2000) and his 1,248 victories over 42 seasons entering 2024 are the most in Oklahoma's high school baseball history.

Turner was a 2024 inductee into the National High School Baseball Coaches Association Hall of Fame.

The Rams' 2013 state title team posted a 36-0 record and pitcher Dylan Bundy was the 2011 Gatorade National High School Baseball Player of the Year after posting a 0.25 earned run average in his senior season. Bundy later pitched for the Baltimore Orioles, Los Angeles Angels and Minnesota Twins.

From the 1940s through the 1980s, teams from the Tulsa Public Schools dominated the local prep baseball scene. When families began moving from the city of Tulsa to suburban communities, the balance of high school baseball power shifted to the suburbs.

The era of baseball dominance by eight teams from the Tulsa Public Schools was mostly during the 1960s and 1970s with eight state titles earned in each decade. The last TPS team to win a state baseball pennant was the 1997 Nathan Hale Rangers.

Pitcher Carl Morton from Daniel Webster High School in southwest Tulsa is the best-known alumnus from the TPS baseball program. He was the 1970 National League Rookie of Year, posting an 18-11 won-lost record for the last-place Montreal Expos.

After being traded to the Atlanta Braves, Morton proceeded to win 15 or more games each year from 1973 through 1975. He was 39 years old when he died in 1983 from a heart attack while jogging near the home of his parents.

The Webster Warriors have won the most state baseball championships of any TPS program, winning seven of their eight titles between 1959 and 1970.

A pair of metropolitan Tulsa high schools has won six state baseball titles. The Bishop Kelley Comets were two-time state champions during the 1970s then won four more since 2004. The Metro Christian Academy Patriots won their state championships in 2001 and 2017.

The Oklahoma Secondary Schools Activities Association (OSSAA) is the governing body for the state's high school athletic programs and its website lists the following breakdown of state high school baseball championships won by teams from the metropolitan Tulsa area:

Suburban High Schools (53)

Berryhill Chiefs: 2 (2007, 2013)

Bixby Spartans: 3 (1978, 2008, 2023)

Broken Arrow Tigers: 2 (1991, 2011)

Catoosa Indians: None

Claremore Zebras: 4 (1993, 1999, 2003, 2005)

Collinsville Cardinals: 1 (2010)

Coweta Tigers: 1 (1999)

Glenpool Warriors: None

Jenks Trojans: 4 (1997, 2000, 2002, 2021)

Mannford Pirates: 1 (1984)

Owasso Rams: 14 (1973, 1975, 1987, 1998, 1999, 2001, 2003, 2004, 2007, 2008, 2009, 2013, 2015, 2022)

Sand Springs Sandites: None

Sapulpa Chieftains: None

Sequoyah (Claremore) Eagles: None

Skiatook Bulldogs: 1 (2004)

Sperry Pirates: 7 (1981, 1982, 1983, 1990, 2006, 2008, 2009)

Union Redskins: 7 (1979, 1989, 1990, 2005, 2006, 2010, 2018)

Verdigris Cardinals: 6 (2002, 2011, 2012, 2013, 2014, 2016)

Tulsa Public Schools (32)

Booker T. Washington Hornets: None

Central Braves: 5 (1947, 1948, 1950, 1955, 1960)

Charles Mason: 1 (1977)

East Central Cardinals: 1 (1970).

Edison Eagles: 2 (1961, 1971)

Nathan Hale Rangers: 6 (1966, 1975, 1976, 1983, 1994, 1997)

McLain Scots: 1 (1967)

Memorial Chargers: 3 (1980, 1981, 1984)

Will Rogers Ropers: 5 (1954, 1968, 1973, 1978, 1979)

Webster Warriors: 8 (1958, 1959, 1961, 1962, 1964, 1969, 1970, 1985)

Tulsa Private Schools (9)

Bishop Kelley Comets: 6 (1976, 1978, 2004, 2006, 2011, 2018)

Holland Hall Dutch: 1 (2021)

Metro Christian Academy Patriots: 2 (2001, 2017)

Chapter Seventeen

College Baseball History

Oral Roberts University Golden Eagles

ORU is Tulsa's only active collegiate baseball team and have created a legacy of success in Division I competition, winning 26 regular season conference championships, 26 conference tournament championships and qualifying 29 times for NCAA postseason tournaments, including consecutive appearances from 2015 through 2018.

The program's pinnacle was reaching the 1978 College World Series in Omaha, Nebraska after upsetting the Oklahoma State Cowboys and Southern Illinois Salukis in regional play. ORU routed the North Carolina Tar Heels in their Omaha debut, 11-0, and held an early 5-0 lead over perennial national title contender Arizona State before falling, 7-6, and then being eliminated with a 5-3 loss to the Miami Hurricanes.

A total of 22 Golden Eagle baseball players have reached the major leagues and there have been 44 All-Americans with nine of those earning First Team All-American honors.

Counting ORU's tenures in the Mid-Continent and Southland Conferences and Summit Leagues, 14 individuals earned Conference Player of the Year awards and 14 pitchers were named Conference Pitcher of the Year.

Dennis Bigby, who went on to play in the Toronto Blue Jays' organization, was the Mid-Continent Conference Pitcher of the Year in 2004 and 2005 and also earned Mid-Continent Conference Player of the Year honors in those same years when he also played first base and designated hitter. While at ORU, he had a 41-9 won-lost record with a 2.92 earned run average and also hit 24 home runs.

Other multiple winners were catcher David Castillo (Mid-Continent Conference Player of the Year in 2002 and 2003) and pitcher Alex Gonzales (Southland Pitcher of the Year in 2011 and Summit League Pitcher of the Year in 2013).

Three men have had their jersey numbers retired as a salute to their career achievements at ORU.

Former head coach Larry Cochell (jersey number 1) holds the program's record for most career victories (428 over 10 seasons), most victories in a season (51 in 1983) and highest career winning percentage (.712). From 1977 through 1986, his ORU teams produced seven First-Team All-American players and as mentioned earlier, his 1978 team reached the College World Series.

Cochell won 1,331 games over 39 seasons and is just one of three college baseball coaches to take three different schools to the College World Series. After leaving ORU, he achieved that feat with the California State-Fullerton Titans and the Oklahoma Sooners.

Jim Brewer (jersey number 29) was ORU's pitching coach from 1979 through 1986 and played a key role in developing a pitching staff that three times led the nation in lowest earned run average. Seventeen of his pupils were drafted by major league teams.

The Broken Arrow High School alumnus spent 12 of his 17 major league seasons with the Los Angeles Dodgers, was a member of their 1965 World Series championship squad and was played for the National League in the 1973 All-Star Game.

Pitcher Mike Moore (jersey 22) is ORU's most famous baseball alumnus, spending 14 years in the American League and being the first player chosen overall in the 1981 MLB Amateur Draft, going to the Seattle Mariners. He won 28 games in three years at ORU and held the school record for career victories prior to turning professional.

Moore pitched for Seattle from 1982 through 1988 and then was a member of the Oakland Athletics (1989-92) and Detroit Tigers (1993-95). Born in the small southwestern Oklahoma town of Carnegie (1,723 population in 2010), Moore won 19 games for Oakland's 1989 World Series champions.

ORU also has a proud history of other successful players and coaches.

Relief pitcher Todd Burns attended ORU in 1982-84 and finished his college career as ORU's all-time saves leader. He helped the Oakland Athletics win three consecutive American League Western Division pennants (1988-90) and was nicknamed "The Mad Hatter" because he always tugged and readjusted his baseball cap before every pitch.

Catcher Tom Nieto (1981) was part of a team that was ranked as high as fifth in the national college baseball polls. He spent seven years in the major leagues and was part of the Minnesota Twins' 1987 World

Series champions. Nieto later spent over a decade as a minor league manager, mostly in the New York Yankees' organization.

Second baseman Keith Lockhart (1985-86) spent 10 years in the big leagues and was part of the Atlanta Braves' 1999 World Series championship team.

Keith Miller (1982-84) was a utility player at ORU who later played nine seasons in the major leagues with the New York Mets (1987-91) and Kansas City Royals (1992-95).

Pitcher Alexander "Chi Chi" Gonzalez played for the Texas Rangers in 2015-16 and has been with the Colorado Rockies since 2019. Gonzalez was the first player chosen by the Rangers and the 23rd overall selection in the 2013 MLB Amateur Draft.

Catcher Jose Trevino was a three-time All-Conference selection (2014-16) with the Golden Eagles and has played for the Texas Rangers since 2018. He was a 2017 Texas League All-Star playing for the Rangers' Double-A Texas League affiliate, the Frisco RoughRiders.

Matt Whatley was the 2017 recipient of the Johnny Bench Award, which is presented to the most valuable catcher in collegiate baseball. Among the prior winners of the Johnny Bench Award is Buster Posey, a Florida State University product who became a five-time National League All-Star and played for three World Series champions as a member of the San Francisco Giants.

With the 2017 Golden Eagles, Whatley threw out 43 per cent of would-be base stealers. He was no slouch on offense, posting a .302 batting average with 22 extra-base hits, drove in 49 runs and his 50 bases on balls were the most by any ORU baseball player in nearly a decade.

Whatley was also a three-time All-Summit League selection and was named twice to the Summit League's All-Academic Team. He was a third-round draft pick of the Texas Rangers and quickly became a rising star in the Rangers' minor league system.

Sunny Golloway was ORU's coach from 1996 through 2003, winning six Mid-Continent Conference championships and leading the Golden Eagles to NCAA Regional Tournament appearances from 1998 through 2003. His ORU teams posted an amazing 117-15 record in league games. Golloway went on to coach the University of Oklahoma Sooners from 2004 through 2013 and the Auburn University Tigers from 2014 through 2015.

Rob Walton succeeded Golloway in 2004 and enhanced ORU's baseball heritage during his nine-year tenure. His teams won 367 games and played in the NCAA Tournament all nine seasons, highlighted by the aforementioned 2006 appearance in the NCAA Super Regional at Clemson. Walton was also chosen five times as the Summit League Baseball Coach of the Year.

During Walton's time as an assistant coach or head coach at ORU, the Golden Eagles produced 16 All-Americans with 12 pitchers won conference Pitcher of the Year honors and 45 players being drafted by big-league teams. Walton, who played collegiately at Oklahoma State University, returned to OSU after the 2012 season to serve as pitching coach.

Ryan Folmar was promoted to head baseball coach in 2013 and entering the 2023 season, he posted a 319-210 career head coaching record and was a five-time winner of the Summit League's Coach of the Year award. Folmar previously spent nine years as Walton's assistant coach and hitting instructor.

Entering the 2021 season, Folmar had posted a 250-167 won-lost record along with being honored as the Summit League's Coach of the Year from 2015 through 2018. In 2018, he became the fifth coach in Golden Eagles baseball history to win 200 or more games.

Home games are played at J.L. Johnson Stadium on the eastern edge of ORU's campus. The facility hosted NCAA Regional Baseball Tournaments in 1978, 1980 and 1981 as well as 17 conference championship tournaments. The stadium dimensions are 330 feet down each foul line, 375 feet to left center and right center and 400 feet to center field.

University of Tulsa Golden Hurricane

While baseball is no longer a sport at the University of Tulsa, the Golden Hurricane fielded baseball teams from 1948 through 1980 and is best known for its 1969 and 1971 appearances in the College World Series, played in Omaha, Nebraska.

TU reached the CWS finals in 1969, thanks to upset victories of perennial powers UCLA and Texas but the fell in the finals against Arizona State, 10-1. Then in 1971, the Golden Hurricane made another strong run and finished third to eventual national champion University of Southern California.

Coach Gene Shell was the architect of the Golden Hurricane's baseball success, posting a 478-199 record from 1966 through 1980. By comparison, TU had a 155-169 record over 18 seasons under seven different coaches prior to Shell's arrival.

Under his leadership, TU won seven Missouri Valley Conference championships, finished second five times and his 1972 squad was the nation's top-ranked college baseball team. His teams won 30 or more games six times along and also won 40-plus games in two other seasons.

Chapter Eighteen

Additional Tulsa-Area Players in Major League Baseball

Many other individuals who were not mentioned earlier in this book have connections to Tulsa and professional baseball. To be listed in this section, he must have either played for any of Tulsa's professional baseball teams, been born in the metropolitan Tulsa area, attended a public or private school in the metropolitan Tulsa area or have been an established resident of metropolitan Tulsa for at least 10 years during the player's major league career.

In alphabetical order, here are their names and achievements:

Jerry Adair: The Sand Springs native spent nine of his 13 major league baseball seasons with the Baltimore Orioles then contributed to the Boston Red Sox winning the 1967 American League championship. He primarily played second base and made up for inconsistent hitting with solid defensive play and an accurate throwing arm.

After Adair's playing career ended, he was an assistant to manager Dick Williams on the Oakland Athletics' World Series championship teams from 1972 through 1974. Adair was also a college baseball and basketball standout at Oklahoma State University during the 1950s. He was inducted into the OSU Baseball Hall of Fame in 2001.

Jim Baumer: The Broken Arrow High School graduate served as the general manager of the Milwaukee Brewers from 1975 through 1977. During the 1980s, he worked for the Philadelphia Phillies as a player scout and as a team vice president. Baumer's evaluation of player talent helped lay the foundation for the Phillies' National League championships teams of 1983 and 1993.

Baumer batted .600 as a high school senior in 1949 and signed a $45,000 "bonus baby" contract to play for the Chicago White Sox. By comparison, Mickey Mantle's 1949 signing bonus with the New York Yankees was $1,500. However, Baumer's playing career was derailed by arm injuries and he played briefly for the 1949 White Sox and the 1961 Cincinnati Reds.

Archie Bradley: Yet another Broken Arrow High School alumnus, Bradley played for the Arizona Diamondbacks from 2015 through 2020 and in following seasons, would pitch for the Cincinnati Reds, Philadelphia Phillies, Los Angeles Angels and Miami Marlins.

Bradley was Arizona's first selection and the seventh player chosen overall in the 2011 MLB amateur draft. He defeated Los Angeles Dodgers ace Clayton Kershaw to win his Diamondback debut in 2015 but shortly after that game, he was struck in the face by a line drive and coupled with a shoulder injury, spent the rest of the season with Arizona's Triple-A affiliate in Reno, Nevada.

After being in the starting rotation for his first two seasons, Bradley was converted into a closing relief pitcher and his 18 saves was tops among Diamondbacks pitchers in 2019.

In the fall of 2018 when the Broken Arrow High School Tigers won their first Oklahoma high school football championship in over 100 years of competition, Bradley donated $5,000 to help pay for championship rings for that team's players.

Jim Brewer: The long-time Los Angeles Dodgers relief pitcher and Broken Arrow High School graduate spent 12 of his 17 major league seasons with the Los Angeles Dodgers then served as Oral Roberts University's pitching coach from 1979 through 1986. The left-handed hurler was best known for a wicked screwball pitch that gave right-handed batters fits.

During his Dodger career (1964-75), Brewer was a member of the 1965 World Series championship team and played for the National League in the 1973 All-Star Game. He also posted 20 or more saves four times between 1968 and 1973. He also played for the Chicago Cubs and California Angels.

Under Brewer's guidance, ORU pitchers three times led NCAA baseball teams with the lowest earned run average by a pitching staff and 17 pitchers were drafted by major league teams. Seventeen of his pupils were drafted by major league teams. In appreciation of Brewer's contributions, ORU retired his jersey number (29).

Dylan Bundy: The Owasso High School graduate Dylan Bundy was the first player picked (fourth overall) by the Baltimore Orioles in the 2011 MLB Amateur Draft and in 2012, he worked his way from the bottom of the minor leagues to finishing the year in the majors leagues.

After spending three seasons in the minors and overcoming a series of injuries, Bundy played for the Orioles from 2016 through 2019, joined the starting rotation and appeared to have a bright future. Then injuries to an ankle and his groin resulted in a disastrous 2018 season in which he led American League pitchers in two dubious categories: most losses (16) and most home runs allowed (41).

In December of 2019, Bundy was traded to the Los Angeles Angels for four minor league players. During the coronavirus-shortened 2020 season, Bundy became the ace of the Angels' pitching staffing, leading the team with a 3.29 ERA, 72 strikeouts (while walking just 17 batters) along with a 6-3 won-lost record in 11 starts. Bundy signed a free agent contract with the Minnesota Twins prior to the 2022 season.

Bundy was the 2011 Gatorade National High School Baseball Player of the Year as an Owasso Rams senior when he struck out 158 batters while allowing just five bases on balls over 71 innings with a 0.20 earned run average.

Todd Burns: This pitcher attended Oral Roberts University and later helped the Oakland Athletics win three consecutive American League Western Division pennants from 1988 through 1990. He was nicknamed "The Mad Hatter" because he tugged and readjusted his baseball cap before every pitch.

His best season with Oakland was 1988 when he posted an 8-2 won-lost record and a 3.16 earned run average. After playing four seasons with the Athletics, he spent two years with the Texas Rangers and retired in 1994 after playing for the St. Louis Cardinals.

Burns played for ORU from 1982 through 1984, finishing his college career as ORU's all-time saves leader, posting a stingy 1.74 career ERA and earned First Team All-American honors in 1984. He currently operates a baseball and softball training clinic in Huntsville, Alabama.

Dick Calmus: This right-handed pitcher signed with the Los Angeles Dodgers directly after graduating from Webster High School and became known as a "bonus baby"; the term used for major league teams that sign very young players and pay them astronomical (for those times) cash bonuses.

Calmus posted a stingy 2.66 earned run average in 1963 when the pitching-rich Dodgers won the World Series. Dodger legend Sandy Koufax had a locker next to Calmus that year. But arm injuries ended the dreams of a long major league career, so Calmus returned to the Tulsa area, serving as a pitching coach at Oral Roberts University and as the head baseball coach at Jenks High School.

His nephew, Rocky Calmus, played college football for the University of Oklahoma Sooners and won the 2001 Butkus Award as the top linebacker in college football.

Jose Cardenal: The Cuban native lived in Tulsa during offseasons in his 18-year big-league career and was renowned for his steady hitting productivity, stolen base skills and outstanding defensive abilities when playing in left field or center field.

He had 1,973 base hits in his 18-year big-league career, 329 stolen bases and a .275 batting average. He also had 10 seasons with 20 or more stolen bases and consistently ranked among his league's top outfielders in putouts, assists and starting double plays.

Cardenal played for nine teams during his MLB career, most notably with the Chicago Cubs from 1972 through 1977. He batted .290 or higher for five consecutive seasons with the Cubs and had six base hits in seven at-bats in the first game of a May 2, 1976 doubleheader against the San Francisco Giants. He later served as an assistant coach with the Cincinnati Reds, St. Louis Cardinals, New York Yankees and Tampa Bay Devil Rays.

Bobby Cox: He is the only Tulsa-born baseball player to be enshrined (2014 induction) in the Baseball Hall of Fame in Cooperstown, New York. His 2,504 career victories as a major league manager are the fourth highest such total in the sport's history. Twenty-five of those seasons (1978-81 and 1990-2010) were with the Atlanta Braves and the other four (1982-85) with the Toronto Blue Jays.

During Cox's two tenures with the Braves, that team won 14 division titles, five National League pennants and the 1995 World Series crown. He also won the Associated Press Manager of the Year award four times (1985, 1991, 2004 and 2005) and his jersey number (6) was retired by the team in 2011 as a salute to his success.

He still holds the dubious distinction of being ejected by umpires from more regular season and postseason games (161) than any major league baseball manager.

Cox also served as the Braves' general manager and played key roles in developing the careers of future All-Stars Chipper Jones, Tom Glavine, Steve Avery, David Justice and Dale Murphy.

Cox's family lived in Tulsa for the first year of his childhood before eventually winding up in California. He spent 10 years playing minor league baseball (mostly in the Los Angeles Dodgers' player development system) along with playing for the New York Yankees in 1968 and 1969.

Tim Flannery: He played second base for the San Diego Padres' 1984 National League championship team. After playing for the Padres from 1979 through 1989, Flannery served as a coach for the Padres (1996-2002) and San Francisco Giants (2007-14). He was on the Giants' World Series championship teams in 2010, 2012 and 2014 before serving as a TV analyst for Giants' telecasts.

Flannery was born in Tulsa where his father, Ragon Flannery, served as the pastor of now-closed East Tulsa Christian Church at the intersection of East 15th Street and South Indianapolis Avenue. Ironically, that church sat 10 blocks west of the site of what used to be Oiler Park.

Flannery is also part of a roots music band, Tim Flannery and The Lunatic Fringe, which frequently performs in the San Francisco Bay Area and in northern California. He has shared the stage with such diverse artists as Linda Ronstadt, Jackson Browne, Mike Weir of The Grateful Dead, Willie Nelson, Merle Haggard, Judy Collins, Bonnie Raitt and Jimmy Buffett.

Brian Flynn: The 6-foot-7 left-handed pitcher from Owasso was Oklahoma's 2008 High School Pitcher of the Year. As a high school senior, Flynn posted a 9-1 won-lost record, a 0.79 earned run average and struck out 126 batters in nearly 71 innings while allowing just 21 bases on balls. After playing for Wichita State University's perennial college national championship contenders, Flynn was drafted by the Detroit Tigers.

Flynn played for the Miami Marlins in 2013 and 2014 after leading the Triple-A Pacific Coast League in 2013 with the lowest earned run average by a starting pitcher (2.80). Then he became a middle relief pitcher with the Kansas City Royals from 2016 through 2019.

Roy Foster: The only MLB player from Tulsa's Booker T. Washington High School, Foster was a left fielder for the Cleveland Indians from 1970 through 1972 and was chosen by *The Sporting News* as its 1970 American League Rookie Player of the Year.

In 1970, Foster batted .268 and finished second on the Indians in home runs (23) and doubles (26) in addition to driving in 60 runs. But the combination of poor fielding performances and multiple injuries ended his big-league career just two years later.

Ron Gardenhire: The Okmulgee native spent 13 seasons as manager of the Minnesota Twins (2002-14), won six American League divisional pennants and was inducted in 2022 to the Minnesota Twins Hall of Fame.

His Twins' teams posted winning records in eight of 13 seasons and won 90 or more games four times. His 1,068 career victories as a Twins manager are surpassed only by Tom Kelly's 1,140 wins over 16 seasons.

Gardenhire won the 2010 American League Manager of the Year award and finished among the top three vote-getters for that honor on six other occasions. He served as a minor league manager in Minnesota's player development program and as an assistant coach before replacing Kelly as the Twins' manager.

He returned to the majors in 2018 as manager of the Detroit Tigers until abruptly retiring late in 2020 due to health-related issues. He never had a winning season during his tenure with the Tigers.

Gardenhire played shortstop for the New York Mets from 1982 through 1985 but a series of injuries led to the end of his playing career and a new career path as a coach and, eventually, as a manager.

Denver Grigsby: The Sapulpa native spent three seasons (1923-25) with the Chicago Cubs and 14 seasons as a minor league standout, most notably with the Kansas City Blues. He posted a respectable .289 batting average in his MLB career along with a .310 batting average for his minor league career.

Grigsby's professional baseball career began near Tulsa and ended in Tulsa. After his pitching led the Sapulpa High School Chieftains to three consecutive state championships (1920-22), the New York Yankees signed him to a pro contract and moved him to the outfield where he competed with Babe Ruth for a spot on the roster.

The Yankees released Grigsby the following year and after the left-handed hitter swatted four home runs in a single game for the Class D Sapulpa Sappers of the Southwestern League, the Chicago Cubs signed him to a contract. He played for the Cubs from 1923 through 1925 with 1924 being his most productive season. That year, he batted .299 over 124 games and had the dubious distinction of leading the Cubs in most times hit by a pitch (six).

Grigsby spent eight seasons (1926-33) with the Kansas City Blues of the American Association with 1929 being his finest minor league season. His .345 batting average was tops on Kansas City and his 33 doubles ranked third on the team. His professional career ended with the 1935 Tulsa Oilers, where he led the team in walks (72) but batted only .228.

Grigsby later ran a service station on Route 66 on the eastern edge of Sapulpa which is still standing. He passed away in 1973 and is buried in Sapulpa's South Heights Cemetary.

Zach Jackson: A graduate of Berryhill High School, Jackson made his MLB debut in 2022 with the Oakland Athletics. He posted a 2.50 ERA in 19 appearances with the A's in 2023 before an arm injury prematurely ended his season.

At Berryhill (a small suburb southwest of Tulsa), Jackson earned second-team High School All-American honors as a senior; posting a 13-1 record, a stingy 0.38 ERA and 147 strikeouts in 72.2 innings. In the classroom, he had a perfect 4.0 grade point average was the valedictorian of his graduating class.

Jackson played for the University of Arkansas Razorbacks from 2014 through 2016 and was converted to a relief pitcher with occasional starting assignments. He was part of the 2015 Razorback team that reached the NCAA Men's College World Series. Jackson posted a 10-7 collegiate won-lost record with a 3.24 ERA and 197 strikeouts in 155.2 innings.

He was a third round draft choice of the Toronto Blue Jays in the 2016 MLB draft and spent four seasons in their minor league system. His best season was with Triple-A Buffalo in 2019 with a 9-0 record and a 3.97 ERA.

Josh Johnson: A graduate of Jenks High School, Johnson pitched for the Florida (now Miami) Marlins from 2005 through 2011 and played for the National League in the 2009 and 2010 All-Star Games.

The 6-foot-7 right-hander had a 15-5 record and a 3.23 earned run average for the Marlins in 2009 along with 191 strikeouts in 209 innings. The following season, he posted the National League's lowest earned run average (2.30) along with an 11-6 record and 186 strikeouts in nearly 184 innings.

But three major arm/elbow injuries that required surgery derailed comeback attempts with the Toronto Blue Jays and San Diego Padres. Johnson's professional career ended in 2015.

Dallas Keuchel: This left-handed pitcher who attended Bishop Kelley High School is the only native Tulsan to win the Cy Young Award as the American League's best pitcher. He was the primary force in the Houston Astros rebounding from a 70-92 record in 2014 to winning the American League Western Division in 2015, the team's first-ever World Series championship in 2017 along with the 2018 American League championship.

Keuchel played for the Astros from 2012 through 2019, joined the Atlanta Braves midway through the 2019 season and has pitched for the Chicago White Sox from 2020 through 2022.

Known for a large beard that was the result of a dare with a couple of teammates, Keuchel emerged as the ace of the Houston Astros' pitching staff in 2015, leading the AL in victories (20), innings pitched (232) and shutouts (2) and finishing second in lowest earned run average (2.48). Even more impressive was his amazing 15-0 record in regular-season home games.

After an injury-plagued 9-12 record in 2016, Keuchel rebounded with a 14-5 record along with a stingy 2.90 earned run average for the 2017 World Series champions. And during the Astros' flight to the

2018 AL pennant, Keuchel started in an American League-leading total of 34 games.

Keuchel led the Bishop Kelley Comets to two state high school championships then played college baseball at the University of Arkansas. In 2009 with the Razorbacks, he posted a 9-3 record that was highlighted by two victories at the College World Series.

Pete Kozma: This Owasso High School alumnus played shortstop for the St. Louis Cardinals from 2011 through 2015. In subsequent seasons, he would play for the New York Yankees, Texas Rangers, Detroit Tigers and Oakland Athletics as well as the Perth Heat in the Australian Baseball League.

During the Cardinals' flight to the 2013 National League championship, Kozma's 98 double plays led all NL shortstops and his fielding percentage of 98.4 percent (only nine errors while handling the baseball 561 times) was the league's second-highest. Kozma was always known as an effective defensive infielder but a lack of consistent hitting led to reduced playing time with several MLB teams.

Keith Lockhart: This second baseman spent six of his 10 seasons in the big leagues with the Atlanta Braves and was part of their 1999 National League championship team.

He was also a pinch-hitting specialist who delivered clutch hits for the Braves during postseason play from 1997 through 2002. His postseason career batting average was .280 compared to a .261 average in regular-season games. He also spent two seasons apiece with the San Diego Padres and Kansas City Royals.

Lockhart played only two seasons at Oral Roberts University (1985-86) but his .325 batting average, 19 home runs and 53 stolen bases were good enough to earn induction into its Athletic Hall of Fame.

Joey McLaughlin: The only McLain High School graduate to play in the majors, this relief pitcher spent two seasons with the Atlanta Braves then pitched for the Toronto Blue Jays for five seasons before ending his career with a one-year stint with the Texas Rangers.

McLaughlin's best seasons were with Toronto in 1981 and 1982. In 1981, he led Blue Jays relief pitchers with 10 saves while posting a 2.85 earned run average. Then in 1982, he had a team-leading eight saves and his eight victories tied him with two others for most victories that year by a Toronto relief pitcher.

His two sons, Joey Jr. and Jeff, later pitched for Oklahoma City University.

Keith Miller: He primarily played at second base during his nine-year major league career (New York Mets in 1987-91and Kansas City Royals in 1992-95) but was known for his solid defensive play along with timely hitting. His best offensive season was 1982, his first season with the Royals, in which he batted .282 and ranked third in the American League in the dubious category of most times being hit by a pitch (14).

After his playing career ended, Miller became a sports agent catering to baseball players and currently lives in Milford, Michigan. Among Miller's current clients are Jonathan Papelbon (Washington Nationals relief pitcher), David Wright (New York Mets third baseman) and Dustin Pedroia (Boston Red Sox second baseman).

Mike Moore: ORU's most famous baseball alumnus spent 14 years in the American League after being chosen by the Seattle Mariners as the first overall in the 1981 MLB Amateur Draft. He won 28 games in three years at ORU, held the school record for career victories prior to turning professional and his jersey number (22) was retired by the Golden Eagles as a salute to his collegiate career.

Moore pitched for Seattle from 1982 through 1988, for the Oakland Athletics from 1989 through 1992) and the Detroit Tigers from 1993 through 1995. He won 15 or more games four times with his best big-league season, coming with Oakland's 1989 World Series championship team. He won 19 games with a career-best 2.61 earned run average, played for the American League in the All-Star Game and finished third in voting for the American League Cy Young Award.

Born in the small southwestern Oklahoma town of Carnegie (1,723 population in 2010), Moore most recently served as a volunteer assistant coach for the Lookeba-Sickles (average daily high school attendance of 256) when it played in the 2014 Oklahoma Class B High School championship tournament. Moore was inducted into the Oklahoma Sports Hall of Fame in 2019.

Carl Morton: This Tulsa Webster alumnus who once played outfield in the minor leagues won the 1970 National League Rookie of the Year Award and spent four seasons each as a pitcher with the Montreal Expos (1969-72) and Atlanta Braves (1973-76).

During Morton's standout 1970 season, he posted an 18-11 record along with a 3.60 earned run average as well as tossing 10 complete games; four of those being shutouts. Making his feat more remarkable was the fact that he gave up a league-leading total of 125 walks to opposing batters. Despite winning 15 or more games in three of his four seasons in Atlanta, Morton's control problems persisted as he led NL pitchers in 1974 and 1975 in most base hits allowed, giving up 290 or more hits in each of those seasons.

Morton returned to Tulsa and died at the age of 39 in 1983 after suffering a heart attack while jogging near the home of his parents.

Les Moss: This Tulsa Oilers batboy and Central High School student was playing for a local American Legion team in 1941 when he signed a professional contract with the St. Louis Browns at the age of 16. As a catcher, Moss would spend 10 of his 13 big-league seasons with the St. Louis Browns/Baltimore Orioles. His best offensive season was 1949 when his .291 batting average was third-highest on the Browns.

As a minor league manager, Moss led the Montgomery Rebels to Southern League pennants in 1975 and 1976 then his revival of the Triple-A Evansville Triplets earned the Minor League Manager of the Year award from *The Sporting News*. But his brief tenures as a big-league manager didn't go so well: 39-50 in parts of two seasons with the Chicago White Sox and Detroit Tigers.

Lance Parrish, the eight-time All-Star catcher, has credited Moss' teachings at Evansville in 1978 as laying the foundation for his 19-year major league career. Parrish had his best minor league season that year (25 home runs, 90 runs batted in) and Moss likened Parrish's throwing arm to that of Johnny Bench.

Tom Nieto: This catcher jumped from Oral Roberts University to the professional ranks after just one season with the Golden Eagles. He was a First Team All-American that batted .354 and hit 14 home runs to help boost ORU to the number five spot in the 1981 national college baseball rankings and a 45-10-1 record.

Nieto spent seven seasons in the major leagues, highlighted by postseason play with the St. Louis Cardinals and Minnesota Twins. He played for the Cardinals' 1985 National League champions and was part of Minnesota's 1987 World Series champions.

He later served as an assistant coach with the New York Mets, as a minor league manager for affiliates of the New York Yankees, Cincinnati Reds, St. Louis, Minnesota and the Los Angeles Angels of Anaheim.

Charlie O'Brien: The standout from Bishop Kelley High School was the catcher for 13 Cy Young Award winners during his 15-year major league career. Among the superstar pitchers that trusted O'Brien's pitching strategy through the years were Greg Maddux, Roger Clemens, Dwight Gooden and Bret Saberhagen.

After playing for the Wichita State University team that reached the 1982 College World Series finals, his longest tenures with an MLB team would be four years apiece with the Milwaukee Brewers (1987-90) and the New York Mets (1991-93). During a stretch between 1990 and 1997, O'Brien ranked among the top five catchers in a league with the highest percentage of catching runners trying to steal a base.

His greatest baseball legacy, however, is his invention of a catcher's helmet similar to the one worn by ice hockey goalies. That device protected the top, sides and back of the head, the throat and deflected a foul ball before hitting the catcher's face. Equally important was a redesigned visor that gave a catcher much better peripheral vision.

O'Brien's autobiography, *The Cy Young Catcher*, was published in 2015 and is filled with stories about his baseball career, teammates and memorable events on and off the baseball diamond.

Brad Penny: The pitcher from Broken Arrow High School played in the majors from 2000 through 2014, played for the National League in two All-Star Games and pitched for a pair of World Series champions: the 2003 Florida Marlins and 2012 San Francisco Giants.

The 6-foot-4 right-hander's best seasons were with the 2006 and 2007 Los Angeles Dodgers, winning 16 games in each of those years and playing in the All-Star Game. He finished third in voting for the 2007 National League Cy Young Award, given to that league's best pitcher. Assorted arm injuries would plague Penny in ensuing years and he retired in March of 2016 after trying a comeback with the Toronto Blue Jays.

Penny earned a spot in baseball lore in 2005 when he challenged a Dodger batboy to drink a gallon of milk in one hour. The batboy did it, then threw up and was suspended for six games when the team's officials found out what happened.

Dave Rader: Born in Claremore, Rader was a catcher who spent the first six of his 10 MLB seasons with the San Francisco Giants. He was a solid defensive catcher throughout his career, frequently ranking among the National League's top catchers in numerous categories. Early in his career, he was a consistent hitter, posting consecutive .291 batting averages in 1974 and 1975.

Rader was the first player chosen (18th overall selection) by the Giants in the 1971 amateur draft and the runner-up for the 1972 National League Rookie of the Year. A later highlight was his being the catcher for Ed Halicki's no-hitter against the New York Mets on August 24, 1975.

Rader finished his career with one-year stopovers with the St. Louis Cardinals, Chicago Cubs, Philadelphia Phillies and Boston Red Sox.

Mark Redman: A standout pitcher at the University of Oklahoma, the current Catoosa resident pitched for eight MLB teams from 1999 through 2008. The highlight of his collegiate career came in 1994 when he was chosen as the Big 8 Conference Newcomer of the Year and played for the Sooners' College World Series championship team.

Redman's longest big-league tenure was three seasons with the Minnesota Twins (1999 through 2001), followed by two seasons with the Detroit Tigers. His best single season was as part of the 2003 Florida Marlins' World Series championship team when he posted a 14-9 record along with a career-high 151 strikeouts. With the 2006 Kansas City Royals, Redman posted an 11-10 record and played in the All-Star Game.

Steve Rogers: Thanks to his All-Star career as the pitching ace of the Montreal Expos, 27 years of service to the Major League Baseball Players Association (the players' union) and induction into a Baseball Hall of Fame, he is the most successful baseball player to come from metro Tulsa's high school or collegiate baseball programs.

Rogers played 13 seasons with Montreal (1973-85) and was a five-time selection to the National League's All-Star Game roster. He won 15 or more games in five seasons with a career-best 19 victories in 1982. He also led the NL in lowest earned run average (2.40 in 1982), complete games (14 in 1980) and twice led the league in shutouts (five each in 1973 and 1979).

Rogers was also the runner-up to San Francisco Giants outfielder Garry Mathews for the 1973 National League Rookie of the Year award and placed among the top five vote-getters on three different occasions for the NL Cy Young Award. By comparison, his career earned run average of 3.17 is lower than two legendary pitchers: Nolan Ryan and Steve Carlton.

During his TU career, Rogers was nicknamed "The Springfield Rifle" in recognition of his Missouri hometown along with his precise style of pitching. He was the ace of the Golden Hurricane pitching staff from 1968 through 1971, finishing with a 31-5 collegiate record and a 2.06 career earned run average.

That led to him being Montreal's first pick (fourth overall) in the 1971 amateur baseball draft. His rookie season in 1973 started in impressive fashion, highlighted by a stingy 1.31 earned run average over his first 14 starting assignments.

After his career ended, Rogers began a lengthy career as a Special Assistant to the Executive Director of the Major League Baseball Players Association and with the MLB Alumni Association. He was a 2005 inductee into the Canadian Baseball Hall of Fame,

Jordan Romano: This former Oral Roberts University pitcher has been the bullpen ace for the Toronto Blue Jays since 2021. A right-handed hurler from Markham, Ontario, Canada, this right-handed pitcher posted 23 saves in 2021 followed by 36 saves in 2022 and was a member of the 2022 American League All-Star Game roster.

Romano played at ORU from 2011 through 2014 then was a 10th round draft pick of the Blue Jays in 2014 and made his MLB debut in 2019.

Drew Rucinski: The Union High School alumnus pitched for the Los Angeles Angels of Anaheim during the 2014 and 2015 seasons, the Minnesota Twins in 2017 and the Miami Marlins in 2018. Playing for the Ohio State University Buckeyes in 2009, Rucinski's 12 victories that year as a relief pitcher set a school record.

Rucinski played for the NC Dinos in the Korea Baseball Organization from 2019 through 2022 and was instrumental in his team winning the 2020 KBO championship, an event ESPN picked up to fill its baseball programming gap during the Covic-19 pandemic. He went 19-5 in 2020, leading his team and ranking second among KBO pitchers in victories.

Bill Russell: This shortstop spent his entire 18-year big-league career with the Los Angeles Dodgers and lived in Broken Arrow during the offseason. He played on four Dodger National League championship teams (1974, 1977, 1978 and 1981) and played for the National League team in three All-Star Games.

Russell was a durable and dependable player throughout his career but he stared out with the Dodgers as an outfielder before moving to shortstop in 1972 to replace the legendary Maury Wills. He ranked among the NL's top four shortstops in defensive assists in six seasons and was among the top five shortstops in best fielding percentage three different times.

As a hitter, Russell consistently ranked among the National League's best hitters in total singles and sacrifice hits. His best World Series performance was in 1978 with a .423 batting average.

Russell served as the Dodgers' manager for the entire 1997 season and parts of the 1996 and 1998 campaigns, as well. He guided Los Angeles to second place finishes in the NL Western Division in his first two seasons but was replaced midway through the 1998 season, a victim of escalating turmoil between Dodgers executives.

Mike Sember: This shortstop played for the University of Tulsa from 1971 through 1974, earning All-American honors, batting .352 during his collegiate career with 22 home runs and 100 runs batted in and playing two major league seasons with the Chicago Cubs.

Not too shabby, considering that Sember was cut from the baseball team early in his career by Golden Hurricane coach Gene Shell. Sember was later asked to come back to the baseball team and capitalized on that second chance, highlighted by his 2011 induction into the TU Athletic Hall of Fame.

Sember's defensive play was a key part of TU winning consecutive Missouri Valley Conference championships from 1972 through 1974. The Cubs selected Sember in the second round of the 1974 MLB amateur draft and he played for the Cubs in 1977 and 1978.

Steve Sparks: This pitcher from Holland Hall High School spent eight of his nine major league seasons in the American League, using the knuckleball as his most effective pitch. He played four seasons with the Detroit Tigers (2000-03) and his best season was 2001 with a 14-9 record and a league-leading eight complete games.

Sparks also played two seasons apiece with the Anaheim Angels and Milwaukee Brewers and part of one season each with the Oakland

Athletics and Arizona Diamondbacks. He currently works as the color analyst on Houston Astros radio broadcasts and also did pre-game and post-game TV analysis for the Astros' regional TV network.

As a rookie pitcher in Milwaukee's 1995 spring training camp, he earned a place in sports injury infamy. His left shoulder was dislocated in attempt to tear a phone book in half with his bare hands. Since Sparks was a right-handed pitcher, he didn't miss much playing time.

Jerry Tabb: The most decorated first baseman in University of Tulsa history, Tabb batted .397 during his collegiate career, was a First Team Collegiate All-American and the Most Valuable Player in the 1971 College World Series when the Golden Hurricane was the national runner-up to the Southern California Trojans.

Tabb was the Chicago Cubs' first draft pick (16th overall) in the 1973 amateur draft. He posted double-digit home runs total in five of his six minor league seasons with Cubs affiliates, highlighted by 29 home runs and 105 RBIs with Double-A Midland in 1974. Hitting big-league pitching was another story, contributing to playing part of the 1976 season in Chicago and parts of the 1977 and 1978 seasons with the Oakland Athletics.

Playing for the Golden Hurricane from 1971 through 1973, Tabb had a career batting average of .397 with 19 home runs and 144 runs batted in and also led TU to three consecutive Missouri Valley Conference championships. He was the District 5 batting champion in 1971 with a .413 average and hit .401 in 54 games in his final season.

Bob Thurman: Born approximately 20 miles southwest of Tulsa in the town of Kellyville, this full-time outfielder and part-time pitcher (just like Babe Ruth in his early days) was a standout in the Negro League and the Puerto Rican winter leagues.

Nicknamed "The Big Swish" for his long and powerful left-handed batting stroke, Thurman was a member of the Homestead Grays powerhouse from 1946 through 1948. He batted .350 or better in each of those seasons and excelled in 1948 when the Grays won the final Negro League championship. That season, he had a 6-4 pitching record and batted .345. Among his Homestead Grays teammates were Negro League legends such as catcher Josh Gibson, first baseman Buck Leonard and pitcher James "Cool Papa" Bell.

Thurman also played 12 seasons in the Puerto Rican winter leagues and was inducted into the Puerto Rico Baseball Hall of Fame for hitting a career record (for that point in time) 120 home runs. Among Thurman's teammates on the 1954-55 Santurce Crabbers were baseball legends such as Willie Mays, Don Zimmer and Roberto Clemente.

When Thurman finally made his major league debut at the age of 38 with the 1955 Cincinnati Reds as a left fielder and pinch-hitting specialist, he quickly became a fan favorite for his enthusiastic playing style along with home runs in each of his first four games. His best batting average with the Reds was .295 in 1956 and his best power numbers were 16 home runs and 40 runs batted in during 1957.

After Thurman's playing career ended, he worked as a scout for the Reds, the Minnesota Twins and Kansas City Royals.

Jose Trevino: A catcher who played collegiately at Oral Roberts University, Trevino played for the Texas Rangers (2018-2021) and has been the New York Yankees' starting catcher since 2022. Trevino earned a 2022 American League Golden Glove award for his defensive excellence. Then he pleasantly surprised Yankee fans with a career-high 11 home runs and getting 31 of his 43 runs batted in with runners in scoring position.

During the 2022 Major League Baseball All-Star game, he became the first ORU player to get a base hit in an MLB All-Star game. The Corpus Christi, Texas native was a three-time All-Conference selection (2014-16) with the Golden Eagles and a sixth-round draft pick of the Texas Rangers in 2014.

Don Wallace: The Sapulpa native played mostly as a second baseman and pinch-hitting specialist for the American League's California Angels in 1967. The left-handed hitter and defensive standout was especially skilled at hitting to the opposite field during his professional and collegiate careers.

As a junior at Oklahoma State University, Wallace played shortstop for the 1961 Oklahoma State University baseball team that reached the finals of the College World Series. He was named to that year's College World Series All-Tournament team and earned bachelors and master's degrees at OSU.

Tyler Wells: The 6-foot-8 Tulsa-born pitcher made his major league debut in 2021 with the Baltimore Orioles as a middle reliever and moved into the team's starting rotation in 2022. Wells spent three seasons in the lower levels of the Minnesota Twins' minor league system before joining the Orioles.

Wells played high school baseball at Yucaipa (CA) High School and collegiate baseball at California State University-San Bernardino.

Rick Wrona: This catcher from Bishop Kelley High School spent three of his six big-league seasons with the Chicago Cubs (1988-90) and was part of the Cubs' 1989 National League Eastern Division championship team. He was a fifth-round draft choice of the Cubs in 1985 and also spent one season each with the Cincinnati Reds (1992), Chicago White Sox (1993) and Milwaukee Brewers (1994).

Rick played collegiate baseball at Wichita State University from 1983 through 1985 and played for the Shockers' NCAA Tournament teams in 1983 and 1985. In 1984, he was voted by his teammates as the Most Improved Player.

Rick and his father, Walt, earned a place in Tulsa's sports history as the only father-son duo to play for the city's minor league baseball teams. Walt was a catcher for the Tulsa Oilers from 1948 through 1951 and Rick spent part of the 1991 season as a catcher for the Tulsa Drillers.

Chapter Nineteen

Youth Baseball Teams in the National Spotlight

Not every youngster gets the opportunity to play in the big leagues but two Tulsa teams brought home national championships while two other teams advanced to either the national tournament or the regional finals of the hallowed Little League World Series. The Babe Ruth League has players ranging from 13 to 18 years of age while the Little League World Series features players that are 11 or 12 years old.

Here are their stories:

1959 Babe Ruth League National Champions

Led by two pitchers who would become major league stars in their own way, this team mostly comprised of west Tulsa youth who later attended Webster High School needed extra innings to defeat Sikeston, Missouri, 3-1, in the championship finals. After the game was tied 1-1 at the end of the regulation seven innings, Tulsa struck for two runs in the eight and held on for the victory.

Carl Morton, who would pitch for the Montreal Expos and Atlanta Braves was the winning pitcher in the semifinal contest. Dick Calmus, who joined the Los Angeles Dodgers after his high school graduation, was the winning pitcher in that championship game.

1963 Babe Ruth League National Champions

With most of its roster being high school sophomores from Central and Will Rogers and known locally as the Northside Civitans, this team reeled off 14 consecutive victories in postseason play, capped by 9-0 victory over Puerto Rico in the championship game before 8,350 fans in Farmington, New Mexico.

Tulsa won the quarterfinal game against Farmington, 2-1, but had its hands full. Farmington's pitcher took a no-hitter into the seventh inning. Tulsa then capitalized on a pair of fielding errors and scored the tying and winning runs in the seventh inning.

Left-handed pitcher Eli Gourd, the shortest player on Tulsa's team at 5-foot-4, scattered four hits in a 9-2 semifinal victory over Klamath Falls, Oregon.

Puerto Rico worked its way through the loser's bracket into the showdown against Tulsa on August 24, 1963. Many of the Puerto Rico players were bigger and stronger than the Tulsa team but Gourd's sharply breaking curveball kept fooling the opponents. He scattered six hits in the 9-0 championship triumph.

The team soaked up the celebrity-laden atmosphere during that event. Babe Ruth's widow attended the pretournament banquet and Lefty Grove, arguably one of the greatest pitchers in baseball history, was the guest of honor. Oklahoma native and St. Louis Cardinals All-Star shortstop Pepper Martin and Hall of Fame pitcher Bob Feller also visited with the Tulsa players.

1988 Little League World Series

The Tulsa Nationals were the first local team to advance to this historic event in Williamsport, Pennsylvania. While the sights and sounds brought special memories for all of the players, the on-field results weren't as good as Tulsa lost all three of its games that year.

Tulsa was the champion of the U.S. Central Division and faced the U.S. West champions from Pearl City, Hawaii in the quarterfinals but lost a heartbreaking contest, 3-2.

A two-run double in the fourth inning by Tulsa's Peter Schultz gave the local team a 2-0 lead. It was also the first ball hit out of the infield against Pearl City pitching ace Chad Miyake. Pearl City's three runs came in the sixth inning and were set up by two singles and a walk.

Chris Yoshimoto scored on a passed ball then Skye Nakagawa belted a two-run double that put Pearl City ahead to stay.

In the loser's bracket contests, Saudi Arabia held Tulsa hitless in a 12-1 victory and Panama allowed just one Tulsa base hit in a 7-0 victory.

2018 Little League World Series

The Tulsa Nationals were the first Oklahoma team to reach the Southwest Region finals and came within one game of advancing to the national championship tournament.

Their Cinderella season includes a memorable Southwest Regional victory where the team failed to get a base hit but pulled out a victory thanks to capitalizing on opponent mistakes.

Dylan Baldridge was the pitching ace for the Tulsa Nationals and also helped his own cause with timely hitting during the Southwest Regional contests.

2022 Little League World Series Qualifying Tournament – Waco, TX

Even though Tulsa lost 9-4 to Pearland, Texas in the Southwest Regional Playoff Final and didn't reach the Little League World Series, the actions of a Tulsa player won the hearts of sports fans around the world.

Isaiah Jarvis, a Fort Smith, Arkansas native playing for the Tulsa-based team, was batting against Pearland pitcher Kaiden Shelton with the bases loaded and an 0-2 count. Shelton's pitch got away and violently hit Jarvis on the left cheek. Jarvis was clutching his head while falling to the ground then coaches and medical staffers quickly came to provide aid.

Jarvis recovered and walked without assistance to first base. Meanwhile, Shelton stayed on the mound, kept looking at the ground and couldn't stop crying about what happened.

Then Jarvis did something that truly exemplified good sportsmanship. He walked to the mound and hugged Jarvis and told him, "Hey, you're doing great."

Jarvis' action not only drew a standing ovation from those at the game, the video quickly spread around the world and both young men became household names.

Shelton couldn't continue in the game after the accident but shortly afterwards, would pitch twice in the Little League World Series in Williamsport, Pennsylvania.

Jarvis was honored at the 2022 Musial Awards in St. Louis, an event saluting athletes throughout the United States for outstanding displays of sportsmanship and personal character. Long-time St. Louis Cardinals player Albert Pujols was presented with the Stan Musial Lifetime Achievement Award for Sportsmanship.

Chapter Twenty

Special Baseball Contributors from Tulsa

Two Tulsans that never suited up for a major league baseball game have made significant contributions to the sport while standing on the field. Here are their stories:

George Barr, Umpire

Nineteen of Barr's 24 seasons as a major league umpire were spent in the National League. He was chosen to serve on the umpiring crew for four World Series and two All-Star Games during the 1930s and 1940s.

But his career as a baseball umpire began in a most unusual fashion.

Barr had come to Tulsa from Kansas in 1915, carrying only pocket change and hope for a better life. He worked as the head usher at McNulty Park in 1923 when a member of the umpiring crew didn't show up for that day's game. The other umps asked for volunteers so Barr stepped forward.

That fateful day led to nearly eight years of umpiring in minor league baseball before he was called up to the big leagues.

In Barr's World Series career, he saw the New York Yankees defeat the New York Giants and Brooklyn Dodgers in 1937 and 1949, respectively. He officiated the Yankees' losing to the St. Louis Cardinals in 1942 and the Cleveland Indians beating the Boston Braves in 1948.

He also umpired in two MLB All-Star Games: the 1937 game in Washington, DC won by the American League but marred by St. Louis pitcher Dizzy Dean suffering a career-changing toe injury and the 1944 game in Pittsburgh when future Tulsa Oilers manager Whitey Kurowski drove in two runs for the victorious National League squad.

During Barr's MLB career, he was part of some of the game's most memorable events.

He was the first base umpire when Cincinnati's Johnny Vander Meer pitched a second consecutive no-hitter against the Brooklyn Dodgers at Ebbets Field. He was the home plate ump for Babe Ruth's final game in 1935 and when Jackie Robinson stole home in Brooklyn's 1948 win over the Boston Braves.

Barr's most memorable game was the September 28, 1938 game between the Pittsburgh Pirates and Chicago Cubs. With darkness quickly enveloping Wrigley Field, Barr ordered one more inning to be played. Chicago's Gabby Harnett hit a two-out, two-run home run to give the Cubs a 6-5 victory.

One of baseball's most dramatic walk-off home runs, the "Homer in the Gloamin" was the spark that would lift the Cubs to the 1938 National League championship.

Barr also had moments that he would have preferred to forget about.

He was the umpire for baseball's longest scoreless tie, a 19-inning contest on September 11, 1946 between Brooklyn and Cincinnati. Seven days later, he suffered a heart attack during a game between the New York Giants and Chicago Cubs but recovered.

Then on a rainy day in 1948, Boston Braves All-Star second baseman Connie Ryan was thrown out of the game by Barr for daring to wear a raincoat while standing in the on-deck circle waiting his turn to bat.

After retiring from his umpiring career, Barr continued to give back to the game that he loved by writing the 1952 book *Baseball Umpiring*. It focused on the mechanics of umpiring a baseball game with many of its fundamental techniques still being utilized in today's MLB action. He also contributed to 1951 book *How to Play Basebal* which was published by *The Sporting News.*

He also served as president of three lower-level minor leagues: the Western Association, the Sooner State League and Kansas-Oklahoma-Missouri League. He founded an umpiring school in Hot Springs, Arkansas and spent 14 years as Babe Ruth Baseball League's International Director.

Barr was inducted into the Oklahoma Sports Hall of Fame and the Babe Ruth League Baseball Hall of Fame. He died in 1967 from a heart-related illness.

Myron Noodleman (aka Rick Hader), Entertainer

The 1992 Tulsa Drillers season was the breakout year for Rick Hader, a local school teacher who would become Myron Noodleman, the self-proclaimed "Hippest Nerd in Da Biz" and the last man to wear the crown of the Clown Prince of Baseball.

And if that last name sounds familiar to TV viewers, his nephew is Bill Hader who starred on NBC-TV's *Saturday Night Live* comedy show as well as in numerous comedic and dramatic movies and long-running series.

The Park Ridge, Illinois native traveled to minor league baseball parks large and small to perform comedic routines in the tradition of legendary predecessors Arlie Latham (in the late 1800s), Nick Altrock (1910s), Al Schacht (1920s and 1930s) and Max Patkin (1940s through 1990s).

Hader was familiar with the Tulsa area because one of his six brothers attended Oklahoma State University in Stillwater. He came to Tulsa in 1982 and earned a mathematics degree from Northeastern Oklahoma State University. After earning his teaching certificate from NSU, Hader became a math teacher in Tulsa's Union Public School district.

Prior to coming to Tulsa, he won $1,000 at a 1981 Halloween costume contest at a Chicago bar. His character was a drop-dead duplicate of Professor Julius Kelp, a nerdy character portrayed by Jerry Lewis in the 1963 science fiction-comedy movie classic, *The Nutty Professor.*

Hader's character had a head of black hair containing large globs of gel and was parted down the middle of his head. Groucho Marx-style eyebrows were aided by abundant mascara. There were also white teeth with a blinding shine, heavy eyeglasses and big bow tie.

The suit coat was way too tight, the pants were way too short and long whiter-than-white socks were visible. On top of all that, there was a perpetual smile and witty remarks waiting to burst forth from a mouth that could talk a mile a minute.

Hader said the character's name came to him quickly because Myron sounded like a nerd's name and Noodleman sounded, well, funny.

Other benefits of the gig were being able to choose when to work, where to work and the most important thing: making people laugh.

Comedians often run into a tough crowd but in his rookie season with the Drillers, Hader ran into something tougher: the weather. One of his first performances was at a game which was cancelled in the fourth inning by, of all things, a snow storm.

Word quickly spread throughout minor league baseball how Noodleman's act was both family-friendly and side-splitting funny. He would interact with fans in the stands during the game and occasionally perform rehearsed skits on the field with a team's players and umpires between innings.

Hader's busiest season was 1996 when he did 72 minor league baseball games, including 18 consecutive games during one period. A more typical schedule these days has 50 to 60 minor league baseball games as well as professional basketball games.

Like many minor league baseball players, he had a brief (as in: one game) stint in the majors for the Anaheim Angels. But Hader often said that he considered minor league baseball to be the major leagues for an act like his.

The high point of his baseball comedy career came at Hilton Head, South Carolina on November 11, 2004 when Myron Noodleman was officially named as the fourth Clown Prince of Baseball by legendary major league baseball executive Roland Hemond.

Hader passed away in November of 2017 after a bout with cancer. An online obituary stated that Hader had a gift of making friends and creating laughter, whether through simple conversations or turning a trip to the grocery store into a comedic adventure.

And family members would receive endearing nicknames; one of which was "Lumpy" and was taken from a goofy character named

Lumpy Rutherford from the classic TV comedy series, *Leave It to Beaver*.

Acknowledgements

The leadoff hitter of this extensive lineup is Brian Carroll, the Assistant General Manager and Vice President of Public Relations and Baseball Operations for the Tulsa Drillers baseball team. Brian was the person that provided the encouragement for this particular book as well as my pursuit of writing.

The late Wayne McCombs was Tulsa's pre-eminent baseball historian and contributed a treasure trove of information regarding the era of Tulsa Oilers baseball.

Barry Lewis, the long-time *Tulsa World* minor league baseball beat writer and a past recipient of the Oklahoma Sportswriter of the Year Award from the National Sportscasters and Sportswriters Association, provided contributions about Tulsa's minor league baseball history.

Barry's baseball beat writer predecessors, John A. Ferguson of the *Tulsa World* and Dick Suagee of the *Tulsa Tribune,* were kind enough to take this aspiring high school sportswriter under their professional wings.

Jake Cornwell, Tulsa's "Horsehide Historian" and Adjunct Lecturer at Oklahoma State University provided invaluable contributions related to Oklahoma in the days of Negro League baseball.

The late Len Morton and the late Jack Campbell were long-time radio announcers for Tulsa Oilers baseball. They showed me the ins-and-outs of broadcasting, the value of baseball statistics and the important of keeping up with scores coming across the old Western Union ticker.

Cal Sharp, the owner and Creative Director of Caligraphics Design designed this book's cover. To see more of Cal's amazing works, visit http://www.caligraphics.net

My wife, Denise Townsend Lindblad, provided the inspiration and motivation to complete this project when life kept throwing me Nolan Ryan-like fastballs and curveballs.

About the Author

Elven Lindblad is the author of the Books About Tulsa series and has over 50 years of professional experience in print and electronic sports journalism and information research. He lives in Broken Arrow, Oklahoma and is a member of the Society for American Baseball Research and the Tulsa Historical Society.

Elven's services are frequently used by local, national and international sports media outlets. His research skills have also been utilized in diverse industries such as local and national health care organizations, private education, background screening and financial institutions.

His email address is booksabouttulsa@gmail.com.

Selected Bibliography

The author conducted extensive research through all of these sources in an attempt to ensure that the information contained in this book is as complete and accurate as possible. The author assumes no responsibility for omissions, errors, inaccuracies or any other type of inconsistency. If there appears to be a slight against any individual or organization, it is completely unintentional.

Books and Media Guides

McCombs, Wayne. *Let's Goooooooooo, Tulsa! The History and Record Book of Professional Baseball in Tulsa, Oklahoma – 1905-1989.* Self-published. 1990.

Texas League. *2016 Media Guide and Record Book.* Tom Kayser, editor. 2016.

Internet Sites

Babe Ruth League: www.baberuthleague.org

Baseball Almanac: www.baseball-almanac.com

Baseball Cube: www.thebaseballcube.com

Baseball Hall of Fame: www.baseballhall.org

Baseball-Reference.com: www.baseball-reference.com

Big 12 Conference: www.big12sports.com

Centers for Disease Control and Prevention: www.cdc.gov

ESPN: www.espn.com

Everything Explained Today: www.everything.explained.today.com

Fox Sports: www.foxsports.com

Fun While It Lasted: www.funwhileitlasted.net

Little League Baseball World Series: www.llbws.org

Minor League Baseball: www.milb.com

Musial Awards: www.musialawards.com

National Sportscasters and Sportswriters Association: www.nssafame.com

National Weather Service: www.srh.noaa.gov

Negro Leagues Baseball Museum: www.nlbm.com

Oklahoma Secondary Schools Activities Association: www.ossaa.com

Oral Roberts University: www.oruathletics.com

Roger Maris Museum: www.rogermarismuseum.com

Society for American Baseball Research: www.sabr.org

Southwest Tulsa on Historic Route 66: www.southwesttulsa.org

Sports Broadcasting Hall of Fame: www.sportsvideo.org

SRO Agency: www.sroagency.com

Texas Collegiate League: www.texascollegiateleague.com

The Baseball Zealot: www.thebaseballzealot.com

Tim Flannery: www.timflannery.com

Tulsa City-County Library: www.tulsalibrary.org

Tulsa Drillers: www.tulsadrillers.com

Tulsa Historical Society: www.tulsahistory.org

Tulsa People Magazine: www.tulsapeople.com

Tulsa State Fair: www.tulsastatefair.com

Tulsa TV Memories: www.tulsatvmemories.com

Tulsa World: www.tulsaworld.com

World Health Organization: www.who.int

Newspaper and Magazine Articles

Avallone, Michael. "Hoskins Broke Barriers in Texas League." April 13, 2020. Accessed January 29, 2021. www.milb.com.

Bernreuter, Hugh. "Keith Miller Honored to be Part of Wendell Nehmer's Means Stamping Legacy." *Michigan Live*, January 28, 2012. Accessed April 9, 2016. www.mlive.com.

Colon, Bob. "McLaughlin Family Veins Bleed Balls and Strikes" *Daily Oklahoman*, May 23, 2003. Accessed February 26, 2016. www.newsok.com.

Connors, Bill. "Jim Baumer Was 30-1 Favorite to Outshine Mantle." *Tulsa World*, April 19, 1992. Accessed March 4, 2016. www.tulsaworld.com.

Costello, Rory. "Willard Brown." Society for American Baseball Research, Accessed July 19, 2017. www.sabr.org.

Eaton, Doug. "Legacy of Success." *Tulsa People*, May 2016. Accessed May 4, 2016. www.tulsapeople.com.

Eaton, Doug. "Richard 'Dick' Calmus." *Tulsa People*, April 2015. Accessed April 29, 2016. www.tulsapeople.com.

Friend, Tom. "Flannery Comes of Age: Surviving Personal Trials Has Helped Him to Mature." *Los Angeles Times*. May 14, 1985. Accessed April 5, 2016. www.latimes.com.

Haisten, Bill. "For Bob Carpenter, a Hall of Fame Election, a New Baseball Contract and the End of a 40-year Run in College Basketball." *Tulsa World*, December 22, 2016. Accessed December 24, 2016. www.tulsaworld.com.

Haisten, Bill, "Strike Wrecks Macko's Clubhouse Lifestyle," *Tulsa World*, August 30, 1994.

Haudricourt, Tom. "One for the Books: Pitcher Hurts Shoulder Ripping Phone Directory." *Milwaukee Sentinel*. March 16, 1994. Accessed April 4, 2016. www.jsonline.com.

Hersom, Bob. "Where Are They Now? Tulsa Native Rick Wrona." *Daily Oklahoman*, August 10, 2005. Accessed January 8, 2016. www.newsok.com.

Hoover, John E. "Hometown Hero: Keuchel Becomes First State Native to Win Cy Young." *Tulsa World*, November 19, 2015. Accessed November 21, 2015. www.tulsaworld.com.

Hoover, John E. "Ballplayers Reunite to Celebrate 50 Years." *Tulsa World*, June 16, 2013. Accessed March 28, 2016. www.tulsaworld.com.

Hoover, John E. "Lockart: A Glove of Love." *Tulsa World*, January 8, 2002. Accessed February 27, 2016. www.tulsaworld.com.

Kerber, Fred. "How a Dare Escalated into Dallas Keuchel's Glorious Beard." *New York Post*, October 6, 2015. Accessed February 9, 2016. www.nypost.com.

LaWell, Carolyn. "A Taste of Tulsa." *A Minor League Season*, June 11, 2012. Accessed February 24, 2013. www.aminorleagueseason.com.

Leventhal, Josh. "Best Baseball Parks in the Minors." Baseball America, May 17, 2015. Accessed May 25, 2015. www.baseballamerica.com.

Lewis, Barry. "Drillers' Impressive First Half Has a Rough Ending." *Tulsa World*, June 25, 2023. Accessed December 17, 2023. www.tulsaworld.com.

Lewis, Barry. "Drillers Set Experienced Roster for 2022 Season." *Tulsa World*, April 5, 2022. Accessed April 5, 2022. www.tulsaworld.com.

Lewis, Barry. "Old Baseball Park Comes Back to Life for an Afternoon at Expo Square." *Tulsa World*, April 1, 2022. Accessed April 5, 2022. www.tulsaworld.com.

Lewis, Barry. "Double-A Central Honors Four Drillers." *Tulsa World*, October 9, 2021. Accessed October 30, 2021.www.tulsaworld.com.

Lewis, Barry. "Most Rewarding Season for Drillers Manager Scott Hennessey Despite Missing Playoffs." *Tulsa World*, September 25, 2021. Accessed October 30, 2021.www.tulsaworld.com.

Lewis, Barry. "Drillers Update: Bryce Osmond captures TCL strikeouts title." *Tulsa World*, August 4, 2020. Accessed February 2, 2021. www.tulsaworld.com.

Lewis, Barry. "Tulsa Drillers 2017 Season Review: Scott Hennessey Does 'Unbelievable' Job Guiding Team to Brink of Texas League Title." *Tulsa World*, September 21, 2017. Accessed September 29, 2017. www.tulsaworld.com.

Lewis, Barry. "Drillers Manager Ryan Garko Resigns to Take College Job." *Tulsa World*, July 23, 2017. Accessed August 1, 2017. www.tulsaworld.com.

Lewis, Barry. "New Manager Ryan Garko Learned From Drillers Legend Bobby Jones."*Tulsa World*, January 27, 2016. Accessed January 30, 2016. www.tulsaworld.com.

Lewis, Barry. "Drillers Roster Set for Season Opener." *Tulsa World*, April 4, 2016. Accessed April 7, 2016. www.tulsaworld.com.

Lewis, Barry. "Drillers Loading Up With Young Talent for the '16 Season." *Tulsa World*, April 3, 2016. Accessed April 7, 2016. www.tulsaworld.com.

Lewis, Barry. "Drillers Will Remain Dodgers Affiliate for at Least Two More Years." *Tulsa World*, August 4, 2016. Accessed September 27, 2016. www.tulsaworld.com.

Lewis, Barry. "History Repeat: Drillers Season in Review." *Tulsa World*, September 11, 2016. Accessed September 27, 2016. www.tulsaworld.com.

Lewis, Barry. "2008 Drillers Were Launching Pad for Cubs." *Tulsa World*, October 26, 2016. Accessed October 26, 2016. www.tulsaworld.com.

Lewis, Barry. "Garko to Return for Second Season as Drillers Manager." *Tulsa World*, December 22, 2016. Accessed December 24, 2016. www.tulsaworld.com.

Lewis, Barry. "Highlights and Lowlights for 2017 Drillers." *Tulsa World*, September 21, 2017. Accessed September 29, 2017. www.tulsaworld.com.

Lewis, Barry. "Two Popular Former Drillers Honored." *Tulsa World*, July 27, 2014. Accessed August 9, 2014. www.tulsaworld.com.

Lewis, Barry, "Drillers Have Chance at 2nd-Half Title," *Tulsa World*, June 15, 2014.

Lewis, Barry, "White Among Hall Inductees," *Tulsa World*, July 28, 2013.

Lewis, Barry, "Driller Players Developed, But Playoffs Didn't," *Tulsa World*, September 11, 2011.

Lewis, Barry. "Oklahoma Centennial: Top 100 Greatest Oklahoma Baseball Players." *Tulsa World*, July 8, 2007. Accessed March 30. 2016. www.tulsaworld.com.

Lewis, Barry, "Tulsa Baseball: Celebrating 100 Years," *Tulsa World*, July 3, 2005.

McCallion, Sarah. "Pitcher Brings Baseball Flair to Tulsa Business." *Tulsa Business and Legal News*, March 27, 2014. Accessed January 9, 2016. www.tulsaworld.com.

O'Neill, Dan. "Larry Jaster: Dominating the Dodgers Like No Other." *St. Louis Post-Dispatch*, August 22, 2011. Accessed July 31, 2013. www.stltoday.com.

Shapiro, Michael. "Twins SP Devin Smeltzer Deals Six Shutout Innings in MLB Debut After Cancer Battle." *Sports Illustrated*, May 29, 2019. Accessed July 4, 2019. www.si.com.

Stevenson, Stefan. "Ten Things You Might Not Know About Pudge Rodriguez." *Fort Worth Star Telegram*, July 26, 2017. Accessed August 1, 2017. www.star-telegram.com.

Unruh, Jacob. "Former Oakland Athletics Pitcher Mike Moore Back in Small-Town Oklahoma Helping Coach Lookeba-Sickles." *Daily Oklahoman*, October 9, 2014. Accessed April 2, 2016. www.newsok.com.

"Ex-Umpire Has Memories of Days, Times Gone By," *Altus Times-Democrat*, May 18, 1969.

"Indians Beaten by Rangers, 14 to 6," *Tulsa World*, January 10, 1927.

"Oilers Win First From Indians," *Tulsa World*, May 31, 1921.

"Oilers and Indians Split Home Finale," *Tulsa World*, June 1, 1921.

"Sure Bet at Shortstop for Hens?" *Toledo Blade*, March 23, 1965.

"North Tops South at TL All-Star Game," *Tulsa World*, June 25, 2014.

www.ingramcontent.com/pod-product-compliance
Lightning Source LLC
Chambersburg PA
CBHW070501160726

48003CB00004B/1360

9798330211708